Readings in Inflation Accounting

Readings in Inflation Accounting

Edited by

P.T. Wanless M.Sc., B.A.
Lecturer in Economics,
University of Strathclyde

and

D.A.R. Forrester M.A., B.A., A.C.M.A.
Lecturer in Accountancy and Finance,
University of Strathclyde

A Wiley—Interscience Publication

JOHN WILEY & SONS
Chichester · New York · Brisbane · Toronto

British Library Cataloguing in Publication Data:

Readings in inflation accounting.
1. Accounting and price fluctuations
—Addresses, essays, lectures
I. Wanless, P.T. II. Forrester, David A.R.
657'.3 HF5657 79-40741

ISBN 0 471 27657 X

Printed and bound in Great Britain

INTRODUCTION

The aim of this book is to fill a gap in the range of books on inflation accounting by bringing together a number of articles on major aspects of this wide subject. As teachers and scholars, we were concerned that no book of readings in inflation accounting were available. We felt that such a collection would be valuable, partly as a supplement to the available textbooks, but more importantly because we felt that students, teachers, practitioners and other interested parties would be stimulated and educated by ready access to some of the significant contributions to the debate on inflation accounting. None other being available, we were prompted to compile one ourselves.

In compiling a book of readings in so major and extensive a subject as inflation accounting, some topics are inevitably neglected. We have confined our selection to recent books in the English language and we include nothing on the history nor on the legal or fiscal implications. Our final selection consists of thirty items presented here in ten sections. In our Biblography, we list a large number of other works, classified according to the major themes with which they deal and annotated to provide a guide to further reading.

The first section is entitled "Inflation Accounting and the Economy". The aim of this section is to show the place of inflation accounting in the context of both economic causes and effects and accounting theory.

We begin with a paper, presented to a conference here by Paul Bareau, which deals with the origins and evils of inflation. Alternative explanations of inflation may be found in socialist texts such as "L'Inflation au Coeur" by M. Rocard and J. Gallus (Gallimond, Paris, 1975). More recent data and deeper historical perspectives are given in "Inflation" by Michael Jefferson et al., (John Calder, London, 1977). Such books confirm the diagnosis of inflation as cause or symptom of a deadly social disease. Mr. Bareau's paper provides a microscopic aid to diagnosis, or - as he preferred to put it - some help in accounting for inflation.

We follow Mr. Bareau's paper by a wide ranging review of Professor W.T. Baxter's recent book on inflation accounting. The discussion of the book and its intellectual background reveals that inflation accounting is not just a sub-set of accounting theory, but a central issue: for in its discussion, the profession is forced to re-examine the fundamental principles on which the preparation of accounts has been based.

Our second section, paradoxically it may seem, is "On Not Accounting for Inflation". Professor R.N. Anthony tests accounting alternatives for their ability to report accurately the income or profit of firms in 'steady-state' constant output conditions. He demonstrates that current cost accounting accurately reports steady-state income if market prices are based on current costs, while historical cost does not; but historical cost accounting is the appropriate method if prices are based on historical costs. To understand Professor Anthony's argument, the reader should focus on his calculations of interest paid and his assumptions about the impact of inflation on the cost of capital. Since he found little evidence that firms actually price on the basis of current costs, he concludes that the case for current cost accounting is not proven and that "we should not get into this morass unless there is persuasive evidence that this is the way the economy actually works."

Professor Yuji Ijiri gives a lucid and witty exposition of the case for historical cost accounting. Using his considerable knowledge of accounting theory, he examines the advantages and disadvantages of accounting practices in five hypothetical countries. In country A, income is measured by comparing opening and closing net worths, measured at current prices. Country B is very similar, but continuous records are also kept in physical units. Ijiri argues that in both countries, the accounting record is deficient and places shareholders at the mercy of company managements, since accounting values are unverifiable and management is unaccountable. In Country C. assets are basically valued at historical costs, but publically reported profits are measured on a current cost basis; the lawyers are kept busy on lawsuits over the division of profits, arising from challenges of the "correctness" of the unverifiable current cost figures. In country D, historical cost accounts are presented to equity investors, but not to managers, since historical costs are considered irrelevant for managerial decision-making. Managers protest bitterly against the unfairness of being expected to allocate resources without any guidance from the historical record. Country E is the only country relying solely on a historical cost system, and Professor Ijiri adduces five propositions affirming the value of historical cost in producing verifiable figures, in promoting managerial accountability and in aiding managerial decision-making.

The third paper in this section is a rather different one. It is the only paper dealing exclusively with any aspect of management accounting in a time of inflation. Messrs. Abel and McLenon describe how the American Cost Accounting Standards Board has tried to deal with the problems which inflation caused for the costing of long-term contracts, especially government defense contracts. Inflation accounting was rejected as a means of defending the interests of suppliers; instead, the C.A.S.B. has made interest foregone on the capital tied up in defense projects a recognised cost of the project. (This paper could equally well have been included in Section IX, for the C.A.S.B. approach closely resembles the ideas expounded by one of the editors in Reading 29.)

Section III is "On General Price-Level Adjusted Accounting", an approach also known under a variety of names and initials, such as G.P.A., current purchasing-power accounting or C.P.P., stabilised accounting, indexation and revalorisation. This approach retains all the usual accounting conventions except for the use of the monetary unit as a standard measurement. A general price index is used to correct for instability in the monetary unit due to changes in the general purchasing--power of money over time. Thus like is compared with like in the matching of costs and revenues and accounts are prepared in stable purchasing-power units of accounts, not unstable monetary units. (These views of G.P.A. do not prevail unchallenged. Ijiri (1976) denies that G.P.A. is based on the same accounting conventions as historical cost accounting; Gynther (esp. 1966 & 1974) and others have challenged the relevance of using a general price index when accounting for a single enterprise with its individual pruchasing pattern. Ryan (1972) doubts if it is possible to contruct a stable purchasing-power unit of account. (See Bibliography, A & C.)

The first reading in Section III consists of the text of the British accounting profession's recommendations for C.P.P. accounting, including an explanation of why the profession at that time favoured C.P.P. rather than some form of current cost accounting. These proposals were never put into practice, being overtaken by subsequent events in the United Kingdom. Then follows R.L. Mathews' strong critique of C.P.P.; his remarks are especially aimed at the method discussed and used in a research study published by the American Institute of Certified Public Accountants (Bibliog.D.) but are applicable to C.P.P. in general. We then include a paper by George Staubus, who writes on C.P.P. in the context of how the definition of capital influences accounting conventions and asset valuations. (For more detailed discussion on this point, see Gynther (1967, 1970, 1971), Bibliog. A.) Staubus' paper is especially interesting since it was written in the United Kingdom at a time when interest in C.P.P. was already beginning to decline, after the Government sponsored Sandilands Committee had reported in favour of current cost accounting. We conclude Section III with a case-study in which C.P.P. accounting is applied to the U.K. mechanical engineering industry.

Section IV focuses "On Gains and Losses on Monetary Liabilities and Assets'. The problem is whether, during inflation, the profits and losses made, in real terms, by debtors and creditors should be recognised. These gains and losses arise when loans are agreed in monetary terms and interest rates do not fully anticipate inflation. As the value of the monetary unit declines, so too does the real burden of debt, impoverishing the creditor and enriching the debtor. Loyd Heath examines ways of measuring such changes in wealth, but shows that there is no unambiguous dividing line between monetary and non-monetary items. The empirical work from P.T. Wanless shows that these problems of classification are by no means trivial, but may leave opportunities for considerable manipulation of inflation-adjusted profits; moreover, reporting gains on debt as profit is of dubious value if the borrowed funds are subsequently lost because of unskillful investment. (For related evidence, see Briscoe and Hawke (1976), Bibliog. C.)

Section V is "On Current Cost Accounting Theory".The English-language literature on which we have drawn was ante-dated by Continental, especially Dutch work, which had some influence on Dutch accounting practices, and to which we turn in Section VI.

It is symptomatic of a general confusion about inflation that G.P.A. and current cost accounting are popularly represented as being alternative methods of "inflation accounting". The general public and the popular press appear to consider a rise in any price as "inflationary" while to the inflation specialist, the term "inflation" should only be used to describe a general rise in the money prices of all goods. Current cost accounting is concerned with recognising changes in the money prices of individual goods and assets. The case for current cost accounting would remain valid even if there were no inflation, wheras the case for G.P.A. would not.

To understand the intellectual basis of current cost theory, we must delve into the theory of value. Theorists in this area distinguish two concepts of value - value as reflected in market price, and value in terms of the subjective utility derived from the possession and enjoyment of a good. The existence of market imperfections, such as transactions costs, operations of middle-men, etc., meansthat two possible market prices exist; the seller's price, usually called net realisable value; and the buyer's price, usually called replacement cost. The subjective value of a producer's good is in principle measured by the net present value of expected future cash-flows to be earned by the asset.

Thus, current cost accountants must select from three measures of value to value one asset. Much discussion has turned on when and under what circumstances one measure should be preferred to the others. A widely cited and extremely influential contribution was made by Edwards and Bell (1964; see Bibliog. A); we wished to represent their work in our readings, but we felt that to take any short extract from their book would be to do less than justice to that magnum opus. To represent their contribution therefore, we have included a paper by E.O. Edwards which takes a retrospective view of their work. We complement this with a paper by Professors Bedford and McKeown, who with no words wasted, discuss the relative merits of replacement cost and net realisable value. We also include Professor Edward Stamp's paper which tries to rescue accounting theorists from the embarrassment of having to admit that, under certain circumstances, it may be appropiate to use a subjective and therefore unverifiable measure of value. Rescue is effected by invoking the principle of conservatism and arguing that since " in normal circumstances" either net realisable value or replacement cost or both will be lower than net present value, subjective value can never represent accounting value. As Professor Yoshida points out in his criticism of Professor Stamp's approach, this presumes that firms are always profitable and never make mistakes in investment.

A further problem arises: what to do if current costs change while a firm is holding an asset prior to use in production or sale? Accounting convention usually proscribes the recognition of unrealised increases in value (although this convention is honoured less in practice than in principle). Many theorists believe that increases in current costs should be recognised in the balance-sheet, but should not be treated as part of profit. But if theorists assert that business income is the change in net worth of a firm's assets between balance-sheet dates, then all increases in asset values should be included in profit. Edwards and Bell have argued that increases in current costs should be reported as profit to the extent that such increases are not due solely to increases in the general price-level; moreover such changes in values of assets held should be reported as a separate component of profit. Thus if an asset's current cost rises faster than the general price-level, a "holding gain" is reported; if current cost rises more slowly, a "holding loss" must be reported. These proposals are still very controversial and we have included a paper by Professors Drake and Dopuch to try and cast some light on these matters.

Finally in Section V, we have included a very short paper by R.J. Chambers to represent the views of those who believe that the only valid accounting value is net realisable value. Chambers' views are explained at greater length in his 1966 book (Bibliog. G). Basically, Chambers rejects the "going concern" convention usual in accounting, because it is static and therefore irrelevant to the activities of the normal firm which must continually adapt to a changing environment in order to survive and make profits. Since, in a market economy, adaptation is achieved through exchange, Chambers argues that net realisable values (for which he coins the term "current cash equivalents") are the only acceptable values.

Section VI is "<u>On Dutch Replacement Value Accounting</u>". Dutch theory has been influenced since after World War I by the work of Theodore Limperg, whose advocacy of the use of current costs in accounting was essentially motivated by his opposition to the idea of subjective value derived from utility theory, which in his day was still a relatively new and revolutionary doctrine. In a sense, Limperg was the last of the classical economists. As we have seen, opposition to the use of subjective values in accounting has still not died away. Limperg's ideas are expounded by Professor Mey (himself once a collaborator of Limperg's) and Professor Burgert provides a critique.

We also include two papers on accounting practice in Holland. The report by Dr. Klaasen shows to what extent some form of current cost accounting is used by firms in Holland, and how they go about doing so. The paper by Geoffrey Holmes is a short and uncomplicated account of the replacement value accounting in use in the international Philips group of companies.

Section VII consists of "Case-studies in Current Cost Accounting". We include these because they may help to indicate the state of the evidence on the practicality of current cost accounting. The two case-studies of individual companies by Professor Gress and Mr. Gray, and the exercise in establishing current costs reported by Professor McDonald suggest that the problems of finding and using current costs are not insurmountable. However, Charles Tritschler's paper on French asset revaluations suggests that the benefits were less apparent to those who had to implement the procedures than to the fiscal and accounting theorists. Revaluation was not widely adopted, in spite of the availability of Government-prescribed specific price-indices to aid in revaluation and in spite of the tax-savings which could be made if revaluation were adopted. (Further case-studies are listed in the Bibliography.)

In Section VIII, attention is focused "On British Developments in Current Cost Accounting". Because these developments have been and continue to be very controversial, and because of the influence which British accounting developments exercise over accounting throughout the rest of the English-speaking world, we felt that they should have a whole section to themselves.

These developments were heavily influenced, of course, by the Report of a Government Committee of Enquiry into inflation accounting (the Sandilands Report). Emeritus Professor Baxter gives a scholarly and lucid survey of the Report and this is followed by extracts from the British accounting profession's proposals for implementing current cost accounting. These proposals were rejected, however, as a result of an emergency general meeting of the members of the Institute of Chartered Accountants in England and Wales, who voted a resounding 'No' to the proposals. Dr. Tweedie's paper gives some indication of the climate of opinion in the aftermath of this 'grass-roots' revolt. However, the Accounting Standards Committee rallied in spite of the blow, and the rejected current cost proposals were replaced by a far simpler set of 'interim guidelines' (the so-called 'Hyde guidelines'). While simpler to understand and implement, these guidelines essentially abandoned the principles of current cost accounts, being based on a form of replacement cost accounting based on selected price indices. We reproduce these guidelines, which represent the latest stage in the inflation accounting debate in Britain.

Section IX proposes "Radical Alternatives" which seek to improve accounting procedures in ways which would automatically avoid the problems encountered by conventional accounting in a time of inflation. Professor Lawson is a well-known advocate of cash flow accounting. By definition, all items contributing to cash flow in 1984 are measured in terms of 1984 prices, so that the adoption of cash-flow accounts, which have other advantages, seems to solve the inflation accounting problem. One of the editors puts forward his own proposals in Reading 29, proposals for improving accountability by making interest forgone on capital an explicit accounting cost (cf Reading 5). Since interest rates reflect the market's anticipation of inflation, this proposal would automatically incorporate some element of inflation accounting.

"World-wide Developments in Inflation Accounting" are covered in Section X. This section describes recent moves and practices in a variety of countries, English-speaking and otherwise, up to early 1977. The editors are aware that this item will be out of date by the time the book is printed, but we have included this section to give the reader some insight into the variety of inflation accounting attitudes and practices which may be found once national boundaries are crossed.

We follow our last section with a guide to further reading in the form of an extensive, annotated classified bibliography. We hope this bibliography will assist those readers who would like to pursue individual themes and ideas further.

These are the thirty-two readings which we offer to our readers. We offer no apologies to anyone who feels we have left any thing out. Our intention, stated at the beginning of this introduction, is to stimulate and educate, and we believe that this extensive collection of readings achieves those objectives, and gives an excellent coverage to the major areas of interest and controversy in inflation accounting. To complete our coverage, the latest United Kingdom proposals on current cost accounting, ED 24, are given as an addendum.

P.T. Wanless

D.A.R. Forrester

University of Strathclyde, May 1979.

Contents

Note: In deference to the original intentions of the various authors, conventions for giving references follow the conventions of the original texts from which these readings are taken.

I Inflation, Accounting and the Economy

1 Inflation and the Economy

Paul Bareau

The main purpose of this one day conference is to consider the adjustments to accountancy conventions and techniques that are required in the world of inflation in which we live - and are likely to live in the foreseeable future. We have some veritable heavyweights of the profession, both philosophers and practitioners, to guide us through the subtleties and techniques of inflationary and replacement accounting.

I am no accountant; but the way for my entry into this conference was opened by our chairman, Professor Briston and his colleagues, who chose the overall title of the conference: "Accounting for Inflation". Whether intentional or not, here is a convenient <u>double entendre</u> which allows me to account for inflation, to assess its causes, to consider whether it will persist, to ask whether there are politically and socially feasible cures for it; in short to set the scene and ask the basic question whether this conference is worth while, whether it may not be concerning itself with a hopefully transient, ephemeral phenomenon.

Let me in one respect set your minds at rest - and in another confirm your fears; this conference is justified not only in terms of the conditions of inflation we have recently had to endure and are still enduring, but given the prospect that they will persist and will, in the short run at least, get worse. Let me give you the sorry sequence of increases in the consumer prices index in the United Kingdom over the past six years, starting with 1968, 4.5 per cent; 5.5 in 1969; 6.4 in 1970; 11.0 in 1971 (the after effect of devaluation in 1969); 6.5 in 1972; 13 per cent in 1973.

There is an ominous build up of momentum and acceleration in this series which, alas, is not going to be denied by 1974. Allowing for the price increases flowing directly from the present Budget proposals, the leap-frogging effect of the threshold clause legacy of the previous government, the still very partial impact on consumer prices of the much higher level of oil and other raw material prices, I estimate that for 1974 we shall improve (if that is the word) on the 1973 performance by at least 5 percentage points. That would take us to an 18 per cent rate of inflation - one which if maintained would halve the value of the currency in 3½ years and would reduce the value of the £ to that of the present penny in 20 years.

What is most ominous in this situation is that we have made the great moral capitulation before this enemy. We have tacitly admitted that we have to accept and live with this continuous erosion in the value of money. We are talking of living in an indexed world where salaries, wages, pensions, bank balances, overdrafts, taxes, would all be linked to the cost of living index. This tacit admission was symbolised in the previous government's insertion of the so-called threshold clause in Phase 3 of its proposals for prices and income controls. That clause is certain to be triggered off this summer: given the required increase in the cost of living, wages and salaries will be subject to upward adjustment and the leap-frogging of prices and incomes will be given another spurt. This is but one of dozens of examples of the manner in which we are erecting a built-in machinery for generating perpetual inflation.

Another example of this acceptance of inflation as part of our way of life is to hand in the very conference in which we are participating and which is concerned with the adjustment of principles and practices of accountancy to the realities of changes in the value of money - one-way changes, alas.

If we are to analyse the causes and peer into the future progression of the disease and its possible cures, we have first of all to admit that we are dealing with a world-wide phenomenon. Inflation is rampant throughout the world and in some highly industrialised countries - Japan, for example - the fever is even more virulent that it is here. We must, therefore, try to distinguish between those contributory forces to inflation which are world wide in their character, and those which derive from essentially domestic policies and initiatives.

The most potent international cause of inflation can be seen in the vast and accelerating increase in world reserves and international liquidity. Let us once more take 1968 as our starting point. Since that year the world reserves of gold, foreign currencies (almost wholly dollars and sterling) and Special Drawing Rights, have increased from $75 billion to $178 billion. Virtually the whole of that close on 2½ fold expansion has been in U.S. dollars held as reserves by countries outside the United States.

When the Bretton Woods system was launched at the end of the Second World War, it was based on the principle of fixed parities, expressed in terms of gold but adjustable where the currency concerned had become fundamentally over or undervalued. External reserves were to be held in gold and gold-convertible currencies, while the dynamic, flexible element in internal reserves was to be supplied by credit facilities made available by the International Monetary Fund to each of the member countries according to their quotas.

Things did not work out according to plan. In the abnormal conditions experienced after the war it was inevitable - and indeed desirable - that the major task of providing additional reserves should fall on the dollar.

The United States were the dominant economy and with their generous and enlightened initiative they put their strength and their currency to work in rebuilding the shattered post-war world. Through the Marshall Plan and reconstruction loans they reinforced the economies and currency reserves of former allies and foes alike. They made possible the miracle of European recovery - and one could wish that this fact were more readily and widely acknowledged today.

But practices and policies which are virtuous in one set of circumstances can persist and become less admirable in other circumstances. The U.S. balance of payments deficits which were so constructive and desirable in the years of post-war reconstruction in Europe, Japan and elsewhere, persisted and began to swamp the world with excessive dollars. Some of these went into the reserves of monetary authorities and provided the backing of domestic currency inflations. Others drifted into the Eurodollar market and provided the wherewithal out of which the world boom of the late 1960's and early 1970's was financed.

That boom in production and trade involved a demand for and consumption of primary commodities - and not least, of oil - to which the somewhat belated response has been the sharp rise in raw material prices to which we are being called upon to accustom and adjust ourselves. The large volume of liquidity in the Eurocurrency markets which, as I have pointed out, underpinned the boom and the rise in commodity prices is now preventing the change in the terms of trade between industrialised and primary producing countries from having its normal corrective anti-inflationary effect. This is because of the ease with which the deficits of the countries importing oil and other high priced materials can be financed by borrowing in the large and still expanding Eurocurrency market. I do not condemn the policy of recycling the oil surpluses so as to finance the deficits of oil importing countries. I do, however, wish to stress that the blithe manner in which Britain, France, Italy, Japan and others are piling up external debt to finance not capital investment, but current consumption, is one more nail in the coffin of any hope of effective international counter-inflationary action.

Here, then, are some of the major, universal forces contributing at the moment to persistence of inflation in all countries. Are we, therefore, to agree with those who argue that the first priority, in dealing with the problem of inflation, must be given to the reform of the international monetary system? The old Bretton Woods system has, indeed, broken down and must be reconstructed. Much work has been done on its reconstruction; but every aspect of that work has been conditioned by continuing divergencies of domestic economic policies. Hence the impossibility of going back to a system of stable exchange rates; the acceptance of floating exchanges as a permanent feature of the system; the phasing out of the monetary role of gold and with it of the impersonal discipline which gold convertibility used to ensure in a less permissive age. The Committee of Twenty to whom the work of reform has been entrusted has, at every stage of its labours, been reminded of the fact that international monetary reconstruction, like charity, begins at home.

Let us, therefore, turn to the home base, to our own affairs here in the United Kingdom, and try to account for our inflation.

Basically, it is a question of attitude and priorities. Attitudes - in that the disciplines required to ensure the integrity of money have weakened in common with other moral disciplines. In a permissive age we have allowed the undermining of discipline to extend to the realms of economic and, particularly, monetary policy. In our political and economic priorities Governments give the highest places to full employment, the maximisation of economic growth, social security and a very lowly place to the stability, the integrity of money. This may well be one of the inevitable implications of Parliamentary democracy as we know it - and in this respect Britain does not, by any means, stand alone. This worsening of the monetary discipline is common to most countries of the world and is the basic, philosophic factor that should have been added to the tally of external, universal forces behind the momentum of world inflation.

Attitudes and philosophies are inanimate. They have to be translated into policies and actions. And here, let us again turn to the United Kingdom home base. The inflation of the past years has been accompanied by an inordinate increase in the money supply. I will not bemuse you - or myself - with the various concepts and definitions of money supply: M 1 - M 3 etc. Suffice it to say that whichever we choose, it has been expanding too fast - much faster than the national product. A galaxy of so called "monetarists" have proclaimed the self-evident truth that the rate of growth in the money supply must be reduced if inflation is to be checked. But to argue that the whole solution of the problem of inflation is to be found in the appropriate control of the money supply is naive in the extreme; it avoids the real question, namely the reasons for the excessive growth, the inflation of the currency.

Those reasons are the obsession with growth, the related aversion to more than minimal unemployment and the monopolistic power of the trades unions which has been able to extract wage increases well in excess of the concurrent increases in productivity.

There is no need to go back too far in economic history. Let us take the fiscal and monetary policy of the Heath Government, elected in mid-1970 on a programme dedicated to the principles of a self-reliant society, relying on market forces, providing greater rewards for efficiency and success, and penalties for failure. That did not last long. By the autumn of 1971 a number of lame ducks had been rescued and under the compulsion of rising unemployment we saw the major U turns, the easing of credit policy under the provisions of Competition and Credit Control, and the parallel easing of fiscal policy in the pursuit of a higher rate of economic growth than had ever been sustained over any appreciable period in this country.

This led to a rapid deterioration in the balance of payments and, in the conditions of full employment and consumer boom of 1972 and 1973 to inordinate increases in wages and retail prices. The rate of increase in money supply accelerated and to meet the rapidly worsening inflationary situation the Government sought refuge in an attempt to control wages and prices by legislation. We are all too familiar with the subsequent sequence of events.

The fallacy of this policy - this obsession with growth - was and is the belief that growth can be created by the appropriate monetary and fiscal policies. The real sinews of economic growth are to be found in such things as good management; readiness to invest in new plant; readiness on the part of the workers to operate the new plant; good human relations in industry; absence of restrictive practices whether through cartels on the part of employers or the whole paraphernalia of luddite practices on the part of employees. The danger lies in assuming that the appropriate monetary and fiscal policy can be a substitute for these real factors in the growth and prosperity of the economy. If these basic factors are not present, and the pursuit of a rate of growth which in the circumstances is unobtainable and certainly unsustainable, is attempted by a permissive, expansionist monetary and fiscal policy, this will assuredly land us in the kind of inflationary mess in which we find ourselves to-day.

Our new political masters have not, so far, improved on the pathetic performance of their predecessors. The Budget left a reduced but still excessive borrowing requirement. Food subsidies, rent freezes, and artificial attempts to get interest down in order to prevent an increase in mortgage rates may be good political manoeuvreing, but they are not relevant to the basic problems of inflation - indeed, they are in the long run counter-productive because they increase the Budget deficit, the borrowing requirement, which stimulates the growth in the money supply.

As for the social compact, I remain sceptical. The evidence of the past years tends to confirm the proposition that full employment, collective wage bargaining by powerful unions, and the stability of prices are a wholly imcompatible trio.

What then of the prospect and the possible remedies? What I have said so far will hardly prepare you for optimism or hope of easy solutions.

And yet, if only the people understood the evil that is facing them, if they were made to understand by effective articulate leadership, they would, I believe, respond to a call for honest money. But so far there is no adequate understanding of the social and political as well as economic damage which inflation begets. We shall hear much more in this conference of the economic damage, of inflation's distortion of truth in planning and accounting. But socially, inflation - and the injustices it creates - is a destructive force. It can convert a reasonably affluent, contented society into a resentful, envious, improvident and perhaps aggressively and defensively militant society. The political consequences follow. Lenin remarked "if you want to destroy capitalism and bourgeois democracy, begin by debauching currency". He knew - he had done it in Russia.

Does this suggest that the only solution of our inflationary problem lies in a drift to increasing State intervention and ultimately to a much more authoritarian type of government? That would be a very depressing note on which to conclude. But the fact remains - and history provides many precedents - that inflation at the kind of rates which we in this country are now approaching leads to dictatorships, whether of the left or of the right. The Austrian economist, Schumpeter, writing 40 years ago, argued that there is an irreconcilable incompatibility between democracy and capitalism. If there is such incompatibility it lies in the tendency of Parliamentary democracy to beget inflation. I retain enough faith in human intelligence to believe that if the dangers were spelt out, explained and the grim alternative set out, the fight for honest money could yet be won. But it would be - it will be - a long battle and meanwhile we must prepare ourselves to live and work with inflation, to adapt our techniques of financial management and accounting to this temporary, I hope, way of life.

2 Accounting Values and Inflation

D. A. R. Forrester

Introduction

At the time of the first British draft Standard on Inflation Accounting, the Research Committee of the Institute of Chartered Accountants in England and Wales sponsored this study by an Edinburgh graduate in Commerce, a Scots Chartered Accountant, and a Professor in America, South Africa and London, - all of which are the accomplishment of Baxter. His retiral from the Chair of Accounting at the London School of Economics in 1973 after a quarter of a Century was marked by a Festschrift, which revealed his influence through the status of the contributors, as well as some of the strengths and weaknesses of the School[1].)

The present book demonstrates its author to be a scholar, gentle man and wit; but it reveals the problems faced by one with these attributes in dealing with the malaise which threatens Western Civilisation, and in resisting the successive debauching of currencies. Of the Light Touch, the whimsical phrase, and the simplified or personalised illustration, there are examples throughout a book written neither by a ponderous academic nor a myopic researcher. Some 200 double-columned pages contain good working illustrations, and diagrams as well as text. In the first page, there is reference to a child's measurements, to barter economy, and to fairy-tale consequences of a surplus of treasure. The following chapters discuss general and specific price-changes, their measurement; concepts of wealth and income, revaluation and stabilisation, gain and loss on money; time-lag errors due to price-changes which intensify trade-cycles, so it is claimed, through the accountant's lethargic reporting and historic cost conventions. Then come longer chapters on asset revaluation, on the valuation of depreciating assets and revaluation mechanics. As is appropriate for readers who learned accountancy rather than auctioneering and valuation, the author seeks to convey his message with simplicity and clarity, sometimes by means of new terms, such as "Coma", an abbreviation for the lower of Cost or Market value, or "Relief Value", as the application of Deprival value to liabilities in assessing the benefit the firm would receive if it were relieved of a burden. (p 139) Once or twice only does a punning play on words carry lightness of touch too far.

COST THEORY

Those wishing to discuss values under inflation must inevitably consider prices and costs. Costs - to this reviewer - reflect the efforts which converge on products or services up to the present or up till transfer of ownership, at which times comparison may be made with alternatives - values in exchange, value in esteem or value in use. This Aristotelian view has been modified at the London School of Economics by a Cost Concept with the following characteristics, according to J.M. Buchanan:- 2)

1) - Cost is subjective, existing only in the mind of the decisionmaker:
2) - Cost can be measured only by the chooser, since we cannot observe subjective mental experience;
3) - Cost is based exclusively on anticipations;
4) - Cost must be borne exlusively by the decision-maker;
5) - Cost can be dated at the moment of final decision or choice;
6) - Cost can never be realised, because through choice the alternatives rejected can never be enjoyed.

Such beliefs may explain Baxter's preference for a personalised illustration, rather than for robust and auditable procedures. More clearly they explain numerous passages distinguishing values to be used in decision-making from those used in income or profit-measurement: these Baxter holds need not be the same. The former requires "sacrifice budgets" (p. 51). The time element in depreciation is not an avoidable cost of a job, and should be left out of decision-budgets, writes Baxter (p. 147) but should be included with other fixed costs in the Income Statement. (In passing, we may query his choice here of "budget" - a term which for two centuries has been used for annual forecasts against which actual income and expenditures are set.) Baxter admits that the main reason for valuing in accounting is of course to find figures for annual statements (p. 120), but on the next page states that in selecting principles of valuation he is "in a no man's land between accounting, economics, and appraisal, and cannot expect much help from any of them."

Appraisers, we are told, move from the known to the unknown, estimating the sales price of a house from knowledge of the prices of similar houses at recent dates. (p. 122) But we seek in vain, from Baxter and all other writers in this area, for a clear message on the degrees of specificity and market imperfection which might prompt preference for the information content of the historic cost of an asset, or at which incidences of general or specific price-changes we would be wise to prefer the "synchronous" (current prices of supposedly similar land) to the "syntopous", or past prices of the specific land. Perhaps too long have we generalised, and sought to prescribe for current conditions without stating precisely when emergency adjustments can be abandoned, let alone analysing why this world-wide emergency is upon us.

AMNESIA INSTITUTIONALISED

The reader is treated throughout this book to spasmodic apologetics. These focus in the pages just referred to. "The good manager" writes Baxter, "must treat bygones as bygones, and cost all inputs in current terms; yet where historical figures persist in the accounts, the bygones tend to creep into even sophisticated budgets."

Two hundred and fifty years ago almost identical words were used by Bernouilli in insisting that short-term experience in gambling does not modify long-term odds. The phrase itself creeps everywhere from Jevons' "Theory of Political Economy" (1871, republ. Pelican, p. 186) who preferred subjective utilities, as reflected in marginal market demand, to any labour theory of value. The decision-making model, and its sub-set the L.S.E. Cost-concept, are thus rooted in the Bernouillis' mathematics of gambling and in Jevons' economics apposite to the inherited conventions and imperial institutions of Victorian commerce, which may be "marketable" in class-rooms but not necessarily relevant to real-life business today.

We cannot blame the L.S.E. for all anti-historicism - for Henry Ford preferred to treat History as Bunk, and novelists give fictional report of a more widely disseminated amnesia:-

"As all of us who had been subject to the mind-improvement discipline know, the act of deliberate memory is so exhausting.. as to be well nigh unsustainable...whether this applies to the very young for whom the discipline is automatically the major part of their education, I do not know. I have however noticed a strong aversion among them from recalling any event or conversation that occurred more than about one week ago, physically manifested in a glassiness of eye, a tendency to stammer, a

twitching of hands and feet".
("The Golden Age" by Constantine Fitzgibbon, p40)

Particularising, one may feel that Baxter has an aversion against understanding what happened more than a league away from his tradition and dogma. Here is his treatment of the historical cost principle, the upholding of which against current values "is far less respectable than the other objectives. Our historical cost 'principle' is really not much more than a belated reationalisation, thought up by theorists anxious to justify a procedure that in fact just grew from the bookkeeper's daily routine. This procedure became widespread because it was well suited to the needs of times. There seems no good reason why we should not now adapt it to present needs". (p.120)

Thus as an alternative to the conspiratorial theory of history, or to R. Turvey's careful analysis referred to on pp. 50 and 143, we have Baxter's Topsy - it just growed - theory of history! The approach here advocated instead is that practices, like money should have continuing but adaptive functions, and historical costs, after shrinking to Direct or even incremental cash-expense cores, should have additional elements of private and social costs cumulated on, to aid both external and internal accounting from which trends may be extrapolated and the future best explored.3)

Baxter smells some dangers out: for depreciation, even the usual rule -of-thumb methods use extimates of life-spans and scrap proceeds:-

"in fact they rely also on sweeping assumptions about the future - all the more dangerous because they have never been spelled out." (p. 149) Of course when it comes to valuing work-in-progress, replacement costs could be estimated assuming the firm will work at its most efficient level of activity, and the rates derived would resemble those of full standard cost. (p. 134) But when it comes to the essentials of the ongoing, through-flow production model, developed by the accountant to cope with nonliquidation situations, then Baxter asserts the universal applicability (and availability?) of market prices. Although around the margin, market prices may change, and although batch-size will affect unit prices, Lifo or Fifo hypotheses are beneath contempt:-

"one can hardly argue that economic magnitudes depend on such piffling trivialities as physical sequence (real or assumed). A concept that stumbles here must tend to be discredited in toto".

Again "None of the family can be defended as more than a convenient make-shift: to link value with a past physical event is an affront to economic logic." (p. 77)

In a note, Viscount Simonds' opinion in the Anaconda American Brass case (1950) is quoted as giving an agreeable air of sophistication to Lifo, which "still has all the faults inherent in value theories based on cost." (p.92)

And so the sags and bags of the tradition in which Baxter is entrammelled become ever more apparent: "Accounting is more and more finding that in some areas (notably management decision) figures cannot be both sure and informative. We must give up some sureness if we are to get more information. Precision are sureness are good things, but they are less so in some contexts than in others. When for instance, tax assessment depends on an income figure, they are important since they affect the size of cash payments; and therefore a strait-jacket of rigid rules may be here defensible." (p. 119)

In general, unlike physical measures, "values stem from human wants and so must be elusive. We should approach our task with limited expectations and some pessimism." (p. 120)

One notes there is no mention here of the need to judge impartially and objectively against human wants and sectional claims. And there is another side to Baxter's modesty: for those outside the subjectivist tradition there is contempt: for Capital Allowances used in calculating tax, "the procedure depends on legal rules, not economic goals, and so lies beyond the reach of reason." (p. 146)

FULL COSTS

Let us further establish our suggesion that costs meet and must marry values otherwise established at "the present", or moment of accountability and decision, or on the mutual decision represented by a sale. Costs reflect effort and skill, where we may differentiate:- the efforts of society to enable productive firms to be formed to exist; the efforts of firms to acquire and maintain their productive capacity; the efforts of producers to acquire and convert materials to goods; and the efforts of salesmen to convert these goods into value satisfactions deliverable by the firm at a profit. (This last phrase is Roger Falk's). Accountability prompts that each of these, in appropriate order, should be attributed, first to products or cost units, and secondly, for the remainder, to periods. Good stewards will not fear or resist the charging of thes costs, so that the process of adding value is reflected in increasing stock values, and Profit statements show a progressive reduction of Income or Gross Product by Direct Costs to give Contributions, further reducted by Overheads fully attributed to give Gross and Net Profits, and then by Costs of Capital to give Superprofit or Residual Income. Accounting procedures and company structure should promote such very full cost charging. But it requires to be matched at least periodically by a contrary and complementary policy prompting reassessment of results and market values from which are derived and reported Provisions against future, specific losses and expense. (So far we have spelt out the Continental approach, modified only by the inclusion of Cost of Capital.[4]) But we go further and claim that if the firm is to continue through slumps and booms, without state intervention to cream off boom year profits and dole out subventions to enable survival and ability to continue employment in bad years, not to mention ability to pay dividends, the principles must be developed for reserve building robust enough to satisfy owners and participants and be subject to impartial audit. To this we return later.

In these terms we would interpret Baxter's requirement that managers should cost all inputs; and such Reports would offer an alternative picture "of the relative prowess of different firms, industries and regions" (p. 118) The model we have described is required not to facilitate any centralisation of decision-making through improved contemporary values of selected, tangible assets being made available to stock exchange or ministry, but is necessary and sufficient for responsible and informed and auditable decentralised decisions. A possibility of conflicting pressures on the auditor is mentioned by Baxter when he suggests that it is to everyone's advantage to value year-end stocks highly (has he forgotten the tax-payer?), while a bias to keep fixed asset and depreciation charges low is equally to be guarded against by the auditor. (p. 174)

Interestingly Baxter is committed to very full cost charging for fixed assets. These are the subject of Chaps. 10 and 13, which are based on his previous monograph on Depreciation. We can only here summarise his case, for which we have more than sympathy, that depreciation is not to be related to any fall in market values of the asset during the accounting period, but to the behaviours both of the depreciable assets <u>and</u> of the secondary assets in which the depreciation provisions have been retained, either with a specific funding and investment outside the business, or by "enriching the whole net asset structure" (pp. 94 and 148) Baxter's treatment therefore inclines towards annuity and sinking fund methods, although he is significantly loath to modify depreciation rates downwards as interest rates increase, without reasons given! (p. 98)

In search of the value to the firm or "deprival value" of fixed assets, he suggests that 'budgeting' and cashflow projections are essential, based on relevant flows, interest rates and an assumed knowledge of the future. (pp. 148-9) Relevance is extended:- "the growth of the firm's secondary assets is thus part and parcel of the depreciating asset's story. Their earnings enter into its cashflow just as surely as say the scrap-receipt; and so, rather surprisingly, these seemingly remote secondary flows influence the depreciation calculation. The 'interest' of the annuity method should presumably be interpreted as reflecting these secondary earnings and not the rate of return from the primary asset". (p. 151)

Later he prefers phrases such as cost of capital or secondary earnings as more helpful than interest, in that they suggest the high rates appropriate to business projects rather than the low rates earned on less risky investments. (p. 159) But there is no mention here of interest rates which must anticipate inflation, or of the ideas of Defliess or Anthony that these rates may under circumstances be used to modify acquisition costs of assets.[5])

Instead Baxter recommends a "full service charge", or cost reflecting the whole yearly sacrifice through investing in an asset, covering depreciation and repairs and cost of capital, less earnings on depreciation provisions. (p. 151): and this is approximated by straightline depreciation plus interest for the year, plus the yearly average of relevant repairs. (p.109, note 5).

Perhaps we criticise a potential ally! For a sentence o two, interest does appear as a modifier of asset values alternative to general or specific price indices:- "The notion that an asset can be subject to both depreciation and increase is unfamiliar. The easiest way to explain it is perhaps to use a backward looking argument, and say that the full cost of the asset to date consists not only of the initial investment but also of Cost of Capital; so this invisible cost should each year be added to the asset's value as 'interest' on the opening balance for the year, and thus increases its value". (p.157)

Thus when Baxter accepts some continuity of past and future, and aims for some similarity between an asset's 'story' in the accounts and its decision-model, the congruence is to be emphasised and welcomed. More usually he appears oblivious to the dual role of accounts, in providing both planned recording and recordable form for planning and commitment (as perhaps was H. van der Haas in describing "The Enterprise in Transition" (Tavistock, 1967) p. 174))

INTEREST AND INFLATION RATES

If interest or Cost of Capital thus enters deeply into one aspect of Baxter's proposals, we may ask why he ignores or denies their ability to anticipate inflation. He seems convinced that inflation always transfers wealth, with shareholders "reaping an agreeable harvest". (p.37) Similarly the home-owner with a mortgate is in a "snug position" during inflation, "the obverse of the rentier's discomfiture", which is shared by those on fixed income, (or with little short-term "deprival value", we may add, if they adopt 'industrial action'). Yet Baxter recognises that holding gains tend to dry up, as lenders become wary, and as interest rates rise with inflation. (p. 43) He wisely notes the impact of taxation on interest rates which are raised in an attempt to ensure maintenance of capital and even some real return. (p.42) Trustees would have to transfer much revenue to ensure preservation of capital values. (p.44) Index-linked contracts are briefly considered, especially for government borrowing, where indexation related to net national product per person, he feels, would save the Treasury's face, since this varies with inflation and productivity. (p.43)

The state, he notes, is special beneficiary from fixed interest borrowing, and thus has little incentive to control inflation. But it is also suggested that investment trusts get the benefits from gearing as well as spread. (Here the cynic might suggest that the discounts on net assets at which investment trust shares are traded may measure the market's negative valuation of such gearing, of professional investment decisions, and/or of impersonal institutional investment in general!) Needless to say, for all these circumstances Baxter commends "stabilised accounts", suggesting that "gain or loss on money can have immense importance for individuals, firms and society. Yet ordinary accounts make not the least attempt to measure it. Here is one of the strongest arguments for stabilisation". (p.34)

How far stabilisation of accounts, or indeed indexation of contracts, would make life more tolerable is not entirely clear, although some adoption of the former, Baxter suggests, might well prompt strong and probably beneficial political pressures against inflation. (p.40) Meanwhile Victorian maxims need qualification: prudence should be less taught to children than price-trends. "It pays to run head-over-heels into debt when inflation is coming" (p.39) The course of addiction becomes clear, the cure less so: and we must look elsewhere for advice on what to do when common sense and firm money win the day. Meanwhile we are all prompted to become speculators and gamblers. (p.40) If accounts showing surpluses on revaluation suggest that managers have been clever to buy land and property [6], Baxter writes that this could be better entitled a "nominal gain from avoiding money assets". (p.37) (With wisdom after the event, one might suggest that such gains on property be converted into Australian dollars, before that property boom bursts!) Surely Paish should not only be quoted but trumpeted, when he writes of the declining attractiveness at times of rising prices in owning productive assets rather than non-productive, while the hoarding of goods is seen as a better hedge against inflation than investing in enterprise) p.178) - for a time! Faced by such symptons, are stabilised accounts even a palliative?

We have so far illustrated the wit but imperfect wisdom with which such matters have been treated. We now must turn to deeper matters involving the accounting model, or theories of accounting which underlie our basic financial statements. Here some may choose to test the depth of Baxter's teaching, noting that he was less known till recently as author of books than as editor or as writer of articles which have been not infrequently reproduced by those of his School. He first wrote on the present subject in Feb. 1949 and May 1952 [7] In the mid '50s appeared articles on historical accounting's contribution to the trade cycle, which form Chap. 11 of the present book. [8] He duplicated American studies of the effects of inflation on steel companies with British evidence in 1959.[9] Since then he has written on replacement costs. [10] capital maintenance, [11] and has become advocate of deprival values. Thus inflation accounting is no novel area for him: his book focuses the results of decades of work.

ACCOUNTING THEORY

Little sense is imparted to the reader of developing wisdom or techniques. Could not reference have been made to the inter-war monetary policies which gave rise to the Continental "stabilised accounting" techniques confessedly adopted by Sweeney? We must turn to Professor Stamp for any acknowledgement of the work of Limperg. [12] For his "deprival values", Baxter and the Sandilands Report both acknowledge debt to "The Valuation of Property" (Michie, 1937) by J.C. Bonbright, here called "massive and incomparable". But Bonbright discusses a very large range of theories, including "fire insurance values" which will compensate the insured for their deprivation. And there may be found, in Vol. I page 47, criticisms of Irving Fisher's macro-accounting, with its calculation of national wealth by a summation of quantities multiplied by the prices of the small quantities actually exchanged on the markets - a criticism which is readily extendible to price inflators or deflators. Only five continental writers feature in Baxter's two and a half pages of bibliography, prompting the conclusion that his accounting theory is little likely to have been influenced from across the Channel.

Anglo-Saxon weaknesses therefore emerge clearly. Although the stabilities of the pound sterling and the dollar long protected us from the need to consider monetary theory, Baxter's first chapter is summarised with the caption - "Our Irrational Faith in Money". Paradoxically, many seem now more attracted to cash-flow accounting than to balance sheets and profit and loss accounts which we seem unable to treat seriously. Baxter may seem to suffer from a doubting dualism, which attempts to give equal importance to profit and net worth measurements, and in despair turns elsewhere.

Income is referred to early on as growth in wealth during a period, rather than during a production or adding value process. This definition, Baxter says, is not widely used, and accountants prefer to compare revenues and costs; but since the balance sheet approach "seems to fit the facts and clarifies the problems of price changes" he makes much use of it. (p. 19) Perhaps he makes the shop-keeper's mistake of regarding assets as familiar and easy to list and number or weigh. Costs and revenues he finds less clear, since they are mere "measures of asset changes. So probably we see more of the truth when we compare the net assets at two dates than when we try to visualise the stream of arrivals and departures". (p.53) This view, he notes, is contrary to current preference for income statements, regarding balance sheets as cold stores for unripe costs and revenues. Where the problem may seem to begin with the classification and quantification of resources, positive and negative, Baxter takes refuge in a naive dualism where "to belittle the values in the balance sheet is also to belittle the values in the profit and loss account". (p.65)

Balance Sheets are give more extended treatment in the chapter on Asset Revaluation: people turn to them for an impression of the firm's general nature, size and ownership sturcture, as for help with problems of asset strength, liquidity, etc. Share purchase decisions are informed by balance sheet data, we are told, often mediated through ratios of earnings on capital employed, etc. which he says without revaluations lose whatever virtue they may otherwise possess. Without any differentiation of primary from secondary share-exchange markets, he suggest that non-current values must affect decisions there. "This harms us collectively as well as individually; because we lack clearer pictures of the relative prowess of different firms, industries and regions, the nation's flow of capital may be misdirected". (p.118)

Stewardship and other arguments against perpetual indexations are ignored or charicatured, in complete insensitivity to the tradition of accountability:- "the prime duty of the man who prepares any form of statistics is to make them as accurate as possible regardless of seemingly bad consequences". (p.178)

But if accountants surrender traditional areas of competence, and hope to become statisticians and valuers, then Baxter's nominal modesty from one viewpoint is seen to disguise an accountant's ambitious "we": "Values stem from human wants and so must be elusive. We should approach our task with limited expectations and some pessimism". (p. 120) (In case of doubt, of course, we can always call in the professional valuers).

PROFITS FOR ALL SEASONS

As in The Corporate and the Trueblood Reports, so in Baxter we find a claim to find economic realities regardless of the lawyers, which must be grounded in ideas of Equity revealed to Anglo-Saxon auditors! Above equity and truth, we seem to place utility: "Probably indeed it is a mistake to suppose that there is a 'true' income...some of the rivals are preferable to others because they are more useful. And useful means not only honest but informative...each version of profit may light up some aspect of the firm's progress better than other versions, or suit one kind of firm better than other kinds". (p. 23)

Or indeed one version may suit one person's greed more than another! There can be little wonder that British profits, thus ill-defined, have been ill-defended in comparison with neighbour countries. We find in such subjectivity base for resistance neither against unjustified and unauditable retentions policies by British directors, nor against distribution constraints imposed by short-sighted, time-and-vote-serving governments. (Just such self-financing was encouraged in Nazi Germany). Baxter writes some sentences on profits concepts for legal purposes; and indeed finds the ordinary accounting concept has merit in being familiar, cautious except in times of inflation, and sensible in reducing the scope for bickering about tax and dividend payments. But "judicial blessings on this score do not make it more true than any other version. Nor should they stop us from trying to improve it, for judges must in time give weight to reform that becomes accepted business practice". (p. 23)

The notes refer to Hicks' confession, in which all those who follow him too closely should join, of doubt whether in the end "we have not been chasing a will-o-the-wisp". [13]) Another lengthy quotation in the footnotes suggests that periodic income may not be an effective tool of financial planning and control: past pre-occupations therewith may be as outmoded as blood-letting: after balance sheets came profit statement; and he quotes "we may now be de-emphasising the income statement in favour of fund flows, or cash-flows. Each of us sees the future differently no doubt. But my own guess is that, so far as the history of accounting is concerned, the next twenty-five years may subsequently be seen to have been the twilight of income measurement".

In this pronouncement the sense is clear, the tense less so! The seer quoted by Baxter is David Solomons, Professor at Wharton, but still displaying certain signs of his L.S.E. origins, and addictions.

All this may be briefly compared with Continental emphasis - of Nicklisch who considered chiefly the assets as the controllable area and source of subsistence of the business man. Schmalenbach, on the other hand, focussed on the Results and Returns, projection of which enabled present values of the firm to be assessed. (He influenced the Finnish author, whose cynicism on constituent asset valuation promts Baxter to doubts which at the extreme places both Balance Sheet and Income Statement beyond reform: perhaps in the end, he writes, we shall accept such counsels of despair! p. 180) But Schmalenbach linked cash and profit flows coherently, while his antagonist Wilhelm Rieger took a proprietorial view, reading the Balance Sheet from Capital to Assets, and then back to Capital.

The above summary we owe to Otto Bredt,[15]) who went on to suggest that firms no longer operate within Balance Sheet constraints. Finance replaces the personal capital of the market, the economist's capital as means of profuction, and the Business Economist's capital which dictates his room for manoevre.

Finance, Bredt suggests, is felt to be something which must fulfill our needs. Some asset or other is desired, and so finance is required. "And thus the dam against an insatiable appetite for assets has been ever more widely breached in business and in both public and purely private sectors. The channel to an inflationary flood is opened".

MEASURES FROM UTOPIA

For Baxter, things are simpler. Since the main reason we work is to earn our living, and since the end of production is consumption, so he feels we can ignore alike joy at work and any particular interests of the investor. With Hicks' definition of income as potential consumption, the consumption-power criterion is found as corollary. (p. 23) Indeed, as in medieval philosophy, real and nominal become somewhat divorced from commonsense. Real-wealth units are for Baxter expressed in constant purchasing-power, price-indexed baskets. In discussing the availability of gains, he suggests that value changes on current money assets and liabilities might be added to income and dividends, but not those on non-current money items. General price changes, he suggests, make Realisation harder than ever to define in cautious terms. Gains realised conventionally can be lost if left as a money asset - they are not certainly 'realised' till cash dividends or tax is paid. Facetiously he suggests that profit on non-money assets is not realised until it is turned into money assets, and gain on money assets is not realised until it is invested in non-money assets! (p. 47)

Brief reference is made to indexing present values back - we might note to a time when the pound was not a volatile measure of value. (pp. 34 & 36) But the preference for current costs, contemporary values and, still more, for cash-flows and projections - "when conditions cease to be stable, one should again use the perpetuity approach" (p.152) - tends to push all accountancy into ever quicker sands. The contrast between old and new is here poignantly made. No longer is the pound sterling the stable measure; rather our problem is to convert the British Branch results into the Utopian dollars of the Head Office: "With stabilised accounts, in effect we pretend that the ordinary accounts are those of a foreign branch, and we convert them into the units of a conceptual head office in a far off, happy land with stable money. Index factors based on the price-level of any convenient time take the place of exchange rates. In simple examples, the mechanics are much the same as for the Utopian firm". (p. 31)

The present reviewer finds no time of inflation 'convenient' for this or any other palliative. Moreover he finds it odd that British authors have not had the humility to support proposals which originated in Germany in the 1920s for converting volatile local currency transactions in terms of the strongest currency available.

ACCOUNTING AND TRADE CYCLES

As further test, we may examine Baxter's view that unadjusted, reported profits have contributed to trade-cycles. His illustrations hypothesise boom to slump cycles of about 14 years - too long, of course to be materially affected by delays in the external reporting of up-or down-turns in profitability, these delays extending to 16 or 18 months in the absence of interim reports. Baxter makes no plea in this regard for the monthly results advocated in Cologne in the 1920s. Instead he emphasises that depreciation charges based on historic costs will be too high when slumps prompt lower replacement costs, and will be too low as profits boom, together with plant replacement prices. Presupposed of course is not continuing inflation, but demand affecting prices, down as well as up in far-off, pre-ratchet and government-intervention days. Part of the effect comes from charging depreciation to products or periods by multi-year apportionments of initial cost, regardless of whether the investment was optimally timed, and with no clear separation of unused capacity-costs which Limperg commended and which facilitates the tracing of trade cycle effects.

Perhaps the Victorians were wiser in regarding depreciation less as a constant product-unit or period cost, and more as an appropriation to reserves made openly or in secret to smooth divisible profits over the years and cycles. Thus Baxter's problem with regard to depreciation may be at least in part one of our own, blind making.

More serious, however, is thought to be the time-lag in charging cost-of-goods against sales: this depends on the purchase-to-sales stock-holding period, which itself may vary if there are speculative increases or decreases in stock levels. Baxter's theory suggests that when goods are costed at lower, earlier price levels, then high profits will be reported and will intensify boom expectations, up until a break when glutted markets reject further price increases: thereafter goods costed at peak prices, according to the Cost or Market "Coma" rule, will reduce profits as the slump intensifies, and may continue to repress recovering results.

All this has been understood in the Limperg School, and is received doctrine among students of trade-cycles or 'conjunctures', who have noted, with Baxter, tendencies analogous to an accelerator which makes the system less stable. But does the argument fit into the 'stagflation' situation, when organised labour tries to ride the slumps with state intervention on monetary and employment matters, gaining higher wage rates during booms, leading to a ratchet effect on costs and prices? Even agricultural and raw material prices are now less determined by the trade cycle, with international funds and institutions seeking to mitigate the most immediately undesirable effects. In the 1930s, and even later, state or international bankers' action was not considered the only solution: Business economists and others sought pricing and reserve building policies which would help the firm, the workers and the economy as a whole.

On the accounting front, one solution was to create hidden reserves in booms and to release them to maintain confidence during slumps. Just as the monetary policies of the 1920s prompted the Great Collapse - as J. Rueff, M. Friedmann and A. J. Schwarz have variously shown - public concern and legal investigation tended to focus on Secret Reserve manipulations, in such cases as that against Lord Kylsant of the royal Mail Coy. Contemporaneously price restraints by cartells and states reduced the availability of the contracyclical policies advocated by Schmalenbach. He suggested that as demand increased to absorb productive capacity, prices should be enterprisingly raised and profits earned adequate to enable fixed costs in slump years at least partially to be covered. Even today such reserve manipulations remain part of Swedish tax and stabilising policy: at first glance they appear to be better rooted in economic sense, and to be potentially more effective than Baxter's pleas for Current Cost Accounting. But both the Schmalenbach/Swedish and the Limperg/Baxter policies require thorough comparison in the light of current monetary and institutional, political and public opinion circumstances.

RESERVE BUILDING

Updating of policies which have these inter-War roots may focus less on income measurement and the external reporting of Contributions, Gross or Net Profits, and more on the principles of reserve building to maintain capital and employment. Reserves are not yet in all sectors disclosed. Even provisions against stock losses or debts and VAT unrecoverable do not appear in Anglo-Saxon Accounts. It may therefore be presumptious to pretend that external disclosure in this or other fields is a feasible or desirable panacea. Only when the variety of decisions, fundings, and manipulations possible is clear, with an assessment of inter-active effectiveness, can one suggest what information should reach which levels or areas, from whom, and whether by restricted or open transmission.

Reserves of course in the present context have ambivalent meaning. Baxter suggests that inflation has given a fillip to accounting theory, especially for those with vested interests in historical costs "so easily gathered in a ledger".

Confused by a mixture of specific and general price changes, questions of whether inflation charges are costs or appropriations have been raised. (p.62) But price-level theory cannot be content with upward trends alone. Deflation credits may also require to be debited to the owner's equity, "ideally from an inflation allowance created on the upswing of the price cycle" (p.61) Current cost accounting of course has focussed on cost adjustments, has fumbled with reserve building, and has not proceeded to the forms of asset holding optimal for survival, adaptive ability and maintaining employment at times of reduced prices and margins.

It is thus not enough to refer whimsically to a qualified audit report, proposed in 1951:- "Subject to the capital market providing sufficient resources to make good the drain that has occurred through wrong price-policy, through inflation and through the taxation of capital made to masquerade as income, in our opinion such balance sheet and profit and loss account give a true and fair view, etc". (p. 63)

It may be necessary rather to clarify information models and hierarchies of accounting, pricing, asset-buying, and selling and financing decisions which are capable of being implemented within the firm, at Board level, at Treasury and Bank levels, and on international commodity and monetary markets. Decision-makers must feel confident in their adaptations, trusted by those affected - not blindly but on the basis of educated understanding and willing participation. Moreover the discharge of decision-making duties at most if not all levels should be capable of audit, as in Sweden in the company sector. A programme to deal with a changing economy, the stresses in which have long been intensified by monetary debasement, thus requires research in field wider than accounting practices and the elaboration of coherent policies on clear and contemporary bases. An educational challenge of training, retraining and worker-orientation is then to be faced, accompanied by a clarification of audit procedures and reports, and of the constitution and varied qualifications of audit committees.

THE FIRM

Since the firm appears as anti-social unless regulated, among government interventionists, or as in equipoise, with neither growth nor decline from the point of view of capital maintenance, we may refer to Baxter's views on its role and survival. He clarifies that no speculation can be profitable if specific price indices are universally applied; and then list circumstances or points favourable to the special index case: given inflation, there is a cash strain of replacements; there is a presumption that future receipts will be unchanged, and thus higher input prices spell lower future profits, and once the holding gain is recorded, thereafter the rise is an unrelieved misfortune. Then, significantly, he suggests that the special index man distinguishes firm and owner, the latter being more interested in the purchasing power of his returns. Continued existence and growth, regardless of social and economic contribution, he notes, will appeal to employees, and to managers who are paternalist in their attitudes to shareholders and other 'outsiders', while they build up what are, by real wealth standards, secret reserves. (pp. 70-72)

Baxter quotes Barker on the "organising idea" rather than real corporate personality of firms - and could have gone on to justify limited life companies (as Turnbull has done in Abacus, June, 1973.) The maintenance of a viable set of physical assets must appeal to managers, who may be too authoritarian in measuring profit in a way that suits themselves rather than the owners of the firm, and which moreover fosters reinvestment regardless of its fruitfulness, and so may lead to inefficient use of resources. (p. 73)

The special index man must choose policies reflecting prices of the one asset, the firm's assets, or the industry's assets. To help him, he has "some rather woolly concept of maintaining an activity level that is satisfactory to various human beings - perhaps the level that keeps workers in jobs, preserves management's morale and provides customers with their usual purchases". (p. 72) For standard products, methods and activities, of course, standard costing systems can, and perhaps regularly do, facilitate revaluations to current prices, as Baxter admits. (p. 174)

On final balance, the impression gained of our author is of a wit and clear exponent, scholar of national status and gentle man, unwilling to thrust his argument beyond somewhat narrow, professional and technical bounds: unwilling, too, effectively to stamp on nonsense, or to establish new modes of co-operation and mutual confidence between state and firms, between employers and employees and consumers. For him, much of the controversy is summarised in a cautious conservatism which seeks reformed accountancy methods to maintain business capital, and is opposed to a sleepy conservatism which supports older methods that may erode it: "The outcome of the argument will show which strain of conservatism is dominant". (p.64) More radical thinking, we have submitted, is necessary to span the breadth and depth of the malaise represented by inflation, and to prompt sensible, effective but far from politically radical cures rather than palliatives. This book is priced in sterling, and written by an author of sterling reputation. Its value is not to be assessed only in terms of the author's efforts of brain or pen, or measured by the publisher's costs, but in its significance to those who can read and understand.

FOOTNOTES

(1) "Debits, Credits, Finance and Profits" ed. Edey and Yamey (Sweet and Maxwell, 1974).

(2) "The L.S.E. Concept of Cost" (Weidenfeld, 1973).

(3) cf. "Holding Gains or Holding Costs - The Case for Current Cost of Capital Accounting", Management Accounting, March 1977.

(4) Continental Principles are worked out most fully in U. Leffson's "Grundsaetze Ordnungsmaessige Buchfuehrung" (IdWp. 1972).

(5) "Accounting for the Cost of Interest" by R.N. Anthony (Lexington, 1975).

(6) Things are fairly bad when Cost and Management Accountants are urged to jubilate at their Institute's property speculations. cf. "Stop-Inflation Accounting" (The Accountant, June 10th 1976).

(7) To the Manchester Stat. Socy. and in the Westminster Bank Rev.

(8) Economica, May, 1955.

(9) Accountancy, May and June, 1959.

(10) Jour. A/cinq Res. Autumn, 1967.

(11) Journal UEC, 3, 1967.

(12) The A/cant's Mag. 1971, p. 285.

(13) "Value and Capital" (OUP, 1946) p. 176.

(14) Quote from the Accounting Rev. July, 1961, p. 118.

(15) In Zeitschrift fuer betriebswissenschaftliche Forschung, 1973, p. 27.

II On Not Accounting for Inflation

3 A Case for Historical Costs

R.N. Anthony

Whatever the disagreement over the precise objectives of financial statements, there probably is general agreement that they are supposed to report the economic events and the economic status of an enterprise as realistically as possible - they are supposed to "tell it like it was". The essence of the current debate between the historical-cost advocates and the proponents of replacement cost is, I believe, a disagreement on what actually constitutes economic reality.

What really does happen in the company about which the financial statements report? Some companies grow and prosper and other companies are less successful and fail. The factors responsible for prosperity or failure are complicated, and the actual financial statements reflect this complexity.

In order to focus on the accounting issue, we must separate out the influence of extraneous factors. We can do this by looking at a steady-state company, one that neither grows nor shrinks, but remains at a constant level of production and unit sales indefinitely.

We can then test alternative accounting concepts by examining whether they accurately report this steady-state situation. The essential characteristic of such a company is that its revenues will just equal all its costs, including the cost of capital. If revenues exceed all costs, the company will shrink. So if, under one accounting concept, the income statement reports that a steady-state company is growing or shrinking, then we know that this concept does not provide a realistic picture.

I shall first describe a steady-state company in an environment of price stability and show the accounting that accurately reports what has happened in this company. With the price-stability model as a baseline, I shall next examine alternative accounting concepts (historical-cost and replacement-cost) for companies in an inflationary environment, and, by applying the same test, find out which concept reports what actually has happened. And finally I shall report some evidence that suggests which of these two concepts is more realistic.

PRICE STABILITY MODEL

Company A operates in an environment that has no inflation. To make the model as economical as possible, let's say that Company A has only a single asset. It was purchased at the beginning of Year 1 at a cost of $1,200 and has a useful life of three years. Half of the funds for the purchase of this asset were provided from debt and half from equity investors. The $600 of debt is a three-year bond, with interest payable annually at a rate of 4% (2% after taxes, assuming a 50% income tax rate). The $600 of equity comes from investors who expect a return of 10%.

The company's only operating cost is the depreciation on its asset, which on a straight-line basis is $400 per year. In order to operate at a steady rate, Company A's annual revenues must equal all its costs, which are: depreciation, $400, income tax on operating income, $72, aftertax interest cost, $12, and equity cost, $60 - a total of $544.

The company pays out all its net income as dividends. It must do this if it is to be a steady-state company, for if it retains any earnings, it will grow. Since depreciation is a noncash cost, the company will accumulate cash, but for the sake of simplicity let's assume that it earns no interest on this cash.

At the end of Year 3, Company A uses $600 of the $1,200 cash it has generated during the three years to retire its debt. It takes the remaining $600 plus $600 obtained from a new three-year debt issue and buys a new machine for $1,200. It repeats the process indefinitely.

Exhibit 1 shows the income statements and balance sheets for Company A. They are simple, and obvious. The income statement for each year reports that profit is equal to the dividend and, consequently, that Company A remains in a steady state. The balance sheet shows the debt and equity capital that investors have committed to Company A and the assets acquired with this capital.

EXHIBIT I

STEADY-STATE COMPANY A

PRICE STABILITY

Years	0	1	2	3	4	5	6
Income Statements							
Revenue		$ 544	$ 544	$ 544	$ 544	$ 544	$ 544
Depreciation		(400)	(400)	(400)	(400)	(400)	(400)
Operating Income		144	144	144	144	144	144
Tax @ 50%		(72)	(72)	(72)	(72)	(72)	(72)
Aftertax operating income		72	72	72	72	72	72
Interest expense (aftertax)		(12)	(12)	(12)	(12)	(12)	(12)
Net income		60	60	60	60	60	60
Dividends		(60)	(60)	(60)	(60)	(60)	(60)
Retained earnings		$ 0	$ 0	$ 0	$ 0	$ 0	$ 0
Balance sheet, end of year							
Cash	$ 0	$ 400	$ 800	$ 0	£ 400	$ 800	$ 0
Plant	1,200	800	400	1,200	800	400	1,200
Total assets	$1,200	$1,200	$1,200	$1,200	$1,200	$1,200	$1,200
Debt	$ 600	$ 600	$ 600	$ 600	$ 600	$ 600	$ 600
Equity	600	600	600	600	600	600	600
Total liability and equity	$1,200	$1,200	$1,200	$1,200	$1,200	$1,200	$1,200

Incidentally, I am basing Company A's rate of debt interest on the widely accepted generalization that the riskless cost of capital is approximately 2%. I have added 2% more for the risk premium of debt in an industrial company, making the pretax interest rate 4%. The 10% cost of equity capital includes a risk premium of 6 percentage points above the pretax cost of debt. Considering that our company is a steady-state company with correspondingly low risk, 10% may be on the high side, but the percentage has no effect on the conclusions to be drawn.

Of course, in most companies the cost of equity capital cannot be determined, but in a steady-state company the cost of capital is a readily determined equilibrium percentage. At a higher percentage, additional equity capital will be attracted to the company, and the company will grow. At a lower percentage, the original investors would have been unwilling to commit their funds.

INFLATIONARY CONDITIONS

Now let us examine what happens if, instead of price stability, we have inflation. How will a steady-state company set selling prices under inflation?

The answer - and this is my central point - is that in an inflationary economy a company can price in either of two ways and still fulfill all the conditions of remaining a steady-state company.

In examining these two alternatives, we shall continue to assume a situation in which a company has a single asset which originally cost £1,200. We shall further assume that the company operates in an environment in which equipment replacement costs are increasing 6% a year, and, for simplicity, that the increase occurs at the beginning of each year. We shall increase the tax cost of debt to 10%, which is an allowance of an additional 6 percentage points for inflation, because the general belief is that the cost of debt increases so as to offset the rate of inflation.[1] We shall also assume that the cost of equity capital is 16%, or 6 percentage points above its no-inflation cost.

Note that the alternatives to be examined involve different companies from the company in Exhibit 1. If we were to use the same company, we would have to examine its transition from a non-inflationary to an inflationary economy. This is a special, one-time phenomenon, and there is no need for us to complicate our analysis by considering it.

Historical-cost Pricing

Company B sets selling prices on the basis of historical costs. In each of the first three years that it uses the machine with a historical cost of $1,200, it sets selling prices so as to recover its depreciation of $400, its income tax on operations of $126, its after-tax debt interest cost of $30 ($600 x 10% x 50% tax), and its cost of equity capital of $96 ($600 x 16%), a total of $652. Its revenue must therefore be $652.

At the end of Year 3 it purchases a new machine, at a cost of $1,430, representing the three-year effect of inflation. As is its practice, the company finances this purchase half with debt and half with equity, so it incurs a three-year debt of $715, uses the $600 cash that it has remaining, and obtains new equity of $115 for the balance.

Each one of these moves is entirely consistent with our assumptions and with the practices that at least some businesses follow. We need not examine the question of why Company B sets selling prices so as to recover only the historical cost of its assets. As I will show there is ample evidence that some companies do price this way.

A criticism of this statement has been that a company may set selling prices on the basis of historical costs because generally accepted accounting principles are based on historical costs. The implication is that managers are stupid, that accounting governs management decisions rather than reflects the results of management decisions. But managers are not stupid; companies that price to recover historical costs do so because their managers conclude that this is the best pricing policy given the competitive conditions.

Additional Equity

Having established a satisfactory debt/equity ratio, Company B can obtain new debt financing consistent with it. Furthermore, if the cost of equity capital in this environment is 16%, Company B, with its demonstrated return of 16%, can obtain additional equity capital when it needs to do so.

One may argue that the necessity of raising additional equity capital implies that this is not in fact a steady-state situation. My point is that the company's physical productive capacity remains unchanged, it neither grows nor shrinks in size. In the fourth year, it has more dollars of capital, but it needs this capital to maintain its same physical size.

One could also claim that in a period of inflation the real value of a given amount of shareholders' investment decreases and that shareholders will therefore expect an increasing rate of return on the amount of their investment. The fact is, however, that this consideration is what made the cost of equity capital under inflation equal to 16% compared with 10% in a condition of price stability. To require an additional increment would be double counting.

Having aquired a new machine, Company B now sets selling prices in Years 4, 5, and 6 to recover the historical cost of this machine, which is $1,430. Its operating costs are the annual depreciation cost of $477, and to this it must add a provision for taxes of $150 on its operating income, and a profit margin sufficient to cover the aftertax interest expense of $36 and the 16% return on the $715 of equity, which is $114. So its selling prices must produce total revenue of $777.

(I realise it may seem unrealistic to assume that a company can increase its selling prices in Year 4 as sharply as the above calculations indicate is necessary. Since the only cost in Company B is depreciation of a single asset, the effect of the plant replacement is much more abrupt than would be in the case in a real company in which there are many other cost elements and many assets, with replacements spread over a period of time).

At the end of Year 6, Company B has accumulated $1,430 of cash. It uses $715 to pay off its debt. It uses the remainder plus $852 of new debt and $137 of new equity to purchase a third machine, which costs $1,704.

Income Statement Test

The financial statements describing this situation are shown in Exhibit II. They are prepared in accordance with current generally accepted accounting principles, that is, depreciation is based on the historical cost of the asset and amounts are stated in actual dollars.

(Throughout this analysis the financial statements are given in actual dollars. The question of whether the amounts should be restated in dollars of constant purchasing power is a quite separate issue and is not discussed in this article).

Recall that our test was that in a steady-state company, profits must equal the cost of equity capital, as shown by the fact that when dividends are equal to the cost of equity capital, retained earnings are zero. Company B is a steady-

EXHIBIT II

STEADY-STATE COMPANY B

HISTORICAL-COST PRICING AND HISTORICAL-COST ACCOUNTING

Years	0	1	2	3	4	5	6
Income statements							
Revenue		$ 652	$ 652	$ 652	$ 777	$ 777	$ 777
Depreciation		(400)	(400)	(400)	(477)	(477)	(477)
Operating income		252	252	252	300	300	300
Tax @ 50%		(126)	(126)	(126)	(150)	(150)	(150)
Aftertax operating income		126	126	126	150	150	150
Interest expense (aftertax)		(30)	(30)	(30)	(36)	(36)	(36)
Net income		96	96	96	114	114	114
Dividends		(96)	(96)	(96)	(114)	(114)	(114)
Retained earnings		$ 0	$ 0	$ 0	$ 0	$ 0	$ 0
Balance sheet, end of year							
Cash	$ 0	$ 400	$ 800	$ 0	$ 477	$ 954	$ 0
Plant	1,200	800	400	1,430	953	476	1,704
Total Assets	$1,200	$1,200	$1,200	$1,430	$1,430	$1,430	$1,704
Debt	$ 600	$ 600	$ 600	$ 715	$ 715	$ 715	$ 852
Equity	600	600	600	715	715	715	852
Total liability and equity	$1,200	$1,200	$1,200	$1,430	$1,430	$1,430	$1,704

state company, and its income statement, prepared on a historical-cost basis, reports that retained earnings are zero in each and every year. The income statements report reality.

We therefore can conclude that the principles used to construct this income statement are correct, and specifically that in these circumstances depreciation should be based on the historical cost of the asset. (The balance sheet shows an increase in the monetary amount of assets, but we know that there has been no change in the physical amount of assets; the monetary amounts reflect changes in the price level. Our test is an income statement test, not a balance sheet test).

Retained earnings

One may argue that Company B would be well advised not to pay out all its profits as dividends. If it retained earnings sufficient to provide for the cost of the new equipment at the end of Year 3, the company would not need new equity capital from outside investors. This view is sound, and we could create a more complicated model with retained earnings, but such a model would in no way change the cost of equity capital or alter the fact that profit was equal to the cost of equity capital in the situation being analysed.

One might propose a model in which the company replaces an equal fraction of its plant each year, which, given my assumptions, would have the company paying out all its income as dividends and raising new equity capital at the same time. Of course this is unlikely to happen. Instead, the company would retain earnings sufficient to provide at least part of the additional equity capital. But whether earnings are retained or distributed, the fact is that the company has earned 16% on equity capital, and the income statement correctly reports this fact. This situation is, of course, the extreme case; in reality, companies do not replace an equal fraction of their plant each year.

REPLACEMENT-COST PRICING

Another way in which a company can price in an inflationary environment is to match its selling prices to current costs. We shall now examine Company C, which does this. Company C has the same interest and dividend requirements as Company B, but its selling prices are higher than Company B's because the depreciation component is based on the replacement cost of the asset.

EXHIBIT III

STEADY STATE COMPANY C

REPLACEMENT-COST PRICING AND HISTORICAL-COST ACCOUNTING

Years	0	1	2	3	4	5	6
Income Statements							
Revenue *		$ 700	$ 750	$ 804	$ 842	$ 904	$ 968
Depreciation		(400)	(400)	(400)	(476)	(476)	(476)
Operating Income		300	350	404	366	428	492
Tax @ 50%		(150)	(175)	(202)	(183)	(214)	(246)
Aftertax operating income		150	175	202	183	214	246
Interest expense (aftertax)		(30)	(30)	(30)	(34)	(34)	(34)
Net income		120	145	172	149	180	212
Dividends		(96)	(96)	(96)	(120)	(120)	(120)
Retained earnings		$ 24	$ 49	$ 76	$ 29	$ 60	$ 92
Balance sheet, end of year							
Cash	$ 0	$ 424	$ 873	$ 0	$ 505	$1,041	$ 0
Plant	1,200	800	400	1,430	954	478	1,703
Total assets	$1,200	$1,224	$1,273	$1,430	$1,459	$1,519	$1,703
Debt	$ 600	$ 600	$ 600	$ 681	$ 681	$ 681	$ 775
Equity	600	624	673	749	778	638	928
Total liability and equity	$1,200	$1,224	$1,273	$1,430	$1,459	$1,519	$1,703
* Calculation of revenue							
Replacement value		$1,272	$1,348	$1,430	$1,516	$1,607	$1,703
Depreciation (1/3)		(424)	(449)	(476)	(505)	(536)	(568)
Tax on operating income		(150)	(175)	(202)	(183)	(214)	(246)
Aftertax interest and dividends		(126)	(126)	(126)	(154)	(154)	(154)
Revenue		$ 700	$ 750	$ 804	$ 842	$ 904	$ 968

This depreciation works out to one third of $1,272, or $424, in Year 1; to one third of $1,348, or $449, in Year 2; and to one third of $1,430, or $476, in Year 3. Income tax continues to be calculated on the basis of historical costs. The question of changing the basis of income taxation is not an accounting question, and we are here focusing only on the accounting issue.

Whether taxes based on replacement costs would be lower than current taxes which are based on historical costs adjusted for accelerated depreciation, the investment credit, and the Asset Depreciation Range, is an interesting question, but it is irrelevent for our present purpose. The tax on operating income works out to be $150 in Year 1, $175 in Year 2, and $202 in Year 3.

The company must also recover its aftertax interest cost of $30 and its required profit of $96. It therefore prices its products so that revenues are the sum of the above amounts: $700 in Year 1, $750 in Year 2, and $804 in Year 3. Stated another way, unless Company C earns revenue of $700 in Year 1, it will not generate the $424 of cash that it needs to provide for the replacement cost of the machine.

At the end of Year 3 Company C will have accumulated $1,349 of cash. It will use $600 of this cash to pay off its debt and will have $749 to apply to the purchase of the replacement machine. Since the new machine costs $1,430, the company will need to borrow only $681 of debt to finance it, which is somewhat less than its intended debt/equity ratio of 50-50. Its annual aftertax interest cost will then be 5% of $681, or $34, and the annual dividend requirement will be 16% of $749, or $120. Data for Years 4, 5, and 6, covering the life of the replacement machine, can then be calculated in a similar manner.

The only debatable point about the financial statements for Company C, shown in Exhibit III, is the fact that the cost of equity capital has been calculated on the original amount of the shareholders' investment. As the balance sheet shows, the recorded amount of shareholders' equity increases each year, and one may argue that shareholders expect a 16% return on the total amount.

This is a weak argument. The increase in shareholders' equity reflects only the temporary accumulation of funds that will be used to acquire new equipment. It does not represent an additional investment by the shareholders.

Debt/Equity Shift

Note that by basing its prices on replacement cost, Company C has accumulated cash that will provide for the equity portion of the purchase price of the replacement machine when it is acquired at the end of Year 3, so an additional equity investment is not required as was the case with Company B.

Note also that Company C actually has accumulated more cash than it needs in order to maintain its 50-50 debt/equity ratio. This is because replacement-cost pricing does not take into account the fact that the debt obligation is unaffected by inflation. This inadequacy is a hidden defect in most replacement-cost models, but I shall do no more than call attention to it.

Note also that the income statements indicate that profits increase each year and that they exceed dividend requirements by $24 in Year 1, $49 in Year 2, and $76 in Year 3. Our company is nevertheless a steady-state company in the sense that its physical size remains unchanged. It holds the additional cash and uses it later on for the purpose of replacing the machine.

Wrong Signal

The advocates of replacement-cost accounting point to Exhibit III as an example of what is wrong with conventional accounting, and they are correct. This exhibit gives the wrong signal. It indicates that the company is growing in size because its profits exceed the cost of its equity capital. Accordingly, some recommend that accounting should be done on the basis of replacement costs.

In replacement-cost accounting, the gross amount of plant is restated each year at its replacement cost, and annual depreciation expense is based on this replacement cost. Since this was the basis of pricing used in Exhibit III, the annual depreciation amounts are the same as the replacement depreciation amounts shown at the bottom.

When assets are written up to replacement costs, a holding gain is created. This gain is separated from the results of operations in the period; for simplicity, we shall credit it directly to shareholders' equity on the balance sheets, although some people advocate showing it on the income statement below the operating profit.

Exhibit IV shows the financial statements for Company C on a replacement basis. (The income tax is still based on historical cost as in Exhibit III, however.) In each year, profit is just equal to the dividend requirement, and so we conclude that replacement-cost accounting is appropriate under these circumstances.

COMPARISON OF ALTERNATIVES

In comparing Exhibits II, III, and IV, and in contrasting them to our bench mark in Exhibit I, it is apparent that the income statements in Exhibit III do not tell a valid story. The reported amount of retained earnings in this exhibit indicates that the company is growing, whereas with the policies described we know that it is in a steady state. It will accumulate cash from prices based on replacement costs, and it will use this cash to buy higher-priced replacement machines. If it distributed this cash to shareholders or used it for other purposes, its intention of using the cash to replace equipment, which was the justification for basing selling prices on replacement costs, would be nullified.

The critics of conventional-cost accounting are therefore right: Exhibit III should be discarded, and Exhibit IV, which is prepared in accordance with the replacement-cost concept of accounting, should be adopted because it gives the correct picture in these circumstances.

But - and this is the all-important "but" - this conclusion is valid only if a company prices so as to recover its replacement costs. If a company prices to recover historical costs as Company B does, conventional accounting gives a correct picture of its situation as shown in Exhibit II. By contrast, if the income statements in Exhibit II were converted to a replacement-cost basis, they would signal, incorrectly, that the company was shrinking in size.

We can conclude from this demonstration, therefore, that the correct answer to the question of whether accounting should be based on historical costs or on replacement costs is: it depends. If a company prices so as to recover its historical costs, historical-cost accounting is appropriate. If a company prices so as to recover replacement costs, replacement-cost accounting is appropriate.

SOUND STANDARD

The trouble is that such a conclusion does not provide a sound basis for an accounting standard. Unfortunately,

EXHIBIT IV

STEADY-STATE COMPANY C

REPLACEMENT-COST PRICING AND REPLACEMENT-COST ACCOUNTING

Years	0	1	2	3	4	5	6
Income Statements							
Revenue		$ 700	$ 750	$ 804	$ 842	$ 904	$ 968
Depreciation		(424)	(449)	(476)	(505)	(536)	(568)
Operating income		276	301	328	337	368	400
Income tax		(150)	(175)	(202)	(183)	(214)	(246)
Aftertax operating income		126	126	126	154	154	154
Interest expense (aftertax)		(30)	(30)	(30)	(34)	(34)	(34)
Net income		96	96	96	120	120	120
Dividends		(96)	(96)	(96)	(120)	(120)	(120)
Retained earnings		$ 0	$ 0	$ 0	$ 0	$ 0	$ 0
Balance sheet, end of year							
Cash	$ 0	$ 424	$ 873	$ 0	$ 505	$1,041	$ 0
Plant, gross	1,200	1,272	1,348	1,430	1,516	1,607	1,703
Depreciation	(0)	(424)	(873)	(0)	(505)	(1,041)	(0)
Plant, net	1,200	848	475	1,430	1,011	566	1,703
Total assets	$1,200	$1,272	$1,348	$1,430	$1,516	$1,607	$1,703
Debt	$ 600	$ 600	$ 600	$ 681	$ 681	$ 681	$ 775
Equity	600	672	748	749	835	926	928
Total liability and equity	$1,200	$1,272	$1,348	$1,430	$1,516	$1,607	$1,703

there is no reliable way of identifying companies that price on one basis or the other. Prices are seldom clearly based on historical costs, or alternatively on replacement costs. Many factors influence the actual selling price, and most companies could not honestly say that they use one approach or the other.

In particular, if the choice of an accounting method were left to individual companies, as is the case with inventory-valuation and depreciation methods, there is no assurance that companies would make that choice in accordance with the principle stated above, rather than in accordance with the perceived benefits of reporting income in one way or the other.

Thus the choice of an accounting standard must be made on the basis of the general tendency in the economy rather than on the situation in specific companies.

MAINTENANCE OF CAPITAL

Advocates of replacement-cost accounting assume that prices are based on replacement costs and that ongoing companies must recover the replacement cost of assets through operations if they are to "maintain capital".

For example, John C. Burton Jr., the former chief accountant of the Securities and Exchange Commission, say quite categorically, "It is obvious that matching historical monetary cost against current revenue will not give a good approximation of the long-run average net cash inflow at current activity levels under conditions of rapidly changing cost."[2]

In proposing disclosure of replacement costs, the SEC stated: "The Commission believes that these data will make it possible for investors to obtain a better understanding of the current costs of operating the business which cannot be obtained from historical-cost financial statements taken alone and that such an understanding is necessary in order to make informed investment decisions."[3]

And Britain's Sandilands Report is based on a similar premise.[4]

But as the experience of Company B clearly demonstrates, this assumption is wrong. A Company can operate indefinitely by recovering its historical costs plus the cost of its capital. It must indeed obtain additional debt and equity capital in an inflationary economy, but if investors believe that the company will earn an adequate return, they will be willing to supply that capital. The return that they require is higher in an inflationary environment than in a non-inflationary one, but this is reflected in the higher debt and equity rates, and need not be reflected again by using replacement-cost depreciation.

EMPIRICAL EVIDENCE

While much has been written and said about how people think prices should be arrived at, the real question is how prices are set. We therefore turn to evidence that shows how companies actually set prices.

Since pricing practices are so diverse, and since the relationship between selling prices and cost varies from being quite close in some cases, such as cost-type contracts, to none at all in others, such as perfume and prize-fight tickets, one can cite examples in support of any theory.

Obviously, such anecdotal evidence does not provide the answer we need. An accounting standard must apply to all companies, or at least to a broad category of companies. For evidence suggesting what that standard should be, we need data on the general relationship between costs and prices.

Nevertheless, as near as I can determine, the principal evidence that supports the view that prices are based on replacement costs is anecdotal evidence. Plenty of businessmen wish that prices were based on replacement costs because they obviously prefer higher profits to lower profits. But wishing doesn't make it so. There are undoubtedly individual companies that both have a policy of recovering replacement costs and are successful in implementing this policy, but there are no data that I know of showing that the number of such companies is large.

Inconclusive Data

So far as I know, no macro studies have been made on this specific question. There have been many macro studies of prices - that is, analyses of price movements in the economy as a whole or in some segment of it, but they had other objectives. These studies do contain some useful information although they are not conclusive.

In one excellent survey, Aubrey Silberston summarizes 153 British and American studies of prices.[5] While some reference is made to the tendency for prices to vary with changes in the costs of labour and material, the subject of depreciation is not even mentioned. Silberston's primary concern was the controversy about marginal costing versus full costing, and most of the period covered in his survey was not characterised by significant inflation. Either or both of these facts may account for the absence of information that bears directly on the issue of current interest.

In October 1970, the Federal Reserve Board and the Social Science Research Council sponsored a conference on the econometrics of price determination. Participants were leading econometricians, indluding Otto Eckstein and Lawrence Klein, who are responsible for two of the leading American econometric models. I think it is not an exaggeration to say that this conference considered and evaluated all the significant macro evidence about prices that was available at the time.

In the 397 page conference report there is no evidence whatsoever that prices were influenced by the replacement cost of capital assets.[6] To the extent that depreciation entered into the equations at all, only historical-cost depreciation was relevant.

William D. Nordhaus studied fluctuations in total industry profits from 1948 to 1973.[7] Like most economists, he regards reported profits only as "nominal" profits, so he corrected them for changes in price levels. After he had done so, and after taking cyclical fluctuations into account, he found that profits had declined over that period. A decline in profits adjusted for price-level changes indicates that prices are not based on replacement costs. However, Nordhaus's study was not designed to answer this specific question, so, again, the evidence is indicative at best.

Actual Practices

There are, however, several straws in the wind which lead me to believe that companies do tend to price on the basis of historical costs:

1. Some $50 billion of cost-type procurement contracts are awarded annually by the federal government, all based on historical costs for depreciable assets. The Cost Accounting Standards Board has considered, and rejected, a proposal to provide increased depreciation allowances based on replacement costs.

2. Similarly, large health care payments totalling perhaps $50 billion annually are made on the basis of cost calculations

that include historical costs. Hospital charges do include an allowance for capital improvement in excess of historical costs, but this is in recognition of the cost of improved technology, not for the replacement cost of the same technology.

3. Many private-sector contracts contain escalation clauses for labour costs and material costs, but few contain escalation clauses for increases caused by higher replacement costs of existing equipment. Some of these contracts are quite long-term, eight years or more, for example, for construction of a nuclear power plant.

4. Similarly, many building rental agreements contain escalation clauses for certain cost elements, but not for replacement costs of the building itself.

5. Financial lease rates are based on the historical cost of the equipment leased at the time the lease begins; usually, they are not adjusted upward for increases in replacement costs during the lease period. "Historical cost" in this context may be either the original cost of the equipment, or the amount that the lessor paid for used equipment.

6. The price control formulas used in the early 1970s allowed only for historical-cost depreciation. The Price Commission (which included two well-known economists) never once debated the merits of allowing replacement-cost depreciation.

7. Public utilities are greatly upset at the prospect of being required to adopt replacement-cost accounting or price-level-adjusted accounting, and advocates of such accounting currently tend to say that they should be exempted as exceptions to the general rule. Why should they be exceptions to the general rule? Is it not plausible that their revenues, which are based on historical costs, are adequate to keep capital flowing into the industry, and that their performance is faithfully measured by traditional historical-cost accounting methods?

8. Managers are said to have difficulty in understanding the results of an inflation adjustment to their data. Why should this be if they have been pricing according to replacement costs all along?

9. Businessmen make resource allocation decisions on the basis of fairly well developed and generally understood capital budgeting models. All such models require that the investment should recover its actual costs plus a satisfactory return. No such model of which I am aware demands that an investment should, in addition, earn enought to cover the replacement

costs of the succeeding acquisition.

10. Although Philips' Gloeilampenfabrieken N.V. and a few other Dutch companies have used replacement-cost accounting for many years, there has been no great rush, even by other Dutch companies, to swing over to the practice. In the Soviet Union, all fixed assets have been revalued as of a given time (most recently in 1972). In some Latin American countries, most successfully in Brazil, all assets are indexed upward, and in these countries, selling prices are based on the adjusted costs, not on historical costs. In most other countries, even those with high inflation, depreciation continues to be based on historical costs.

Thus such evidence as we do have supports the view that prices are based on the historical cost of fixed assets, not the replacement cost.

Advocates of historical costs, of which I am one, should not even have to search for such evidence. The burden of proof should be on those who propose a change. Replacement cost advocates have offered no evidence - except wishful thinking - to support their position.

IN SUMMARY

If a company's selling prices are such that it recovers its historical costs plus its cost of capital, then the company can continue to operate indefinitely, and its annual profit is best measured by the difference between revenues and historical costs.

If a company's selling prices are such that it recovers its replacement costs plus its cost of capital, then the company can also continue to operate indefinitely, but in this case its annual profit is best measured by the difference between revenues and replacement costs.

There is no objective way of classifying a give company into one of these two categories. We must therefore act on the basis of general tendencies, and the general tendency seems to be that prices are based on historical costs.

Unless replacement-cost advocates can furnish evidence that this is not so, we should continue to use historical-cost accounting. And this evidence must be especially strong - strong enough to counteract the fact that replacement-cost accounting would be extremely difficult to implement and would increase the subjectivity of reported net income. We should not get into this morass unless there is persuasive evidence that this is the way the economy actually works.

FOOTNOTES

(1) John Lintner, "Inflation and Security Returns," Journal of Finance, May 1975, p. 259.

(2) John C. Burton "Financial Reporting in an Age of Inflation," Journal of Accountancy, February 1975, p. 69.

(3) "Notice of Proposed Amendments to Regulation S-X to Require Disclosure of Certain Replacement Cost Data in Notes to Financial Statements," SEC 57-579, August 21, 1975.

(4) Inflation Accounting: Report of the Inflation Accounting Committee, Cmnd Document 6225, Her Majesty's Stationery Office, London, 1975.

(5) Aubrey Silberston, "Surveys of Applied Economics: Price Behavior of Firms," The Economic Journal, September 1970, p. 511.

(6) The Econometrics of Price Determination Conference, 1970 (Washington, D.C.: Board of Governers of Federal Reserve System, 1972).

(7) William D. Nordhaus, "The Falling Share of Profits," Brookings Papers on Economic Activity, 1974: 1, p. 169.

Author's Note:

I appreciate the constructive criticism of Robert T. Sprouse and the financial support of the Associates of the Harvard Graduate School of Business Administration.

4 A Defense of Historical Cost Accounting

Yuji Ijiri

Introduction

It is truly remarkable that historical cost accounting has been the principal methodology of accounting over several centuries. Unfortunately, however, familiarity often breeds contempt, and attacks on historical cost accounting have been launched from various corners of business and accounting especially since the beginning of the second half of this century.

The argument that I am going to present in this paper in defense of historical cost accounting is addressed not only to those who attempt to eliminate it completely from the field of accounting but also to those who recognize the significance of historical cost accounting only to a very limited extent. However, it is not addressed to those who evaluate highly the contribution by historical cost accounting but nonetheless advocate the need for improving it and supplementing it by other procedures. I, myself, do not consider historical cost accounting to have all the answers for the whole field of accounting. Nevertheless, I do believe that the contribution made by historical cost accounting is really significant and that it will continue to make significant contributions to business in the future as well.

It is difficult to recognize the value of something to which we are very much accustomed. However, if the best way to recognize the value of the air is to try to stop breathing or to move into a highly polluted area, perhaps we can apply the same principle and imagine what the business world might look like without historical cost accounting.

In the next section, I shall present the accounting practices of five hypothetical countries, A through E. The role of historical cost accounting will be increased gradually as we move from Country A through Country E. Then in Section III, I shall summarize my argument for historical cost accounting imbedded in the accounting practices in these countries.

II. A Defense for Historical Cost

In order to obtain some insights into the significant role that has been played by historical cost accounting, let us consider what might happen if we substituted current cost accounting for historical cost accounting. I use current cost accounting because it is the alternative to historical cost accounting which has been most strongly advocated. However, a similar type of argument as the one presented in this section is also applicable to other kinds of proposed alternatives to historical cost accounting.

The firms in Country A do not keep any records on the historical flows of resources. Instead, the accounting practices of this country require that a firm take a physical inventory of all assets and liabilities at the end of each year and evaluate them at the current costs. Income for the year is then calculated as the difference in the net worth at the end of the year and the net worth at the beginning of the year, after adjusting for capital transactions (new stock issues, dividends, etc.). The historical records of the resource flows are not required since the history of how resources came under a firm's control (e.g., how much was paid for the resources) is totally irrelevant in the current cost valuation.

The investors in this country are completely at the mercy of the management, because they are only told the results of the operations of the firm with no recourse to check how the results have been produced. The management can spend the firm's resources in any way they want without leaving any trace of where the resources came from and where they went, since in this country, past records are considered to be of no interest. Instead, a considerable effort is made in each firm at the year-end to list every asset and liability of the firm and evaluate them at their year-end prices. A balance sheet is then prepared at current cost and the income for the year is calculated as stated above.

Undoubtedly, this is the most primitive way of recording and reporting in current cost accounting. However, even in this balance sheet method of calculating income, if the valuation method is based on historical cost, the investors can implicitly impose the condition on the firm that historical records of transactions be kept, since without records of historical resource flows it is not possible to evaluate resources in historical costs. This automatic control feature of historical cost accounting is completely lacking in Country A.

While current cost accounting does not have the resource control feature imbedded in its valuation method, the resource control system can be initiated in addition to the year-end valuation. Let us introduce such a control system in Country B while retaining the current cost valuation method.

The accounting practice in Country B is slightly more civilized. The valuation method used in this country is/also the current cost basis as in Country A, but in Country B, it is required to keep records in physical units on the increase and the decrease in every type of resource. The firm takes a physical inventory of all assets and liabilities at the end of each year, but unlike Country A, the physical inventory is only a means of verifying the accuracy of the records rather than the sole basis for preparing the financial statements.

The reason that the records are kept in physical units is that current costs change over time and the year-end prices cannot be anticipated during the year. Historical costs are considered to be of no value, hence, they are completely eliminated from the records.

Although in this country it is required to keep records for changes in each type of resource in physical units, it is not required to keep records on how much of the resources (inputs) were spent to obtain how much of the other resources (outputs). For example, it is required to keep a stock ledger indicating in the respective physical units the balance and changes in each item in the inventories, and to keep a cash ledger for every cash receipt and disbursement. It is not required to keep a record on how much was paid for materials, since it is irrelevant for the current cost valuation. In other words, records on the balance and changes in each resource type are kept independently from those in other resource types in a single-entry fashion, instead of relating inputs and outputs as observed in the double-entry bookkeeping system. In this sense, firms in this country do not have records of "transactions", as currently exist in the United States and elsewhere, although records of every change in every type of asset and liability are properly kept.

This lack of transaction records in Country B presents a serious weakness in resource management and control not only in purchases, but also in production, in sales and in all other activities of a firm. Note that such a situation cannot occur if historical cost accounting is used. When a firm receives 100 units of materials, it must determine how much money has been or is going to be paid for those materials, since otherwise their historical cost cannot be determined. Similarly, when 50 units of finished goods are produced, a firm must determine how much material was used for the finished goods in order to determine their historical cost. Thus, every increase and decrease in resources is "chained" by means of input-output relationship in historical cost accounting. The double-entry bookkeeping system offers an effective means of recording this relationship.[1]

Of course, it is possible to chain the changes in resources in physical units, and there is no reason why the double-entry bookkeeping system cannot be utilized to accommodate such a transaction as

Dr. Materials	100 units
Cr. Cash	$4,000

although the equality of the debit entry and the credit entry is no longer maintained.[2] Similarly, there is no reason why some sort of estimate of the year-end current costs cannot be used as a basis of recording as in standard cost accounting, although it would become necessary to set up such estimates or standards for all kinds of assets, including fixed assets. But, the fundamental difference between historical cost accounting and current cost accounting is that in the firmer, the chaining of inputs and outputs is the basis for the valuation, while in the latter, such an automatic control feature is missing.

At the very minimum, the significance of the custodianship function of historical cost accounting seems unquestionable. Actually, the function of accounting in controlling the resources of a firm is the most fundamental one with which accounting began several centuries ago. Since then, the role of accounting has been expanded considerably. But, the important question now is whether the custodianship function has become insignificant. Knowing that millions of investors are relying upon the custodianship function of accounting when they invest in a firm, how can one discuss accounting without considering this important function?

However, the significance of historical cost accounting is far from being limited to the custodianship function, as we shall see in the next example.

Let us now observe the accounting practices in Country C. Here, the importance of historical cost accounting in resource control is fully recognized, and it is required to keep records on the resource flows, based on the historical costs. However, for the purpose of income distribution in the form of dividends, bonuses to officers and employers, income taxes, refunds to customers of a firm in a regulated industry etc., it is required to base the determination of income on the current cost method of valuation.

Here, the income figure is used not just as information but as a means of solving conflicts of interest in income distribution. Therefore, the process of income determination must be carried out in the least disputable manner. Otherwise, tremendous pressures will be put on accountants, and the process of income determination will become a process of political negotiations rather than a process of systematic calculations. A flood of law suits will arise out of disputes over income figures, and the social cost of accounting will become phenomenal.

It is extremely important that the basis of income determination be least disputable if the income figure is to be used as a basis of income distribution. Unfortunately, however, accountants in Country C will find current cost income (income determined under the current cost valuation) far more disputable and therefore less suitable as a basis for income distribution than historical cost income.

Current cost accounting is based on contemplated transactions. In order to determine current cost income, it is first necessary to set up a method of determining uniquely which contemplated transaction should be used as a basis of valuation. This is because there are numerous transactions that may be contemplated with respect to the replacement or the disposal of a given resource. Various outside offers may be received, market prices at various domestic and foreign markets may be quoted. Which alternative should be used as a basis? The highest, or the lowest, or an average? How should the search area, to get offers or find prices, be determined? Notice that it is not enough to determine whether a contemplated transaction is reasonable, since in many cases there is more than one contemplated transaction that is considered to be reasonable. In order to avoid disputes over the income figure, there must be a means of determining a unique transaction among all transactions that may be contemplated with respect to a given resource.

Historical cost accounting avoids this problem, since it is based on the actual transaction that was chosen by the firm. Of course, both in historical cost accounting and in current cost accounting, there is room for disputes over the interpretation of the financial effects of the transaction. But, at least the former is less disputable than the latter by not having the problem of selecting one out of numerous transactions that can be contemplated.

The second factor which makes current cost income more

disputable than historic cost income is the non-additivity of current costs. The historical cost of Resource A and Resource B is by definition the sum of the historical cost of Resource A and Resource B. If A is purchased at $10 and B at $15, the historical cost of A and B is defined to be $25.

This additivity does not exist in current cost valuation, insofar as the price of a resource is not necessarily equal to the sum of the prices of its components. If the current cost of Resource A is $20 and Resource B is $30 but that of A and B together is $60, should we use $50 or $60 as the current cost of Resource A and Resource B? Similarly, in evaluating a large quantity of merchandise, the price for the entire lot can be quite different from the sum of the prices for the sublots, even if the lot consists of only one homogeneous product due to quantity discounts, ease or difficulty in purchasing or selling a large lot etc. Also, the competent-by-competent valuation of a plant can be quite different from the valuation of the plant as a whole. What is more serious is the problem that the component-by-component evaluation of the assets of a firm or its subsidiary can be considerably different from the valuation of the firm or its subsidiary as an organism. This problem of determining the level of aggregation at which resources in the firm (or the firm itself) should be evaluated is a serious one that must be resolved in order to avoid disputes over current cost income.

However, there is a diametrically opposite problem in historical cost accounting. Instead of the above aggregation problem in historical cost accounting, the problem is one of disaggregation, or allocation. Suppose that Resources A and B are purchased together for $20, but at the end of the year the firm only had Resource A. How much of the $20 should be assigned to Resource A? Depreciation is a typical problem of this kind. However, accountants have devised many methods, however arbitary they may be, by which such allocations are carried out objectively. Furthermore, it must be noted that disaggregation problems occur only when resources purchased originally as a group are split among periods, departments, or products, whereas the aggregation problem in current cost accounting discussed above always occurs. It even occurs when only one kind of resource is at issue, as in the homogeneous product case mentioned above.

Therefore, to those who think that current cost accounting eliminates the messy problem of depreciation and other joint cost allocations, it must be pointed out that in current cost accounting there is the much messier problem of aggregation and that any rules derived to specify the aggregation level (e.g., a plant should be evaluated as a whole, but a subsidiary should be evaluated as the sum of the values of its assets) are just as arbitrary as the depreciation methods.

The third problem which makes current cost income less suitable for use in income distribution then historical cost income is the difficulty in specifying and verifying the level of likelihood that a contemplated transaction may actually take place. Nobody has proposed to evaluate assets of a U.S. firm based on the market prices in China when everybody knows that such a deal can never take place. How likely should a contemplated transaction be and how should the likelihood be verified? It would be easy for firms to exchange phony offers in order to help each other get a favorable income figure, unless there were a safeguard against such chicanery. But how could one verify whether an offer made by Firm B to purchase or rebuild a plant of Firm A at $1 million was bona fide or phony unless the deal had actually been consummated? If current cost income is used as a basis for income distribution, endless disputes would arise over the seriousness of such offers.

Attempts to remedy these three problems in current cost account may perhaps be worthwhile if it can be shown that current cost income leads to more "equitable" distribution of income than historical cost income. This is extremely difficult to show. On the contrary, historical cost accounting, which refuses to recognize holding gains and losses, seems to be more in line with the fundamental spirit of the law aimed at solving conflicts of interest, namely, the maintenance of the status quo until changes (in income) are proven necessary beyond any reasonable doubt. Contemplation alone is not subject to reward or punishment by law regardless of its content, because it is too weak a foundation for a legal relationship among interested parties. To stand the heat and pressure of legal disputes over income distribution, the realizable income concept is far too weak compared with the realized income concept.

From the examples of accounting practices in Countries A, B and C, it is obvious that historical cost accounting has been and will be the most effective method of accounting in the area of resource control and distribution. Accounting has two fundamentally different functions to perform; one function is to protect the equity of interested parties of a firm and the other is to provide relevant data to decision - makers (inside and outside the firm) to help them make decisions on resource allocation. Accounting oriented toward the former function is called equity accounting, and accounting oriented toward the latter function is called operational accounting.[3]

Obviously, more rigorous rules are required in equity acccounting than in operational accounting. The rules of the latter emphasize the relevance and timing of data in relation to the decision at the expense of verification and objectivity. In fact, it is of secondary importance whether financial data produced in equity accounting are properly supplied to interested parties, insofar as the parties can trust accountants that their system has been operating properly. In equity accounting, the primary importance is the system itself and not the financial data per se.

The significance of equity accounting should not be undercut by the recent shift of emphasis toward decision making and operational accounting. For the proper functioning of our economy, it is essential to have a system which assures the investors not only that the total resources invested in the firm are properly controlled (the custodianship function) but also that each investor's share is properly protected from other investors and other interested parties of the firm. Equity accounting is aimed at exactly this objective. This is the area in which accounting has traditionally developed. Although operational accounting is playing a more and more important role in business, the significance of equity accounting and the central role of historical cost accounting in equity accounting should be fully recognized.

In the above argument, the area in which I believe historical cost accounting has played and will play an indispensable role was expanded from custodianship accounting to equity accounting. I would now like to expand it further to include at least a part of operational accounting, since I do believe that information provided by historical cost accounting is useful for management and investment decisions, although I fully realize the need for additional types of information. In order to highlight the contribution of historical cost accounting in operational accounting, let us imagine Country D in which historical cost data are completely barred for use by management and investors.

In Country D, equity accounting is based on historical cost accounting, but accountants in this country believe that historical cost data are useful only in equity accounting and are of no use for decision making purposes. They even consider such data to be misleading if provided to the management and the public. As a result, the records prepared in equity accounting are shielded from everybody except a special audit agency of the government which thoroughly audits the records of each firm and issues a report. Financial statements prepared under historical cost accounting are made available only to the audit agency. The management and the public are given only the audit report, which includes the income figure and an opinion by the audit agency that proper records were maintained and the income figure was derived properly. This income figure is then used for all purposes of income distribution.

Although the management and the public do not receive any historical cost data other than the income figure verified by the audit agency, they are well provided with current cost data. Financial statements prepared on the current cost basis are published regularly and made available to the public to help them make investment and other decisions. The management is also provided with a set of current cost data whenever necessary, although historical cost data are barred entirely in operational accounting, since they are considered to be misleading or at least of no use.

What would happen in a country like this? I can offer only my conjecture of what would happen if historical cost data were eliminated entirely from the business world.

Vicious complaints would arise, first from the management and then from the public. The management would argue strongly against the accountants who hold that historical cost data are useless. They would argue that management is a dynamic process which requires a careful study of the past in order to predict the future. To substitute current cost data for historical cost data is like wiping out their past experiences. They would want to know the price of the material at the last purchase so that they can compare it with the price they have to pay presently. Historical cost data provide useful information, they would say, not only when they are compared with current cost data, but also when they are compared with other historical cost data, as in the analysis of trends, seasonal cycles, comparisons with other departments or firms, etc. Of course, they would not deny the usefulness of current cost data, but they would be opposed to the idea that historical cost data are useless.

Complaints from the public on the financial statements under the current cost basis would be raised for a different reason. As in the case of Country C, current cost data offer much more room for manipulation than historical cost data. Furthermore, data in operational accounting are under less severe rules and regulations than those in equity accounting. Therefore, the public would quickly discover that every firm attempted to paint a bright financial picture of the firm in the minds of the public in order to attach more investment to the firm under favorable terms and to raise the market price of its stock. The demand for the disclosure of financial statements based on historical costs would grow stronger and stronger since these types of statements are regulated by more rigorous rules and are far less subject to manipulation. The public would consider current cost data to be a good supplement to historical cost data but not a substitute.

I leave it to the reader to judge how long the practice of barring historical cost data could be continued in this hypothetical country.

Finally, I would like to point out that the issue of asset valuation is only one of the many issues that accountants should explore in developing an accounting system for society. I do not object to current cost accounting if one can show that its benefit to society is greater than its cost of implementation. Remember, however, the bill to society for establishing and running such a system can be enormous, considering the cost of assessment, calculation, and auditing (all of which must be done every year) as well as the cost of solving disputes if the firm or the accountants are challenged on the reliability of data or are accused of intending to mislead the public. (Financial statements under historical costs are prepared as a by-product of equity accounting, hence, insofar as equity accounting is considered to be indispensable, the additional cost fo publishing financial statements is negligible relative to the cost incurred under current costs).

I believe we should explore other ways of providing useful information to the investors instead of limiting our attention to valuation problems only. Let us explore such a possibility in Country E.

In Country E, historical cost accounting is recognized not only as the basis for equity accounting but also as an important souce of data in operational accounting. Thus, historical cost data are made available to the management for their use in decision making. Also, financial statements based on a historical cost valuation are published for the public.

However, accountants in this country also realize that historical cost data are only a modest portion of data needed by the management and the public in making decisions on resource allocation. Unlike the accountants in Country D who attempted to improve the data of operational accounting by changing the valuation method, accountants in Country E try to expand the kinds of data they record and report.

For example, they have succeeded in establishing a recording and reporting system on the commitment basis.[4] This is an attempt to better control contracts and other financial commitments that management makes, and also to provide information in financial statements on outstanding sales, purchases, construction contracts, etc. These commitments are reasonably good indicators of how the financial situation of the firm is going to actually change, unlike data in current cost accounting which are derived from contemplated (replacement or disposal) transactions that the firm is almost certainly not going to undertake. The change to the commitment basis of accounting was initiated both to protect the equity of interested parties (equity accounting) by placing contracts and other financial commitments under the same control as regular resources and also to provide relevant data to the management and the public in making their decisions (operational accounting).

Another direction in which accountants in Country E are attempting to move is toward a more timely reporting system. They feel that reporting financial data annually is too infrequent to be of much use to the public in this day of computer technology. A committee was appointed whose members were selected from public accounting firms, industry, financial analysts, etc., to set up rules detailing the facts that must be immediately disclosed to the public and the conditions of their disclosure.

Efforts were made to specify the rules in such a way that they could be applied most objectively in determining the need for disclosure and the contents to be disclosed. Major events that were considered by the committee included mergers and acquisitions, construction of major plants, introduction of new product lines which would substantially change the product mix of the firm, major contracts and their cancellations etc.

Rules for immediate public disclosure are very difficult to derive for two different reasons. One is that the interest of the management in protecting their trade secrets from disclosure to competitors and the public must be weighed against the investors' and the public's interest in timely information of major events of a firm. The second is concerned with a method for releasing the information to the public in the most equitable manner. When information dealt with by accountants was not so "hot", this was not a problem. But as accountants work with more and more crucial information to the investors, this second problem becomes more and more serious. The committee is still studying the rules for immediate public disclosure from these two angles.

I do not have the answers to these two difficult problems, but I am certain that these are the crucial problems we must face if we continue to make an effort to provide relevant data to investors for their investment decisions.

Although these difficulties with operational accounting exist for the investors and the public, operational accounting for management seems to hold no major barrier to unlimited progress. It appears that the most promising area in which accountants can concentrate their efforts is to develop integrated accounting and management information systems by coordinating their efforts with developments in the computers and systems area. The benefit to the investors and to society that can be derived from such efforts are indirect but certain.

III. CONCLUSION

I shall summarize the arguments presented in the previous section in the following five propositions.

Proposition 1

Historical cost valuation is the only valuation method which includes, as an integral part of its valuation procedure structured on the double-entry bookeeping system, the essential requirement of equity accounting that every actual change in the resources of an entity be recorded by relating inputs and outputs so that it can be traced and identified whenever necessary.

Proposition 2

Historical cost valuation provides data that are less disputable than data provided under other valuation methods currently being proposed, an essential requirement in equity accounting.

Proposition 3

Historical cost valuation by refusing to recognize holding gains and losses, is in line with the spirit of maintaining the status quo unless changes (in income) are proved to be necessary beyond any reasonable doubt. This spirit is essential for solving conflicts of interest and maintaining order and stability in society.

Proposition 4

Historical cost valuation provides data that are useful for decision-making by insightful managers and investors insofar as history is the only basis for predicting the future.

Proposition 5

Historical cost valuation is among all valuation methods currently proposed, the method that is least costly to society, considering the social costs of recording, reporting, auditing, settling disputes, etc.

FOOTNOTES

(1) See Yuji Ijiri, The Foundations of Accounting Measurement (New York: Prentice-Hall, 1967), Chapter 5 on the inseparable relationship between the double-entry bookkeeping system and historical cost valuation.

(2) Ibid.

(3) Ibid.

(4) See Yuji Ijiri, "On the Commitment Basis of Recording Transactions", to be published in the Proceedings of Scandinavian-GSIA Joint Faculty Seminar, University of Goteborg, Sweden, 1971.

5 Recognising the Cost of Capital in Government Contracting

Rein Abel and Paul McLenon

Standard No. 414 of the Cost Accounting Standards Board deals with the cost of money as an element of cost of facilities capital. This article gives a brief account of its development. It also examines some of the issues that emerge when attempts are made to deal with inflation and rate of return on capital employed in a cost based contract pricing environment.

Cost Accounting Standard No. 414, "Cost of Money as an Element of the Cost of Facilities Capital",[1] is an example of an explicit measurement of a non-transactional cost. This Standard went into effect on October 1, 1976. It followed another Cost Accounting Standards Board proposal to recognize an imputed cost desinged to measure the impact of inflation,[2] which was withdrawn at the time Standard No. 414 was officially proposed by the Board.

The purpose of Standard No. 414 is to provide the procurement agencies with a means to identify and recognize explicitly an imputed contract cost, the "cost of money as an element of the cost of facilities capital". This cost should be distinguished from other possibly related concepts such as interest paid and a firm's average cost of capital. In essence, the Standard seeks to measure the net book value of noncurrent assets used in the production process and then employs the assets so measured as a base to which an interest rate periodically determined by the Secretary of the Treasury is applied.[3] Therefore, the amount computed is not related to interest paid nor is the source of a contractor's financing taken into account in that computation. The amount of "cost of money" so computed is allocated to individual contracts generally on the same basis as overhead expenses and other indirect costs.

It should be noted that although Standard No. 414 prescribes a method for measuring a contract cost, the Cost Accounting Standards Board does not determine whether it should be treated as an allowable contract cost by the procurement agencies. This decision has to be made by these agencies presumably in conjunction with a reorientation of their existing profit policies. By the effective date of Standard No. 414, only the Department of Defense had given a clear indication of its intention to treat the "cost of money", measured in accordance with the Standard as an allowable contract cost.

Some Earlier Developments

The basic idea of Standard No. 414 is not novel, and the concept of adequate return on capital employed can be traced back to the beginning of modern economics. To quote Adam Smith in his Wealth of Nations originally published 200 years ago:

> In exchanging the complete manufacture either for money, for labor or for other goods, over and above what may be sufficient to pay the price of the materials, and the wages of the workmen, something must be given for the profits of the undertaker of the work who hazards his stock in this adventure.[4]

Notwithstanding the general acceptance of this basic economic principle, the question of whether, in Government contracting, explicit recognition of return on capital should be given in profit or as a cost has been debated for a long time. Some of the earlier effort has gone into trying to convert interest paid into an allowable contract cost. Other attempts have dealt with proposed changes to the "weighted guidelines" used by certain procurement agencies in the contract profit negotiation process. More recently the Department of Defense introduced experimentally in its Defense Procurement Circular 107 a method for "specifically recognizing contractor capital to be employed in contract performance".[5] Application of the circular was voluntary and the experiment was eventually terminated when it became evident that in its existing format it would be used rather infrequently.

Meanwhile the need to deal with return on capital and the somewhat allied problem of inflation in Government contract costing became increasingly more evident. In these circumstances the Cost Accounting Standards Board became convinced that standards would be required to deal with these topics. The commitment was made public by the Chairman of the Board, Elmer B. Staats, in the course of congressional hearings dealing with an earlier cost accounting standard. In response to a question from Senator Cranston inquiring "how realistic is it to ask the Board to come up with capital cost Standards and inflation cost Standards?" Mr. Staats replied: "We think it is very realistic, and we have given these two Standards the highest priority among all the other work we are doing".[6] Subsequently the staff of the Board developed two draft Standards, Nos. 413 and 414, to deal with the two topics under consideration.

Proposed Standard No. 413

These two staff research efforts dealt with economic factors which had not been recognized in contract costing. For this reason the CASB staff could not benefit from reviewing the practices followed by various contractors. Accountants who were interested in negotiated contracting tended to avoid the broad conceptual issues related to these two topics and were frequently more attuned to consider accounting matters on the basis of narrow views related to likely impacts on prices.

The research process dealing with the inflation Standard was unusual. The staff arranged a series of discussion meetings. Participants in these meetings dealt with a group of issues which were to be considered in the development of a possible Cost Accounting Standard to measure the impact of inflation as a contract cost.

The CASB's decisions on these issues were announced in the Federal Register for October 9, 1975, which included an unprecedented introductory commentary. The Board had, until this publication, used prefatory comments only at the time of final promulgation of a Standard to provide analyses of comments received on earlier proposals. The October 9 publication on proposed Standard No. 413 had not been preceded by a widely distributed staff draft of a proposed Standard, and the Board recognized that added explanatory material might be helpful. In those early remarks the Board noted (40 FR 47518) the close relationship between the projects to measure the cost of inflation and the cost of capital.

Commentators speaking for a number of Government agencies were strongly critical of the Board's proposal to recognize, as a contract cost, a special inflation-related adjustment to depreciation costs. Commentators who represented contractors tended to favor the basic idea, but to criticize the specific proposal. Almost no one supported the proposal as published. Suggestions from contractors mostly were designed to make the proposal more flexible. The Board has already considered such alternatives. Measurement of the particular impact of inflation on different contractors might be desirable, but the Board determined that it would require the use of objective techniques which could be effectively applied in a contract situation.

The Board announced the withdrawal of proposed Standard No. 413 in the Federal Register for March 5, 1976 (41 FR 9562 et seq.) in conjunction with the publication of proposed Standard No. 414. That announcement included a brief analysis of the issue raised by commentators.

Development and Promulgation of Standard No. 414

While the proposed Standard No. 413 was designed to deal with the impact of inflation as an element of cost in Government contracting, the primary emphasis in the development of Standard No. 414 has been on identifying an adequate rate of return on the contractor capital employed. At the same time, because any market related interest rate necessarily includes some allowance for expected future inflation, at least some provision for the inflationary erosion anticipated in future years is provided by this Standard. The matter will be further discussed in the next section of this paper.

The staff of the Board had been involved in research dealing with imputed interest and/or return on capital since early 1972. The work on the project was accelerated in the fall of 1973, and in June 1974 an "issues paper" on the topic was mailed to a large number of interested parties. At this stage the aim was to narrow the scope of the problem area so that the pertinent issues could be examined in greater detail. Thus the questions posed covered a broad area.

For instance, when dealing with the interest rate to be applied the primary question examined was whether the cost of capital rate should be (a) an across-the-board rate applicable to all contractors, (b) an across-the-board rate applicable to all the contractors in a given industry, or (c) a rate computed individually for each contractor.

Similarly when dealing with the capital base to which this rate must be applied the primary question was whether an attempt should be made to measure capital utilization at the individual contract level or is it sufficient to develop "a uniform rate applicable to the total cost of all the contracts handled in a corporation, division, profit center or productive burden center." In the latter case the cost of capital would be spread among the individual contracts on the basis of their total cost - a practice that would not necessarily reflect the amount of contractor capital actually utilized in the performance of the contract.

The responses to this issues paper were analyzed. The research at this stage of the project involved also certain other steps such as interviews with various interested parties including contractors who had actually tried to implement Defense Procurement Circular 107 procedures. As a result of these efforts a second issues paper was mailed in April 1975. The issues presented in this paper dealt with a much narrower problem area. In fact, the paper outlined the basic framework of a possible Standard.

For instance, it was proposed that a single, across-the-board rate would be applied to all the contractors and thus the question became which single rate would be the most appropriate to use in any future Standard. Second it was proposed that the net book value (historical cost) would be used in computing the asset base and that an attempt would be made to establish a close relationship at the contract level between capital utilization and the corresponding compensation for cost of money. In other words, the broader the approach that would have involved simply computation of cost of capital at the divisional or departmental level and its subsequent allocation to individual contracts on the basis of their total cost was discarded. It was also proposed to follow the precedent of Circular 107 and to provide separate treatment for operating capital (working capital) and facilities capital (fixed assets).

Once again the responses to the issues paper were analyzed and a staff draft Standard was developed which was mailed to interested parties in December 1975. The draft Standard followed the broad framework that had been developed in conjunction with the second issues paper. Besides soliciting general comments on the draft Standard, specific questions were asked dealing with such matters as the estimated implementation costs of the proposed Standard and whether the proposed "cost of money" should be treated as a contract cost or as part of the profit objective. In addition, two methods of dealing with the troublesome question of allocating operating capital to contracts had been included in the draft Standard and the respondents were asked to give their views on the relative merits of these methods.

Once again the staff reviewed the responses to the staff draft and a proposed Standard was prepared for a possible publication in the Federal Register. This proposed Standard was submitted to members of the Cost Accounting Standards Board at a Board meeting held on February 27-28, 1976. After an extensive discussion of the whole matter, including the interrelationship between the proposed Standards 413 and 414, the Board decided to withdraw the proposed Standard 413 and to proceed with the Standard 414. The latter was modified, however, so that its coverage was limited solely to facilities or fixed capital. This reduction in scope was based primarily on the difficulties perceived by the CASB and its staff in dealing, on fairly short notice, with several interrelated issues involved with operating or working capital. Research was to continue on these issues. As mentioned above, the proposed Standard was published in the Federal Register on March 5, 1976.

The Board received some 80 comments on this proposed Standard. Again the comments were analyzed and some relatively minor adjustments were made to the Standard. Subsequently the Standard was promulgated and its final version was published in the Federal Register on June 2, 1976. The publication was accompanied by a set of prefatory comments that dealt with most of the significant questions raised by commentators. The effective date of this Standard was, as expected, October 1, 1976.

Compensation for Inflation in Standards Nos. 413 and 414.

Upon withdrawing Standard No. 413, as Standard No. 414 was first published, the Board stated:

> The Board believes that the proposed Cost Accounting Standard being published today will provide reasonable recognition for the cost of a contractor's investment in facilities, by using the semiannual interest rate established under Public Law 92-41, which also includes a factor for the risk of inflation.[1]

In other words, this statement basically asserts that any inflationary erosion in the contractor's fixed capital will be compensated, at least to a certain extent, by using a market related interest rate in computing the "cost of money" - although this rate is applied to an asset base determined in accordance with the precepts of historical accounting that ignores any price level changes.

The approach is clearly different from the conventional way of dealing with the inflationary problem where the emphasis is on asset revaluation and where these revalued assets are then used as a basis for computing a more realistic depreciation figure. This latter approach was reflected in the subsequently withdrawn Standard No. 413. In other words, Standard No. 414 seeks to recognize current inflationary expectations as reflected in the market related interest rates while the more conventional approach incorporated in Standard No. 413 attempted to deal with the "actual" inflationary erosion that had taken place.

A market related interest rate, such as the one used in Standard No. 414, can be regarded as a currently acceptable compensation offered to the investor for investing his funds for a certain period of time in a given investment environment. The compensation the investor gets is interest or its equivalent. Conceivably the investor makes his decision in the light of a single figure - the expected rate of return. As far as the principal amount of investment is concerned all he expects is the return of the unadjusted monetary amount that he is investing. He does not expect any adjustment to his invested capital to compensate for the inflationary erosion. Therefore, any compensation that he believes is necessary to maintain his invested capital intact must come out of the return that he will obtain on the prospective investment. This applies both to the erosion of his invested capital and also the erosion of the monetary income stream generated by the investment. Thus inflationary expectations are necessarily built into the market related interest rates.

Therefore, in order to understand the different approaches, taken in Standards Nos. 413 and 414, it is important to recognize the two different directions one can take in attempting to deal with the inflationary problem. On the one hand, we have the historical inflationary experiences that, for better or for worse, can be measured by such techniques as indexing and appraisal. Standard No. 413 sought to follow this path. On the other hand, however, we have prevailing inflationary expectations that are reflected in current market related interest rates. It is this second approach that was taken in developing Standard No. 414. Here, a key question is whether current inflationary expectations will turn out to be in line with actual developments. But even if we assume that the future course of inflation differs materially from earlier inflationary expectations, it still seems possible to argue that the eventual emergence of such a difference between original expectations and actual experiences represents a contracting risk shared by both parties which should not necessarily have any impact on contract prices. What matters is that current expectations of investors regarding current negotiations are satisfied; i.e., that the prevailing interest rate is incorporated in the system used to compensate investors.

Some Additional Considerations

Besides offering at least some compensation for the inflationary erosion, Standard No. 414 should also accomplish certain other objectives. Basically, the cost accounting and pricing practices employed in Government contracting prior to the promulgation of this Standard did not effectively recognize contractor investment in facilities capital. At times attempts were made to give some recognition to cost of capital when the "weighted guidelines" method was used for determing the profit objective. However, this recognition seems to have been somewhat haphazard and it is questionable whether, in general, sufficient heed was paid to the relative capital intensity of the various contractor operations.

It was noted earlier that the Cost Accounting Standards Board does not determine whether a specific item of cost is allowable for Government contract cost accounting purposes. The Board deals with allocability and not with allowability of contract costs. Nevertheless, the very nature of the Board action frequently acts as a strong inducement for procurement agencies to change their policies in such areas as cost allowability and profit determination. Standard No. 414 has been particularly significant in this respect. It was noted earlier that at least one procurement agency, the Department of Defense, has decided to treat the cost of money, measured in accordance with Standard No. 414, as an allowable contract cost. In addition, the Department has decided to discard its old "weighted guidelines" used in computing the prenegotiation profit objective and to employ a new set of guidelines designed to operate in conjunction with Standard No. 414.[8] These new "weighted guidelines" recognize explicitly contractor investment in facilities capital, and they reduce somewhat the weight traditionally given to such items as the total contract cost and its various component parts.

According to public pronouncements by Defense officials the expectation is that, in the aggregate, the increased cost resulting from recognition of cost of money on facilities capital as an allowable contract cost should be offset by a decrease in anticipated profits of a roughly similar magnitude. The emphasis here is, however, on the word "aggregate". In other words, while there is an expectation that the aggregate dollar outlay by Defense for a given volume of contracts would not change, it is also expected that the net result of applying Standard No. 414 and the new profit policy would be to channel more of the procurement dollar in the direction of capital intensive contractors. Correspondingly, contractors whose operations employ only a relatively modest amount of facilities capital would have to endure some loss in their traditional share of the Defense procurement dollar.

The "offset" argument advanced in the previous paragraph is, in essence, a short run argument. In the long run Standard No. 414 should have a significant impact on the investment policies of Government contractors. The inability of contractors to be sure that contract prices included adequate recognition for the cost of money has led, over the years, to a situation where according to most observers investment in facilities capital devoted to Government contract work has become inadequate. The lack of explicit recognition of cost of capital has tended to act as an effective deterrent to the necessary investment by contractors. Implementation of Standard No. 414 and the new profit policy adopted by the Department of Defense should remove that deterrent. Thus as additional investments are made, production costs should fall - a fact which in a cost based pricing environment will be immediately reflected in lower contract prices.

Finally, promulgation of Standard No. 414 may encourage improvement in other cost accounting practices in a way that would at first seem unrelated to this Standard. One consequence of the policy of nonrecognition of cost of capital in Government contracting has been the existence of a consistent strong incentive to recognize costs at the contract level as soon as possible. In a cost based pricing environment such an early recognition of costs tends to lead to a corresponding early revenue recognition and to enhanced cash flows. Thus any cost accounting precepts that could be used to favor cost deferral had to stand up to strong economic pressures that favored immediate expensing. And if the asset acquired was capitalized the same pressures generally dictated that it be written off over as short period of time as possible - frequently quite irrespective of the economic life of the asset. As the cost of money on facilities capital is explicitly recognized, it seems reasonable to expect that such considerations should become less important in the selection of proper cost accounting practices for application in a given set of circumstances.

FOOTNOTES

(1) Federal Register, Vol. 41, No. 107, June 2, 1976, pp. 22241-22251.

(2) Proposed Cost Accounting Standard No. 413, Federal Register, Vol. 40, No. 107, October, 9 1975, pp. 47517-47519.

(3) The rate is determined twice a year by the Secretary of the Treasury, pursuant to Public Law 92-41 (85 Stat. 97). It takes into consideration "current private commercial rates of interest for new loans maturing in approximately five years".

(4) Adam Smith, An Inquiry into the Nature and Causes of the Wealth of Nations (New York, N.Y., The Modern Library, 1937). p.48.

(5) Much of the research that went into developing DPC 107 has been summarized by Lauren D. Lampert in "Defense Industry Profits Contract Capital Employed". National Contract Management Journal 7 (Fall 1973) pp. 93-114.

(6) Hearing on Cost Accounting Standard No. 409 before the Subcommittee on Production and Stabilization of the Senate Committee on Banking, Housing and Urban Affairs, 94th Congress 1st session, 181 (1975).

(7) Federal Register, Vol. 41, No. 45 March 5, 1976, p. 9562.

(8) For details of the new profit policy see Department of Defense, Defense Procurement Circular No. 76-3, September 1, 1976.

III On General Price-Level Adjusted Accounting

6 Statement of Standard Accounting Practice No.7 Accounting for Changes in the Purchasing Power of Money

The statement which follows differs from conventional statements of standard accounting practice in that it is 'provisional', that is, it does not involve a binding obligation to disclose and explain in annual accounts departures from the procedures contained in it, nor does it oblige auditors to mention such departures in their report. However, there is general recognition that financial statements adjusted for the effects of inflation are essential for efficient management and it is in the interest of shareholders that they should be provided with that information by the directors. It is believed that the procedures outlined in this statement will receive substantial support from major companies. In this statement, references to 'standard' mean 'provisional standard' throughout.

PART 1 - EXPLANATORY NOTE.

Inflation, which is the decline in the purchasing power of money as the general price level of goods and services rises, affects most aspects of economic life, including investment decisions, wage negotiations, pricing policies, international trade and government taxation policy.

2. When the annual rate of inflation appears low, there is a tendency for business undertakings to regard the problem as not serious enough to warrant any action. Nevertheless, over a period of years even a modest rate of progressive inflation can have a significant effect if there are assets and liabilities with lives extending over a number of years. When the annual rate of inflation

rises to a persistently significant level, business undertakings become more aware of the problem and there is a demand, such as we are experiencing now, for action.

3. It is important that managements and other users of financial accounts should be in a position to appreciate the effects of inflation on the businesses with which they are concerned - for example, the effects on costs, profits, distribution policies, dividend cover, the exercise of borrowing powers, returns on funds and future cash needs. The purpose of this statement is the limited one of establishing a standard practice for demonstrating the effect of changes in the purchasing power of money on accounts prepared on the basis of existing conventions. It does not suggest the abandonment of the historical cost convention, but simply that historical costs should be converted from an aggregation of historical pounds of many different purchasing powers into approximate figures of current purchasing power and that this information should be given in a supplement to the basic accounts prepared on the historical cost basis.

Scope

4. While it is desirable that all companies should provide information on the effects of inflation it is recognized that:

(a) such information is probably of greater significance in the case of listed companies;
(b) the work involved in producing the information, although not great, may be proportionally heavier for smaller companies;
(c) there is a need to phase the work of introducing inflation adjusted accounts, which is likely to be greater initially than when once established, so as not to overload the accounting resources of companies generally.

Accordingly, the practice described in this statement, whilst recommended for all companies, is to be regarded as standard initially only for the annual accounts of listed companies.

5. The first presentation of the supplementary statement required by this standard or of figures derived therefrom, should be in the company's annual accounts. Interim accounts or the preliminary announcement of the results for the year are not suitable places for the first

presentation of such figures as they do not provide an adequate opportunity to explain their significance. While the standard applies only to the annual accounts of listed companies it is desirable, where practical and as the relevant figures become available, that the practice of providing this supplementary information should be extended to include other financial statements such as interim accounts, preliminary announcements of figures for the year, ten-year summaries, profit forecasts and prospectuses.

The Historical Cost Convention

6. The annual accounts of companies are prepared substantially on the basis of the historical cost of the items dealt with. In addition, some companies periodically revalue some of their assets to current values. The effect is that items are recorded in terms of the purchasing power of the pound at the date when the asset was acquired or revalued, the liability was incurred, or the capital obtained.

7. This convention has the advantage that the recorded historical cost is derived from factual monetary transactions, and its use helps to limit the number of matters within the accounts which are subject to the exercise of judgement. However, that advantage is impaired where the purchasing power of the monetary unit used changes significantly over a period of years. The need to show the effect of inflation on conventional accounts has become of pressing importance.

The Need for Supplementary Information

8. The purchasing power of the pound, in common with other currencies, has altered materially, and in recent years the rate of change has increased. There is clearly a need to reflect the effects of such changes in accounting statements but there is debate about the best method of achieving this object.

9. It has been suggested that readers of annual accounts can make sufficient and suitable mental adjustments for the effects of changes in the purchasing power of the pound. Such adjustments, however, can be no more than crude estimates because:

(a) the rate of change in the purchasing power of money has not been constant;

(b) the effect of change in the purchasing power of money will vary between companies according to:
   (i) individual ratios of monetary to non-monetary items (for an explanation of these terms see paragraphs 14 to 19 below); and
   (ii) different patterns over the course of time in the acquisition of assets, incurring and raising of capital.

10. Most users of annual accounts outside a company will not be in a position to make the required adjustments for themselves. Only the directors of a company are in a position to provide suitable information to enable users of accounts to understand the effects of inflation on the results and financial position.

The Proposed Method Compared With Other Methods

11. The method proposed in this statement (the 'current purchasing power' or 'CPP' method) is concerned with removing the distorting effects of changes in the general purchasing power of money on accounts prepared in accordance with established practice. It does not deal with changes in the relative values of non-monetary assets (which occur also in the absence of inflation). It should therefore be distinguished from methods of 'replacement cost' or 'current value' accounting which deal with a mixture of changes in relative values and changes due to movements in the general price level. (Detailed comment on the differences between CPP and replacement cost accounting is given in Appendix 1) (not reproduced).

Summary of the principal aspects of the statement of standard accounting practice

12. The main features of the standard are:

(a) companies will continue to keep their records and present their basic annual accounts in historical pounds, i.e., in terms of the value of the pound at the time of each transaction or revaluation;
(b) in addition, all listed companies should present to their shareholders a supplementary statement in terms of the value of the pound at the end of the period to which the accounts relate;
(c) the conversion of the figures in the basic

accounts into the figures in the supplementary statement should be by means of a general index of the purchasing power of the pound.

(d) the standard requires the directors to provide in a note to the supplementary statement an explanation of the basis on which it has been prepared and it is desirable that directors should comment on the significance of the figures.

13. The form of the supplementary statement is a matter for the directors of the company to decide, provided that they conform to the standard accounting practice (part 3 below). There are a number of ways in which the information required may be shown. An example of a possible presentation is given in Appendix 2 (not reproduced). This example includes some ratios as the effect of changes in the purchasing power of the pound on them may be even more significant than on the underlying absolute figures.

Monetary and Non-monetary Items

14. In converting the figures in the basic historical cost accounts into those in the supplementary current purchasing power statement a distinction is drawn between:

(a) monetary items; and
(b) non-monetary items.

15. Monetary items are those whose amounts are fixed by contract or otherwise in terms of numbers of pounds, regardless of changes in general price levels. Examples of monetary items are cash, debtors, creditors and loan capital. Holders of monetary assets lose general purchasing power during a period of inflation to the extent that any income from the assets does not adequately compensate for the loss; the converse applies to those having monetary liabilities. A company with a material excess on average over the year of long- and short-term debt (e.g., debentures and creditors) over debtors and cash will show, in its supplementary current purchasing power statement, a gain in purchasing power during the year. This is a real gain to the equity shareholders in purchasing power but it has to be appreciated that there may be circumstances in which it will be accompanied by a dangerously illiquid situation or by excessively high gearing, and for this reason any such gain should be shown as a separate figure.

16. It has been argued that the gain on long-term borrowing should not be shown as profit in the supplementary statement because it might not be possible to distribute it without raising additional finance. This argument, however, confuses the measurement of profitability with the measurement of liquidity. Even in the absence of inflation, the whole of a company's profit may not be distributable without raising additional finance, for example because it has been invested in, or earmarked for investment in, non-liquid assets.

17. Moreover, it is inconsistent to exclude such gains when profit has been debited with the cost of borrowing (which must be assumed to reflect anticipation of inflation by the lender during the currency of the loan), and with depreciation on the converted cost of fixed assets.

18. Non-monetary items include such assets as stock, plant and buildings. The retention of the historical cost concept (see paragraphs 6 and 7) requires that holders of non-monetary assets are assumed neither to gain nor to lose purchasing power by reason only of changes in the purchasing power of the pound (but see paragraphs 21 and 22 below).

19. The owners of a company's equity capital have the residual claim on its net monetary and non-monetary assets. The equity interest is therefore neither a monetary nor a non-monetary item.

The Conversion Process

20. In converting from basic historical cost accounts to supplementary current purchasing power statements for any particular period:

(a) monetary items in the balance sheet at the end of the period remain the same;
(b) non-monetary items are increased in proportion to the inflation that has occurred since their acquisition or revaluation (and conversely, reduced in times of deflation)

21. In the conversion process, after increasing non-monetary items by the amount of inflation, it is necessary to apply the test of lower of cost (expressed in pounds of current purchasing Power) and net realizable value to relevant current assets, e.g., stocks, and further to adjust the figures if necessary. Similarly, after restating fixed assets in terms of pounds of current purchasing power, the question of the value to the business

needs to be reviewed in that context and provision made if necessary. Other matters that will need to be considered include the adequacy of the charge for depreciation on freehold and long leasehold properties and whether it may be necessary to include in the deferred tax account in the supplementary statement, an amount for the corporation tax (in the Republic of Ireland, income tax and corporation profits tax) on any chargeable gain which would arise on a sale of the assets at the date of the balance sheet at the amount shown in the supplementary statement.

22. In applying these tests, and during the whole process of conversion, it is important to balance the effort involved against the materiality of the figures concerned. The supplementary current purchasing power statement can be no more than an approximation, and it is pointless to strive for over-elaborate precision.

Index to be Used

23. In the United Kingdom there are a number of indices which might be taken as indicators of changes in the general purchasing power of the pound. For the post-war years they include the following:

(a) the gross domestic product (GDP) deflator;
(b) the total final expenditure (TFE) deflator;
(c) the consumers' expenditure deflator (CED) (formerly referred to as the consumer price index);
(d) the general index of retail prices (RPI).

24. The choice between these indicators is in principle quite finely balanced. The first reflects changes in total home costs and the second changes in the prices of total final output (including investment goods and exports). But final changes in the purchasing power of the pound are, as in this statement, more often conceived in relation to the purchasing power of money spent by individuals on the goods and services purchased for their own personal use and for this reason indicators of the third or fourth type are considered to be more appropriate. The RPI has certain practical advantages over the CED: unlike the CED it is not subject to retrospective revision and it is available monthly by about the middle of the following month (the CED is an annual index available in March of the following year). For these reasons it has been decided that for periods covered by the RPI in its present form (i.e., since the beginning of 1962) the indicator to be used should be the RPI.

25. On the basis of a recommendation from the Central Statistical Office, the use of the following indices is specified for the relevant periods:

for periods up to end-1938, the Ministry of Labour cost of living index;
for periods between end-1938 and end-1961, the consumers' expenditure deflator;
for periods from 1962 onwards, the general index of retail prices.

Figures for these indices spliced together to form a continuous series will be found in Appendix 4. The figures quoted are annual averages and as the financial year-ends of companies vary an index number will be required for each month-end. An adequate approximation can be obtained by using an appropriate index of retail prices to adjust the annual index. Appropriate retail price indices for each month from December 1914 to December 1966 will be found in Method of Construction and Calculation of the Index of Retail Prices (Department of Employment and Productivity, HMSO). Figures for later months may be obtained direct from the Central Statistical Office, or from the Monthly Digest of Statistics (obtainable from HMSO), or Trade and Industry (published by the Department of Trade and Industry and also obtainable from HMSO).

26. In the Republic of Ireland, the general index of retail prices should be taken to refer to the quarterly Consumer Price Index compiled by the Central Statistics Office, Dublin. The four separate index series, which have been compiled since 1922, have been linked together to form a continuous annual average series (base January 1974 = 100). The Irish Consumer Price Index may be obtained directly from the Central Statistics Office, Dublin, or from the Irish Statistical Bulletin (obtainable from the Government Publications Office, GPO Arcade, Dublin 1). The method of calculating the current index (base November 1968 = 100) is described in the Irish Statistical Bulletin, March, 1969. Where a company's year-end falls at a date other than that to which the index is compiled, it will be necessary to interpolate or extrapolate the values of the index to approximate to the value at the company's year-end.

Overseas Subsidiaries and Associates

27. It is possible that some companies may experience difficulties in obtaining the information necessary to produce the current purchasing power supplementary statements from some of their overseas subsidiaries or associates.

In such cases, directors will have to weigh the materiality of the items concerned against the cost of obtaining the necessary information. The reasons for the treatment adopted and the magnitude of the items involved should be disclosed in a note to the supplementary statement.

PART 2 - DEFINITION OF TERMS

28. Monetary items are assets, liabilities, or capital, the amounts of which are fixed by contract or statute in terms of numbers of pounds regardless of changes in the purchasing power of the pound.

29. Non-monetary items are all items which are not monetary items, with the exception of the total equity interest (i.e., share capital, reserves and retained profits). The total equity interest is neither a monetary nor a non-monetary item.

30. Conversion is the process of translating figures from historical pounds to pounds of current purchasing power.

31. Updating is the process of trnaslating figures of an earlier accounting period from pounds of current purchasing power at one date to pounds of current purchasing power at another, later, date.

32. Basic accounts are those prepared substantially in accordance with established conventions on the basis of historical cost and include those in which some or all fixed assets have been revalued and/or some or all current assets are shown at estimated realizable value.

33. A listed company is one which has some or all of its securities admitted to the official list of a recognized stock exchange. A recognized stock exchange has the meaning given to it by the Companies Act 1967 (i.e., 'any body of persons which is for the time being a recognized stock exchange for the purposes of the Prevention of Fraud (Investments) Act 1958'), together with the Belfast Stock Exchange, which is recognized under the Northern Ireland Prevention of Fraud (Investments) Act 1940, and any stock exchange prescribed by the Minister for Industry and Commerce of the Republic of Ireland under the Companies Act 1963 (at present this is the Stock Exchange - Irish).

PART 3 - PROVISIONAL STANDARD ACCOUNTING PRACTICE

Scope of this Statement

34. This accounting standard applies to the published annual accounts of listed companies. But the method of presenting the effects of changes in the purchasing power of money which is described is capable of application to every type of business, and its general adoption is recommended as good practice in the interests of more informative reporting.

Accounts to be Restated in a Supplement

35. All accounts laid before the members of listed companies in general meeting should be supported by a supplementary statement showing in terms of pounds of purchasing power at the end of the year to which the accounts relate the financial position at that date and the results for the year.

36. The supplementary statement should be prepared by converting the basic accounts by the application of a general index of prices as described in paragraph 40. The supplementary statement need not give a converted figure for each item in the basic accounts but may be in reasonably summarized form. The supplementary statement should contain separate figures, if material, for depreciation and for the loss or gain on holding monetary items (i.e., the net loss or gain in purchasing power resulting from the effects of inflation on the company's net monetary assets or liabilities).

37. In the case of a listed holding company presenting group accounts in the form of consolidated accounts, the supplementary statement need deal only with the consolidated accounts.

38. The supplementary statement should contain a note outlining the method of conversion used including the treatment of accounts originally prepared in foreign currencies.

39. The auditors should report on the supplementary statement.

Index to be Used

40. The index to be used in the conversion process should be:

(a) in the United Kingdom:

for periods up to end-1938, the Ministry of Labour cost of living index;

for periods between end-1938 and end-1961, the consumers' expenditure deflator;
for periods from 1962 onwards, the general index of retail prices based on January 1974 = 100.

(b) in the Republic of Ireland, the official consumer price index.

41. The figure for the index at the beginning and end of the accounting period and the date of the base of the index should be shown in a note to the supplementary statement.

Corresponding Amounts

42. In all supplementary statements, except the first, prepared in accordance with this standard, all corresponding amounts shown for the preceding year should be 'updated' (see definition paragraph 31) so that they are restated in terms of the purchasing power of the pound at the end of the year under review.

43. It is not necessary to provide corresponding amounts in the first supplementary statement produced in accordance with this standard, but their provision is recommended.

Date from which Effective

44. While this standard is provisional and not of binding effect, it should nevertheless be regarded as persuasive in content and the member bodies of the ASSC strongly recommend its adoption in accounts as soon as possible and preferably not later than the first accounting period beginning after June 30th, 1974.

(Appendices 1 to 4 not reproduced)

7 Price-Level Changes and Useless Information

R.L. Mathews

The American Institute Price-Level Study

Accounting Research Study No. 6 was prepared as the result of a directive by the American Institute's Accounting Principles Board to the Director of Accounting Research. After stating that the Board "...agreed that the assumption in accounting that fluctuations in the value of the dollar may be ignored is unrealistic," this directive instructed the Director "to set up a research project to study the problem and to prepare a report in which recommendations are made for the disclosure of the effect of price-level changes upon the financial statements. In this study, special attention should be paid to the use of supplementary statements as a means of disclosure."[1]

The directive thus indicated the broad lines along which the study was to proceed; it restricted the inquiry to an examination of the effect of "fluctuations in the value of the dollar" (or, by implication, the effect of changes in the general price level as opposed to the effect of price changes affecting specific items or groups) and it emphasized the need to use supplementary statements to disclose the effects of these price-level changes. This effectively tied the hands of the Director of Accounting Research since it required him to ignore two of the major issues which arise in any consideration of the price-level problem; (1) the kind of adjustment which is to be made in response to price changes and (2) whether or not the adjustment is to be recorded in the double-entry accounting records and the primary accounting reports derived from those records. The emphasis on the use of supplementary statements was itself unduly restrictive although it might have been justified by the view that supplementary statements "have marked advantages in a period of education, experimentation, and transition."[2] The restriction of the study to general price-level changes was no doubt likewise inspired by a desire to moderate the pace of change in accounting methods, perhaps to be accomplished by adhering as closely as possible to historical cost data. But the result of such a constraint will be nothing short of disastrous if, as seems likely, it diverts attention from the effects of specific price changes (which can be shown to be highly significant for the individual business enterprise) to the effects of relatively unimportant general price-level changes (which, in any case, cannot be properly evaluated with respect to the individual business unless something is already known of the effects of specific price changes).

Price Changes in the Principles Study

The earlier A.I.C.P.A. Accounting Research Study No. 3 acknowledged the need to look beyond general price-level changes;[3] its authors recommended that:

> Changes in resources should be classified among the amounts attributable to:
>
> 1. Changes in the dollar (price-level changes) which lead to restatements of capital but not to revenues or expenses.
> 2. Changes in replacement costs (above or below the effects of price-level changes) which lead to elements of gain or of loss.[4]

In discussing the measurement of inventories and cost of goods sold, Sprouse and Moonitz[5] argued that, because future exchange prices are indeterminable or uncertain, and because past exchange prices are out of date or relate to different points on the time scale, all that remains logically is "...the possibility of using a current exchange price, or replacement cost." This "...eliminates the need for any assumption as to the flow of actual costs incurred." It may also be presumed "...that current (replacement) costs represent at least the minimum economic value of those items (in the inventory) to the enterprise." Further, following Edwards and Bell,[6] Sprouse and Moonitz argued that the use of current replacement cost makes it possible to distinguish between holding gains and losses (the differences between historical costs and current costs) and profit from operating margins (the difference between sales price and current replacement cost).[7]

Sprouse and Moonitz also quoted Edwards and Bell with apparent approval in discussing the measurement of plant and equipment and depreciation. Although realizable value may be irrelevant, and although it may be difficult to establish a current market price for specific assets, they showed that it is misleading to carry such assets at their acquisition costs because this has the effect of combining "(a) the gains (losses) attributable to changes in prices between acquisition and usage with (b) the gains (losses) attributable to operations in a current market."[8] Operating profit will be enhanced by the fact that the firm is buying its assets cheap and using them dear, but this fact will not be revealed unless the firm has regard to "the current (replacement) cost of the services rendered by these assets and the separate classification of the related gain or loss."[9]

Sprouse and Moonitz therefore observe that "it is technically feasible to reflect changes in some assets in a more timely fashion, and thereby give more current information in the balance sheet," and they propose "a classification that distinguishes among (a) the amount attributable to changes in the dollar (price-level changes), (b) the amount attributable to the acquisition of goods and services prior to their utilization, and (c) the amount attributable to sales in a current market."[10]

This distinction between general price-level changes, specific price changes and operating results was, significantly, ignored in the Price-Level Study which began to quote the foregoing passage of the Principles Study but stopped abruptly after (a), thereby creating the impression that the Principles Study had made no reference to specific price changes. And whereas, as we have seen, the Principles Study had made one or two approving references to and had drawn on the ideas of Edwards and Bell, the Price-Level Study ignored their book except for including it, along with some two hundred other items, in a selected bibliography. In the present writer's view the Edwards and Bell book is one of the most important works on accounting to appear in a generation. Since it pays special attention to the problem of changing prices, it is difficult to understand how any discussion of the price-level problem in accounting can fail to be influenced by it.

Changing Prices and the Price Level

The authors of the Price-Level Study may reasonably claim that they are entitled to define "price-level changes" and "price-level adjustments" in any way they please, and there are undoubtedly terminological advantages in using the term "price-level changes" to denote changes in the general price level and "price changes" to denote changes in the prices of specific items or groups. But they are not justified in claiming that the meaning they ascribe to the term "price-level adjustment" is the only one which is appropriate to use and that other definitions are open to abuse:

> In some discussions, for example, the term (price-level adjustment) refers to an approximation of current replacement cost by the use of index numbers that measure the changes in prices of specific commodities. This usage probably arose because the term "replacement cost" came into disfavor in the early 30's when it became clear that the writeup of asset values during the 20's, which were supposedly based on replacement costs as determined by appraisals, had often resulted in flagrant overvaluations. Because many accountants today still associate the term with its former abuse, there is a tendency to avoid it. Adjustment for "price-level" change, on the other hand, does not carry overtones from the past. As a result, the objective measure of changes in either the price-level or the prices of specific commodities by use of index numbers has been referred to as a "price-level adjustment." The label, however, is properly applied to the former, but not the latter.[11]

Whether or not one feels that the term replacement cost is appropriate for the purpose of measuring specific price changes (I prefer the term current cost or current value) it is possible to disagree with the assertion that the term price-level adjustment should be used only to describe changes in the general price level applied to historical cost data. In making this assertion, indeed, and in concentrating on the effects of general price-level changes, the authors of the Price-Level Study preclude the possibility of undertaking the kind of analysis which is necessary to reveal the accounting effects of price changes. This is because adjustments designed to measure changes in the general price level only acquire meaning if they are calculated by reference to data which have themselves been valued on a consistent basis.

Current and Constant Price-Level Adjustments

It will be argued below that consistency for this purpose implies current values or values determined by adjusting all items in financial statements to the current prices prevailing during (in the case of income statements) or at the end of (in the case of balance sheets) the accounting period in respect of which the financial statements have been prepared. There are thus two kinds of price-level adjustments which may be referred to respectively as current price-level adjustments and constant price-level adjustments,[12] which may be made in respect of each financial statement. Of these it is the former which needs to be calculated by revaluing, in terms of current prices, every item in a financial statement expressed in prices of a past accounting period (namely, certain costs such as cost of goods sold and depreciation, and certain assets such as inventories and fixed assets). This revaluation is most significant and it can only be carried out by recognizing specific price changes. The second kind of price-level adjustment, on the other hand, involves the application of a general price index to the current values so determined. This constant price-level adjustment makes it possible for financial statements of different periods to be prepared on a comparable basis, but the information which is derived as a result of this second adjustment is of relatively minor significance (for purposes either of decision-making by managers or appraisal by stockholders and investors) compared with the information that results from the current price-level adjustment. Nevertheless, it will be shown later that financial statements expressed in terms of a constant price level may be compared more meaningfully than those which have been adjusted in accordance with the procedures recommended by the authors of the Price-Level Study. This is because in the latter study a general price-level index is applied to historical cost data which are themselves expressed in terms of the prices prevailing in different periods or different points of time.

It is one of the main purposes of this paper to show that, by failing to make a distinction between current and constant values, the adjustments proposed in the Price-Level Study lose all meaning. It is not a defence of the Price-Level Study to say that it

> ....is not aimed at resolving the relative merits of historical (acquisition) cost for inventories and fixed assets, with or without correction for general price-level effects, as compared with the systematic use of current replacement costs, whether calculated on the basis of direct quotations of market prices or by the use of special index numbers.[13]

Likewise the authors of the Price-Level Study are not justified in claiming that the effect of ignoring specific price changes is to simplify and add precision to analysis:

> For the sake of simplicity and precision in analysis, this study assumes that replacement costs are not to be introduced into the financial statements. With or without replacement costs, the measurement and disclosure of the effects of changes in the purchasing power of the dollar (as measured by the index of the movement in all prices) is still desirable.[14]

The measurement and disclosure of all the effects of general price-level changes may be desirable, but it will be shown that the adjustments involved in such analysis are meaningless unless they are applied to data that are themselves expressed in terms of the current prices prevailing in any particular period or point of time. Where technological changes are occurring it may be difficult to assess current prices as measured by the current replacement costs of particular assets, but an estimate may be made on the basis of the current replacement costs of equivalent assets (or more particularly the current replacement costs of assets capable of providing the same services as existing assets). Even allowing for errors in estimation the calculation will inevitably be more meaningful than one which applies a general price-level index to historical cost data.

Before we proceed to a detailed evaluation of the Price-Level Study approach, the method of adjustment which the authors recommend will be described and contrasted with the alternative accounting data for price changes recommended in this paper and called the current valuation approach. It will be shown that the two approaches give exactly the same constant price-adjusted data if all prices change at a uniform rate, but that: (a) many more calculations are involved in the Price-Level Study approach than in the current valuation approach; (b) the Price-Level Study approach fails to provide important information, namely current price-adjusted data, in respect of periods other than the base period; and (c) the Price-Level Study approach, unlike the current valuation approach, cannot be incorporated in the double-entry accounting system. It will be shown further that, if prices do not change all at a uniform rate, the current valuation approach permits an analysis of differential price changes whereas the Price-Level Study approach does not. Because all prices normally do not change at a uniform rate, the results obtained from the Price-Level Study approach are meaningless for purposes of analysis and business policy.

Price-Level Study Adjustment Procedures

The actual technique of adjustment used in the Price-Level Study follows the procedure which was adopted in the American Accounting Association's study of price-level changes.[15] So far as the balance sheet is concerned, the technique involves a restatement of every item other than monetary items on a current common dollar basis. This, in turn, requires non-monetary items to be adjusted in accordance with the proportionate change that has occured in the general price-level between the time of original record and the date of the balance sheet. Since monetary items (defined as financial assets and liabilities) are automatically expressed in terms of current dollars, no adjustment is necessary for these. The Price-Level Study shows that "a gain or loss on the monetary item occurs as the purchasing power of the dollar decreases or increases because the dollar as legal tender does not change," and that it is necessary to adjust the owners' equity in the balance sheet by the amount of this gain or loss. This gain or loss on monetary items also needs to be taken into the income statement as an adjustment to operating profit which has been calculated, on the basis of a restatement, in terms of common dollars of revenues and expenses.

The Price-Level Study approach to the problem may be illustrated by reference to the following analysis which is essentially the same as that used in the Study except that we shall assume that M represents net monetary assets, whereas in the Price-Level Study a distinction is made between M (monetary assets) and L (liabilities). Other symbols are used, N (non-monetary assets), R (residual equity) and p (the proportionate rise in the general price level between Time 1 and Time 2).

At Time 1 the balance sheet of the firm may be represented as follows:

$$M + N = R$$

If the firm engages in no transactions between Time 1 and Time 2, but the general price level rises by p, the Price-Level Study suggests that the change in the price level over the period may be recognized by multiplying every item in the balance sheet by (1 + p):

$$M(1 + p) + N(1 + p) = R(1 + p) \qquad (1)$$

But the net monetary assets are the same at Time 2 as they were at Time 1. Although their purchasing power has changed, their legal significance, in terms of Time 2 prices, is represented by their unadjusted face value. The Price-Level Study shows that it is therefore more meaningful to express equation (1) in a slightly different form (in effect we are subtracting Mp from both sides):

$$M + N(1 + p) = R(1 + p) - Mp \tag{2}$$

An Alternative Procedure - Current Price-Level Adjustments Followed by Constant Price-Level Adjustments

Now the loss on monetary assets Mp is equal to the difference between Rp and Np; it occurs because every item in the balance sheet is being revalued except M. This suggests that the change in the general price level could have been reflected in the balance sheet in another way; by restating N in terms of the current price level, making no adjustment to M or R, and adding to R an amount Np equal to the difference between the restated and the original value of N:

$$M + N(1 + p) = R + Np \tag{3}$$

where $Np = Rp - Mp$.[16]

Equation (3), like equation (2), records each item in terms of the price level prevailing at Time 2, and a change in the general price level between Time 2 and any other point of time (say Time 3) can be recognized by inflating every item in the balance sheet (M, N(1 + p), R and Np) by the proportionate change in the general price level so that every item will then be restated in Time 3 prices. That is to say, a constant price-level adjustment can be easily superimposed on the current (general) price-level adjustment that has been made in equation (3). It is apparant, however, that a balance sheet adjusted in accordance with equation (3) bears a close resemblance to a balance sheet which records changes in specific prices which, of course, affect only the operating assets represented by N.

The Current Valuation Approach

If we suppose that the proportionate rise in the current value of non-monetary assets N between Time 1 and Time 2 is represented by r, then the application of a current price-level adjustment, based on specific price changes, would result in N being revalued to N(1 + r) and a revaluation reserve Nr being added to the residual equity:

$$M + N(1 + r) = R + Nr \tag{4}$$

In equation (4) every item is stated in terms of current prices prevailing at Time 2. If the general level of prices and current costs both rise, again by p and r, between Time 2 and Time 3, it is possible to restate the Time 2 balance sheets, as expressed in equations (2) or (3) and (4) respectively, in terms of Time 3 prices as follows:

General Price-Level Adjustment (Price-Level Study Approach)

$$M(1 + p) + N(1 + p)^2 = R(1 + p)^2 - Mp(1 + p) \tag{5}$$

or

$$M(1 + p) + N(1 + p)^2 = R(1 + p) + Np(1 + p) \tag{6}$$

Current (Specific) Price Adjustment followed by Constant Price-Level Adjustment (Current Valuation Approach)

$$M(1 + p) + N(1 + r)(1 + p) = R(1 + p) + Nr(1 + p) \tag{7}$$

In terms of a numerical example, the comparison between the different methods may be made as in Table 1 in which it is assumed that $p = r$. It will be seen from Table 1 that the Price-Level Study approach involves adjusting all the non-monetary items in accordance with the changes in the price level p, and calculating a monetary loss Mp to maintain equilibrium in the balance sheet by deducting from the funds or equities side the amount that, in effect, has been deducted from the assets side as a result of not revaluing M. The current valuation approach only revalues N, adding the amount of the revaluation Nr as a separate item to the funds or equities side of the balance sheet. Having ensured that every item is thus expressed in terms of current prices, it is then a relatively simple matter to apply the general price-level index p to the data to express them in terms of constant Time 3 prices.

If the rise in current cost r over the relevant period is the same as the rise in the general price level p, then it is clear from a comparison of equations (3) and (4) or (6) and (7), or from the numerical example, that the Price-Level Study method of adjustment gives the same result as the current valuation method. In the Appendix to this paper the detailed results obtained in the Price-Level Study example (pp. 121-133) are compared with the results that are obtained when the current valuation approach is applied to the same data. It will be seen that, provided the proportionate increases in the general price level are the same as the proportionate increases in the specific prices of inventories and fixed assets (as is assumed in the Appendix), the two approaches give identical figures, in terms of constant prices, for balance sheet values and net changes in residual equity.

Evaluation of Alternative Approaches to the Problem of Accounting for Price Changes

If prices all rise at a uniform rate, the two approaches thus yield the same constant price-adjusted data. Even under these circumstances it would appear that the current valuation approach has the advantage of requiring a smaller number of calculations; this is evident if one compares the adjustment calculations in the Appendix with the adjustment calculations on pp. 123-131 of the Price-Level Study.

But, as has been emphasized, prices do not change at a uniform rate, and managers, proprietors and investors are substantially more interested in the differential effects of price changes on the profitability and financial position of business enterprises than in the hypothetical effects of price-level changes which postulate, in effect, that relative price changes may be ignored. The current valuation approach outlined and discussed in greater detail in the Appendix analyses the effects of differential price changes while still permitting, if desired, a restatement of all items in terms of constant money values. It is an advantage of the current valuation approach, therefore, that it permits an analysis of the effects of both specific and general price changes, whereas the Price-Level Study approach restricts attention to the constant price-level adjustments and prevents any analysis of the effects of differential price changes from being made.

But perhaps the conclusive objection to the Price-Level Study approach is that it is impossible to ascribe any sensible meaning to the adjusted figures which appear in the supplementary statements. When a firm commences business there may be some justification for regarding its funds as representing generalized purchasing power. At that time its undeployed assets may be said to be consistently valued in terms of current prices and, at least until the time the firm buys operating assets and begins its business activities, may reasonably be regarded as having an infinite range of alternative uses and may therefore be represented as generalized purchasing power. But once the firm's funds are invested in specific assets and it begins to engage in specialized kinds of operating activity, these conditions no longer hold. The passage of time means that some items cease to reflect current values; there is no longer a consistent basis of valuation. Moreover, the fact that most operating assets are, to a large extent, specific to the firm means that they cannot be even notionally regarded as representing generalized purchasing power. Even the funds which flow into the business as a result of its operating activity cannot be regarded as constituting generalized purchasing power since most of these funds are immediately re-invested in operating assets which are related to the particular kinds of economic activity which the firm undertakes.

As prices change, the historical cost figures which record cost of goods sold, depreciation, inventories and fixed assets come to reflect neither their current value in use to the firm nor their current value in exchange. The historical cost figures differ in significance as between items in the income statement or balance sheet and even different components of the same item may not be valued on a consistent basis.

The application of a general price-level index to historical cost data subject to these limitations merely perpetuates the problem. Suppose, for example, that a machine with an expected service life of two years and an expected scrap value of nil is purchased for $100 in Year 1, and that an identical machine is purchased for $200 in Year 2. Suppose also that, although there is no further change in the price of machines, the general price level (which stood at 100 in Year 1) increases from 150 in Year 2 to 200 in Year 3. The application of the Price-Level Study method of adjustment and straight-line depreciation would require depreciation on the first machine in Year 2 to be valued at $100 in terms of Year 3 prices, while depreciation on the second machine in the same year would be recorded at $133 in terms of Year 3 prices. The date of purchase of the machine, that is to say, affects the adjusted cost figure in the same arbitrary way as it affects cost calculated on a straight historical cost basis. By adopting the current valuation approach, on the other hand, and making a current price-level adjustment followed by a constant price-level adjustment, the distortion resulting from the different time of purchase is removed. The historical cost depreciation charged on the first machine is adjusted to its current cost in Year 2, namely $50 x (200/100) = $100, and this figure may be subsequently adjusted to constant Year 3 prices by applying the general price-level index as follows: $100 x (200/150) = $133. This is the same as the adjusted value, in terms of constant Year 3 prices, of the depreciation charge on the second machine.

The same point may be made by reference to the land example in the Price-Level Study.[17] This assumes that three pieces of "similar" land, the sizes of which were 10, 15 and 5 acres respectively, were each purchased at different points of time (Time 1, Time 2, and Time 3) for $10,000; the general price-level index stood at 100, 125 and 75 at Times 1, 2 and 3 respectively, and by Time 4 had risen to 200. The replacement cost or appraisal value of the three pieces of land at Time 4 was $3,000 per acre, or $90,000. Under these circumstances, the Price-Level Study suggests, the following price-level adjustment is necessary to express each purchase in terms of the so-called current dollar:

Purchase	Unadjusted Cost	Multiplier	Adjusted Cost
	$		$
First	10,000	200/100	20,000
Second	10,000	200/125	16,000
Third	10,000	200/75	26,667
	30,000		62,667

Alternatively the adjustment could have been made in terms of the base period dollar:

Purchase	Unadjusted Cost	Multiplier	Adjusted Cost
	$		$
First	10,000	100/100	10,000
Second	10,000	100/125	8,000
Third	10,000	100/75	13,333
	30,000		31,333

It is then argued that

> Either of these calculations shows the cost of each parcel of land in proper relation to the cost of the others, that is, the adjusted amounts indicate the relative sacrifice which the purchaser made in acquiring each parcel, and the relative significance to the seller of the amounts received. The amounts of $31,333 and $62,667 represent the same amount of general purchasing power and either will be comparable to other similarly adjusted items on the financial statements.[18]

But the purchaser of the land is not likely to be the least bit interested in an assessment of his relative sacrifice expressed in this way. If he is farming the land he will be interested in its value in use as represented by its current replacement cost, and if he is holding the land for resale he will be interested in its value in exchange as represented by its market selling value. Because the three pieces of land are similar these will be the same for each piece, namely $3,000 per acre. He will be badly misled if he measures his sacrifice in using or selling the different pieces of land by reference to the adjusted figures calculated on the basis of the Price-Level Study approach, which are as follows in terms of Time 4 prices:

Purchase	Acres	Adjusted Cost	Adjusted Cost per Acre
		$	$
First	10	20,000	2,000
Second	15	16,000	1,067
Third	5	26,667	5,333

The value of the third piece of land, on a per acre basis, cannot sensibly be regarded as being five times as great as that of the second piece of land, or two and two-thirds that of the first piece, as these figures suggest.

The only reliable guide to policy is given by the current replacement cost or market selling value of the land (in this case assumed to be the same) and these show the current per acre value of the three pieces of land to be $3,000 in each case:

Purchase	Acres	Historical Cost	Current (Time 4) Value	Current (Time 4) Value per Acre
		$	$	$
First	10	10,000	30,000	3,000
Second	15	10,000	45,000	3,000
Third	5	10,000	15,000	3,000
	30	30,000	90,000	3,000

The foregoing example is used in the Price-Level Study to illustrate the distinction between what are described as "replacement costs and price-level adjustments" and to show "...that price-level adjustments of accounting data are not the same thing as the adoption of replacement costs, either in theory or in the nature of the results."[19] Although the possibility of using a replacement cost instead of an original cost basis of accounting seems to be admitted,[20] the problem of accounting for specific price changes seems to be treated as a problem that is independent of and secondary to the problem of accounting for changes in the general price level. The difference between the original cost ($30,000) and Time 4 replacement cost ($90,000) of the land in the foregoing example is thus analysed into two parts, $32,667 representing the adjustment of original cost to "a current common-dollar basis," and $27,333 representing an "appreciation in value."

This method of assessing the significance of price changes is not very helpful because different time periods are involved for each piece of land and because, as we have seen, the adjustment for the effects of specific price changes. The analysis of the differential effects of specific and general price changes acquires more meaning if attention is directed to differences between amounts expressed in terms of constant prices between any two points of time. These differences may then be analysed by reference to the changes that have occurred in specific prices and the general price level respectively. In the land example, the following analysis indicates the significance of the change in value of land between Time 3 and Time 4:

Purchased	Time 3		
	Unadjusted Cost	Current Time 3 Prices	Constant Time 4 Prices
	$	$	$
First..........	10,000	20,000	53,333
Second.........	10,000	30,000	80,000
Third..........	10,000	10,000	26,667
	30,000	60,000	160,000

Purchased	Time 4		
	Unadjusted Cost	Current Time 3 Prices	Constant Time 4 Prices
	$	$	$
First..........	10,000	30,000	30,000
Second.........	10,000	45,000	45,000
Third..........	10,000	15,000	15,000
	30,000	90,000	90,000

It will be seen that the value of the land in Constant Time 4 prices has fallen from $160,000 at Times 3 to $90,000 at Time 4. There would have been a loss of generalized purchasing power of $100,000 (in Time 4 prices) if the current value of the land had not changed, but there was an offsetting gain of $30,000 arising from the increased replacement cost of the land, leaving a net reduction in value, in terms of Time 4 prices, of $70,000.

To the extent that it regards changes in specific prices as a separate problem, and one which can be ignored for purposes of making price-level adjustments, the Price-Level Study adjustment technique must be regarded as failing in its purpose. The following justification which is advanced for the technique certainly lacks validity:

> ...all the revenues and expenses in the earnings statement for any one year will be expressed in dollars of the same size and not in a mixture of dollars from different years. Similarly, the various balance-sheet items will all be expressed in terms of a common dollar. Since both the results of operations and financial position will be stated in terms of the same "common dollar," a calculation of a rate of return on invested capital can be made in which both numerator and denominator are expressed in the same units.[21]

Data which are measured in different units to begin with cannot be converted to a common basis of measurement merely by applying a common conversion factor. Historical cost figures, that is to say, cannot be converted to a uniform basis of valuation merely by applying a general price index. The above examples relating to depreciation and land values make nonsense of the assertion made in the Price-Level Study that figures in financial statements which have been restated in terms of a common dollar "...can logically be compared and more meaningful conclusions can be drawn than from the original unadjusted cost figures."[22]

The current valuation approach which has been described in this paper is undoubtedly more radical, insofar as its attitude to the conventional historical cost and monetary postulates of accounting are concerned, than the Price-Level Study method of adjusting historical cost data; but it has the advantage that its adjustments, unlike those of the Price-Level Study approach, can be integrated with the traditional double-entry records and the reports which are derived from them. The Price-Level Study approach not only involves dual sets of data, but it results in a breaking of the nexus between the basic double-entry records and accounting reports. In the long run, this is likely to cause confusion in the minds of users of accounting data and to discredit the accounting information system as a whole. It may be true, as the Price Level Study suggests, that supplementary statements have advantages "in a period of education, experimentation and transition,"[23] but at least the possibility should be open for incorporating the adjustments for price changes in the basic accounting data when the need for such adjustments is eventually recognized. This possibility does not exist with the Price-Level Study approach. The current valuation approach, on the other hand, can be incorporated in the double-entry system immediately; if this is regarded as too radical a departure from conventional practice, the current valuation approach may be used to prepare supplementary statements of current values (with or without constant price-level adjustments) and the incorporation of the adjustments in the double-entry system can be left until such time as there is general acceptance by accountants and businessmen of the need for price-adjusted accounting data.

The Price-Level Study, with its emphasis on constant or common dollar comparisons, also seems to assume that the analysis of accounting data can be carried out most effectively by comparing items or groups in accounting reports on an inter-temporal basis, that is to say by studying trends in constant price-adjusted figures. Even if we ignore the inherent limitations which, as we have seen, attach to such constant price-level data, the point needs to be made that current value data are more significant for purposes of analysis and managerial decision-making than data expressed in terms of a constant money value. This is because managers, proprietors and investors are all essentially interested in evaluating the operating performance and financial structure of business enterprises, or changes in financial structure or operating performance over time. Such evaluation can only be carried out on the basis of structural analysis of accounting reports, i.e., by a comparison of items or groups with other items or groups in reports relating to the same period (or point of time) and which have been valued on a comparable basis. Trends in individual items or groups, even if they have been expressed in terms of a constant price level, are of secondary importance. A comparison of profits over Years 1, 2, and 3, all expressed in terms of the Year 3 price level, is thus not nearly so significant as a comparison of the percentage relationship between current income and the average current value of stockholders' equity in each of the three years. Likewise an examination of trends in fixed assets over time, even if these have been restated in terms of a constant or common dollar, is not nearly so revealing as a study of trends in the relationship between the current value of fixed assets and the current value of total assets. These structural relationships can be calculated each year without reference to changes in the general price level, and can be compared meaningfully as between different businesses. Although similar relationships can be calculated from data that have been adjusted to a constant-dollar basis, it is more difficult to attach a meaning to the latter for reasons that have already been discussed.

The Price-Level Study approach to the problem of accounting for price changes has thus little to commend it, and if persisted with is likely to do positive and lasting harm to the cause of consistency and common sense in accounting. Its laborious calculation procedures result in data that are likely to be just as misleading to managers, stockholders and other interested parties as historical cost data. If the accounting information system is to produce meaningful data we must recognize the effects of all price changes on business enterprise accounts, not merely the effects of changes in the general level of prices. If they are to make rational decisions, businessmen must have access to accounting data expressed in terms of current values, and accountants must accept the responsibility for providing the information that is needed. The accountancy profession will be discredited, and its influence in the world of business will inevitably decline, if it continues to confine its records and reports to historical cost data in either an unadjusted or a patched-up form.

APPENDIX 1

Comparison of Price-Level Study Approach and Current Valuation Approach (in $)

	Time 1					Time 2					Time 3				
	Index of General and Specific Prices														
	100					150					225				
	Historical Prices	Time 1 Prices (AICPA)	Current (Specific Prices	Constant Time 3 Prices Applied to Historical Prices (AICPA)	Constant Time 3 Prices Applied to Current (Specific) Prices	Historical Prices	Time 2 Prices (AICPA)	Current (Specific Prices	Constant Time 3 Prices Applied to Historical Prices (AICPA)	Constant Time 3 Prices Applied to Current (Specific) Prices	Historical Prices	Time 3 Prices (AICPA)	Current (Specific Prices	Constant Time 3 Prices Applied to Historical Prices (AICPA)	Constant Time 3 Prices Applied to Current (Specific) Prices.
M	10	'10	10	22.5	22.5	10	10	10	15	15	10	10	10	10	10
N	20	20	20	45.0	45.0	20	30	30	45	45	20	45	45	45	45
	30	30	30	67.5	67.5	30	40	40	60	60	30	55	55	55	55
R	30	30	30	67.5	67.5	30	45	30	67.5	45	30	67.5	30	67.5	30
Mp							-5		-7.5			-12.5		-12.5	
Nr	—	—		—	—	—	—	10	—	15	—	—	25	—	25
	30	30	30	67.5	67.5	30	40	40	60	60	30	55	55	55	55

FOOTNOTES

(1) The Staff of the Accounting Research Division, Reporting the Financial Effects pf Price-Level Changes (New York: American Institute of Certified Public Accountants, 1963), hereinafter called the Price-Level Study, p.1.

(2) Ibid, p.4.

(3) Robert T. Sprouse and Maurice Moonitz, A Tentative Set of Broad Accounting Principles for Business Enterprises (New York: American Institute of Certified Public Accountants, 1962), hereinafter called the Principles Study.

(4) Principles Study, p.55. Logically it would seem that the sequence should be reversed, since restatements in terms of changes in the general price level can only be sensibly made in respect of data which have already been adjusted for changes in replacement costs.

(5) Ibid., p.29.

(6) E.O. Edwards and P.W. Bell, The Theory and Measurement of Business Income (Berkeley and Los Angelos: University of California Press, 1961).

(7) Principles Study, p.29.

(8) Ibid., pp. 33-34.

(9) Ibid., p.34.

(10) Ibid., p.17.

(11) Price-Level Study, pp.4-5.

(12) In the Price-Level Study exception is taken to the use of the term constant dollars and preference is expressed for the term common dollars, on the grounds that the former term can only be used if the base is constant, whereas in revaluing accounting data a final-year base is used and this changes each year. But the restatement of different reports in terms of the prices of the period of the most recent report may still be characterized as a restatement in terms of constant final-year prices, even though another set of constant final-year prices will be calculated in the following period.

(13) Price-Level Study, p.5.

(14) Ibid., p.xii.

(15) Perry Mason, Price-Level Changes and Financial Statements - Basic Concepts and Methods, American Accounting Association, 1956; Ralph C. Jones, Effects of Price Level Changes on Business Income, Capital and Taxes, American Accounting Association, 1956; Jones, Price Level Changes and Financial Statements - Case Studies of Four Companies, American Accounting Association, 1955.

(16) This point is also made by R.J. Chambers, Towards a General Theory of Accounting, University of Adelaide, 1961, p.35.

(17) Price-Level Study, pp. 26-28.

(18) Ibid., p.27.

(19) Ibid., p.31.

(20) Ibid., "The possibility of shifting from an original cost to a replacement cost basis of accounting exists even though the value of the dollar remains constant."

(21) Ibid., pp.14-15.

(22) Ibid., p.25.

(23) Ibid., p.4.

8 Price-Level Accounting: Some Unfinished Business

George J. Staubus

The great longevity and the volume of written and spoken words associated with the debate on general price-level accounting suggests that little more should be said or written on the subject. But recent literature still indicates that some points have not been made clearly. One of these relates to the choice of the capital maintenance concept, and measure of it, that ties in most closely with the objective of accounting. Another is the legitimacy of including gains on long-term and short-term debt in income. A third is the roles of current value accounting and price-level restatements and the need for both. A brief review of the logical basis for price-level restatements will serve as a foundation for the subsequent discussion.

Measurements of flows, such as the revenues, expenses, gains and losses that constitute business income, require comparisons of measurements of stocks at two points in time. Many expense measurements, for example, involve adding a beginning balance and current acquisitions, then subtracting an ending balance. For the result to be clearly interpretable the three measurements must be made in a common unit. And when different line items are added and subtracted on an income statement common units are also desirable.

Accountants traditionally have considered all units of money which are denominated in the same currency to be comparable. Thus, all money accounts expressed in Deutschmarks are considered subject to addition and subtraction without any adjustment; 'a DM is a DM is a DM'. This means that the number of monetary units is the focus of our concern; what the money units will buy is ignored. The alternative view is that Deutschmarks, and pounds sterling and United States dollars, are significant because of what one can buy with them, and since this - their purchasing power - varies over time, 'a DM is not a DM is not a DM'. The size of the monetary unit actually varies so that adjustments must be made to express measurements relating to different dates in a common unit. Preparing financial statements in monetary units adjusted for the changes in a purchasing power index, or price level index, may be called 'price level accounting', 'general purchasing power accounting', 'accounting in units of general purchasing power', 'current purchasing power accounting' or 'common unit accounting'. The latter term will be used here to apply to the currency of any country, to avoid implying the use of a particular type of index, and to suggest the basic objective of the procedure in a short phrase. Under whichever name one may prefer, common unit accounting is, in the mid-1970s, under serious consideration in major English-speaking countries as an alternative to accounting in numbers of monetary units of varying sizes.

Common unit accounting is intended to make all monetary amounts appearing on any one financial statement, and on any articulated set of financial statements presented at one time, comparable in terms of purchasing power. Thus, if \$95 is subtracted from \$100 the \$5 remainder can be read as five dollars with the purchasing power that dollars have as of the date of the financial statement. While application of current value measurement methods (excluding historical cost) do express all measures on one balance sheet in monetary units of the same purchasing power, such a measurement system does not achieve common purchasing power measurements on an income statement or on comparative balance sheets. A 'scale adjustment' for changes in our measuring instrument - the monetary unit - must be made in order to achieve purchasing power comparability of measurements made at different times under inflationary conditions.[1]

The Index Choice and Capital Maintenance

The general objective of common unit accounting - to report in units of equal purchasing power - was clarified in the above introduction, but the specifics of this objective were not discussed. Now we need to face up to questions such as, 'Whose purchasing power?' and 'Power to purchase what?' Since the need for restating nominal units to purchasing power units is particularly important for the computation of income, rather than for the preparation of a balance sheet, it may be helpful to give some attention to the distinction between capital and income.

While the term 'capital' has many meanings, all of them relate to stocks of wealth (or interests in such stocks) while income relates to changes in stocks of wealth, or flows of wealth. The term 'capital maintenance' means having the same amount of capital at the end of a period as at its beginning so that the entity may 'break even', or have zero income. Once we have clarified what it means to maintain capital at its previous level, the computation of income follows. Income is the excess of ending capital over the amount needed to maintain capital at a constant (beginning) level. To paraphrase the definition by J.R. Hicks, income is the amount one can consume during a period and still be as well off at the end of the period as at the beginning.[2] Or, income is what can be consumed (or paid out by a corporation) and still maintain the original amount of capital intact.

What is required to maintain the original amount of capital intact? How much must we have at the end of the period in order to feel that we have maintained our capital? One possible answer to this is, if the net assets of the firm are worth as many dollars at the end of the period as the firm's net assets were worth at the beginning, capital has been maintained. This is the money capital concept of capital maintenance. It was, implicitly, rejected in the introduction when we turned to the purchasing power concept. Hereafter, we assume it is not acceptable. Having as many dollars at the end of the period as we had at the beginning is not the same as being as well off - if the purchasing power of the dollars has changed.

Another possible concept of capital maintenance is physical capital maintenance. In this view, if we have on hand as many units of materials, finished products and machine services as we had at the beginning of the period, or if we have enough cash to buy such equivalent physical assets, we have maintained our capital. By this approach, income realized by the sale of an asset may be computed by deducting from its selling price the number of monetary units that it would take to replace the asset sold. This concept of capital maintenance requires the use of the replacement cost method of measuring expenses and would require that the holding gain (or loss) be excluded from income. Thus, if two widgets were purchased at the beginning of the period for $6 each, one was sold for $9 when its replacement cost was $7, and the other is still on hand at the end of the period with a replacement cost of $7.50, the income for the period would be $9 less $7, or $2. No income would be recognized on the unsold widget. In circumstances which would make it difficult to determine and record the replacement cost of each commodity, a narrow (specific) price index reflecting changes in the prices of commodities of the category of the ones being measured could be used to approximate specific replacement cost.

Now let us consider the implications of the physical capital maintenance concept. If the cost of goods sold is determined by replacement cost, how does a trader who buys and sells securities, or a commodities speculator, earn any income? If a trader is buying and selling in the same market, replacement cost at the time of sale (the measure of cost of goods sold) must be the same as selling price, so no income is ever recognized. Or, consider the case of the two trading companies, X and Y. Suppose X invests in commodity A which rises in price and Y invests in commodity B which falls. If the cost to be matched with revenues upon sale are replacement costs, A and B will appear to have performed equally well, that is they will show equal incomes: zero. In effect, if capital maintenance means that we must be able to replace what we sold or consumed in the course of business, it makes no difference which assets we buy and hold. But surely we are better off holding assets which rise in price than we are holding assets whose prices fall! It is difficult to imagine anyone choosing a physical concept of capital maintenance in the face of this evidence.

A variation on the physical concept of capital maintenance is the use of an index of prices of commodities purchased by the firm (including raw materials or merchandise and plant assets such as machinery and buildings). Such an index would measure changes in the power of the monetary unit (e.g. dollar) to purchase the things the firm is required to purchase to stay in business. Such a concept of purchasing power might appear to be an appropriate one for implementation of the general purchasing power restatement proposal. On closer examination, however, this idea is essentially a physical capital maintenance approach and is subject to the evaluation in the preceding paragraph. If it were adopted, a firm holding a set of assets that fell in price would look just as good as a firm that held a rising 'portfolio' of assets.

It has been argued that a firm does not have income until it has provided for maintaining the same productive capacity and carrying the same inventories as it had at the beginning of the period. According to this argument, if prices pertaining to our industry rise faster than average prices in the economy, and if income taxes and dividends are based on a computation of income that does not provide for replacing the physical assets (or their services) consumed, then 100% payout of reported income would require either borrowing more money or contracting the physical operations of the firm. But could not a firm be driven out of business by such policies?[3]

This argument does not recognize that maintenance of physical capacity is not necessary to maintain the real earning power and investment value of the firm. A phenomenon associated with mobility of capital is the tendency towards a common rate of return on capital in firms with similar risk levels if there is freedom of entry and exit. Thus if companies X and Y start out with equal capital, but X's assets rise in price more than Y's, and if owners' capital is retained (or added) to permit the financing of the higher priced assets, in fluid capital markets and under competitive conditions, X's earnings must rise more than Y's so as to provide a rate of return on investment that is comparable for the two firms. Otherwise, capital would tend to flow out of one industry and into the other. In other words, maintenance of physical capital in a more inflationary industry will tend to increase the industry's real earning power. If the capital has greater earning power, it is a larger quantum of capital, so capital has been more than maintained. The firm purchasing power concept of capital maintenance is rejected.[4]

The decision-usefulness approach to accounting issues has not been mentioned in the above discussions of possible capital maintenance concepts. When the Hicksian concept of income is associated with the objective of producing accounting data that are useful to the readers of financial statements, it becomes apparent that it is the users' purchasing power with which accountants should be concerned. If we agree that the managers are working for the owners and that employees make only limited use of financial statements, the major groups of users who appear to warrant substantial consideration here are investors (owners and creditors, including suppliers) and taxing authorities. It is investors' well-offness that managers are trying to maximize and that governments are trying to tax.

People invest in enterprises in order to increase the utility of their wealth - to have greater purchasing power than they would otherwise have. Investors like to know their income so they can know how much they can consume without eating into their capital. From a longer-term perspective, an individual needs to predict his life-time income and know his beginning capital if he is to spread his consumption and bequests in a pattern that equalizes marginal utility and maximizes total utility. Knowledge of his income in the recent past and knowledge of his present capital (after including income to date) are helpful in predicting future returns available for consumption expenditures. If an investor owning an interest in a business is taxed on a return of capital by a taxing authority who intends to be taxing income, of if he spends for personal consumption a cash return which he believes to be income but is in fact a return of capital, accounting is not providing the information that is most relevant to those decisions, viz. the change in the purchasing power of the investor's wealth. For an investor's multi-period investment, consumption decisions, for income taxation decisions and for decisions regarding managers' success in achieving owners' objectives - for all of these basic uses of income information, capital is maintained when the investor has end-of-period wealth with the same consumption purchasing power as he had at the beginning of the period and income is an increase in the investor's stock of consumption purchasing power.

The argument that the corporate accountant cannot use the different purchasing power indexes of each individual shareholder must be read as either a weak excuse for inaction or an insistence on a degree of perfection that accountants have not reached in the past and are not likely to reach in the future. Surely a broadly based price index provides a better measure of the change in the measuring unit than the assumption that there is no change at all, as the millions of people who base contracts on such indexes recognize.

The appropriate index to use in restating accounting measurements in units of purchasing power is an index of prices of goods consumed by investors. To this author's knowledge, no such index has been constructed and maintained in any country. The best-known consumer price index in the USA is an index of prices paid by factory wage earners and clerical employees which is not ideal for price level restatements. Fortunately, the Labor Department is planning to commence publication of a new consumer price index in April 1977. It will reflect prices paid by a broader segment of the population but will not be specifically aimed at the investor segment. Still another index appears to be needed.

In practice, the Accounting Standards Steering Committee has chosen the British retail price index and the Irish consumer price index for use in common unit accounting. The

Financial Accounting Standards Board, on the other hand, has, as of this date, selected an economy-wide index- the gross national product implicit price deflator - and similar indexes have been suggested for use in Australia and Canada.

Note that the extent of price change reflected by the chosen index establishes 'par' for changes in specific prices. Assuming that assets are measured at their current values, if the price of a particular asset increases by the same percentage as the index, no real gain or loss occurs; only a greater than average, or less than average, increase would be recognized as an income item. Thus, under a physical concept of capital maintenance, no gain or loss would be recognized when assets were revalued to current replacement cost; the offsetting entry would always be reflected as a restatement of owners' equity. But if an investor purchasing power concept of capital maintenance were accepted, revaluations of specific assets other than in proportion to the change in the chosen index would result in a holding gain or loss on the asset. The chosen index is also used for measuring the loss from holding cash and other monetary assets and the gain from being in debt during inflation.

One other point relating to capital maintenance needs to be made here. Our standard of capital maintenance must be consistent across all balance sheet items if the sums and difference reflected in the residual equity are to be clearly interpretable. For example, we must not apply different indexes in restating monetary and non-monetary items. If a monetary asset must increase in nominal units by the percentage increase in the consumer price index in order to maintain its real value, the same is true of a non-monetary asset. If, on the other hand, an entity purchasing power index is applied to restate non-monetary items, it should also be applied to monetary items. A loss or gain is then reported in the amount of any difference between the restated beginning measurement and the ending measurement, whether the item is monetary or non-monetary, an asset or a liability.

Is the Gain on Debt Income?

Individual members of two of the national standards setting bodies have taken the position, in confidential correspondence, that the restatement of long-term debt is not an income item on a current basis. The best known application of common unit accounting in the United States - that of the Indiana Telephone Company - defers the recognition of such income until the debt is retired. Another position that has appeared in print is that the restatement of debt should be deducted from the value of the assets financed by the debt and thus charged to expense as the asset is depreciated or sold.[5] It is likely that others question the propriety of the majority view - that the shrinkage in the burden of fixed debts as the purchasing power of the monetary unit in which the debt is denominated shrinks, is income when the inflation occurs. Perhaps an example will help clarify this issue.

A static firm holds 1,000 units of a commodity through a period when the price index increased by 10%. The conventional balance sheet remained as follows:

BALANCE SHEET
throughout 19X1

Commodity,		Debt	$40
1,000 units	$100	Residual equity	$60

Upon restatement and revaluation of the debt, this balance sheet reflects income of 4 end-of-period dollars, that is, a residual equity amount $4 greater than is necessary to maintain the residual equity-holders' purchasing power. The income is derived from a gain on the debt. (Restated initial debt minus ending amount: $44 - 40 = $4).

BALANCE SHEET
Restated and Revalued
12/31/X1

Commodity,		Debt	$40
1,000 units	$110	Residual equity	$70

Is this $4 income distributable? Yes, it is, if it is real at all. If the market selling price of the commodity is now $0.11 per unit, the firm can sell 36 units for $3.96 and pay a cash dividend of that amount, or it can pay a dividend in kind by distributing 36 units of the commodity, leaving the following balance sheet at the start of the next period:

BALANCE SHEET
1/1/X2

Commodity, 964 units	$106.04	Debt	$40
		Residual equity	$66.04

If the price level again increases by 10%, a restatement and revaluation of the debt to $40 would leave an income of $4, which could be distributed in the same manner. This practice can continue as long as the price level increases, the price of our commodity keeps pace and the commodity is divisible enough to permit carving off a portion for sale or distribution. The earning power of the company is not reduced below its beginning-of-period level by such distributions. But note two things that common unit accounting does not do: (1) it does not, by itself, account for unrealized gains or losses due to specific price changes different than the index; current value accounting, along with common unit accounting, is needed to reflect this properly; (2) it does not report on liquidity any more than other accrual accounting systems do; a liquidity-oriented funds statement is needed for this purpose.

In other words, a price-level gain on debt represents 'better-offness' of owners and is distributable to them without impairing capital. Like any other accrual basis income, it does not assure liquidity. The potential problem of a profit accompanied by a cash shortage is a risk involved in computing income on any non-cash basis. But it is difficult to see how the use of cash to pay off the debt would make the gain any more distributable. Nor does paying off the debt change the exposure to inflation as the reductions in cash and debt offset each other, leaving the net monetary position unchanged. How can debt retirement (and disbursement of cash) be considered a realization event related to a gain?

We must realize that a complete, systematic approach to common unit accounting requires recognition that the purchasing power significance of nominally constant debt and monetary assets changes with inflation; we cannot recognize restatement on unbalanced parts of the balance sheet and still have a balancing statement. The idea that debtors gain from inflation is as widely accepted as any aspect of inflation accounting; the only possible question (within the context of inflation accounting) is when to recognize it. Accumulating the periodic gains associated with a long-term debt issue until its retirement and reporting them as one amount in the profit and loss account at that time is just as uninformative as ignoring 'unrealized' gains and losses associated with changes in market prices of securities held by an investment company - a practice which accounting theorists rejected long ago. The simple, intuitive answer seems best in this case.

The Roles of Current Value Accounting and Common Unit Accounting

The number of prominent people who confuse the roles of current value accounting and common unit accounting is almost frightening. We shall refrain from embarassing them by mentioning their names. One of the most common manifestations of such confusion is a statement to the effect that one or the other of these systems is the preferred solution to the inflation accounting problem. Another type of loose statement that implies confusion in the mind of the speaker is a comment on 'replacement cost accounting', without any indication of whether the revaluations are to be treated as income or not. As we stated in the discussion of capital maintenance, revaluation to replacement cost without recognition of income effects imples that a commodities trader has no income and that it makes no difference whether a business holds commodities which rise in price or fall - surely an unacceptable position. The alternative of recognizing all revaluations as gains or losses affecting income is to deny that the changing purchasing power of the monetary unit is significant to financial statement users. To what, then, is any form of replacement cost accounting, by itself, a solution? The following exercise, which the author has used for years in teaching, may be helpful.

An Exercise in Current Value and Common Unit Measurement

At the beginning of period one, when a consumer price index stands at 100, Jane Doe purchases a share of X Company stock for $100. At the end of period one, Doe still holds the stock, its market price is $108 and the price index is at 110. Early in period two, while the price index is still at 110, Doe sells the stock for $106.

What is her income in period one? in period two? for the venture? Make these income calculations under several different methods. Which measurement method yields asset and income numbers that appear to be most relevant to (a) a prospective lender's decision regarding lending money to Doe, (b) a judgment of Doe's performance as a portfolio manager, (c) the taxation of Doe's income, and (d) Doe's decision as to how much she can consume and still be as well off at the end of each period as she was at its beginning?

	Variable units		Common units	
	Historical cost	Current market	Historical cost	Current market
Period one				
Beginning	$100	$100	$110	$110
End	100	108	110	108
Income	$ 0	$ 8	$ 0	$ -2
Period two				
Beginning	$100	$108	$110	$108
End	106	106	106	106
Income	$ 6	$ -2	$ -4	$ -2
Venture Income	$ 6	$ 6	$ -4	$ -4

The following comments pertaining to this exercise are offered:

1. Note that the choice between historical cost and current market value affects the timing of the reported income.
2. The choice between traditional variable dollar accounting and common dollar accounting affects the total income over the life of the venture.
3. The difference between common dollar and variable dollar income over the life of the venture is $10 which is equal to the percentage change in the general price index times the beginning owner's equity stated in beginning dollars. This is a simple example of the general rule that the lifetime earnings of an entity, or on an investment, as of the dates originally recorded, are larger under variable unit accounting than under common unit accounting by the sum of the products of periodic inflation rates times beginning-of-period, common unit residual equity amounts.

This may be considered a simple test of the relevance of data produced by different measurement methods - relevance to the types of uses suggested just before the tabulated solutions. Assuming that no serious qualifications on grounds of cost, reliability and so forth are warranted in this simple case, the reader's choice of solutions indicates his view of the relevance of the alternative sets of data to the types of decisions listed. The author believes the common dollar, current market column includes the most relevant information.[6] Doe's investment does not appear to have been successful in either period one or period two and she should not be required to pay any income tax on this venture. Each of the other three columns yields manifestly less useful results. Furthermore, there is no apparent reason why the absurdities of the other solutions in this simple case are any less absurd in more complex situations.

Common unit accounting is necessary to eliminate the effects of changes in the significance of the measuring unit by restating all old measurements for comparison with current measurements in calculating income. Current value accounting is required to distribute income due to differential price movements over the periods in which it occurs. If you only wish to accomplish one of these objectives, at least choose the right tool for the job.

FOOTNOTES

(1) While most readers have found this simple explanation unnecessary at this stage of the debate, the author's contacts with prominent accounting authorities suggests that misconceptions still exist. In mid-1975 a member of the Sandilands Committee indicated in conversation, that 'price levels do not change; only prices of individual goods change'. The point is that the significance of the monetary unit to individuals does change and the changes can be measured with useful accuracy by a price index. Perfect measurement of the change is not necessary for common unit accounting to be helpful.

(2) J. R. Hicks, Value and Capital (Oxford: Clarendon Press, 1946), p. 172.

(3) An excellent statement of this position has been made by Lawrence Revsine and Jerry J. Weygandt, 'Accounting for Inflation: the Controversy', Journal of Accountancy, October 1974, pp. 72-78. Another prominent advocate of the specific entity capital maintenance concept is R. S. Gynther. See his 'Why Use General Purchasing Power?', Accounting and Business Research, Spring 1974, pp. 141-157, and earlier works.

(4) As an aside we may observe that, if the price of a commodity rises faster than a general price index over a considerable period (presumably due to a supply constraint), its sales volume typically will decline (if there is any elasticity of demand) so the company my be able to maintain its share of the market without maintaining the same physical volume of operation. In any event, a company's 'right' to maintain its physical level of operations surely is weak compared to its duty to maintain the amount of consumer purchasing power which its shareholders have entrusted to it.

(5) Marvin M. Deupree, 'Accounting for Gains and Losses in Purchasing Power of Monetary Items' in Staff of the Accounting Research Division, 'Reporting the Financial Effects of Price-Level Changes', Accounting Research Study No. 6 (American Institute of Certified Public Accountants, 1963), pp, 153-165.

(6) For an early formulation of the current accounting, common unit accounting proposal, see George J. Staubus, A Theory of Accounting to Investors (University of California Press, 1961), pp. 116-127.

9 Mechanical Engineering E.D.C. Engineering and Price-Level Accounting

(Here are considered the effects of inflation on company finances and the distortions arising from accounts based on historic cost. Inflation adjustment methods are outlined and applied to sample companies. Eds.)

Depreciation and the renewal of assets

Depreciation is intended to represent the cost of using up capital during a period of time; the actual depreciation charge for a particular year is based upon an accounting convention. Even without inflation there are, however, substantial difficulties in determining the appropriate valuation for assets on which to base that charge. In practice assets are rarely simply replaced. When an item of equipment is 'replaced', the new asset may well incorporate some element of higher productivity deriving from technological progress. Thus per £1,000 expenditure in constant price terms, the output potential of the new asset (also in constant price terms) may well be greater than that of the asset replaced.

The situation is, however, likely to be further complicated in times of inflation. A depreciation provision based on the historic cost of an asset is unlikely to be sufficient to provide for its replacement, or to maintain the real value of the business in terms of current purchasing power. If the historic cost shown in the accounts is adjusted to the prices ruling at the time when the balance sheet is struck, this may well provide a more realistic basis from which to calculate the depreciation provision required than the historic cost of the asset concerned. Failure to make such an adjustment to asset values is likely to lead to an underprovision for their replacement, and hence to an overstatement of profits and retentions.

Depreciation charges are, however, in a sense only accounting transactions; there need be no corresponding movement of funds in reality. There is no direct link between them and actual cash requirements for replacement investment in any one period. The investment outlay depends on the age, condition and economic characteristics of the assets. Thus at least in the short term, under-provision for depreciation may not necessarily create cash problems for companies planning to replace assets.

A company's expenditure on the replacement of fixed assets is related to original purchases made some years previously. In the absence of inflation, and other things being equal, replacement expenditure for a company with an increasing stock of fixed assets will be less in relation to present total stock of fixed assets, and hence to its depreciation provision, than that of a company whose stock of fixed assets is not, in real terms, increasing. Thus even in times of inflation depreciation provisions based on historic costs may be sufficient to meet companies' immediate needs for the replacement of assets.

In the long run, with a constant rate of real growth of assets and a constant rate of inflation, the historic cost (straight line) depreciation charge will exceed current replacement requirements if the real rate of growth of assets exceeds the rate of inflation. It will be less than current replacement requirements if the rate of inflation exceeds the real rate of growth.

Since the majority of companies still do not explicitly adjust for inflation in calculating depreciation provisions, it might have been expected that after some years, serious financing problems would have arisen for them. That they have not done so up to now can be explained largely by the fact that for most of the post-war period the rate of inflation has been fairly similar to the real rate of growth of the industry - about 4 per cent a year.

The situation has, however, changed markedly since 1969. The rate of inflation has increased to nearly 8 per cent a year as measured by the Consumer Price Index, but there has been no similar growth in the industry. Indeed the Index of Mechanical Engineering production increased by only 1 per cent between 1969 and 1971, compared with an average growth between 1948 and 1969 of 4 per cent a year. In these circumstances, historic depreciation charges, however adequate they may have appeared to be in the past, are clearly unlikely to have been so in recent years. By the same token, especially in recent years there must have been serious overstatement of real profits and retentions.

Inflation and working capital

Inflation also creates purely paper profits arising from stock appreciation and at the same time results in increased requirements of working capital. A rise in the value of stocks due to inflation normally inflates profits by the amount of the rise. But to the extent that the profits increase reflects simply the rising replacement cost of stocks rather than skilful purchasing or an increase in the volume of business, the gain is a paper gain only; the profit will be fully absorbed in keeping stocks at their original volume in the face of higher prices. A truer figure for profits is obtained if the contribution of inflation to the rise in the value of stocks is deducted.

If companies use FIFO (first-in, first-out) accounting and base prices on the book cost of materials and components actually used such prices are also likely to be inadequate to provide for the replacement of stocks at new, higher prices. If market conditions allow, companies may try to anticipate rising replacement costs of stocks by determining selling prices on the basis of the replacement rather than the historic cost of stocks. Few companies are, however, likely to have been in a position to anticipate the full extent of the increase in the rate of inflation in 1969.

It is also likely that as sales rise in money terms, so will amounts outstanding in the form of debtors. When the rate of inflation accelerates, cash coming in will tend to lag behind the value of invoiced sales even if the credit period remains constant. Most firms try to balance increases in amounts outstanding from debtors by increases in amounts outstanding to creditors. But as debtors, which reflect turnover, will normally exceed creditors, which are linked to material and other purchases, there will be a net cash outflow in times of inflation, and particularly in times of accelerating inflation such as occurred in 1969 and1970.

This, together with the inflated value of stocks will need to be financed by additional borrowing or from retained profits.

Inflation and borrowing

We have seen in Chapter 2 how the equity owners' proportionate stake in mechanical engineering companies appeared to have been eroded between 1965 and 1971. Because the appreciation in the value of the assets financed by a loan accrues to the equity owners, not to the lenders, the position of the equity owners of a company can be protected by borrowing, provided that the return on any borrowed funds (including the appreciation in the value of the assets) exceeds the cost of borrowing.

This approach can also be extended to cover all monetary items in the balance sheet, including cash holdings, debtors, creditors and any other claims expressed in fixed monetary values, as well as fixed interest borrowing of all sorts. Companies with net monetary assets lose in inflation; those with net monetary liabilities gain. Other things being equal, therefore, it is desirable for companies to minimise monetary assets, and maximise monetary liabilities. By the same token, it is necessary to make allowance for this in adjusting profits for the effects of inflation. Chapter 2 showed how our sample companies extended their position of net monetary liability between 1965 and 1971.

Excessive short term liabilities in relation to liquid assets can, however, result in an inability to meet day to day obligations. There are also risks in the longer term in increasing the gearing of a company's capital structure by increasing the proportion of fixed monetary liabilities in total liabilities. The extent of these risks depends on the return which a company is normally able to earn on its total assets and the stability of that return. Financial institutions normally set limits to the level of long term loans they are willing to provide to individual companies by reference to assets and income cover for capital and interest. These limits are considerably tighter in the UK than in some other countries, eg Japan. Furthermore, banks are seldom willing to finance the whole of a company's increased working capital requirements. Public authorities may also from time to time exert pressure on the banks to cut down on their lending, which may come at an awkward time for a company. There are, therefore, limits to the extent to which companies can pass on the burden of inflation to lenders, even if interest rates are in real terms relatively low.

Inflation and taxation

In computing a company's profits for corporation tax purposes, no allowance is made in the UK for any of the ways in which inflation results in an overstatement of real profits as described above. When profits have been adjusted for inflation, at least in the mechanical engineering industry where real profits are generally lower than profits reported on a historic cost basis, the proportion shown to have been taken by tax is increased considerably. Indeed any retention shown in the accounts as prepared on a historic cost basis, may disappear completely.

It can be argued that corporation tax has been set at a low level and tax allowances at a high level which in effect allows for the average rate of inflation which the UK experienced up to 1968. The acceleration in inflation especially from 1969 to 1971, however, greatly increased the pressures on real cash flow and profits.

General principles for adjusting accounts for inflation

Having examined the ways in which inflation can affect companies finances we now describe in outline how company accounts, as conventionally prepared, can be adjusted to reflect current purchasing power (for the purposes of this study, prices prevailing at end 1971 which is assumed to be the date of the most recent balance sheets).

The first set of adjustments needed stems from the fact that accounts combine records of transactions made at different times and hence, in the absence of revaluations, at different price levels.

As far as the balance sheet is concerned, recorded stocks will reflect purchases on average perhaps a few months before the year end. Only relatively minor adjustments will therefore be needed to such items. For fixed assets the lapse of time is likely to be on average very much longer. The extent of the adjustments to their valuations are likely to be much greater and will also effect the depreciation charge which is assessed on them. All these historical costs of non-monetary items in the accounts will need to be translated into current purchasing values. It is not, however, necessary for this purpose to adjust the value of monetary items in the balance sheet at the end of the year; these represent claims payable in fixed money units regardless of the date when the claims were incurred or changes in price levels. Examples are cash and debtors, creditors and loans.

The year's profit and loss account transactions may for convenience be assumed to have taken place on average some six months earlier than the balance sheet date. It will be necessary to adjust these items to end year values. Further adjustments will be needed to take account of the increase in the depreciation charge arising from the revaluation of fixed assets, the changes in stock values due to inflation and the net gain or loss from the monetary position.

The adjustments made thus far ensure that all the values recorded in one set of accounts reflect prices at the end of that year. In making comparisons between the situation in different years, however, a second set of adjustments is needed. The item in a 1965 balance sheet need to be revalued to 1971 prices in order to reflect their real purchasing power in that year. For example, if the Consumer Price Index is used for this purpose, 1,000 of 1965 pounds sterling become 1,330 of 1971 pounds. Similar revaluations are needed in respect of all balance sheet and profit and loss account items (monetary and non-monetary) of earlier years in order to make them comparable in terms of purchasing power with those of, say, 1971.

Summary

In times of inflation accounts prepared on a historic cost basis give a distorted picture of a company's real situation. Historic cost depreciation provisions may be sufficient to meet immediate needs for the replacement of fixed assets when the rate of inflation is not greater than the real growth of companies.

Profits will be overstated as a rsult both of the underprovision for depreciation and of purely paper profits arising from stock appreciation.

Because no allowance is made for these effects of inflation on profits in calculating corporation tax liability, the proportion of real profits taken by tax will be substantially higher than appears to be the case.

Whilst to a considerable extent rising values of stocks and debtors may be financed by increased borrowing and resort to trade and other forms of credit there may well be a residual element which companies have to finance out of profits.

Because any appreciation in the monetary value of assets financed by loans or other fixed monetary liabilities accrues to the equity owners', not the lenders, the value of the equity owners' stake in their companies may be protected by borrowing. There are, however, likely to be risks in doing this beyond a certain point.

Accounts of the Sample Companies adjusted for inflation.

The price index used

For the conversion of historic cost accounts to current purchasing values a price index or indices is needed. As it is necessary for our purposes to express the values of all items in the accounts of earlier years in terms of 1971 purchasing power, it seemed appropriate to use a general price index rather than different indices for each of the various items in the accounts. Had our purposes been to prepare replacement cost accounts, different indices for different items might have been appropriate.

We considered using the GDP deflator representing the difference between current price figures of GDP and constant 1963 prices, or the consumer price index published in the National income and expenditure blue book. Appendix F shows the values of these and certain other price indices between 1948 and 1971. It shows that the overall changes in the various indices were broadly similar. Between 1965 and 1971 the overall rise in the consumer price index was 33 per cent, while the GDP deflator rose 36 per cent. The former rose more rapidly than the GDP deflator in 1968 and 1969, but less rapidly thereafter. The effect of using one index rather than another would obviously result in some differences in the adjusted figures and in the year to year changes in them. It is, however, clear that these differences would have been small. The broad pattern of development revealed would have been similar whichever of the indices had been used. The Research Foundation of the Institute of Chartered Accountants have recommended the use of the consumer price index in their discussion paper 'Accounting for stewardship in a period of inflation'. We accordingly decided to use the consumer price index.

Adjustment and revaluation of accounts

In order to obtain a view of the balance sheets, and profit and loss accounts for any one year which is adjusted for inflation, it is only necessary to ensure that all items are recorded on a consistent price basis. The accounts for each year have accordingly been adjusted to the prices ruling at the end of that year. The figures obtained for each year have then been revalued to end 1971 prices in order to make a comparison of changes in real terms between 1965 and 1971. The remainder of this chapter deals separately with these adjustments and revaluations.

The Adjustment of balance sheet items to prices ruling at the end of each year

The detailed workings, on the basis of which the adjustment of the balance sheet items to prices ruling at the end of each year are made, are shown in Appendices B and C. Balance sheet data for all the years 1965-71 inclusive, adjusted to end year prices, are set out in Appendix D. (Here excluded, along with other sources (Eds.)).

The adjustments to fixed asset values

The first stage is to adjust the values of property and plant recorded in company accounts to money values ruling at the dates the balance sheets were struck. The detailed information needed for an accurate calculation of their values - the age of assets still in use, the depreciation rates charged on them and their up to date values - are of course not available publicly. Hence it is necessary to build up estimates. A technique for this purpose based on known relationships between the book value of assets and annual and cumulated depreciation is described in Appendix B.

The adjustment values for gross property and plant, net property and plant and accumulated and annual depreciation, all of which are derived from the same calculation, are summarised for all the years covered by our study in Appendix B, Table B3. The estimates are inevitably imprecise but certainly provide a better idea of values at the balance sheet date than those shown in the accounts.

The adjustments to other balance sheet items

It is possible that part of the entries under goodwill and trade investment are of a nature that would have required adjustment similar to that applied to fixed assets. Detailed information for this purpose was however not available and no such adjustments have been made. The effect of them on the overall picture would have been slight as goodwill and trade investments together account for only 4 per cent of total assets.

The valuation of stocks (including work in progress) shown in the accounts will however be slightly out of date. The appropriate adjustments will not be large but for the sake of completeness and because long manufacturing times may make the adjustment important for some companies, an allowance is made for this. Details of the methods and assumptions used and the calculations from which the adjusted figures are derived are given in Appendix C.

For the remaining items in the balance sheets the historic cost values will not need to be adjusted since they are purely monetary items. For example, debtors (included in 'other fixed and current assets') current liabilities, borrowings and preference shares, reflect fixed monetary claims. In the absence of detailed information about them the same has been assumed to be true of deferred liabilities, and provisions and minorities. Adjusted figures for total assets, capital employed, and equity shareholders' interest are then derived from these figures.

The effects of the adjustments on balance sheet values

Table 1 sets out in summary form the balance sheets of our sample companies in 1965 and 1971 on a historic cost basis and after making these adjustments for inflation. It brings out the fact that the main adjustments are to the figures of fixed assets. The upward adjustment to the valuation of fixed assets in 1965 is £95 million (29 per cent) and in 1971 £213 million (46 per cent), compared with stock value adjustments of £4 million and £8 million in 1965 and 1971 respectively.

Table 1 The effect of inflation adjustments on the valuation of balance sheet items in the sample companies accounts, 1965 and 1971.

	1965			1971		
	Historic cost basis £m	Adjusted to end 1965 values £m	Increase %	Historic cost basis £m	Adjusted to end 1965 values £m	Increase %
Net property and plant	296	391	32	397	610	54
Other fixed assets	34	34	-	68	68	-
Fixed assets	331	426	28	465	678	46
Stocks	349	353	1	512	520	2
Other current assets	370	370	-	633	633	-
Total assets	1050	1148	9	1610	1831	14
Less current liabilities	290	290	-	499	499	-
Capital employed	759	858	13	1111	1322	20
Less borrowings, preference, capital minorities, etc.	199	199	-	404	404	-
Equity shareholder's Interest	560	659	18	707	928	31

In the light of these adjustments, capital employed and the equity shareholders' interest are shown to have been understated in the accounts for 1965, and even more so in 1971. After adjusting for inlation, the figure of capital employed is increased by 13 per cent in 1965 and by 20 per cent in 1971.

The upward adjustments to the values of the equity holders' interest are even greater, 18 per cent in 1965 and 31 per cent in 1971. This is because all of the increase in the value of the companies' assets arising from inflation adjustments is added to the equity holders' interest - all long and short term borrowings and preference capital representing obligations only in fixed monetary terms.

The structure of the balance sheets

Because of the cyclical nature of the industry the structure of the balance sheets of the sample companies can only sensibly be compared at similar points on the industry cycle. As was done for the accounts prepared on a historic cost basis we have therefore compared the positions at the end of 1966 and 1970.

Table 2. shows in further detail the effect of the adjustments for inflation on the structure of the balance sheets in these years. Whilst the proportion of current assets and monetary liabilities in total assets and liabilities is shown to have increased substantially between 1966 and 1970, the unadjusted accounts to exaggerate the extent to which this occurred. On an unadjusted basis current assets increased from 69 per cent of total assets in 1966 to 72 per cent in 1970; on an adjusted basis the figures were 63 per cent and 65 per cent. The corresponding increases for monetary liabilities (all liabilities except the equity) were from 48 per cent in 1965 to 56 per cent in 1971 on an unadjusted basis and from 44 per cent to 50 per cent respectively on an adjusted basis. The reverse of this coin is that the proportion of the equity shareholders' interest in the total assets of the companies was understated and the extent of the decline in their proportionate interest was exaggerated in the accounts. In 1966 on the basis of the accounts their interest was 52 per cent of total assets compared with 56 per cent on an adjusted basis. By 1970 this had declined to 44 per cent on the basis of the accounts, compared with 50 per cent on an adjusted basis.

Table 2 Changes in balance sheet structure after adjustment to prices ruling at the end of each year: 1976-70

	Proportion of total assets and liabilities %					
	1966	(*)	1970	(*)	Difference	(*)
Assets						
Fixed assets:						
Property and plant	34	(28)	32	(25)	-2	(-3)
Other fixed assets	3	(3)	4	(4)	+1	(+1)
Total	37	(31)	36	(29)	-1	(-1)
Current assets:						
Cash	4	(4)	3	(3)	-1	(-1)
Debtors	29	(32)	32	(36)	+3	(+4)
Stock	30	(33)	30	(33)	-	(-)
Total	63	(69)	65	(71)	+2	(+2)
Total assets	100	(100)	100	(100)	-	(-)
Liabilities						
Monetary liabilities:						
Creditors	20	(21)	23	(26)	+3	(+5)
Other current liabilities	6	(7)	5	(6)	-1	(-1)
Short term borrowing	6	(7)	9	(10)	+3	(+3)
Long term borrowing	6	(7)	8	(9)	+2	(+2)
Deferred liabilities etc.	3	(4)	3	(3)	-	(-1)
Preference capital	2	(2)	1	(1)	-1	(-1)
Total	44	(48)	50	(56)	+6	(+8)
Equity Interest	56	(52)	50	(44)	-6	(-8)
Total liabilities	100	(100)	100	(100)	-	(-)

- Nil.
Note: Figures may not add up to totals shown due to rounding.

The adjustment of profits, retentions and cash flow to prices ruling at the end of each year.

It was explained in Chapter 3 that a figure for profits that took account of the effects of inflation on the income and expenditure of the firm would give a better idea of the real financial position of the firm than that shown in accounts prepared on an historic cost basis. Such a figure could be obtained by adjusting the figures in the accounts, first for the effect of price increases during the year; secondly, for any gain or loss as a result of the company's net monetary position; thirdly, for paper profits arising from an increase in the value of stocks; and lastly for higher depreciation from the revaluation of assets on which it is charged.

The detailed calculations needed to derive a profit figure adjusted on this basis are given in Appendix E. A summary of the adjustments made in each year from 1966-71 is also given in Table 12. (It is not possible to make the necessary adjustments to 1965 profits in the absence of 1964 balance sheets). For example, in 1971 profits (pre-interest, pre-tax but after depreciation) of £159 million are subject to the following adjustments:

(a) Profits reported reflect transactions that on average took place some six months before the end of the year, and for that reason are understated in terms of end-year prices. £5 million should be added to allow for this.

(b) The aggregated balance sheets show that monetary liabilities exceeded monetary assets by about £270 million. The gain arising from being a net borrower during 1971 was estimated to be worth £19 million to the sample companies due to the rise during the year in the consumer price index.

(c) Profits were inflated by appreciation of stock values. This is estimated to have added £38 million of paper profit to the reported figure, which should be deducted.

(d) Depreciation was understated because fixed assets were undervalued. £16 million should be deducted from profits to cover higher depreciation. The extent of the undervaluation is shown by the same calculations as used to adjust the values of fixed assets.

The net result of these adjustments is to reduce the reported 1971 profit figure of £159 million to £129 million - a reduction of £30 million - or nearly 20 per cent. Similar calculations have been made for the years 1966 to 1970, as shown in Table 3. The effects of these calculations are also illustrated in Figure 1. It can be seen that over the six years for which profit data are available the adjustments to profits have all been increasing as the rate of inflation has been increasing.

Throughout the period the major adjustment to profits required was to offset the effects of the increase in stock values due solely to inflation. This adjustment has more

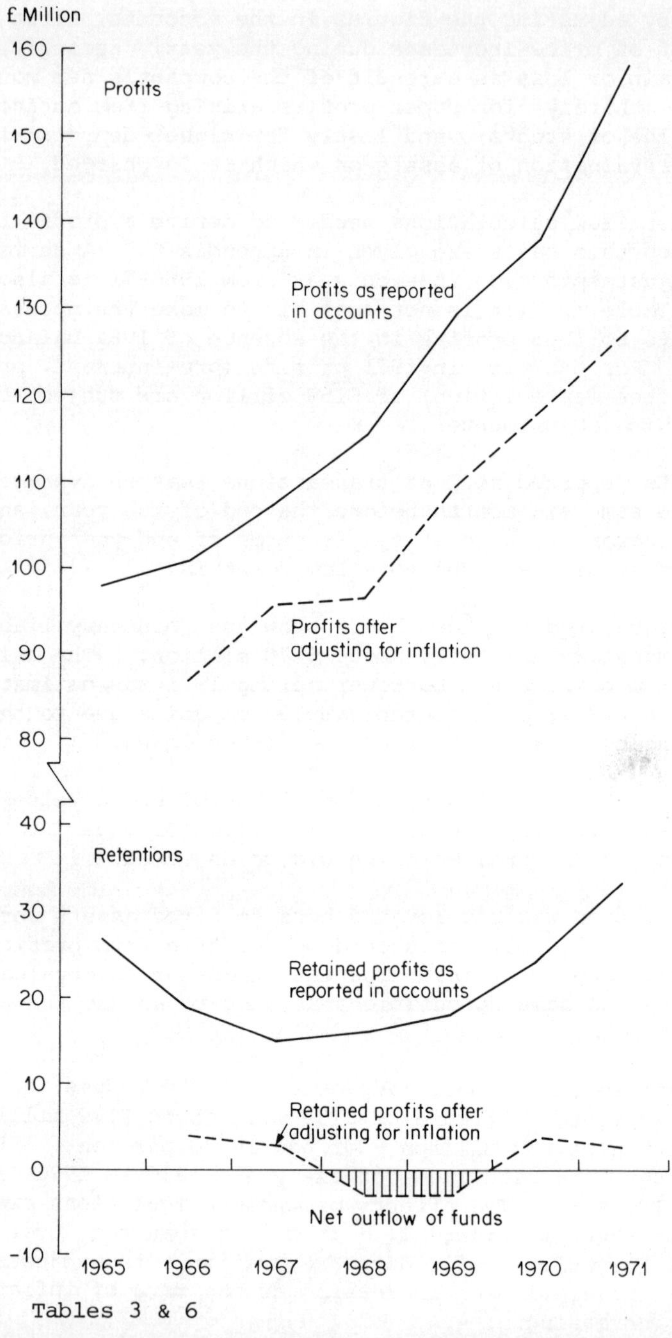

Source: Tables 3 & 6

Figure 1. The effect of adjusting for inflation on the profits and retentions of mechanical engineering companies.

than trebled over the period. Up to 1969 the next largest adjustment was to allow for increased replacement costs for fixed assets. By 1970 and 1971, however, companies had so managed their monetary positions that the adjustment to profits to allow for the advantage of holding net monetary liabilities exceeded the additional depreciation requirement. By 1971, over 35 per cent of the downward adjustment to profits was offset by the holding of net monetary liabilities, compared with an 'offset' of only 21 per cent in 1968.

Table 3 Adjustments of profits to prices ruling at the end of each year: 1966-71, £ million

	1966	1967	1968	1969	1970	1971
Profits reported per accounts	101	108	116	130	139	159
Add						
Adjustment to end year prices	+1	+2	+3	+3	+5	+5
Profit from holding net monetary liabilities	+4	+5	+6	+9	+16	+19
Less						
Appreciation of stock valuues due to inflation	-12	-11	-18	-20	-27	-38
Additional deprecia-tion to allow for increased replace-ment costs	-7	-8	-10	-12	-14	-16
Profits (end year values) As adjusted for gains and losses due to inflation	87	96	97	110	119	129

Return on capital employed

The overall effect of the adjustments of capital employed and profits discussed above on the real return earned by our sample companies is brought out in Table 4. This shows the figures for capital employed, profits and profitability derived from the accounts prepared on a historic cost basis and adjusted to the prices ruling at the relevant year end. Whereas the unadjusted accounts show a gradually increasing profitability, the adjusted figures show both that profitability was lower in real terms than that recorded in the accounts, and also that it was not increasing.

Whereas the accounts show 1968 to have been a profitable year compared with 1966 and 1967, the adjusted figures show it as the least profitable year over the period covered. The marked improvement in profitability in 1971 is also shown to have been almost entirely due to the distorting effects of inflation. On the evidence of our calculations, nearly one quarter (£38 million) of the profits reported in that year, resulted from the appreciation of stock values due to inflation. The table shows that the difference between reported and real profitability was increasing virtually throughout the period from a difference of 2.9 percentage points in 1966 to one of 4.1 percentage points in 1971.

Table 4 Profitability of mechanical engineering companies after adjustment to prices ruling at the end of each year: 1966-71

	1966	1967	1968	1969	1970	1971
Capital employed:						
per accounts (historic cost basis), £m	802	852	891	986	1046	1111
adjusted, £m	903	963	1019	1139	1230	1323
Profits:						
per accounts, (historic cost basis), £m	101	108	116	130	139	159
adjusted, £m	87	96	97	110	119	129
Profitability (profits as a % of capital employed):						
per accounts (historic cost basis) %	12.5	12.6	12.8	13.0	13.1	13.8
adjusted, %	9.6	10.0	9.5	9.7	9.7	9.7
difference accounted for by inflation, %	2.9	2.6	3.3	3.3	3.4	4.1

The impact of taxation

Table 5 shows profits before and after interest

appropriations, and before and after tax and the proportion of taxable profits taken by taxation for the years 1966 to 1971 on a historic cost basis and after adjustment of the profits for inflation. For example £54 million tax was paid in 1971. This represented 41 per cent of profits as shown in the accounts but 53 per cent of inflation adjusted profits. Though there is room for debate on exactly how profits might be taxed on an inflation adjusted basis, this comparison shows that the Revenue gains as the expense of industry as the result of inflation unless special provisions are made. In general the higher the rate of inflation, the greater the advantage to the Revenue and the loss to industry.

Table 5 The impact of taxation after adjustment of profits ruling at the end of each year: 1966-71

	1966	1967	1968	1969	1970	1971
Pre-interest, pre-tax profits:						
per accounts (historic cost basis), £m	101	108	116	130	139	159
adjusted, £m	87	96	97	110	119	129
Less interest, £m	9	11	13	16	23	25
Taxable profits:						
per accounts (historic cost basis), £m	92	97	103	114	116	134
adjusted, £m	78	85	84	94	96	104
Less taxation, £m	39	43	47	55	51	54
Profits after interest and taxation per accounts (historic cost basis), £m	53	54	56	59	65	80
adjusted, £m	39	42	37	39	45	50
Taxation as a percentage of taxable profits:						
per accounts (historic cost basis), %	42	44	46	48	44	41
adjusted, %	49	51	56	58	53	53

Note: Figures do not always add up to totals shown, due to rounding.

Retained profits and net cash flow

Table 6 shows the effects of the adjustment of profits on retentions and net cash flow in each of the years 1966 to 1971. The table shows adjusted figures for profits after tax and interest, retained profits, net cash flow and net cash flow expressed as a percentage of capital employed, and compares these with the figures shown in the historic cost accounts.

Table 6 The appropriation of profits, and net cash flow after adjustment to prices ruling at the end of each year: 1966-71.

	1966	1967	1968	1969	1970	1971
Profits after interest and taxation:						
per accounts (historic cost basis), £m	53	54	56	59	65	80
adjusted, £m	39	42	37	39	45	50
Less dividends and minorities, £m	35	39	40	42	42	46
Retained profits:						
per accounts (historic cost basis), £m	19	15	16	18	24	33
adjusted, £m	4	3	-3	-3	4	3
Net cash flow:						
per accounts (historic cost basis), £m	48	47	49	53	62	74
adjusted, £m	42	43	40	44	56	60
Net cash flow as a percentage of capital employed:						
per accounts (historic cost basis, %	6.0	5.5	5.5	5.4	5.9	6.6
adjusted, &	4.6	4.4	3.9	3.9	4.5	4.5

Note: Figures do not always add up to totals shown due to rounding

It will be seen that retentions never exceeded £4 million on an adjusted basis during the period covered (in 1966 and 1970), compared with a minimum of £15 million (in 1967) shown in the historic cost accounts, Indeed it is calculated that in 1968 and 1969 funds were actually taken out of our sample companies.

Net cash flow does not show so large a reduction as profits or retentions after adjustment for inflation, because of the additional depreciation provision included in the adjusted figures. Nevertheless net cash flow is shown to have been distinctly less than the accounts indicate, especially in relation to the adjusted capital employed. On an adjusted basis it was also slightly lower as a percentage of capital employed in 1971 than in 1965, rather than the reverse as the accounts show.

Revaluation of the accounts to end 1971 prices for each year in the period 1965-71.

We have now seen how the adjustment of company accounts for inflation to the prices ruling when each balance sheet was struck, alters the picture of the balance sheet structures and profitability of companies. The real (i.e. constant price) values of the balance sheet items, profits, appropriations, and cash flow still cannot be compared over time as they are measured at the price levels of different years. It is therefore now necessary to convert all items in the balance sheets and profit and loss accounts to end 1971 price levels. This has only been done in this booklet for 1965 (balance sheet only), 1966, 1970 and 1971 to illustrate the effects of this further revaluation. These years were chosen so that the years at the beginning and end of the period covered, as well as the years of peak strain on liquidity, could be compared.

Comparison of balance sheet items at end 1971 prices

In Table 7, the balance sheet items shown elsewhere have been revalued to end 1971 prices. The table also shows the percentage increases in the value of these items between 1965 and 1971 at end 1971 prices, and compares these with the apparent increases as recorded in the accounts.

In the six years from 1965 to 1971, it can be seen that total assets and liabilities increased by about 18 per cent in real terms, equivalent to about 3 per cent a year. The

Table 7 Changes in balance sheet items after revaluation to end 1971 prices: 1965-71

	£m, end 1971 prices				Increase from 1965-71 As shown by: unadjusted accounts	revalued accounts
	1965	1966	1970	1971	%	%
Property and plant	528	536	590	610	34	16
Goodwill and trade investments	46	47	71	68	100	48
Fixed assets	573	583	661	678	41	18
Cash	66	62	51	75	51	14
Debtors	432	469	589	558	74	29
Stocks	475	479	550	520	47	9
Current assets	973	1010	1190	1153	60	18
Total assets	1547	1593	1851	1831	53	18
Creditors	294	312	432	407	87	38
Other current liabilities	97	101	100	92	27	-5
Current liabilities	391	413	532	499	72	28
Short term borrowing	93	98	162	152	120	63
Long term borrowing	82	102	157	161	164	96
Deferred liabilities etc	56	55	57	68	66	21
Preference capital	37	35	24	23	-18	-38
Equity Interest	888	889	918	928	26	5
Capital employed	1156	1180	1319	1332	46	15
Total liabilities	1547	1593	1851	1851	53	18

Note: Figures do not always add up to totals shown, due to rounding.

unadjusted accounts showed an increase of 53 per cent (over 7 per cent a year). The contrast between the real and apparent growth in total assets is also brought out in Figure 2. From the accounts prepared on an historic cost basis it appeared that most of this increase was due to a nearly 60 per cent increase in the value of current assets, compared with a 31 per cent increase in the value of fixed assets. When the accounts are revalued the percentage increase in both fixed and current assets is about the same. The major increase in assets is still seen to have been in debtors, financed almost entirely by increased creditors and borrowings. This is particularly apparent if the figures for 1966 and 1970 are compared. A £120 million (at end 1971 prices) increase in debtors between these two years was almost exactly balanced by a similar increase in creditors. Virtually all the remaining increase in assets between 1966 and 1970 was financed by a reduction in cash holdings and a more than 50 per cent increase in long and short term borrowing.

Between 1965 and 1971 the equity holders' interest increased by only £40 million or less than 1 per cent a year in real terms, from £888 million to £928 million. Even this increase was in large measure a result of companies' positions of net monetary liability, since retentions were no more than £10 million over the period (see below). The position is in contrast with that shown in the historic cost accounts where the equity interest is recorded as having increased by £147 million or 26 per cent over the period (see Figure 2).

If allowance is made for equity issued by companies for rights and acquisitions during the period the real value of the owners' stake in the companies probably changed very little. Given the widely different rates of growth and performance of individual companies in the industry, it is clear that in a great many cases the real asset value of the owners' holdings must have declined between 1965 and 1971.

Comparison of profit appropriations and net cash flow levels at end 1971 prices

Table 8 shows profits, returns on capital, retentions, and net cash flow in real terms, i.e. after adjustment and revaluation to end 1971 prices, and compares these with the figures shown on a historic cash basis. As can be seen, inflation gives a false impression of the real rise in all these items.

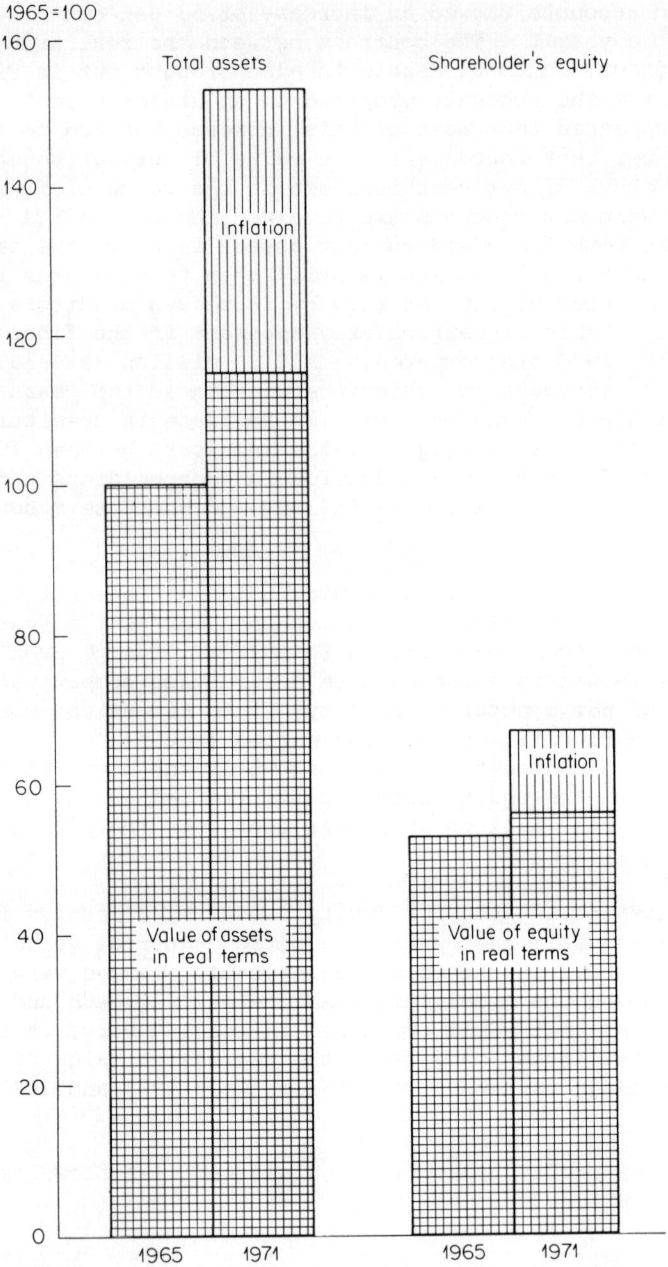

Source: Table 7

Figure 2 Real and apparent growth of total assets and shareholders' equity in mechanical engineering (Total assets in 1965 = 100)

Table 8 Profits, retentions and cash flow after revaluation to end 1971 prices: 1966-71

	1966	1967	1970	1971	Per cent increase from 1966 to 1971
Pre-interest, pre-tax profits:					
per accounts (historic cost basis), £m	101	108	139	159	57
adjusted and re-valued, £m	114	121	128	129	13
Capital employed:					
per accounts (historic cost basis), £m	802	852	1046	1111	39
adjusted and revalued, £m	1181	1216	1319	1332	13
Profit on capital employed;					
per accounts (historic cost basis), %	12.5	12.6	13.1	13.8	+1.3*
adjusted and revalued, %	9.6	10.0	9.7	9.7	+1.0*
Retentions:					
per accounts (historic cost basis), £m	19	15	24	33	74
adjusted and revalued, £m	5	4	4	3	-40
Net cash flow:					
per accounts (historic cost basis), £m	48	47	62	74	54
adjusted and revalued, £m	55	54	60	60	9

* Differences, not % increases

In five years the real value of company profits increased by only 13 per cent, from £114 million in 1966 to £129 million in 1971, while their accounts showed profits nearly 60 per cent higher. Virtually all profits after interest and tax were absorbed by dividends, but in real terms dividends increased by only 2 per cent, compared with a 31 per cent increase shown in the accounts. (The real increase in average weekly earnings in mechanical engineering over the same period is calculated to have been 16 per cent.) This however makes no allowance for rights or acquisitions issues, both of which are likely to have diluted any increase in dividends by spreading payments over a larger group of shareholders.

Over the period as a whole retentions on a revlaued basis were only £10 million compared with £124 million shown in the accounts. As we have already seen (page 30) the figures suggest that funds were actually taken out of the sample companies in 1968 and 1969. In 1971 retentions were only £3 million on a revalued basis compared with £5 million in 1966. By contrast the accounts show a substantial (74 per cent) increase in retentions from £19 million to £33 million between the same two years.

After revaluation, net cash flow is shown to have increased by only 9 per cent, from £55 million to £60 million, between 1966 and 1971. The accounts show a 54 per cent higher level of retentions in the latter year.

Summary and conclusions

The adjustments and revaluations described in this chapter have shown how misleading the picture of the sample companies' operations as reflected in accounts prepared on an historic cost basis can be.

Over the six years 1966-71 it appears on the basis of the price adjustment factors we have used that the profits of our sample of mechanical engineering companies were substantially overstated. This was mainly a result of purely paper profits on stock appreciation and, to a lesser extent, under-provision for the replacement of fixed assets. The reduction made to adjust for these factors were in part offset by additional profits arising from companies' increased positions of increased net monetary liability.

Return on capital employed remained in the range 9.5 per cent to 10 per cent in real terms between 1966 and 1971, rather than rising from 12.5 per cent in 1966 (after 12.9

per cent in 1965) to 13.8 per cent in 1971. The proportion of profits after interest taken by tax was 53 per cent compared with 41 per cent as shown in the accounts.

When the accounts were revalued to end 1971 prices (to reflect current purchasing power), total assets and liabilities are shown to have increased between 1965 and 1971 by about 18 per cent whereas the accounts show a 53 per cent increase. The equity holders' stake increased by only 5 per cent in real terms while the accounts showed a 26 per cent increase.

Also in terms of 1971 prices, pre-interest pre-tax profits increased by 13 per cent between 1966 and 1971 compared with an apparent increase of 57 per cent shown in the accounts. While real earnings in the industry increased by 18 per cent between 1965 and 1971, dividends rose in real terms by 25 per cent (almost all in 1966) though this figure overstates the true increase because no allowance is made for rights and acquisitions issues. Far from expanding their businesses by ploughing back £124 million into them as the accounts show, in fact our sample companies really only retained £10 million of their earnings over the period. Since these are aggregate figures, the implication is that nearly half of them must have run down their businesses quite substantially. As a result of increasing their positions of net monetary liability, companies were able to increase slightly the real value of their equity holders' stake in their businesses.

No doubt slightly different results would have been achieved by using different price indices. Nevertheless the data in Appendix F (not given here) suggest that these differences would not have been all that great. Certainly we are confident that the broad picture revealed by our adjustments to the accounts would not have been altered significantly.

In the light of the evidence contained in this report the importance of allowing for the effects of inflation (when considering the picture represented by company accounts) hardly needs underlining. Misleading information can lead to bad decisions - by managements, investors, creditors, Government and trades unions. The marketing director needs to take inflation into account in making his pricing decisions if sufficient profits are to be made to maintain the real value of the business. The finance director needs to take it into account when assessing the provision he needs to make for the replacement of fixed and other assets and in the management of the company's monetary position. The whole Board needs to take it into account in preparing their business plans and future investment programmes.

Investors, including companies who are considering merging with, or taking over other companies, need to take it into account when examining the financial records of prospective partners. (The quality and age of fixed assets and the extent to which a company's capital is provided by loans can, as we have seen, considerably distort reality when recorded in accounts prepared on a historic cost basis). The same applies to creditors. Government needs to consider its implications for the taxation of companies as well as in placing contracts. (Some European countries allow adjustments to be made for inflation in computing company tax liability). Trade union representatives need to understand its implications for the future viability of the business in which they work.

We hope this booklet will help them all better to understand the impact of inflation on the mechanical engineering industry and particularly on the way in which its performance is recorded in conventionally prepared accounts.

IV On Gains and Losses on Monetary Liabilities and Assets

10 Distinguishing Between Monetary and Non-Monetary Assets and Liabilities

Loyd C. Heath

General price-level accounting literature distinguishes between two types of assets and liabilities: monetary and nonmonetary. This distinction is important because assets and liabilities classified as monetary are accounted for differently in general price-level accounting than those classified as nonmonetary.

The purpose of this paper is to clarify and sharpen the distinction between monetary and nonmonetary assets and liabilities for general price-level accounting. This is done in several steps. First the conceptual basis of general price-level accounting is examined and the distinction between general price-level accounting and conventional accounting is discussed. This is necessary because the criteria for distinguishing between monetary and nonmonetary assets and liabilites developed later in the paper is tied to the purpose or objective of price-level accounting. Second, an example is introduced to illustrate the nature of general price-level gains and losses and how these gains and losses differ from gains and losses now reported in general price level-accounting. Third, the definition used by several authorities for distinguishing between monetary and non-monetary items are examined and evaluated critically in the light of the theoretical concepts developed earlier. The paper concludes with proposed new criteria for distinguishing between monetary and nonmonetary items in general price-level accounting.

THE CONCEPTUAL BASIS OF GENERAL PRICE-LEVEL ACCOUNTING

Accounting is concerned with measurement of certain monetary properties of rights, obligations and events. Before discussing what is meant by the term "general price-level accounting" as used in this paper, it is necessary to discuss certain basic concepts in general and monetary measurement in particular.

Measurement in General

Measurement involves determining the equivalence of some quality between different objects or events. Thus we might say that John is 15 pencils tall, meaning that the ratio between the length of a pencil and John's height is 15 to 1. This type of statement conveys some information but it is not as useful as it might be because the standard of the unit of measurement has not been specified. Pencils vary in length and unless the heights of various persons are measured by the same pencil or in terms of a standard pencil, comparison of heights by comparing pencil length equivalents can be very misleading. Mathematical operations such as adding, subtracting, multiplying or dividing heights measured in pencils to determine how much taller one person is than the other, or to determine average height may yield misleading results unless a measuring unit with a clearly identified standard is used.

Standards are specified for many types of measurement. A metre, for example, is defined as the distance between two microscopic lines on a specific bar of platinum-iridium kept in Paris under specific physical conditions. This bar is the standard used for measurement of length.

Monetary Measurement

Accountants are seldom concerned with measurement of length: they are concerned with the measurement of monetary properties such as costs, values and obligations. The measurement concepts discussed above, however, are also applicable to measurement of these monetary properties.

Accountants measure monetary properties in monetary units such as dollars or pounds sterling. Monetary units are measures of command over goods and services just as a foot, a metre, or a mile is a measure of length. There is seldom any confusion between the abstract concept of a foot as a unit of length and the tangible instrument used to measure length (e.g., a ruler) but the abstract concept of a monetary unit is often confused with money, a tangible "thing" used in exchange. Haines comments as follows on this point:

> There is ... a difference between the monetary unit, which measures the price of goods, and money, which is a means of buying them. The difference is somewhat similar to that between a standard of measurement such as a foot, and an instrument of measurement, such as a ruler. A ruler may have a length of 1 foot, but so

> does my shoe, the Columbia Encyclopedia and acoustical ceiling tile. None of these including the ruler, is a standard of measurement. Similarly, a dollar bill may have a value of $1, but so does a pound of steak, a movie admission, and a necktie. None of these, including the dollar bill, is a standard of value. Money buys goods; the monetary unit measures their price. The monetary unit is an abstract concept; money is a physical substance.[1]

General Price-Level Accounting

The essential difference between general price-level accounting and conventional accounting lies in the standard of the monetary unit in which measurements are made and financial position and results of operation expressed. The standard of the unit used in general price-level accounting is more precisely specified than that used in conventional accounting.

The standard used in conventional accounting is not usually explicitly identified, but a standard is implicit in the type of monetary measurements made and reported. It is the amount of goods and services which can be purchased with a given amount of money. Those who use financial statements are assumed to understand and appreciate this equivalence between money on the one hand and goods and services on the other; if they did not, monetary measurements would convey little or no useful information.

The standard of the monetary unit used in conventional accounting is rather crude because the equivalence between a given amount of money and goods and services varies from time to time. Intertemporal comparisons of monetary measurements made in this type of monetary unit can, under certain conditions, be just as misleading as comparisons of length measurements made in terms of pencils.

The standard of the monetary unit used in general price-level accounting, on the other hand, is more precisely specified. The time at which the equivalence between money and goods and services is established is identified by calling the measuring unit 1960 dollars, or the like. This is merely a shorthand way of expressing the concept that the standard of the measuring unit is the amount of goods and services in general which $1 would have bought in 1960, 1968, or some other year.

THE NATURE OF GAINS AND LOSSES

Accounting is a means of portraying conditions and events that happen in the "real world." The end product of accounting, financial statements, may be likened to maps. Like all maps, financial statements are useful only if they accurately portray the territory (i.e., the real conditions and events) which they purport to portray. Consequently, the first step in formulating a distinction between different types of assets and liabilities for general price-level accounting should be to survey the "territory" - to examine the nature of changes in financial position experienced by the holders of different types of assets when general price-level measurements concepts are used to measure financial position. This is done by means of a simple example.

Types of Losses from Holding Assets

At the beginning of a period (T_1) a firm had total resources of $10. Half of this, or $5 was used to purchase potatoes; the other half was held in cash. At the end of the period (T_2) the potatoes were sold for $6. The general price level doubled during the period.

If general price-level measurement concepts are used to measure the financial position of this firm, it suffered a loss of general purchasing power during the period equal to that of 9 T_2 dollars. At the beginning of the period it held $10 which had general purchasing power equal to 20 T_2 dollars, and at the end of the period it held 11 T_2 dollars.

This loss is composed of two elements. First, there was a loss in purchasing power equivalent to that of 4 T_2 dollars from buying, holding, and selling potatoes. This is the excess of the general purchasing power paid for the potatoes (10 T_2 dollars) over that received for them (6 T_2 dollars). Second, there was a loss of general purchasing power equivalent to that of 5 T_2 dollars from holding $6 cash during the period. At the beginning of the period it had general purchasing power equivalent to 10 T_2 dollars; at the end of period it had general purchasing power equivalent to 5 T_2 dollars. The loss from buying, holding, and selling potatoes in this example will be referred to in the following discussion as an operating loss; the loss from holding money will be referred to as a general price-level loss.

Operating Losses

Even though there was inflation during the period in which the potatoes in this example were bought, held, and sold, and even though the amount of inflation was used to calculate the loss from potato transactions, it would be misleading to say that the operating loss in this example was "due to" or "caused by" inflation. It was, in fact, the joint result of two things: (1) a 20 percent rise in the money price of potatoes (from $5 to $6) and (2) a 50 percent fall in the purchasing power of the monetary unit in which prices are expressed.

A simple analogy should help clarity this point. To say the winner of a race won because his elapsed time was 3:59 or to say he won because his challengers' elapsed time was 4:00 are equally misleading statements; both events were necessary to produce a winner and a loser. Similarly, to say the holder of potatoes lost general purchasing power because prices in general doubled or to say he lost purchasing power because the price of potatoes rose only 20 percent are equally misleading; both events were necessary to produce the result. The only accurate statements are that the winner won the race because he ran faster than his challenger and the potato holder lost general purchasing power because the price of his potatoes rose slower than prices in general.

The $4 loss of general purchasing power from buying, holding, and selling potatoes in the example cannot be separated by "variance analysis" into components such as that portion due to inflation and that portion due to change in the price of potatoes. It has been argued, for example, that there was a $1 gain from a change in the price of potatoes and a $5 loss from inflation. The $1 gain is computed as the difference in the price of potatoes at the beginning and at the end of the period and the $5 loss is then the difference between the $1 price gain and the $4 loss of purchasing power.

The fallacy in this analysis is that the $1 gain is computed by comparing a price measured in T_1 dollars with a price measured in T_2 dollars. The standards for these two measuring units are different and prices measured in one cannot be compared with, added to, or subtracted from, prices measured in the other; both must first be stated in terms of units with a common standard.

The same argument about the cause of losses from buying, holding, and selling potatoes during a period of inflation would be equally applicable even if the monetary price of potatoes had not changed at all. If the price of the potatoes in this example had remained at $5, there would have been a loss equal to 5 instead of 4 T_2 dollars but it would be equally true that no part of this loss could be attributed to inflation alone. There is no way to tell whether the price would have remained at $5 had there been no inflation and there is no way to divide the operating loss between amounts caused by inflation and amounts caused by specific price changes.

General Price-Level Losses

The other part of the loss in the above example, that due to holding money, was due to a different causal force than the operating loss described in the previous section.

The monetary unit in an exchange economy serves as a common denominator and all prices typically are expressed in terms of it. Because of this the price of money is rigidly fixed at unity and cannot fluctuate. As Halm puts it:

> Money, as the unit of account, is distinguished from commodities by the fact that its price cannot change; its price is always one. Prices of commodities, on the other hand, as a rule are free to fluctuate. Price rigidity, therefore, is a characteristic quality of money.[2]

This characteristic of money is important in considering the nature of the loss suffered by the holder of money. It was pointed out above that no part of the loss from buying, holding and selling potatoes could be attribted to inflation alone; it was a function of two variables; (1) the monetary price of potatoes and (2) the general purchasing power of the monetary unit. The loss from holding money, however, was not a function of two variables; it was due solely to changes in the general purchasing power of the monetary unit because the monetary price of money cannot change.

REPORTING GAINS AND LOSSES

The discussion so far has been in terms of real events, not how to report these events in general price-level financial statements. The purpose of this section is to consider these reporting problems.

Gains Similar to Losses

Although the events in the above example resulted in losses in financial position, if there had been deflation instead of inflation or if the money price of potatoes had risen faster than the general price level there would have been gains rather than losses. These gains differ only in sign from the losses identified above. Consequently, the discussion in this section is in terms of gains and losses rather than losses alone.

Reporting Operating Gains and Losses Separately from General Price-Level Gains and Losses

If financial statements are to be of maximum benefit in providing a starting point for predicting future profits and losses, gains and losses due to one causal force should be reported separately from those due to other forces. Consequently, operating gains and losses should be reported separately from those due to price-level changes.

Realization Criteria

The second reporting problem to be considered is when gains and losses should be recognized as income. The simple example discussed above raises no income recognition problem because the firm held only cash at both the beginning and the end of the accounting period. Problems of income recognition are really valuation problems and a firm that holds only cash on the measurement dates has no valuation problem. But what if the firm in this example had not sold the potatoes? Should a loss from holding potatoes then be reported? And, would the answer be any different if there had been a gain instead of a loss?

Consider the income recognition criteria now used in conventional accounting. Gains are typically recognized only when an asset is sold; losses are recognized when a price decline occurs. These same criteria can and should be applied to operating gains and losses in price-level accounting. The amount of an operating gain or loss will normally be different if general price-level accounting measurement concepts are used in place of conventional accounting measurement concepts, but operating gains and losses are of the same general type as those gains and losses now reported in conventional accounting. Both are expressions of differences between acquisition costs and selling prices even though acquisition cost and selling prices are measured in different units in price-level accounting.

The recommendation that the same income recognition criteria now used in conventional accounting also be used in general price-level accounting should not, however, be interpreted as an endorsement of these criteria. There have been many serious proposals to change them in recent years. Proposals to introduce "current values" into accounting are really proposals to change the timing of when income is recognized; the total amount of profit or loss reported over the lifetime of an enterprise would be the same whether assets were valued at historical costs or "current values." It is important that the accounting profession consider these proposals to change currently accepted criteria for income recognition but these proposals should not be confused with general price-level accounting. Price-level measurement concepts are appropriate whether assets are valued at historical cost, "current value" or any other amount and the only point here is that it would be misleading to change currently accepted income recognition criteria in the name of general price-level accounting. Whether to introduce general price-level measurement concepts and whether to change extant income recognition criteria are separable problems.

Currently accepted criteria for income recognition cannot meaningfully be applied to general price-level gains and losses from holding money during a period of changing general price levels. Money is not "sold" in the sense that other assets are sold and it would be meaningless to apply currently accepted criteria by carrying money at "cost" until is is "sold." New criteria must be developed. Since price-level gains and losses from holding money are a direct result of general price-level changes alone and since they can be measured as readily and as precisely when price levels change as in some future period, there is no reason for deferring them. They should, therefore, be reported in the same period in which the price-level changes occur.

DEFINITION OF MONETARY ITEMS

Up to this point the discussion has been restricted to accounting for gains and losses from only two types of assets: potatoes and money. The nature of gains and losses from holding potatoes and money has been analyzed and recommendations have been made on how to report these gains and losses in general price-level financial statements based on this analysis. Next it is necessary to generalize from this analysis and to identify other assets that should be accounted for in the manner prescribed above for potatoes and those that should be accounted for like money.

The accounting treatment prescribed above for money is similar to that recommended for assets referred to as "monetary" by Sweeney, [3] Jones, [4] Mason, [5] the staff of the Accounting Research Division of the American Institute of CPA's in Accounting Research Study No. 6[6] and the Accounting Principles Board in its Statement No. 3.[7] Similarly, the accounting treatment prescribed above for potatoes is basically the same as that recommended for assets referred to as "nonmonetary." The definitions of monetary and non-monetary items used by these authorities are examined and evaluated below but before doing this it is imprtant to point out that merely assigning the names "monetary" and "nonmonetary" to two classes of items does not adequately identify the types of items which belong in each class. In fact, use of these terms tends to cloud the issue because they are familiar to many readers in contexts other than that under consideration here. As Cohen and Nagel point out: "Familiar or ordinary words...carry penumbras of suggested meanings which obstruct the process of rigorous deduction."[8]

It might be desirable to coin new words to refer to "money-type" and "potato-type" items to avoid the "penumbras of suggested meanings" associated with the terms "monetary" and "nonmonetary" but since the terms monetary and nonmonetary are so widely used in general price-level accounting literature to refer to the general concept under consideration here, they are retained in this discussion. During the discussion, however, it should be remembered that distinguishing between different types of assets is basically a problem of classification and the merits of any classification criteria depend on the purpose or objective of classification. Classification criteria developed for one purpose are not necessarily the most useful for other purposes. Assets called "monetary" for some purposes might be better classified as "nonmonetary" for general price-level accounting.

The Essential Characteristic of Monetary Assets

The essential characteristic of an asset classified as monetary for general price-level accounting is that its holder gains or loses general purchasing power during inflation or deflation simply as a result of general price-level changes. In other words, its holder gains or loses general purchasing power as a direct result of general price-level changes alone. This is the characteristic that led to the conclusion that money should be accounted for differently than potatoes in the above example. Money has this characteristic; potatoes do not.

Monetary assets could, of course, be defined in terms of this "essential characteristic" as assets whose holders gain or lose general purchasing power during inflation or deflation simply as a result of general price-level changes. This definition is not, however, very helpful to one who wishes to prepare general price-level financial statements. Further elaboration is needed to identify which assets have this characteristic and which do not. Before attempting to do this, however, it is useful to review critically the definitions of monetary assets used by others.

Definitions of Monetary Assets Used by Other Writers

Mason defines monetary assets as "cash or...any claim to money."[9] The basic problem with this definition is that it is based on an implicit assumption that the reader understands what is meant by "cash" or "money." In other words, it is based on the assumption that the words "cash" and "money" have singular universally agreed-upon definitions which partition all items into either cash or not cash or into money or not money. This, however, is not the case. As Boulding points out:

> Just where to draw the line - just what is money and what is not - is diffucult to define...The quality of being "money" is a matter of degree rather than of kind, and under certain circumstances even things like diamonds or cigarettes behave like money...It is important to realize however, that wherever this line is drawn will be a more or less arbitrary point. Consequently arguments as to whether a certain thing is or is not money are usually a waste of breath.[10]

Consider foreign currency holdings, for example. Foreign currency might be considered cash or money for some purposes but it does not have what was described above as the "essential characteristic" of a monetary asset. The holder of foreign currency does not gain or lose purchasing power during inflation or deflation simply as a result of general price-level changes. The price of pounds sterling in terms of dollars, for example, like the price of potatoes, can and does fluctuate even though complex institutional arrangements have been established to dampen these fluctuations. Consequently gains or losses from holding foreign currency during a time of inflation or deflation, like gains and losses from holding potatoes, can only be attributed to the fact that the price of this currency in terms of the domestic monetary unit of account rose faster or slower than the general price level.

The phrase "claim to money" in Mason's definition also causes problems. Some types of claims to money do and some do not meet the "essential characteristic" test. Also some assets meet the test even though they are neither money nor "claims to money." The holder of a merchandise gift certificate, for example, does not have a claim to money; he has a claim to merchandise. But since his claim is fixed in terms of money, he is affected by inflation or deflation in the same way the holder of a claim to money is affected. A lease tied to gross sales of the lessee or a promissory note tied to net profits of the maker are both "claims to money" but neither should be accounted for as a monetary asset because no part of the gain or loss from holding either of them can be attributed to general price-level changes alone.

Other claims to money do, however, have the "essential characteristic" of a monetary asset. If gains and losses are measured in United States dollars, then claims fixed in terms of a predetermined absolute number of United States dollars by contract, court of law, legislative enactment or administrative settlement by government agency typically do meet the test. Examples are bank accounts, accounts receivable, taxes, bonds or an award of damages arising from litigation. Even in these cases, however, a problem of interpretation may arise. Some of these assets, such as receivables and bonds, have market prices which fluctuate and if financial position is measured in terms of market prices, gains or losses from changes in financial position cannot be attributed to general price-level changes alone and these assets should not, therefore, be considered monetary under these circumstances. Most assets of this type, however, are not accounted for in this way; they are accounted for as claims to fixed amounts of money rather than in terms of their market values. When the financial position of the holder of this type of asset is measured in terms of the holder's claim to a fixed predetermined number of dollars, gains and losses are attributable to general price-level changes alone and these assets should, therefore, be considered monetary.

Jones' definition of a monetary asset is slightly sharper than Mason's. He refers to "claims to...a fixed sum of money"[11] rather than just "claims to money." This would exclude claims to contingent amounts of money such as the lease tied to gross sales of the lessee or the promissory note tied to net profits of the maker mentioned above, but the same basic criticism applicable to Mason's definition is also applicable to that of Jones.

Accounting Research Study No. 6 defines a monetary asset as:

> ... one the amount of which is fixed by statute or contract, and is therefore not affected by a change in the general price-level.[12]

This definition too, falls short of capturing the essence of the concept of a monetary asset. It includes gold - in fact its authors specifically mention that refined gold is a monetary asset where its "price is fixed by government fiat,"[13] yet gains and losses from holding refined gold during inflation or deflation, like gains and losses from holding potatoes, can only be attributed to the fact that the price of these assets rose faster or slower than prices in general. It is just as misleading to say these gains and losses are due to inflation or deflation as it is to say they are due to government control of the price of gold because the fact of the matter is that they are the joint result of both.

The argument that gold should be accounted for as a nonmonetary asset does not, of course, mean that no gains or losses from holding it should be recognized nor does it mean that gold should not be carried at its current market value. As discussed above, the significance of classifying an asset as monetary or nonmonetary lies in when gains and losses from holding it are reported and how these gains and losses are described in the financial statements. The total profit reported over the lifetime of an enterprise will not be affected by whether a given asset is classified as monetary or nonmonetary; only the timing and description of the source of that profit will be affected. An asset classified as nonmonetary may be carried at either historical cost or current market value depending on the appropriate valuation rule. The same total profit would be reported each year if an asset were classified as monetary as if it were classified as nonmonetary and carried at current market value, but the gain and loss from holding that asset would be described differently. If it were classified as nonmonetary, this gain or loss would be reported as part of "cost of goods sold," "gains or losses from market flucutations," or some similar source of gains and losses whereas if it were classified as monetary the gain or loss would be reported as a price-level gain or loss. The objection to classifying gold as monetary lies in labeling gains or losses from holding gold as price-level gains or losses, not in recognizing these gains or losses as income.

The ARS No. 6 definition of a monetary asset not only includes assets which should be excluded; it also excludes assets which should be included. An award of a fixed number of dollars by a court of law to a litigant would meet the "essential characteristic" test described above yet it would not fit the definition of a monetary asset in ARS No. 6 because the amount of this claim was not fixed by "statute or contract."

Perhaps the oldest and one of the best definitions of monetary assets in general price-level accounting literature was by Sweeney. He defined them as:

> (Cash and) other assets (that) are like cash in the fact they remain rigidly and irrevocably set at previously determined money amounts, irrespective of how the value of the money in which they are measured changes.[14]

His phrase "rigidly and irrevocably set at previously determined money amounts" clearly excludes the lease-tied-to-gross-sales-of-lessee type situation and it also excludes refined gold because its "money amount" is not "rigidly and irrevocably set." Although its price is quite "rigid," it certainly is not "irrevocably set." This definition might be interpreted to exclude foreign currency, but it is not as clear on this point as it might be.

The recent statement of the Accounting Principles Board entitled "Financial Statements Restated for General Price-Level Changes"[15] analyzes various types of assets such as bonds, gold and foreign currency in the light of the same "essential characteristic" of monetary assets used in this paper[16] and it is not surprising, therefore, that it comes to the same conclusion on how to classify these assets as this paper. The definition found in the Statement is not, however, as clear or sharp as it could be. Assets are defined as monetary:

> ... if their amounts are fixed by contract or otherwise in terms of numbers of dollars regardless of changes in specific prices or in the general price level.[17]

The major problem with this definition stems from ambiguity of the word "fixed", a word which is commonly used in a number of different ways. Thus, we commonly speak of prices set by government agencies or even by businesses themselves as "fixed". Similarly, we speak of "fixing" the terms of a contract when we mean agreeing on its terms. Consequently, although the complete discussion of monetary items in the Statement makes it clear that the Board did not intend to include assets with "fixed" prices (e.g., gold and foreign currency) or leases merely because the terms have been clearly agreed upon, the definition itself does not clearly exclude them. The phrase "by contract or otherwise" appears to be an attempt to delineate more precisely the meaning of the word "fixed" but it fails because "otherwise" is too broad a word; it includes every means of "fixing" other than by contract and the phrase "by contract or otherwise" includes, therefore, any kind of "fixing" whatever.

This examination of the definitions of monetary assets used by others leads to the obvious conclusion that the distinction between monetary and nonmonetary assets in general price-level accounting has been oversimplified in accounting literature. Most writers have defined monetary items rather loosely, probably because they felt that the distinction between monetary and nonmonetary items is a fairly obvious one that is easily understood.

SUGGESTED NEW DEFINITION

Criticizing the definitions of other writers is probably easier and undoubtedly safer than formulating one's own definition but since a more precise definition is needed, it seems that one should at least be attempted here. The following is therefore suggested:

Monetary assets are those assets whose holders gain or lose general purchasing power during inflation or deflation simply as a result of general price-level changes. Monetary assets include (a) currency holdings of the same monetary unit used in the financial statements being prepared and (b) except for those noted below, claims fixed in terms of the same monetary unit used in the financial statements. The term "claims" as used here includes items fixed in terms of an absolute predetermined number of monetary units by contract, court of law, legislative enactment or administrative settlement by government agency, such as bank accounts, accounts receivable, awards of monetary damages arising out of litigation and tax refunds. It excludes items which merely have a fixed price that can be altered by the same authority that fixed the price initially such as gold and other price controlled commodities. The only claims fixed in terms of the same monetary unit as that used in the financial statements that should not be accounted for as monetary are those accounted for on the basis of current market price rather than on the basis of the claim itself.

This definition appears to avoid the shortcomings of definitions used by others. Monetary assets are defined in terms of the "essential characteristic" developed above. The types of assets that have this essential characteristic are then identified. Foreign currency is excluded by the phrase "of the same monetary unit used in the financial statements." Thus, if financial statements are prepared in United States dollars, only United States dollars and claims to United States dollars are included; if financial statements are prepared in British pounds sterling, only British pounds sterling and claims to British pounds sterling are included. The phrase "fixed in terms of an absolute predetermined number of monetary units" excludes amounts receivable under contracts tied to contingencies such as sales or profits. Price controlled assets are also excluded by precise delineation of the term "claim." It includes awards of monetary damages arising out of litigation and tax refunds by specifically mentioning them but the term "claim" is defined broadly enough to include similar items such as a claim arising out of a private bill of a legislative body.

Monetary Liabilities

The discussion up to this point has been exclusively in terms of assets; liabilities have been ignored. The principles brought out, however, are also applicable to liabilities. If financial position is measured in dollars, an obligor of a liability to pay a fixed number of United States dollars gains purchasing power during inflation in the same way that a holder of a claim to receive a fixed number of dollars loses. Thus, liabilities may be thought of as negative asset holdings and the above statement can be modified to include monetary liabilities as well as monetary assets by merely adding the phrase "obligations to pay a fixed number of dollars" and modifying the clarification of the word "claims" to include "obligations" as well.

Nonmonetary Assets and Liabilities

Identifying monetary assets and liabilities is the major task in distinguishing between monetary and nonmonetary items. Nonmonetary items can simply be defined as all assets and liabilities not defined as monetary. Gains and losses from all assets and liabilities other than monetary are the joint result of their prices rising or falling faster or slower than the general price level.

SUMMARY

This paper examines the conceptual basis of general price-level accounting and concludes that gains and losses from holding money should be accounted for differently than gains and losses from holding potatoes because gains and losses from holding money are due to general price-level changes alone; those from holding potatoes are the joint result of the price of potatoes rising or falling faster or slower than the general price level. The fact that the holder of an asset or obligor of a liability gains or loses general purchasing power due to general price-level changes alone is described as the "essential characteristic" of a monetary item.

The remainder of the article is concerned with identifying the types of assets and liabilities which possess this "essential characteristic." Definitions of monetary assets found in price-level accounting literature are examined critically and found wanting. All are found to be incorrect, unclear or both. A new definition of monetary assets and liabilities is then suggested.

FOOTNOTES

(1) Walter W. Haines, Money, Prices and Policy (McGraw-Hill Book Co., Inc., 1961), p.24.

(2) George N. Halm, Economics of Money and Banking (Rev. ed.; Richard D. Irwin, Inc., 1961), p.5.

(3) Henry W. Sweeney, Stabilized Accounting (Harper & Brothers, 1936), pp. 20-23.

(4) Ralph Coughenor Jones, Effects of Price Level Changes on Business Income, Capital, and Taxes (American Accounting Association, 1956), pp. 9-42.

(5) Perry Mason, Price Level Changes and Financial Statements: Basic Concepts and Methods (American Accounting Association, 1956), pp. 9-11.

(6) Staff of the Accounting Research Division of the AICPA, "Reporting the Financial Effects of Price-Level Changes," Accounting Research Study No. 6 (AICPA, 1963), pp. 8-13 and Appendix C.

(7) Accounting Principles Board, "Financial Statements Restated for General Price-Level Changes," APB Statement No. 3 (AICPA, June 1969).

(8) Morris R. Cohen and Ernest Nagel, An Introduction to Logic and Scientific Method (Harcourt, Brace and World, Inc., 1934), p. 229.

(9) Mason, p. 9.

(10) Kenneth E. Boulding, Economic Analysis (3rd ed.: Harper & Brothers 1955), pp. 311-12.

(11) Jones, p. 9 (emphasis added).

(12) ARS No. 6, p. 138 (emphasis in the original).

(13) Ibid., p. 139.

(14) Sweeney, p. 16.

(15) APB Statement No. 3.

(16) Ibid., par. 18-23.

(17) Ibid., par. 18.

11 Monetary Gains in Current Purchasing-Power Accounting

P. T. Wanless

Introduction

The Report of the Inflation Accounting Committee (1) in the United Kingdom has had two immediate effects. First, it undermined whatever favourable reputation Current Purchasing-Power Accounting (CPP) had enjoyed since PSSAP 7 (2) was issued. Second, it has brought spirited defence of CPP accounting by its proponents. If that defence is to succeed, however, it will need to change from castigation of the Sandilands Report and the form of current cost accounting it proposes to the demonstration that CPP statements are both meaningful for users of accounting reports and easily prepared for all types of business entities.

One of the major complaints about Sandilands' current cost accounting has been that it fails to calculate and report a gain or loss on monetary items as does CPP accounting. But even with CPP accounting, that calculation is open to criticism. This study exposes the consequences of loose descriptions in PSSAP 7 of "monetary" and "non-monetary" items, and how different strategies regarding their definition can produce quite different results.

The Case-Study

CPP accounting was applied to the accounts of the Scottish Cooperative Wholesale Society Ltd. for the fifteen accounting years beginning in January 1958 and ending in January 1973. Inflation accounting of some sort has been applied to other cooperative ventures, but the only other published study of which I am aware is the application of replacement cost accounting to a student housing cooperative in the U.S. (3) However, the Scottish Society study is interesting in that it covers the operation of a large concern for an extended period. In 1973 the Scottish Society had a sales turnover of around £100m and total assets of around £175m (both figures are in historical cost terms).

The Scottish Cooperative Wholesale Society Ltd.,

A cooperative venture is a form of business organization which seeks to avoid the exploitation of one class by another. Cooperative ventures have therefore been traditionally associated with the 'socialist' movement, although in this case a senior executive stated that the aim of the Society was to maximise profits, so that they could pay interest on capital, dividends to members and reinvest to keep the organisation going. The traditional accounting model, with its going concern assumption and its emphasis on profit measurement, seems to fit the Society fairly well.

The Society is a purchasers' cooperative, and distributes profits to members in two ways. Firstly, "dividends" are paid to members in proportion to their purchases from the Society; they are in fact deferred sales discounts, or rebates on purchases, fixed at the discretion of management. Secondly, some of the traders in the Society own "shares". Shares can be redeemed for a fixed monetary value and bear interest at a fixed money amount, rather than being subject to the discretionary dividend paid on shares in a limited liability company. Nevertheless, these shares are quite distinct from fixed-interest debt; the holders of cooperative shares are the owners, not the creditors, of the business.

Activities

From 1868 until 1973, the Scottish Cooperative Wholesale Society Ltd. conducted all its operations in Scotland, while a parallel set of operations was conducted in England and Wales by the Cooperative Wholesale Society Ltd. In 1973, after the close of the period covered by this study, the two organizations merged and currently operate under the title of the Cooperative Wholesale Society Ltd. The two organizations were entirely independent during the period covered by this study.

The Scottish Cooperative Wholesale Society Ltd. (hereafter referred to as SCWS) had three main modes of activity, The Trade Department undertook a wide range of manufacturing and service activities. SCWS also had its own retail outlets, and its own Bank. The Trade Department's products were sold through the Society's own retail outlets, but were mainly sold to other, retail, cooperative societies. The Bank originally existed to channel funds to retail societies, but over the years it became a traditional banking organization and pursued a vigorous investment policy, as well as supplying overdrafts and loans to clients, especially retail societies.

Most of the SCWS turnover came from the Trade Department's activities, which for example provided £91m. of the £100m. (historical cost) turnover in the accounting year ending January 1973. (Henceforth, a reference to a year 19x indicates the accounting year ending in January 19x. Thus 1973 indicates the period from February 1972 to January 1973, inclusive).

But the bulk of the profit came from the Bank; it provided more than half the profit in 1973, and nearly two-thirds in 1972. This indicates the development of the Bank, which had contributed very little to profit in the earlier years of the period studied: less than 1% in 1959 and less than 4% in 1960.

The historical cost accounts can be used to give a conventional indication of the Society's performance in the period 1959-1973. They indicate that profits and profitability tended to rise somewhat until 1964: subsequently, SCWS seems to have shared in the falling profitability of British industry, with some recovery in 1972 and 1973, largely due to the Bank. Sales followed much the same pattern, but the decline did not set in until 1965, and recovery began in 1971. The organization consistenly retained profits to finance expansion: owners' capital - i.e. shares and accumulated retained profits - rose each year between 1959 and 1973, from £11m. to around £25m.

(Details of the way the CPP accounts were prepared are omitted).

Findings

Generally, stated profit was increased by CPP accounting: see Exhibit 1, next page. In earlier years, the most important source of increase was the positive adjustment to sales, etc., which outweighed the adjustments to stocks and depreciation. This was reinforced by a gain on net debt. SCWS was always a net debtor. As time proceeded, the gain on net debt grew in size, until by 1966 it was the major factor in the difference between HC and CPP profit and continued to be thereafter. Profits were still retained under CPP accounting. Equity capital in CPP terms rose from around £23m. in 1959 to £32m. in 1973; all CPP figures are measured at prices prevailing in January

1973. Thus CPP accounting showed equity capital to have risen by less than 40% in fifteen years, while the historical cost capital more than doubled during the same period. Obviously, the purchasing-power of the capital did not double during that time.

Exhibit 1 : Comparison of Historical Cost and Current Purchasing Power Profit.

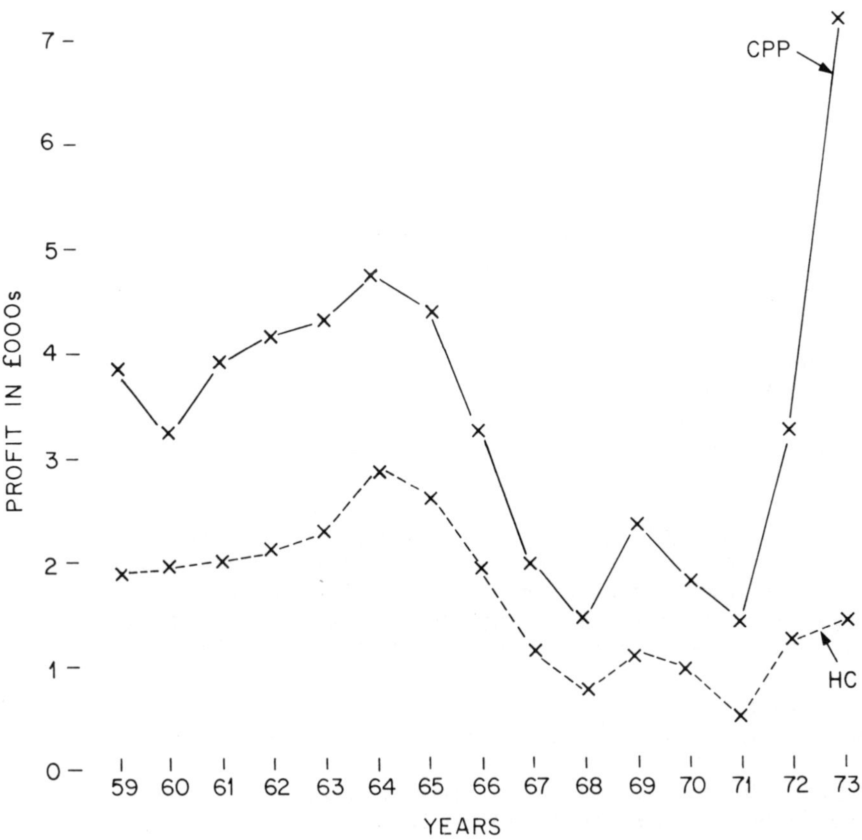

It is worthwhile to consider how one should interpret a difference between CPP and conventional figures. Problems arise because a difference may be due to real factors, to choice of accounting technique, or to a combination of both.

Difference between CPP and HC figures

It was discovered that the difference between the amounts of CPP and HC profit could be substantially influenced by the choice of accounting strategy.

The "original" CPP profit figures were compared with figures calculated under a profit-augmenting strategy - PAS - and a profit-reducing stategy - PRS - for the years 1970-73. The differences were substantial, suggesting that a wide range of profit figures may emerge, depending on the stategy used: see Exhibit 2.

EXHIBIT 2

		CCP Profit (£000)	
Year	PRS	Original	PAS
1970	-145	1,809	2,625
1971	-1,438	1,444	2,760
1972	-771	3,206	5,617
1973	1,701	7,175	11,815

The main methods of affecting the size of the CPP profit lie in the classification of assets either as monetary or as non-monetary, and in the age attributed to stocks and fixed assets. Under the profit-reducing strategy, (i) as many assets as possible were classified in the monetary class, to offset the gain on debt; (ii) attributed ages of fixed assets were increased by one year to increase CPP depreciation; and (iii) the age of stocks was increased by one month to increase the CPP cost of goods sold. In the profit-augmenting strategy, (i) as many assets as possible were classified as non-monetary items to increase the gain on debt; and (ii) the age of fixed assets was reduced by one year to reduce CPP depreciation: no further scope existed for much reduction in the assumed age of stocks.

By far and away the most important source of the discrepancy between original CPP profit and CPP profit under the alternative strategies was the change in the gain calculated in respect of holding monetary items. By classifying more assets as non-monetary items, the stated profit increased substantially; and by classifying more assets as monetary items, a net debtor position may be turned into a net creditor position, and a gain on monetary items changed into a substantial loss.

It is perhaps worth examining this flexibility in more detail. It arises because the basic distinction in the literature between monetary and non-monetary items is not clear-cut. The problem is a familiar one to monetary economists, who know from experience that the distinction between money and near-money is a blurred one. The literature on CPP accounting has not really recognised that these two categories overlap. (4) The Provisional Statement of Standard Accounting Practice, issued by the U.K. accounting bodies defines monetary items as "amounts fixed by contract or otherwise in terms of numbers of pounds, regardless of changes in the purchasing-power of the pound" (para. 15). Non-monetary items are simply "not monetary items" (para. 29).

Many balance sheet items could be placed in either category and satisfy the definition equally well as in another. Consider the class of assets which may be termed 'financial investments'. These include cash, current bank accounts, trade credit, money on short term deposit, loans made to institutions and individuals, debentures, preference shares, equity shares, gilt-edged bonds, sterling certificates of deposit, etc., etc. Only cash and bank accounts are unambiguously monetary items in the context of the definitions in PSSAP 7. All the rest have one value which is fixed, and another which is not. Bonds have a redemption value, shares have a par value, and in addition both have a market price. Shares in unquoted ventures and fixed interest shares in cooperative ventures can be valued at face, or as a proportion of the estimated equity value of the enterprise. Bills can be sold, or discounted. Such ambiguous items accounted for a high proportion of the total assets of SCWS - around 70% in 1970 and 1971, 78% in 1972, and 87% in 1973. This was due to the active investment policy of the Bank.

The figures in Exhibit 2 provide a very interesting example of the scope for manipulating the size of CPP profit. This study has a lesson for those who criticise the Sandilands Report for accounting for inflation without accounting for the gain or loss on monetary items. The lesson is that this gain is the least verifiable item in CPP accounting, and it is the item which could most easily be manipulated. To add accounting for this gain to the current cost accounting recommended by Sandilands is not to combine the best features of CCA and CPP accounting: rather the worst feature of CPP accounting is perpetuated.

The SCWS study raises a further point. It is a clear example in which a reported gain on debt would have proved illusory. Borrowed funds are normally invested in some form or other. Since investments are risky, the investment may be lost. In this case, some or all of the advantage of borrowing funds in a time of inflation will be lost too.

But CPP accounting reports a gain on debt without any offset for losses on unsuccessful projects; indeed, the gain would often be reported before the outcome of the associated debt-financed investment is known.

In 1973, the gain on debt accounted for an impressive 88% of total CPP profit of SCWS. Most of this gain on debt arose from debt incurred by the Bank to finance speculative investment in the finance markets. Total liabilities, excluding trade debts, more than quadrupled in historical cost terms between January 1971 and January 1973. Shortly after balance-sheet date 1973, it became obvious that the Bank had incurred heavy losses. These losses caused SCWS to agree to the merger with the Cooperative Wholesale Society Ltd. Loss of independence was the price of failure. With the benefit of hindsight we know that the gain on debt reported in 1973 by the CPP case-study was largely illusory.

Some writers have suggested that investors use a profit figure as an indicator of progress made by a business and of its ability to pay dividends(5). This case-study suggests that a CPP profit figure cannot always be interpreted in the same way as a conventionally calculated figure, since it may contain a substantial unrealised element. The increase in CPP profit in 1973 cannot be interpreted as a sign of increased wealth, indeed it would be positively misleading to do so, as the subsequent history of the enterprise demonstrates.

Thus the calculated size of the gain on debt may be sensitive to the classification of items as monetary and non-monetary, and the distinction between these two classes is not always clear-cut. This suggests that if any guidelines to accountants in this matter are forthcoming, they will have to be rigid regarding the definitions of monetary items. Without these rigid definitions, there would be little consistency in the gain or loss on these items reported by different firms.

FOOTNOTES

(1) "Inflation Accounting": Report of the Inflation Accounting Committee. Cmnd. 6225. London, H.M.S.O., 1975. Commonly known as the Sandilands Report.

(2) "Provisional Statement of Standard Accounting Practice No. 7" issued jointly by The Institute of Chartered Accountants in England and Wales *et al.*

(3) D.A. Corbin "Accounting and Rising Prices in a Student Cooperative" Accounting Review, Vol. 26, 1951, pp 568-572.

(4) For exceptions, see Loyd C. Heath "Distinguishing Between Monetary and Non-Monetary Assets and Liabilities in General Purchasing-Power Accounting" Accounting Review 1972 (See Rdg. 10. Ed.) and Patrick R.A. Kirkman "Accounting Under Inflationary Conditions" Allen and Unwin Ltd., London, 1974.

(5) e.g. H.C. Edey "The Nature of Profit" Accounting and Business Research, No. 1, Winter 1970, pp 50-56.

V On Current Cost Accounting Theory

12 The State of Current Value Accounting

E. O. Edwards

The demonstrated and likely volatility of prices during this decade suggests a review of current value accounting is in order - where it stands today and what its future might be. The literature indicates a substantial acceptance of current value accounting in accounting theory, but an impressive lack of implementation in accounting practice. The promotion of practical application obviously needs executive direction; why else would a quality product remain on the shelf. Nevertheless, while current value accounting seems to have found a growing number of adherents to its principles, there are yet some major differences, many rough edges, and a few blind alleys exposed in the theoretical literature. I intend first to indicate the currency of the subject, then to bring out some of the conceptual issues involved in current value accounting, next to discuss some of the valuation issues, and finally to identify some of the potential analytical uses of current value data.

THE CURRENCY OF THE MATTER

Economists are agreed that inflation is with us, that it lies ahead, and that it is international in character. To cite some figures (U.S. Department of Labor, 1974) which are undoubtedly familiar to everyone, the Consumer Price Index rose by 6.2% between 1972 and 1973 and by 10.7% between May 1973 and May 1974. The commodity element of that index, leaving services aside, rose by 7.4% and 12.0% respectively during those two periods. During the same periods, on the other hand, the average spendable weekly earnings of those employed in manufacturing having three dependents rose by only 5.4% and 5.7% respectively, suggesting some latent pressure for further price increases as wage earners seek to recoup their losses. Additional inflationary pressures can be inferred from the comparable increases in the Wholesale

Price Index of 13.8% between 1972 and 1973 and 16.4% from May 1973 to May 1974, increases which will almost certainly be soon reflected in the commodity portion of the Consumer Price Index.

What has been less widely discussed, both in the media and the professional literature, is the outlook for differential price changes, for changes in relative prices. I submit that over the next five years the principle economic and accounting challenge will come from substantial and pervasive shifts in relative prices. For example, between 1972 and 1973, while the Wholesale Price Index was rising by 13.8%, the farm products and processed foods and feeds portion of it rose by 30.0% and the industrial commodities portion by only 7.7%. a difference in rate of increase (which is a measure of dispersion) of 22.3 percentage points. The largest prior difference since 1950 occurred in 1953, and that difference was only 7.3 percentage points - against agriculture. Between May 1973 and May 1974, on the other hand, the farm portion of the Wholesale Price Index rose by only 7.7% while the industrial commodities portion rose by 20.1%.

But the dispersion within the Wholesale Price Index would of course be much larger than the figures for these major groups could suggest. Consider a few components of that index for the May 1973 to May 1974 period: refined petroleum products, up 79.5%; iron and steel, up 51.1%; coke, up 44.7%; coal, up 43.7%; all metals, up 28.1%; rubber and plastic products, up 19.9%; heating equipment, up 8.2%; drugs and pharmaceuticals, up 4.9%; but wool products, down 5.0%; eggs, down 8.1%; livestock, down 15.7%; live poultry, down 18.5%; and manufactured animal feeds, down 26.5%. Between the highest and the lowest of those I have cited, the difference in rate of price increase is 106 percentage points. Moreover, this spread is still between groups of commodities and must underestimate the dispersion among individual commodity price movements. Finally, these data apply only to the United States; the dispersion of price changes internationally would be substantially greater.

One can see the economic pressures mounting. The heating equipment manufacturer, caught in a depressed housing market and a 51.1% rise in iron and steel prices, has only been able to increase his prices by 8.2%; the drug manufacturer who may be paying 79.5% more for his refined petroleum inputs is charging only 4.9% more for his product; and the steel maker who is getting 51.1% more this year than the last must nevertheless pay 45% more for his coal and coke. There lies ahead of us a trying period of substantial economic adjustment as these shifting relative prices open up new and possibly international opportunities for some firms while they squeeze others out of international markets and possibly into bankruptcy. The question is whether or not accounting data should record these events as they occur and thereby flag the coming attractions, or only post the closing notices after the audience has gone.

CONCEPTUAL ISSUES

It is tempting in returning to a subject after a long absence, as I am doing, to take up again what seemed to be the most pressing issues in that earlier era (for those earlier views see Edwards, 1954 and 1961, and Edwards and Bell, 1961). But some - perhaps the most fundamental of those issues - while important to the understanding of current value accounting, have retreated from the arena of active controversy, and a few seem to me to be largely of, if I may use the word, historical interest to accounting theoreticians. Other matters now take precedence over them in the theoretical literature.

The first of these issues is the argument that it is sufficient (as well as necessary) to record accounting costs in historical terms. In the midst of rapidly changing prices and values, it gives most of us little comfort to know that the historical cost of every asset now held by business firms throughout the world has not changed since its acquisition. The dictum, "Move ahead but keep your feet in one place," raises serious problems of equilibrium if the head gets too far to the fore. We all know what happens to accounting operating profits during periods of rising prices; they tend to be exaggerated or overstated because the costs charged against current sales are historic and usually lower than current costs. Moreover, the difference between the current and historic cost of inputs will normally be larger the more rapidly prices are rising for two reasons - first, given the time lag between purchase and sale of inputs, prices will rise more; second, inflationary circumstances may lengthen the time lag itself as larger inventories are carried as a buffer against delayed deliveries, the risk of running out, and as a means of making gains in anticipation of higher prices.

Thus, the heating equipment manufacturer whose selling prices have risen by 8.2% while one of his important inputs, iron and steel, has risen by 51.1% may yet show an operating profit by historic cost standards. Yet if prices level off and he can no longer cover current operating losses with holding gains, his competitive inefficiency or lack of opportunity may be revealed. One can argue, of course, that the astute manager or observer will not be misled by overstated operating profits, though certainly the observer and very probably the manager cannot make firm judgements about current costs in a complex firm unless they are actually accounted for. In any event, the argument does not justify - or explain - the overstatement. Even the use of the term "overstatement" suggests a standard other than historic cost, for profits are not overstated by that standard. The standard of comparison is current value accounting.

What seems to have been widely accepted is not, however, the whole set of current value concepts, but rather that one, a central one, which suggests that accounting operating profit should be split into two parts - current operating profit, determined by deducting the current cost of related inputs from sales, and holding gains realized through use, defined as the difference between the current and historic cost of the sale-related inputs. Note that no historic cost data are lost in this disclosure; new information has been provided.

The second issue about which controversy seems to me to have diminished is whether or not adjustments for the price level alone without accounting for individual price changes can do much for either the manager or the external analyst. All this adjustment can do is restate historic costs in terms of current or some base year's purchasing power. The real holding gains (or losses) which are realized when the price of a sale-related input has risen by more (or less) than the price level are still reported as an indistinguishable element of real accounting profit. The task of sorting out current operating profit and holding gains remains and can only be done by accounting for current values - how the prices of sale-related inputs have changes since acquisition - and then asking how much of these gains is real. Moreover, the operating profits of different firms or even of the same firm in different periods cannot be meaningfully compared to reveal genuine differences and trends unless this division, which only current value accounting makes possible, is first attended to. This principle, too, has won its share of adherents.

But these adjustments relate only to the income statement and indeed only to its operating profit section as customarily displayed. The position statement remains in historic cost terms, and improvements in position which result from price changes on unused assets and liabilities are not recorded either in the position or income statement. The issue of reporting current values in the position statement and related realizable gains or cost savings in the income statement seems still to be an issue commanding discussion (Davidson, 1966; Bell, 1971; Enthoven, 1973, Chapter 13).

Current value accounting rests on the principle that relevant, objective current events of the period should be reported on both statements. Current events are not only those related to the acquisition and disposition of assets and liabilities; they also relate to assets and liabilities carried through the period. In other words, the position of a firm is incompletely described if the only changes recorded are those marked by an exchange of assets and/or liabilities - the realization principle - while changes in value not marked by an exchange go unnoted. Of course it is a current event when a gain is realized through the disposition of an asset in the current period; but so too was the accrual of that gain a current event of the periods during which accrual took place. The event of the current period in this example is not the gain, but its realization; the portion of the gain which accrued in prior periods is a current event of those periods.

We are touching, of course, on the definition of income. But must we settle on one? There is no reason in my view why an income statement should not reveal both the accrual of income and its realization. Indeed, both are events of the current period and should be reported. It is only that the events are different and must be distinguished. The important issue in this instance is disclosure; labeling is a secondary matter.

The fourth conceptual issue to which I would draw attention concerns the role of subjective values in the accounting process. In some respects, this is also a valuation option. Since, however, I see a role for both subjective and objective values, their conceptual relationship strikes me as more important than the possible competition between them as a basis for accounting measurement. Subjective values depend entirely on future, or ex ante, events - expected quasi-rents, interest rates, asset and liability values, and time horizons - and are therefore basic to decision making. The essence of decision making is the choice among alternative progressions of future events contained within the decision-maker's set of expectations. That choice being made, never for all time, the chain of expected events associated with it represents the standard which will be tested as actual events unfold. That comparison of actual against expected events is essential to the evaluation of business decisions and of the effectiveness of the decision-making process itself.

Subjective values, depending as they do upon expectations about future events, cannot themselves be objectively measured. But those expectations from which they derive can be stated in objectively measurable and dated dimensions so that their accuracy can be tested against actual events as they transpire. It is the task of effective management to see that expected events are recorded in dated, objective dimensions; it is the task of accounting to record actual objective events as they occur. It follows that present values have no role to play in the measurement of actual events, except as they affect decisions and hence demand and supply in the marketplace and the prices established there.

The last conceptual issue I would mention is taxation - which elements of income should be subjected to income tax? First, it is important to draw a distinction between tax payment and contingent tax liability, along much the same lines as the distinction noted earlier between the accrual and realization of income. If a firm reports the accrual income, it should also report the contingent tax liability on that income; otherwise its position statement will exaggerate the welfare of the firm. Second, if capital gains are to be taxed at different rates from other income - and I am not convinced that such a distinction is justified - those holding gains realized through use and product sale should be treated in precisely the same way as those realized through direct sale. Finally, taxes on income should be levied against real, not money, income, if equity considerations prevail over the anticyclical effects of taxing money income, as it seems to me they should. The problem here is one of relative equity; it is hard to justify taxing business firms on real income, if other entities, such as families and individuals, continue to be taxed on money income.

ISSUES OF VALUATION

Let me turn now to valuation issues on which even more discussion seems to be focused today than on the conceptual issues mentioned above. To a degree, these, too, are conceptual in nature - I do not intend to discuss precise methods of measurement - but at a different level.

Here we do not ask whether current values should be reported but rather which variation of current value should be employed? The issue, however, is not whether one is right and another wrong because the options commonly discussed all have roles to play either in the making of decisions or in their evaluation. Perhaps one day we will be able to account for several concepts simultaneously, but the question today is, If one concept of current value is to be most widely used, which should it be? The options are present or subjective value (already discussed), opportunity cost, and variations of replacement cost.

Opportunity cost can be either subjective or objective in nature. The opportunity cost of an asset is the value it would have in its best alternative use. But that alternative use could be a different pattern of employment of the asset within the firm. The value of the asset in that alternative pattern of use can be determined only be resorting to the present value of the quasirents, expected to be earned in that use, a value which is just as subjective in nature as the present value of the asset in the pattern to which it is committed. If a present value is to be used at all for accounting purposes in these circumstances, it surely should be the highest.

If the alternative considered is to dispose of the asset on the open market, opportunity cost can for the most part be objectively measured as a potential current event. It is, therefore, in an accounting sense, a legitimate method of current cost valuation; it is, if I read them correctly, the method favored by both Chambers (1966) and Sterling(197); it is an exit value, as opposed to an entry value, approach. The issue then is one of entry or exit values in determining current values. Phil Bell and I discussed this matter at some length in our book (1961) and concluded there that entry values were preferable as a normal method of valuation. We did so only after much soul searching and the detailed construction of the concept of realizable profit based on opportunity cost. Our arguments then against the strict application of exit values were essentially as follows:

1. Their use leads to anomalous revaluations on acquisition because of transport costs, installation and removal charges, and imperfect access to markets; immediately upon the purchase, delivery and installation of a new machine or truck its net realizable value is normally substantially less than acquisition cost.

2. Their use implies a short run approach to business operations, posing, as they do, disposition and liquidation values for the position statement; a positive realizable profit

only indicates that it is worth staying in business in the short run, not that it is worth replacing assets and inputs and staying in business over the longer term or as long as current price relationships continue.

3. Their use leads to the anticipation of operating profit before sale by valuing finished goods, and possibly nearly finished goods, in excess of the current costs incurred in their production.

I now think that this argument can be sharpened by drawing a clear distinction between exit prices derived from markets in which the firm is usually a buyer and those derived from markets in which the firm is usually a seller. A firm that values its assets at exit prices derived from markets in which the firm is normally a buyer reports unusual values - those which would obtain in a liquidation situation, at least so far as the assets being so valued are concerned. To employ such values when liquidation is not contemplated is surely misleading. Yet Argument (1) - incurring immediate losses upon acquisition - clearly assumes valuation by exit values in buyer markets for firms having no liquidation intentions. Indeed, Argument (2) is also premised on the assumption that most of the firm's assets would be valued as though they might be disposed of in unusual markets for the firm, though some, particularly finished products, might be valued as though sold through normal channels. Argument (3), on the other hand, clearly assumes exit prices in seller markets and therefore must be considered on different grounds.

I am not convinced of the merit of adopting, as a normal basis for asset valuation in the going concern, exit prices in buyer markets. These are unusual values suitable for unusual situations.[1] I would not object in principle to keeping track of such exit prices at all times and, as Solomons (1966) has suggested, substituting them for entry values when they are the lesser of the two and the firm has taken a definite decision not to replace the asset or even the functions it performs.[2] Indeed, such substitution is necessary if the recent write-downs of computer-leasing and calculator firms are to be justified in advance of actual disposal and if the real position of firms caught holding outmoded style goods is to be reflected in their accounts.

The point at issue, of course, is not whether to value by current entry or exit prices, but when to shift from entry to exit values. The extremes are (1) immediately upon acquisition of any asset or liability and (2) when accounts receivable are converted to cash, or when all services have been converted to cash, or when all services have been performed, whichever is later (Davidson, 1966). The realization principle normally rests on the sale event to signal the displacement of entry values by exit values. The valuation of all finished goods at exit values, a principle against which Argument (3) is directed, identifies an earlier stage - one which is close to sale for the manufacturing concern but at the point of acquisition of stocks in trade for the trading firm.

If the principle was adopted that all assets and liabilities of the going concern should be valued at current entry prices except for those that the firm normally sells, Arguments (1) and (2) above would be disposed of. Such a "usual market" criterion comes close to a rule of "replacement cost or net relizable value, whichever is higher," but it is not - as the example of a firm which is temporarily selling at a loss discloses.

We are left with Argument (3) about which I feel much less strongly, though pragmatic considerations may yet leave it some persuasiveness. There is no strong argument in principle against valuing assets which the firm normally sells at some version of selling prices. The question is only whether we seek to account for cost savings or unrealized gains. The problem is encountered in estimating selling prices. If these are determined by appraisal, given the location and accessibility of the goods in question, we assume again unusual disposal. If, on the other hand, prices are estimated by deducting still-to-be-incurred selling and delivery costs from expected selling prices (discounting both appropriately), we encounter subjective elements. These, I emphasize again, rightly belong in the list of expected events to be tested, and should not serve as the basis for valuing actual events, a position in accord with the American Accounting Association's Committee on Concepts and Standards - Inventory Measurement (1964, p. 708).

The issue of which entry values to use also merits discussion, particularly for long-lived assets. For most short-lived assets, replacement cost can be determined, and that therefore reflects the current entry value of the economy's resources being employed in the firm, which is, I think, what we want to approximate as closely as possible. For many longer-lived assets the cost of identical replacement can also be ascertained in regular markets. The problem arises when identical assets are no longer produced - and technological changes ensure that this will often be the case. I confess to being less than happy with the discussion Phil Bell and I offered on this matter (1961, Chapter 3) and also with those I have read since. The options, when the cost of identical replacement is not market determined, appear to be opportunity cost (an exit value), the cost of optimal replacement, or the cost of obvious replacement.

The argument for opportunity cost is that the asset is not going to be identically replaced, and that therefore it should be written down to its net realizable value and further depreciation should be determined on that basis. But if this is done, it is quite possible, as noted earlier, that subsequent reported operating profits of the firm will suggest that its outmoded assets are just as efficient as the new assets which will probably replace it. Moreover, the firm does intend to replace the functions or services of the asset in question.

Optimal replacement cost, on the other hand, can be determined only by making a comprehensive, hypothetical investment decision which will not in fact be made until some time in the future. (After all, if our firm decides to replace immediately, our problem evaporates). Such a decision when it is made, may also involve the rearrangement of many related functions within the firm and the purchase and replacement of complementary equipment and facilities. The use of optimal replacement cost would not reflect all the value of the nation's economic resources now employed by the firm, but rather the value of a very different and hypothetical set. I don't believe its proponents are many.

The cost of obvious replacement probably comes close to what Parker and Harcourt (1969, p. 19) have called "the cost of currently acquiring the services provided by the asset," or what the American Accounting Association's Committee on Concepts and Standards - Long-Lived Assets (1964, p. 695) called "the purchase price of assets which provide equivalent service capacity." By obvious replacement I mean the clear means currently available for providing the identical physical services, regardless of the operating costs which the hypothetical asset might entail. A refrigerator may be replaced by another of the same cooling capacity and temperature range. Very probably this would not represent optimal replacement. There may also be problems of adjusting for size, temperature control, and asset life. Assuming these can be solved or do not exist, the cost of obvious replacement still has theoretical deficiencies.

A new machine, identical in physical performance, may make an old one obsolete in any of three ways: (1) by raising capital costs and lowering operating costs, (2) by lowering both capital and operating costs, or (3) by lowering capital costs and raising operating costs. By valuing the old machine according to the new one, current cost depreciation will be raised in the first case and reduced in the others. Assuming that operating charges will continue to be charged as actually incurred with the old machine, the operating profits now reported for the old machine as compared with a firm actually using the new one will be lower in the first two cases but higher in the third. In that case the firm employing the old machine has adopted the lower depreciation charges associated with the new machine but retained its own, lower, operating costs. The old machine will appear to be more efficient than the new one. This drawback may not be too serious in a practical sense if my guess is right that few new machines are in fact Type 3, but that is a matter for empirical research, not casual observation. In any event, the drawback is a serious conceptual deficiency.

I have not touched on matters of appraisal, price indices, and averaging formulas as means of approximating cost concepts in practice. Frankly, I regard them as marginal, if necessary, matters which will be satisfactorily resolved once the more important conceptual issues have been settled.

THE ANALYTICAL USES OF CURRENT VALUE ACCOUNTING

If the reluctance to employ current value accounting is rooted in the uncertainty which remains about the issue so far discussed, there is reason for optimism because the degree of uncertainty seems to be diminishing with research and the passage of time. It is also possible, however, that the analytical value of current value accounting data is not considered to be high enough to warrant the cost of producing it. Furthermore, several of the advantages of current value data can be realized only if current value accounting is widely practiced; inter-firm comparisons are an obvious example. In any event, a brief review of the analytical potential of current value data seems in order. I suggest its discussion under three heads: the internal evaluation of business decisions, prediction, and the external evaluation of business performance.

I have already noted the essential role of current value data in providing information on actual current events as a means of identifying and analyzing variances from expected events. The accumulation of current value data is not in itself sufficient for this purpose; a statement of expected events is also required. Such statements can be found in budgets and standard costs, but the events identified in them may not always be dated or stated in dimensions which promote subsequent comparison with actual events. Furthermore, they normally relate to events which compose current operating profit, not holding gains. Statements of expected holding gains and losses are also of importance if business decisions are to be fully evaluated because decisions about operating profit and holding gains are related, not independent in nature. I was delighted, therefore to see the article by Petri and Minch (1974) which provides a framework for the evaluation of decisions on holding gains.

The relationship between operating profit and holding gains is most clearly revealed in the case of inventories. In the absence of price changes, inventory levels are usually determined by purchase lags, delivery patterns, and the acceptable risk of running out. If prices of items in inventory are expected to rise, stockpiling is a natural business response both to make holding gains and to protect against anticipated delivery problems. If prices do not rise, current operating profit will nevertheless be reduced because of the cost of carrying excessive inventories; if they fall, current operating profit may rise, but the increase should be more than offset by holding losses. Without full statements of expected events, the precise causes of changing profit patterns cannot be pin-pointed, nor the sources of error identified and the process of decision making improved. Financial decisions require similar analysis and evaluation.

Improving prediction depends upon the definition of better functional relationships between expectations about future events, "what will be," and past experience, "what has been," in which expectations are rooted. Such functions are the essence of econometric models. But if "what has been" is defined in strictly historic cost terms and reported operating profit represents an amalgam of current and differently dated historic costs, trends over time and comparisons among firms are distorted and the establishment of probable functional relationships is made exceedingly difficult.

Those who attempt to evaluate business performance from outside the firm normally do so largely to improve either private or public decisions. Those whose interests are largely private include present and prospective stockholders, creditors, customers, suppliers, and competitors, and the consultants and security analysts on whom they depend for information and advice. The makers of public policy and those who provide the analytical base for policy decisions are normally employed by governmental or multinational agencies. Private decision makers outside the firm, like the firm itself, can usually be assumed to be striving to maximize their own incomes; policy makers, on the other hand, are charged with representing wider public interests and promoting the general welfare. These two groups evaluate business performance with different purposes in mind. While their evaluations will have much in common, they also differ in important respects.

Those in the private group share an interest in comparative evaluations. The position and performance of a single firm as judged by an absolute standard are normally of considerably less importance to them than its position and performance relative to other firms whether in the same industry, in the same nation, or internationally. It is through comparative evaluations that external investors formulate their expectations about future events, choose their portfolios, and decide on new businesses or lines of activity - and by so doing, collectively influence security prices, interest rates, and the allocation of capital among firms, industries and nations.

These external evaluations of business firms differ from the internal evaluation process discussed earlier in two important respects. In the first place, they do not involve direct comparisons of management expectations with objective accomplishments. Outsiders do not normally have access to management expectations. They seek to judge, therefore, not internal managerial efficiency, but rather managerial efficiency, by comparing performance among firms and over time.

In the second place, outsiders do not have access to managerial accounting data but must rely for their assessments on published financial reports and supplementary data as sources of current events. Making information available to external investors based on current rather than historic cost data is important as a means of improving external private decisions and hence the allocation of a nation's resources among its firms and industries.

Those who make public policy decisions, on the other hand, cannot normally assess business performance exclusively on the basis of reported business profits. In the first place, these may arise only from the efficient production of quality products (which is normally in the public interest) but also from malpractices, monopolistic advantages, and situations of unusual scarcity. When such conditions come to light through the evaluation of business performance, various forms of regulation, antitrust actions, and excess-profit taxes may be employed to protect the public interest.

In the second place, business profits will not normally reflect those benefits which accrue to society from business operations in the form of unmarketable side effects of principal business activities, such as skills former employees take with them. Similarly, business profits will not naturally reflect certain social costs which society may have to bear as a result of business activity because they do not enter the account of the business firm; environmental effects are a widely discussed example. When the divergence between social and private costs becomes large, public policy will usually seek to establish systems of incentives and disincentives which will lead business firms to introduce into their private accounts those social costs and benefits which would otherwise accrue to society but not to the business community. Such incentive systems should induce business firms to modify their behavior in socially desirable directions.

Each firm or industry which is socially efficient should be able to cover the full current cost of its operation even though some of those costs may not usually reach the private accounts through existing mechanisms of the market, falling instead on others. To attempt such assessments requires the valuation of excluded social costs once they have been identified and allocated. There are two basic approaches to this problem - to measure social costs by the damages imposed on society by them or to measure such costs by the current value of the resources which would be required to prevent them from occurring. The point is that such social assessments, complex as they are, can be made more effectively if the operating profits, with which the analysis begins, are reported by business firms in current value terms.

I have not mentioned the advantages of current value data based on entry costs for aggregation into national accounts or for decomposition into input-output co-efficients. Even leaving aside aggregate considerations, the many advantages of current value accounting seem to me impressive.

The end is in sight. There is only the matter of implementation to consider. Why has the "quality product" remained on the shelf? I have no illuminating answers, but one suggestion. Is an industry-wide experiment with current value accounting a feasible first step? Is there a trade association or an industry which might lend its cooperation? Would it be appropriate for the American Accounting Association to take the lead in initiating such an experiment?

FOOTNOTES

(1) It should be noted that exit prices in buyer markets are important to decision making at the micro level, but being unusual, such values cannot be aggregated into anything meaningful for a nation as a whole, either as a component of national wealth or as a basis for valuing gross national product. Such values do not represent the normal flow of resources into product, but rather the unusual disposition of resources, a concept which is both undefined and unenlightening in aggregate form.

(2) Note, however, that Solomons would employ present value if that is less than replacement cost but greater than net realizable value, a recommendation I would oppose for reasons given earlier. Parker and Harcourt (1969, p.18), on the other hand, adopt the Solomons' view.

REFERENCES

American Accounting Association, Committee on Concepts and Standards - Inventory Measurement, "A Discussion of Various Approaches to Inventory Measurement," THE ACCOUNTING REVIEW (July 1964).

___, Committee on Concepts and Standards - Long-Lived Assets, "Accounting for Land, Building, and Equipment," THE ACCOUNTING REVIEW (July 1964).

Bell, P.W., "On Current Replacement Costs and Business Income," in R.R. Sterling, ed., Asset Valuation (Scholars Book Co., 1971).

Chambers, R.J., Accounting, Evaluation and Economic Behavior (Prentice-Hall, 1966).

Davidson, S., "The Realization Concept," in M. Backer, ed., Modern Accounting Theory (Prentice-Hall, 1966).

Edwards, E.O., "Depreciation Policy under Changing Price Levels," THE ACCOUNTING REVIEW (April 1954).

___, "Depreciation and the Maintenance of Real Capital," in J.L. Meij, ed., Depreciation and Replacement Policy (North-Holland, 1961).

___, and Bell, P.W., The Theory and Measurement of Business Income (University of California Press, 1961).

Enthoven, A.J.H., Accountancy and Economic Development Policy (North-Holland, 1973).

Parker, R.H. and Harcourt, G.C., eds., Readings in the Concept and Measurement of Income (Cambridge University Press, 1969).

Petri, E. and Minch, R., "Evaluation of Resource Acquisition Decisions by the Partitioning of Holding Activity," THE ACCOUNTING REVIEW (July 1974).

Solomons, D., "Economic and Accounting Concepts of Cost and Value," in M. Backer, ed., Modern Accounting Theory (Prentice-Hall, 1966).

Sterling, R.R., Theory of the Measurement of Enterprise Income (University Press of Kansas, 1970).

United States Department of Labor, Monthly Labor Review (July 1974).

13 On the Case for Dichotomising Income

David Drake and Nicholas Dopuch

The recent accounting literature reflects an increasing acceptance of the view that income should be separated into two components, holding and operating income. Statements to this effect can be found in the AICPA monograph on accounting principles written by Sprouse and Moonitz[1] and in the reports of the American Accounting Association's Committees on Concepts and Standards.[2] Although the notion of separating the effects of price fluctuations from ordinary transaction income has been discussed earlier,[3] the contemporary source of the idea is the recent book by Edwards and Bell (referred to subsequently as E & B).[4]

In this paper we examine the most modest of E & B's proposals for modifying income - the step they describe as the first "...making income data more useful and realistic." They amplify in the following way:

> The current cost of inputs used in producing output is subtracted from current revenue to yield current operating profit. The difference between this figure and traditional accounting profit comprises realized cost savings, the excess of the current cost of inputs used in production which is sold over and above the original purchase cost of these inputs, and realized capital gains, the excess of proceeds over and above historical costs on the irregular sale or disposal of assets. In other words we simply divide the total profit figure differently, so as to distinguish clearly between the operating and holding components of realized profit.[5]

The modesty of the proposal stems from the fact that the sales realization test is retained as the basis for income recognition even though replacement costs are introduced into the system. The use of replacement cost in this or any other manner should be (and is being)[6] considered as a separate issue.

The E & B proposal, however, implies a second departure from present accounting practice - the use of both historical and replacement costs as a means of dichotomizing income into holding and operating components. This dichotomy is the only aspect of their proposal we consider here although we recognize that each aspect of the proposal may have overlapping effects. For example, one benefit of the use of replacement costs is the timeliness of reporting gains and losses.[7] At one point, E & B link this benefit to their proposal to separate income:

> ...gains (stemming from a wise purchase of inventoriable assets) earned over the entire time span during which the assets were held by the firm are attributed to the period in which the gains are realized...failure to report capital gains and losses (stemming from unwise purchase) as they occur...(leads to) badly distorted balance sheet values....[8]

In our opinion, this advantage of more timely reporting can be obtained from an acceptance of a replacement cost basis of valuation. It does not depend on the dichotomization of income. Thus, the point is secondary to our analysis.

Our general criterion for evaluating the benefits to be derived from these alternative concepts of income is based upon the following: since an income concept is simply an analytical construct for organizing and summarizing information about the economic activities of an enterprise, alternative constructs can be evaluated only in terms of their eventual use. E & B suggest that:

> It is in the evaluation of business decisions.... that the demand for accounting data exists....The improvement of managerial ability and related decision-making processes must lean heavily upon an evaluation of past decisions.[9]

This view of the function of income determination is shared by others,[10] and it suggests to us that the usefulness of an income construct should be determined by its ability to summarize information in a form useful to the ex post evaluation of business decisions.

The principal purpose of our enquiry is to discover precisely how the dichotomization of income aids in the evaluation of past decisions. Our search for those features of the proposal which will improve decision-evaluation was extended beyond the statements by E & B. In considering the views of other advocates of the dichotomy we find three principal justifications:

(1) The two categories of income may be used to evaluate different kinds of decisions.
(2) Operating income is a better measure of the enterprise's "long run" income and it is, consequently, a better forecaster of a firm's future income stream.
(3) The dichotomy will permit better inter-period and inter-firm comparisons of operating performance.[11]

Each of these supposed advantages assumes that the dichotomy improves the ability to predict future results from an evaluation of management's past decisions. Thus, our objective in their analysis is to determine whether a practical application of this proposal is likely to yield these benefits. Our descussion cannot be taken as representing either a clearcut defense or rejection of the proposal to dichotomize income. Any one of the three advantages may be sufficient to justify this departure from historical costs. However, if and when the departure is made, we should be prepared to understand the uses which may be made of the separation of net income into holding and operating components.

1. EVALUATING DIFFERENT KINDS OF DECISIONS

Usually, E & B qualify their statements regarding the significance of their income dichotomy. However, some of their claims suggest that the dichotomy will be useful in evaluating two different types of decisions. For example, they explain that:

> These two kinds of gains (holding and operating) are often the result of quite different sets of decisions ....The difference between forces motivating the business firm to make profit by one means rather than by another and the difference between the events on which the two methods of making profit require that the two kinds of gains be carefully separated if the two types of decisions involved are to be meaningfully evaluated.[12]

Several of the subsequent proponents of the dichotomy have adopted this aspect of the evaluation function as a partial justification for the proposal. The AAA Inventory

Measurement Committee has argued:

> Inventory management decisions should be accounted for more clearly so that the user of the financial statements may readily focus on management's success or failure in dealing with problems of inventory price changes...current income statements fail to isolate trading gains and price gains - gains that usually arise from different types of decision.[13]

In a similar fashion the AAA Committee on the Matching Concept states

> Typically, revenue may be related to at least two efforts of management. On of these is the effort to operate effectively in carrying out the production and/or service functions of the business. The other is the effort to occupy an advantageous position in the market....This (dichotomization of income) would help interested parties to evaluate the effectiveness of management insofar as its buying efforts were concerned; but more importantly, it would remove from the data pertaining directly to operations those amounts realized simply as a result of market fluctuations.[14]

These statements certainly imply that the two categories of income pertain to two different kinds of decisions. We assume that the two kinds of decisions parallel the classical distintion drawn between (1) investment decisions[15] (what resources should the firm acquire and when) and (2) the short-run efficiency decision problem (given a set of resources, how best to utilize). Therefore, a dichotomization of income would be of benefit in the following manner: if the firm actively speculates in prices of assets, holding gains and operating gains should be separated in order that we may determine how efficient the firm is in both this area and in its operations. If a firm does not actively speculate, then the distinction is still necessary. In this case, however, we would wish to determine unambigously the efficiency of the firm's operating decisions. We now consider the feasibility of this distinction with regard to both inventories and fixed assets.

A. Inventory Investment Decisions

Suppose a firm believes that the prices of its inventoried items will remain constant over the next several operating periods. Suppose, also that this firm can predict with certainty the demand for and the costs of carrying inventory, the costs of stockouts, etc. Conceivably, the firm could optimally solve its inventory problem by balancing its storage costs (interest charges included) against the costs of reordering and stockouts.[16] This would allow the firm to determine the amount it should purchase as well as the times at which it should purchase based strictly upon its transaction needs.[17] The firms is speculating to the extent it is investing in anticipation of output prices and input needs. However, its inventory policy cannot be considered to be geared to speculation in inventory prices per se. Now suppose this same firm believed that prices of inventory items were going to rise during the next several operating periods. Presumably, this firm might be motivated to hold more inventory than would be called for in the first solution to its inventory problem. We cannot specify in advance how much or even whether the firm would increase inventory since this depends upon the willingness to trade an optimal lot size for the chance to speculate in inventory prices. The costs of speculating would include additional storage costs and perhaps additional purchasing costs. These additional costs would have to be absorbed by the expected gains from price increases of inventory items.

How would the calculation of holding gains (losses) aid in assessing the firm's decision to speculate in inventory prices? The calculation, as described by E & B, would be based upon the total purchases of inventory and would consist of the difference between the costs of all the items acquired and all the prices at the time the items were used (sold.) For inventory at period end, the gain or loss (unrealized) would be based upon the difference between the costs of the items and the prices current at the end of the period. Therefore, the calculation of holding gains (losses) does not isolate an amount which relates to the price speculation since the measurement does not exclude the amount of inventory the firm would have held regardless of its expectations concering future price increases. More important, this simple method for calculating holding gains (losses) ignores the extra cost incurred in the firm's decision to speculate. These extra costs would be buried in the operating income section. In effect, the firm had to trade operating income for holding income in order to speculate in future price increases. This indicates that the operating and the investment decisions concerning inventory are not completely independent.

Similarly, suppose that the firm anticipated price decreases in the next several operating periods. Here, the firm would consider reducing purchases in order to buy at lower future prices. This decision will also have an effect upon operating income given that the firm had an optimal lot size. The firm could decrease its purchases only at the expense of higher stock-out costs plus higher reordering costs. These added costs are not included in the calculation of holding gains (losses) from price decreases; rather they will appear in the operating section of the income statement (e.g., extra costs in processing back-orders or lower sales). Notice, also, that as prices fall, the calculation of holding losses would be based upon the total inventory the firm acquired. Again, if a firm attempts to speculate in price decreases, the calculation of holding losses does not indicate whether or to what extent the firm acted in a manner consistent with its expectations. Obviously, then, the calculation does not permit an appraisal of the specific decision to speculate.

In short, the recommended method for calculating holding gains (losses) cannot be used to evaluate the decision to speculate in inventory unless we assume that firms purchase all of their inventory items immediately before the units are used (sold). Alternatively, we must adjust the calculation by charging the increased operating costs to the decision to speculate.

Of course, the accountant could modify the calculation to relate it more precisely with the inventory decisions. For example, the accountant could structure the measurement around management's expectations for price movements. If the firm decides to actively speculate in price movements, the accountant could determine the resulting net gain or loss. This modification is certainly feasible for internal reporting purposes[18] since top management can obtain the information necessary to evaluate the inventory decision of its lower-level personnel. Thus, the E & B proposal still has merit for the purposes of internal management. However, if we are to adapt the calculation for external evaluation purposes, another alternative must be selected. That is, it is unlikely that management would report its expectations to external parties.[19]

Conceivably, some insight into management's expectations may be obtained by observing the prior pattern of holding gains and losses reported by a particular firm. We might also observe the reports of holding gains (losses) of different firms and thereby obtain some knowledge about the inventory policies of these different firms. A pattern for an indivdual firm would emerge, however, only if we could assume that the firm's demands for inventory are relatively stable; that its policies regarding the desire to speculate are consistent; and above all, that the firm is reasonably successful in its attempts to speculate. For example, if prices were normally distributed we would expect a successful firm to report more gains than losses. Similarly, we could use these calculations for inter-firm comparisons, only if we could assume that firms have similar operating needs and, therefore, similar inventory requirements. We would then assume that differences in reported holding gains (losses) would reflect only the difference in attitudes toward expected price changes.

We are not sure how valid either inter-period or inter-firm comparisons might be for decision-evaluation and feel that the proponents of the dichotomy of income should demonstrate the usefulness of these comparisons. Moreover, we believe that a comparison of operating incomes and losses, for the two classes are not independent.

B. Capital Investment Decisions

The primary reason for acquiring capital resources is to provide facilities for manufacturing and/or selling products. This reason is analogous to the transaction motive for inventory purchases except that the transaction involves several operating periods. Therefore, by its nature, a capital investment decision entails a considerable degree of speculation. The decision involves a consideration of the capacity needed in future periods, the best mix between capital and other input factors given an expected capacity, the prices of the different input factors, and so on. Depending upon its expectations, a firm's estimates of any one of the many factors influencing an investment decision might be considered a form of speculation. These factors are also interdependent for there is a number of different ways in which a firm can trade one factor against another. For example, a firm may provide for additional capacity by either investing in flexible facilities or by providing for multiple shifts in its operations. A firm may invest in special-purpose assets or in assets which are capable of producing alternative types of outputs. Because of these complications we will not analyze holding gains and losses from the perspective of different methods of speculation. Instead, we will examine the effects on holding income of changes in prices of variable inputs.

One of the most important causes of the recent increase in the price of capital assets has been the more rapid increase in the price of labor, an alternative input.[20] For example, consider U.S. Steel's decision in 1952 to build capital-intensive Fairless Steel Works. This investment decision could not be justified in terms of the current prices at the date of its construction, but:

> Only because labor rates were expected to rise 30 per cent or more in the coming decade was it economic to use such large amounts of capital per worker at the time the plant was built.[21]

Apparently U.S. Steel determined that the incremental capital investment - the amount of investment in excess of that which could currently be justified - would produce future labor savings whose discounted present value was greater than the incremental cost of the capital investment.

This decision was based upon an accurate forecast of relative input prices. Between 1950 and 1960 U.S. Steel's average wage rate increased 100 per cent as measured in nominal dollars and 57 per cent in real dollars.[22] The labor cost per ton of output would have increased 66 per cent in nominal terms and 30 per cent in real terms had U.S. Steel continued its pre-1952 labor-capital input ratio. The magnitude of the real savings on labor costs for U.S. Steel's 1960 output was in the vicinity of 650 million dollars.

How would the total effects of this decision have been reflected in the holding-operating income dichotomy? First, a holding gain would have been reported if U.S. Steel had employed the E & B income system. The prices of capital assets did rise, and we may assume that one of the reasons was because of the increase in labor prices. The discounted value and, hence, the market value of capital goods rose to reflect the savings in payments to labor made possible by the substitution of capital for labor. At least part of the success of U.S. Steel's investment decision would have been reported through the holding income category.

However, some of the important effects of the decision also would have been reflected in the operating income. U.S. Steel initially incurred higher fixed costs relative to output in anticipation of lower variable costs in the future. Thus, the company traded operating income in the period of acquisition and in the early periods of the life of the asset for higher operating income and some holding income in later periods.

We further doubt that the holding income reported by U.S. Steel would be useful in inter-firm comparisons. Consider a hypothetical steel company which invested exactly the same amount in capital facilities as U.S. Steel but for a different reason. This company did not attempt to change the capital-labor mix. Rather, it built a plant with larger (almost twice as large) operating capacity. Between 1952 and 1960, this firm would have reported holding gains of the same magnitude as U.S. Steel, assuming that the method used for calculating the holding gain involved the use of specific price indices as opposed to an appraisal of its facilities.[23] The operating efficiency of this firm in 1960, however, would be vastly inferior to that of U.S. Steel since it would have a much greater proportion of labor per ton of output. Thus, the evaluation of the two investment decisions could not be made without examining both the holding and operating components of income for each firm.

In fact, a firm could invest in capital goods prior to a period of rising prices, report holding gains in that period, and yet have made an incorrect investment decision. In our illustration above, if the anticipated increase in demand for steel products had not occurred, the excess capacity costs - i.e., fixed costs - would have been higher for the amount of output produced. This would have reduced operating income. We can conceive of a situation in which a reduction in operating income, caused by an error in forecasting, could be greater than the reported holding gains.[24] Assuming the excess capacity persists, an incorrect investment decision would result in lower operating income, but at the same time, holding gains would be reported.

It is important to understand the limit of our criticism of the usefulness of the income dichotomy. We have simply attempted to demonstrate that the holding income category is not sufficient to evaluate a specific kind of decision - the decision to hold assets. In general, all investment decisions involve a series of trade-offs. in the case above, we consider the possibility of a trade-off between the prices of labor and capital. It is possible to consider in detail other trade-offs - e.g., flexible versus inflexible facilities; higher output capacity versus lower. The effect would be the same. Holding gains (losses) only reflect the effects of changes in the prices of capital assets over time. The other effects of decisions to invest in a specific mix of input factors must be reported within the operating income statement. Very often it is not even possible to determine the total effects of the decision by merely adding the two components of income since the different trade-off effects could occur in different periods.

C. Operating Income and Decision Evaluation

Our analysis of holding income has led us to conclude that the timing of asset acquisition is not an independent determinant in an investment decision. The particular types of assets to acquire, the appropriate mix of assets, the total quantity of assets, as well as the timing of the acquisition are all vital determinants of a particular investment policy. We cannot assume, therefore, that the current operating income figure is merely a summary of current operating decisions. Rather, the measurement of operating income incorporates the effects of the same kinds of trade-offs we discussed above. Neither the operating income figure nor the holding income figure can be used separately to evaluate two different kinds of decisions.

11. OPERATING INCOME AS A FORECASTER

Our conclusion on the interdependency of investment and operating decisions has implications for a second purported advantage of the income dichotomy. E & B argue that:

> Current operating profit can be used for predictive purposes if the existing production process and the existing conditions under which that process is carried out are expected to continue into the future; current operating profit then indicates the amount that the firm can expect in each period over the long run.[25]

Note that they have carefully qualified their claim concerning the predictive ability of operating income. There must be either a stable production process or, at least, a stable ranking among alternative production techniques.[26]

However, only minor qualifications are made by the Long-Lived Asset Committee concerning the analytical significance of operating income:

> Income from ordinary operations is important to investors in making investment decisions. This amount, when compared with cash dividends, is relevant to an appraisal of the intent of management to contract or expand operating capacity of the firm. Secondly, it facilitates predictions of future income from ordinary operations...[27]

The Realization Committee offers a similar statement:

> Since income from operations and holding gains or losses result from different causes, they can be expected to have different patterns of recurrence. Effective prediction of future income is facilitated by reporting them separately.[28]

At least three separate claims have been made for the predictive ability of operating income. E & B present the most moderate case based exclusively on an assumption concerning the stability of the production process. The validity of this assumption can only be determined by empirical investigations; however, one of the real world forces acting against stability is technological change. In all of their discussions of the income dichotomy Edwards and Bell have ignored this factor.[29]

A second question about the E & B case may be raised by

granting their empirical assumption that productive processes are stable. If this assumption is correct, why should income be dichotomized? Holding gains (losses) would be of little importance in such a stable economy.

The Long-Lived Asset Committee's implication that predictability will be enhanced by the ability to compare dividend policy with operating income is subject to the same stability assumption. The Committee believes the entire amount of operating income can be distributed as cash dividends without diminishing the firm's operating capacity.[30] This would be true only in a stable environment. If technology or factor input prices change, the optimum mix of inputs for a given level of output will also change. Consequently, a change in the relationship between dividends and operating income cannot be interpreted as a change in the investment policy of the firm; the ratio of dividends to operating income is not an unambiguous predictor of future income. The example of the two steel companies is a good illustration of this problem.

Our discussion of the relationship between operating and holding activities also raises doubts about the validity of the Realization Committee's argument for the forecasting properties of operating income. This Committee assumes that the two categories of income are independent and bases its justification for better forecasting on this independence. Again we emphasize that changes in resource prices will result in trade-offs between holding and operating performance. Consequently, a firm's future income stream cannot be predicted from historical cost data on either of the separate components of income.

In conclusion, on a priori grounds, we doubt the argument that dichotomizing income improves the ability to predict a firm's future income stream. However, deductive analysis is not sufficient to resolve this alleged advantage, empirical research is necessary to answer questions about a measurement's forecasting ability.

111. THE INCOME DICHOTOMY AND COMPARABILITY

The third suggested benefit of the income dichotomy is the improvement in the comparability of the performance measures. If improved comparability in the data can be demonstrated, this would be a sufficient justification for the acceptance of the proposal. Much of the traditional accounting approach to decision-evaluation rests on using the measurements in just this way. The implication is that the best available method for evaluating the firm's efficiency is to compare the results of its decisions with the results reported by other firms operating under similar conditions. This view may be contrasted with the alternative of providing information which would be used to evaluate specific decisions at the time they are made. Accounting data reflect only the final results of past decisions.

In this respect, the E & B proposal is consistent with traditional accounting. Indeed, they criticize current accounting practice on these grounds:

> Traditional accounting operating profit cannot be expected to yield identical data for two different periods whose current events are identical. Current operating profit does fulfill this criterion; it depends for its determination on the events which are current in the period under consideration. The figures derived when historically oriented profit concepts are used depend only partly on current events; their measurement is influenced heavily by events of preceding periods, namely, historical costs. Yet it seems reasonable to expect that if a firm operates during two periods with the same endowment of assets, contributes the same factors to the same production and sales processes, sells the same output at the same prices, the firm should report the same profit.[31]

This statement only argues for the use of current operating income in the interperiod comparisons of a single firm's operations. However, the reasoning can be extended to inter-firm comparisons by assuming we are considering two firms alike in all respects except the timing of their asset acquisitions.[32]

The use of a replacement cost basis of asset valuation yields the same quantifications for all like assets. However, replacement cost income could result in two different quantifications for two identical operating performances because of different timing of asset acquisitions. The separation of net income into holding and operating income adds this property of comparability to the operating statements, for changes in asset values are segregated from operating income. In this respect, the proposal is an improvement over the mere recommendation that replacement cost be used as the basis of asset valuation.

This benefit is a controversial one, however, for it still

leads us into the well-known dispute over replacement-cost asset valuation. The proposal adds comparability only to the extent we can resolve some of the issues which have been raised by those originally skeptical of replacement costs.

One of the more frequently quoted criticisms is that changes in replacement costs measure more than changes in the specific price levels of assets. This assumption is implicit in some of the arguments given by E & B. For example, at one point they state:

> A wise management enters an industry at a time when the necessary assets can be purchased at exceedingly favourable prices. As time passes, other firms enter the industry purchasing their assets at substantially higher prices. If all firms now in the industry are equally efficient in their operating activities, the first firm will record a substantially larger "operating profit" than the other firms in the industry. After all, the depreciating charges of the first firm are substantially lower in terms of historical cost than those for the newer firms in the industry. But this excess does not result from the wisdom which the management operates its assets; it is the result of the wisdom which the management displayed at the time it purchased the assets and in its many subsequent (perhaps passive) decisions to hold the asset.[33]

Of course, if the changes in the price of assets also reflect improvements in the quality of the assets, then all firms will not be equally efficient in their operating activities. In this event, the newer firms will be substituting capital for variable input factors, and they should report lower variable costs for the same amount of output than the first firm described by E & B. An adjustment to replacement costs of this first firm's assets would penalize its operating income by assigning a significant part of its net income to holding gains. If, as E & B and others suggest, current operating income is a measure of the ability of the firm to generate income over a long period, then this first firm would be evaluated as being less efficient than its competitors. In fact, it was merely unlucky (unwise) to have purchased its assets when it did!

The criticism assumes that adjustments to replacement costs will be based upon specific price indices; the situation described would not develop if the adjustments were based upon market prices or appraisals of the specific assets. E & B recognize that the use of index numbers will cause this kind of measurement error in their system, but they believe the error is less severe than that produced by the continuing use of historical costs.[34] The important point is that we recognize this limitation in the use of residual measure of current operating income as a basis for comparing the operating decisions of different firms.

Our criticism is immaterial when applied to the use of replacement costs for inventory valuation. The rapid turnover of inventories reduces the magnitude of the error in the application of an index number. In this respect, the proposal could offer more comparability between the measure of costs of goods sold by different firms. We should note, however, that the average cost method which E & B[35] and the AAA Inventory Measurements Committee[36] use as the basis for defining replacement cost does not achieve complete comparability between firms. Consider two firms alike in all respects except the timing of their inventory purchases. By the average cost procedure the two firms will report different costs of goods sold and, consequently, different operating incomes. This deficiency can easily be corrected by defining replacement cost to be used in the measurement of operating income in terms of one measure for all firms, e.g., replacement cost as of the end of the period.

IV. CONCLUSION

By design this review of the holding-operating income proposal has been quite critical. A suggestion has been made for a major innovation to the accounting income report. Although many groups have endorsed the change, their justifications have been rather sketchy. We were able to discover three specific arguments for the proposal. Our examination of these arguments has led us to conclude:

(1) The dichotomy cannot be used for the separate evaluations of different kinds of decisions; holding and operating activities are not independent.

(2) Although further research, primarily of an empirical nature, must be undertaken to fully evaluate the predictive powers resulting from the dichotomy, we remain skeptical of these claims.

(3) Potentially, the most fruitful use of the dichotomy seems to be in the area of improving inter-period and inter-firm comparability.

We have not attempted to give an unequivocal answer to the broad question of whether or not the dichotomy should be accepted. Our analysis indicates that at least one of the claimed advantages of the proposal is capable of validation. If it is validated, this might be sufficient reason to argue for the dichotomy's acceptance. In addition, the discovery of other possible benefits, not yet raised, must be considered. Therefore, our most general conclusion is simply that: the case for dichotomizing income awaits completion.

FOOTNOTES

(1) Robert T. Sprouse and Maurice Moonitz, "A Tentative Set of Broad Accounting Principles for Business Enterprises." Accounting Research Study No. 3 (New York: American Institute of Certified Public Accountants, 1962). p.30

(2) Committee on Concepts and Standards - Inventory Measurement, "A Discussion of Various Approaches to Inventory Measurement," The Accounting Review, Vol. XXXIX, No. 3 (July, 1964), pp. 700-14. Committee on Concepts and Standards - Long-Lived Assets, "Accounting for Land, Buildings and Equipment," ibid., pp. 693-99. 1964 Concepts and Standards Research Study Committee, "The Realization Concept," ibid., Vol. XL, No. 2 (April 1965), pp. 312-22. 1964 Concepts and Standards Research Study Committee, "The Matching Concept," ibid., pp. 368-72.

(3) See, for example, William J. Vatter, the Fund Theory of Accounting and Its Implications for Financial Reporting (Chicago: University of Chicago Press, 1947), pp. 71-74; and Sidney S. Alexander, "Income Measurement in a Dynamic Economy," in Five Monographs on Business Income (New York: Americans Institute of (Certified Public) Accountants, 1950), pp. 73-95.

(4) Edgar O. Edwards and Philip W. Bell, The theory and Measurement of Business Income (Berkeley: University of California Press, 1961).

(5) Ibid., p. 276. This proposal is supported by the majority of the AAA Concepts and Standards Committees.

(6) The most recent exchange on this issue was between Robert L. Dickens and John O. Blackburn, "Holding Gains on Fixed Assets: An Element of Business Income?" The Accounting Review, Vol. XXXIX, No. 2 (April, 1964), pp. 312-29; and Stephen A. Zeff and W. David Maxwell, "Holding Gains of Fixed Assets - A Demurrer," ibid., Vol. XL, No. 1(January 1965), pp. 65-75. In addition, Zeff in a previous article, "Replacement Cost: Member of the Family, Welcome Guest, or Intruder?" ibid., Vol. XXXVII, No. 4 (October, 1962), pp. 611-25, summarizes the controversy in historical perspective.

(7) This is pointed out by Sprouse and Moonitz, op. cit., p.30; and the Committee on Concepts and Standards - Inventory Measurement, op. cit., p. 705.

(8) E & B, pp. 222-23.

(9) Ibid., p.3.

(10) For example, see Committee on Accounting Concepts and Standards Accounting and Reporting Standards for Corporate Financial Statements (Madison: American Accounting Association, 1957), which states that "realized net income of an enterprise measures its effectiveness as an operating unit..." (p.4).

(11) Theses arguments will be cited specifically in later sections. However, we should point out that the discussion by E & B encompasses all three advantages.

(12) E & B, p. 73.

(13) Committee on Concepts and Standards - Inventory Measurement, op. cit., p. 705. Emphasis added.

(14) 1964 Concepts and Standards Research Study, "The Matching Concept," op. cit., pp.370-71.

(15) Our analysis will be restricted to asset management, i.e., it will exclude the problem of debt management. It should be noted that E & B extend the holding income category to the evaluation about the relationship of holding income to asset management are directly applicable to the evaluation of this financial decision.

(16) A more detailed listing of the relevant costs may be obtained from texts on inventory models. For example, see G. Hadley, and T.M. Whitin, Analysis of Inventory Systems (Englewood Cliffs: Prentice-Hall, 1963), pp. 10-21.

(17) Other motives for holding inventory have been described as precautionary, and speculation corresponding to the motives for holding cash proposed by J.M. Keynes. See M.K. Starr and David W. Miller, Inventory Control Theory and Practice (Englewood Cliffs: Prentice Hall, 1962), p.17.

(18) Myron Gordon has outlined some of the necessary techniques to separate these kinds of effects in inventory decisions. See his "Toward A Theory of Responsibility Accounting Systems, N.A.A. Bulletin (December, 1963), pp. 8-9. Also see, Thomas E. Gossett and G.H. Newlove, "Inventory Gains and Losses," Management Services, Vol. II, No. 4 (July-August, 1965), pp. 52-56.

(19) Recently, there have been several suggestions that accountants include a report on the expectations of management.

For example, see Harold Bierman, Jr., "Depreciable Assets - Timing of Expense Recognition," The Accounting Review (October, 1961), p. 618. At this point, the proposal has not achieved general acceptance.

(20) See, for example, John W. Kendrick, "Trends in Product Prices, Factor Prices, and Productivity," The Relationship of Prices to Economic Stability and Growth (Washington, D.C.: U.S. Congress, Joint Economic Committee, 1958).

(21) Yale Brozen, "Economics and Changing Technology," American Economic Review, Vol. XLVII, No. 2 (May, 1957), p. 343.

(22) These calculations are based on data presented in United States Steel Corporation's Annual Reports and the price indices used were the Department of Commerce's in the Economic Report of the President (Washington: United States Government Printing Office, 1965). Although these calculations were based on data from the decade of the fifties, it appears that the substitution of capital for labor is currently continuing. For example, Albert R. Karr, "Steels' Spending," The Wall Street Journal, August 25, 1965, p. 1, examines the current capital expenditure program of the steel industry and concludes that the relative higher cost of labor and technological changes, such as the oxygen furnace, will result in more capital intensive production techniques.

(23) In this review, it has been assumed that the method of deriving the replacement cost of durable capital goods would be specific price level indices. Although E & B suggest specific prices and appraisal values as other alternatives for defining replacement cost, the specific price level index is likely to be the best operational definition of replacement cost.

(24) Again we are assuming that replacement cost is measured with specific price indices. In addition, the illustration assumes that the relative price of capital is rising because of alternative uses available.

(25) E & B, p. 99.

(26) Loc. cit.

(27) Committee on Concepts and Standrds - Long-Lived Assets, op. cit., p. 696.

(28) 1964 Concepts and Standards Research Study Committee, "The Realization Concept," op. cit., p. 320.

(29) E & B, pp. 285-87.

(30) Committee on Concepts and Standards - Long-Lived Assets, op. cit., pp. 695-96.

(31) E & B, p. 3.

(32) The extension is also made by E & B, pp. 222-27.

(33) Ibid., p. 224. Emphasis added.

(34) Ibid., p. 288.

(35) Ibid., pp. 129-55.

(36) Committee on Concepts and Standards - Inventory Measurement, op. cit., pp. 711-14.

14 Asset Valuation and Value to the Firm

Edward Stamp

Definition of Income

One of the best-known definitions of income is that enunciated by Professor Hicks[1] which, modified to meet the special peculiarities of a corporate entity, can be expressed as follows: Income is the maximum value which the corporation can distribute during an accountin period, and still expect to be as well off at the end of the period as it was at the beginning. It is of course assumed for purposes of this definition that no further capital is introduced into or withdrawn from the enterprise during the period.

The crux of this definition hinges upon what we mean by the term "well off". It is clearly a concept which is equivalent to the accountant's notion of equity, or net asset value, and it is evidently a future-oriented concept, since all the benefits from being "well off" reside in the future. In economic terms, well-offness can be defined as the present value, using an appropriate rate of discount, of the expected stream of future net cash receipts of the enterprise. This makes it evident that the concept is a purely subjective one since it not only depends upon expectations of future net receipts, but it is also dependent upon one's (subjective) choice of discount rate. Moreover, as Professor Kaldor has pointed out, although it is a concept of income which aims to maintain capital intact, one has to tread warily since "we cannot first define income as what is left after maintaining capital intact and then define the latter as what is required to maintain income intact, without getting involved in circular reasoning".

Hicks was well aware of this difficulty, and he defined income in ex post terms as the amount of net dividends plus the increment in the money value of the entity's prospect which has accrued during the accounting period; it equals distribution plus capital accumulation. (This definition has been modified slightly from that given by Hicks in order to suit the situation of the corporation as distinct from that of the individual.)

Hicks went on to say, "this last very special sort of 'income' has one supremely important property. So long as we confine our attention to income from property, and leave out of account any increment or decrement in the value of prospects due to changes in people's own earning power (accumulation or decumulation of 'human capital'), income ex post is not a subjective affair like other kinds of income; it is almost completely objective. The capital value of the (entity's) property at the beginning of the period is an assessable figure; so is the capital value of the property at the end of the period; thus, income ex post can be directly calculated."[3]

It should be noted that this concept of income will be objective provided we can find an objective measure of the money value of the entity's capital. And we should observe that if we are successful in our search we will have a concept of income which aims, like historical cost accounting, at the maintenance of money capital intact. However, as we shall see later, it is only in the long run that the two concepts will coincide, and in any given year they are likely to give quite different measures of income.

Thus, if we are to translate the Hicksian concept of income into practical terms, we must define a measurable concept of value which avoids the circularity against which Kaldor warned. It will be noted that the economist's definition links income and value in much the same way that the double-entry system links the income statement with the balance sheet, and this augurs well for the ultimate practicality of the approach we are now following.

What we are looking for is an operational definition of what we mean by the value of an asset to a firm in current terms, that is to say in terms of current prices rather than in historical costs. Whilst we must note the importance of "economic value" (i.e. the net present value of the expected stream of future net receipts attributable to owning the asset in question), since the measure of this value determines whether it is worth while acquiring or retaining any given asset, we must also recognise that the subjectivity of the concept makes it useless for objective accounting purposes.

The two current objectivesvalues which can be attached to an asset are its replacement cost and its net realisable value. What we have to decide is which of these two is the relevant measure of value for use in the determination of income.

The Essential Role of Value in Income Determination

For a solution to this problem we must turn again to the discipline of economics. It is well known that the economist, in assessing the costs and benefits of a course of action, is accustomed to using the concept of "opportunity cost". The opportunity cost of an action can be defined as the value of the most attractive opportunity which has to be sacrificed in order to take the proposed action. This concept is widely used in economics and in business management. Indeed one might say that a successful entrepreneur is born with an intuitive grasp of this concept!

In determining the "value" of an asset one can, as it were, turn the opportunity cost concept on its head,[4] and define opportunity value as the least costly sacrifice avoided by owning an asset. This approach to the problem of measuring the value of an asset to a firm has been adopted by a number of economists, and indeed I am sure that it forms the foundation of Professor Limperg's replacement value theory, which is the basis of the Philips system of accounting (although I cannot verify this directly since his works have not been translated into English).

Although this definition of opportunity value is adequate, a much more pregnant definition was framed by Professor Bonbright, in the following terms:-

> "The value of a property to its owner is identical in amount with the adverse value of the entire loss, direct and indirect, that the owner might expect to suffer if he were deprived of the property."[5]

Let us now consider the significance of replacement cost, net realisable value, and economic value with respect to the concept of value to the owner, or as we shall now call it, Value to the Firm, as defined above.

Economic Value is a subjective quantity and is the net present value of the expected stream of future net receipts attributable to the ownership of the asset. Indivisibilities will frequently make it difficult to form a clear notion of the expected receipts stream and this, combined with the subjective nature of the estimates and of the discount rate to be applied to them, makes this concept quite clearly unacceptable for valuation purposes. However, businessmen must continually attempt the estimates since, if they estimate economic value to be lower than net realisable value, it does not make sense to retain the asset and they will dispose of it.

Thus, the real significance of Economic Value and Net Realisable Value so far as Value to the Firm is concerned, is that if economic value is higher than net realisable value it will pay the firm to retain the asset for use. If, on the other hand, net realisable value exceeds economic value it will pay the firm to dispose of the asset.

Thus we might define a term, to be known as the "Netback Value",[6] representing the highest yield or "netback" which the firm can expect to derive from the asset if it owns it. Netback value will be the higher of economic value and net realisable value. If economic value is the higher, it will pay the firm to retain the asset for use, thus deriving the highest netback. If net realisable value is the higher, it will pay the firm to dispose of the asset.

It is now possible for us to reinterpret Value to the Firm in terms of these other three concepts. If the firm is suddenly deprived of an asset, the maximum loss which it will sustain will be the lower of the replacement cost of the asset and its netback value.

Thus if netback value is higher than replacement cost, it will pay the firm to replace the asset, and the cost of replacement is the maximum value of the loss the firm sustains since this is the amount required to restore it to its position before it was deprived of the asset.

If, on the other hand, netback value is lower than replacement cost, then it would not pay the firm to replace the asset if it was lost, since it could not hope to recover, in netback, the cost of replacement. Thus, under these circumstances the maximum loss which the firm could be said to have sustained as a result of being deprived of the asset is its netback value.

Normally one can assume, in a profitable going concern, that netback value will be equal to economic value. In other words economic value is equal to or greater than net realisable value and it pays the firm to retain assets for use in the ordinary course of business, whether they be fixed assets or inventories, etc. In these circumstances there are only three possible combinations of the three factors arranged in order of size, as follows:-

EV	EV	RC
NRV	RC	EV
RC	NRV	NRV

In the first two cases the Value to the Firm is replacement cost. In the third case it would not be worth while replacing the asset if it were lost, but so long as the firm owns it it is better off using it than selling it. According to our rule, Value to the Firm would be econimic value, but I suggest that since this is a subjective and non-measurable quantity we would not go very far wrong in most instances if we treated Value to the Firm as net realisable value in this case.[7] Management would certainly know that net realisable value was lower than replacement cost, or they ought to know this.

In the other situation, where netback value is equal to net realisable value, three other different combinations are possible:-

NRV	NRV	RC
EV	RC	NRV
RC	EV	EV

In the first two cases Value to the Firm is clearly equal to replacement cost. In the last case it is equally clearly equal to net realisable value. The subjective and unmeasurable nature of economic value is no problem in this instance, since it is presumably known to management that the netback will be greater if they dispose of the asset than if they hang on to it.

We can now see the result of this analysis. We obtain a valuation rule which states, quite simply, that the value of an asset to the firm is equal to the lower of its netback value and its replacement cost. And we can feel reasonably sure that in most cases, in profitable enterprises, this will turn out to be replacement cost. And, if net realisable value is used instead, it will not be on the ground of conservatism but on the ground of economic principle.

If we accept the definition of an asset as a storehouse of future service potential[8] we can see that any attempt to measure the value of an asset must, ipso facto, be an attempt to measure the value of the future service potentials. As we have seen, this leads us into the problem of subjective valuations.

Nevertheless, as we have also seen, it is possible by a process of analysis to derive an operational definition of Value to the Firm which is measurable - provided there is a market economy, and provided there is a reasonable market for the assets in question.

I think it is fair to say that the majority of accounting academics and theoreticians who have studied this question are prepared to accept, in general at any rate, the force of the arguments which I have expounded above. In other words, they would accept that the lower of replacement cost and netback value is a close approximation to Value to the Firm. There is a dwindling band of theoreticians, mainly practitioners, I think, rather than academics, who still favour historical cost, but as I have indicated above I accept the necessity of retaining historical cost, at least for legal purposes, for some time to come.

However, there is one other school of thought which must be considered here. Its most distinguished spokesman is Professor R.J. Chambers, who set forth his ideas in a seminal book, Accounting, Evaluation and Economic Behaviour, published in 1965.[9] Chambers argues that, in principle, the proper basis of valuation is net realisable value, and he rejects replacement cost, as an expedient which should only be used when net realisable value is indeterminate.

As Chambers readily admitted, a great weakness in his argumen is that what he calls a "non-vendible durable", will be written down to zero immediately upon acquisition, according to his theory. Several arrows (in the form of reviews of his book) have been fired in to this Achilles heel, but Chambers, though bloody is yet unbowed.[10] I do not propose to dwell upon this problem at any length, but it is instructive to see how non-vendible durables would be valued according to the principles I have expounded above. A non-vendible durable is a durable tangible asset which is more or less specific to the firm which owns it. It excludes such readily "vendible" assets as office equipment and machinery, automotive equipment, many types of general purpose building etc. As Chambers recognised, highly specialised non-vendible assets have, by definition, a very low net realisable value - to which they would be written down according to his principles.

However, it is obvious that, although the net realisable value may be low, the economic value is presumably high, otherwise the firm would not have invested in the assets, and the presumption is that economic value is higher than replacement cost. Thus, value to the firm would equal replacement cost, unless there was a clear and unmistakable indication that the asset had lost its economic value and was not merely non-vendible but non-economic.

Value, Realisation, and Holding Gains

The implication of an acceptance of Value to the Firm as a legitimate basis for financial reporting is clear. It involves relaxation, but not necessarily abandonment, of the realisation principle.[11] If we accept Value to the Firm as a basis, we are accepting the use of current values prior to the realisation through consummation in a market transaction and, to put this another way, it means that we are recognising gains and losses in value in the periods in which they occur rather than in the period in which they are realised.[12]

On the other hand, such unrealised changes clearly have significance both in the balance sheet and in the income statement. It is convenient to distinguish between the possible ways in which such value changes may be recognised and reported in each of these two financial statements.

If all the assets on the balance sheet are stated in current values (i.e. at Value to the Firm) the balance sheet will show the net tangible equity at a value which is much closer to the "true" value of the total invested capital than does a balance sheet expressed in historical cost. Other important subjective values will, of course, be omitted (in particular, goodwill) but it is unlikely that accountants will ever be able to develop a satisfactory method of measuring such values and, as Professor Sidney Davidson has said, it is better to be approximately right than to be precisely wrong.

I suspect that even fairly conservative accountants are prepared to consider the idea of current values in the balance sheet. After all, many of them have already accepted the idea of recording fixed asset appraisals on the books. The real problem arises when we consider the effects on the income statement.

If price levels are rising, the recording of current values in the asset accounts (in the books and on the balance sheet) necessarily implies higher charges for depreciation and cost of goods sold. This is obvious, and the same thing happens under price-level accounting when the general price level increases, although the principle involved is of course entirely different. The difficulty arises in deciding what to do with the "credit side" (to use terminology with which all accountants will be familiar) of the value increment. These credits represent, in origin, unrealised "holding gains" attributable to holding assets through a price rise.[13] What has to be decided is whether these unrealised holding gains constitute a part of income and if so, whether they constitute income when they are unrealised or only upon realisation (i.e. as the inventory is sold or as the fixed assets are used up). If realised and/or unrealised holding gains are not to be regarded as income we have to decide what is the theoretical justification for treating them otherwise.

We also have to consider the problem that if, for example, specific prices rise faster than the general price level it can be argued (although not necessarily conclusively) that only that portion of the holding gain attributable to the excess of the specific price rise over the general price rise can be regarded as "real", and the balance must be regarded as "fictitious". Clearly, in matters of this kind, a great deal hinges upon our choice of general price index.[14]

The Problem of the Treatment of Holding Gains

If we turn back to our economic definition of income we shall find that it is not of very much help. To say that the income of the firm is the maximum amount that it may distribute while yet remaining as well off at the end of the period as it was at the beginning does not tell us whether holding gains (unrealised and/or realised) are part of income. If we credit them to some form of capital valuation reserve, then they are not income and the definition will tell us so. Alternatively if we credit them to revenue we thereby bring them into capital ("well-offness"), they form part of income, and once again the definition tells us so! We cannot break out of this circle by relying on our definition of income alone, and we shall have to look elsewhere.

Let us first of all consider the situation where an accounting entity holds an asset through a specific price rise without any change in the general price level. That is to say the replacement cost of the asset increases while the entity holds it, but there is no change in the general price level or in the purchasing power of money in this time period. The accounting entity might be a firm holding a stock of inventory or a fixed asset; alternatively it migh be an individual who owns a house or other durable asset. The specific price change has given rise to an unrealised holding gain, and since there has been no change in the general price level all of this holding gain is "real" and non of it is "fictitious".

Suppose the asset is now sold.[15] The result is that what was a real unrealised holding gain becomes a real realised holding gain. Suppose the entity now immediately replaces the asset at the current replacement price. This will require financial resources equal to the original (historical) cost of the asset which has been disposed plus the whole amount of the realised holding gain. Under these circumstances, where replacement is a necessary and deliberate part of maintaining the enterprise as a going concern, I suggest that few people would regard either the unrealised or the realised holding gains as income or as distributable.

On the other hand, if the holding gain had developed and had been realised on an asset extraneous to the general run of the business, it might well be argued that the unrealised and particularly the realised holding gain could be regarded as income. Since there has been no change in the general price level, all of the holding gain is "real", and presumably the accretion of general purchasing power could be used to advantage by the firm, or by its shareholders in a distribution.

This perhaps provides a hint as to where we might look for a solution to the problem. Let us now consider a slightly different example. Let us suppose that our accounting entity buys an irredeemable interest-paying debenture. Immediately after acquisition there is a fall in interest rates and a consequent increase in the replacement value of the debenture. Let us now suppose that interest rates remain constant at the new low level until after the debenture is sold and the proceeds are reinvested. Under these circumstances it would seem inappropriate to credit the unrealised holding gain to income (where it is subject to distribution) since there has been no increase in real resources in relation to maintainable income. If the holding gain were to be credited to income and distributed, then upon disposal of the debenture the firm would suffer, on re-investment, a realised fall in the amount of its income stream (which is equivalent to the quasi rents of real property). And, of course, the present value of the realised fall in the quasi rents will exactly offset the unrealised holding gain.

It is rather easy to understand what is going on in the case of debentures since there is a clear relationship between capital and income in such cases. It is not so easy, in the case of real property, to decide whether changes in replacement cost represent the equivalent of changes in the discount rate or whether they represent improved expectations (which are not possible in the case of fixed interest securities).

I have already referred to Kaldor's warning against the danger of being trapped in a circular reasoning process when thinking about how to define income and value. Yet we cannot escape grappling with this problem, for as Professor Fisher said[16] -

> "It would seem then that income must be derived from capital; and, in a sense, this

> is true. Income is derived from capital goods but the value of the income is not derived from the value of the capital goods. On the contrary, the value of the capital is derived from the value of the income ... Not until we know how much income an item of capital will probably bring us can we set any valuation on that capital at all. It is true that the wheat crop depends on the land which yields it. But the value of the crop does not depend on the value of the land. On the contrary, the value of the land depends on the expected value of its crops."

If we did not live in a market economy, where prices are established by the forces of supply and demand, our accounting problem would be insoluble. But it is the function and purpose of the market to translate expectations into values, and indeed the only reliable and objective test that we have of the value of expectations is the value set in the market place.

The reference to Fisher focuses attention once again upon the intimate connection between the statement of profit and loss and the balance sheet. And I think if suggests that perhaps an answer to the riddle is to be found in a process which blends the matching idea (appropriate to the income statement) with the economist's notions (especially those of Hicks) which effectively define income in terms of balance sheet changes.

Let us first of all consider the matching process in the income statement, and let us confirm ourselves to the cost side of the equation, since we shall be considering realisation when we look at the balance sheet.

As we have already seen, the historical cost approach fails to match like against like, since many of the costs (especially those relating to depreciation and cost of sales) are expressed in historical units of measure of widely differing purchasing powers. Price-level adjustments can correct this, but even they do not give an adequate correction since they fail to take into account specific price changes. If the matching process is to be logical it should clearly match current revenues against the current values to the Firm of the factors of production which have been expended in deriving the revenues. To put it another way, the current value of the output sold should be "matched" against the current cost of the related inputs. If this is done, the resultant income measure is generally known as "Current Operating Profit".[17]

Turning now to the balance sheet, I have argued earlier that it is more logical and more informative, and therefore presumably more useful to the reader, to have the balance sheet expressed in current values. The appropriate basis of measurement would appear to be Value to the Firm as defined above. If this is done, the valuation of assets such as inventories and fixed assets will normally be substantially different from the historical cost valuation, and the excess represents accumulated unrealised holding gains which have accrued since the dates of purchase of the various assets.[18] Upon realisation the current costs will flow into the income statement, where they will be matched against current revenues in the process of determination of current operating profit.

The essence of the problem now is to decide whether, and if so to what extent and in what period, the unrealised gains should be regarded as income; and, further, to what extent and in what manner realised gains should be treated as a part of income. We also have to determine whether it is necessary to divide unrealised and realised gains into their real and fictitious elements by making adjustments for changes in the general price level. If we decide to make such adjustments we have to decide which price index is the appropriate one to use.

Whatever we decide to do, it is clearly preferable to make a segregation between current operating profit and holding gains, since they are attributable to two entirely different types of activity, and any assessment of performance, or attempt to predict future performance, will be facilitated if the segregation is made. It is also important to segregate realised from unrealised changes, since they clearly constitute quite different classes of gain of different "quality", and once again assessment and prediction is facilitated if the segregation is made.[19]

Finally, it is useful to distinguish between holding gains (both unrealised and realised, fictional and real) attributable to assets such as inventories which are purchased for resale, holding gains (unrealised and realised, real and fictional) attributable to fixed assets which are purchased for use rather than re-sale (and where realisation will occur as the asset is depreciated and amortised rather than as it is sold), and realised holding gains on fixed assets which have been sold by the firm (where the excess of the selling price over net depreciated current cost at the time of disposal represents a real capital profit).[20] It is convenient to distinguish between these three categories by denoting them as inventory holding gains, cost savings, and windfalls, respectively.[21]

It will, of course, be appreciated that the measure of the unrealised or realised inventory holding gains, or the cost savings, which have accrued on any given asset up to any particular point in time will be a cumulative figure made up of the net of the gains and losses which have accrued in each of the several years since the asset was purchased. The amounts accruing in any given year are clearly of considerable significance, whether they are realised during the year, and it is customary to describe such annual accretion as a "realisable" inventory holding gain, etc.[22]

A Set of Profit Concepts

It will now be evident that we have managed to break down not only accounting profit but also the economist's concept of profit into their essential components. Readers will find it convenient at this stage to refer to the Exhibit (see following page).

Thus, the concept of profit described by Hicks (unadjusted for changes in general purchasing power) is made up of the sum of current operating profit and realisable inventory holding gains and cost savings. This concept of profit is often described in the literature as Realisable Profit, or Money Profit. The first term is self-explanatory, and the significance of the second will be appreciated later.

If we wish to take account of general price-level changes, it is only necessary to eliminate the fictional from the real portion of the realisable inventory holding gains and cost savings. Real money profit (or real realisable profit) consists of current operating profit plus the real realisable gains, less losses on monetary assets.

Similarly, accounting profit is equal to current operating profit plus both the real and fictional portion of realised cost savings and realised inventory holding gains, together with real and fictional realised capital gains.[23] In the traditional accounting statement of profit and loss, the real and fictional realised capital gains are generally reported separately (without distinguishing between the real and fictional elements thereof), but the realised cost savings and inventory holding gains are "buried" in the reported historical cost figures for depreciation and cost of sales respectively. Thus it is impossible for the reader to see to what extent reported profits are attributable to accumulated inventory holding gains and cost savings.

EXHIBIT

ANALYSIS OF COMPONENTS OF VARIOUS MEASURES OF PROFIT

(a) Components

Code No.	Description	
COP	Current Operating Profit	
1	Real Realisable Holding Gains	i.e. unrealised & realised, accruing in current period
2	Fictitious ,, ,, ,,	
3	Real Realisable Cost Savings	
4	Fictitious ,, ,, ,,	
5	Real Realised Capital Gains	Fixed Assets
6	Fictitious ,, ,, ,,	
7	Real Realised Cost Savings	
8	Fictitious ,, ,, ,,	
9	Real Unrealised ,, ,,	
10	Fictitious ,, ,, ,,	
11	Real Realised Holding Gains	Inventories
12	Fictitious ,, ,, ,,	
13	Real Unrealised ,, ,,	
14	Fictitious ,, ,, ,,	
15	Loss on holding Monetary Assets in current period	
16	Holding Gain element in (5 + 6)	

Notes: (1) Terminology ("gain" etc.) assumes rising price levels, with the rise in specific prices greater than rise in general price level. The terminology (and algebraic sign) changes if these conditions are varied, but not the underlying principles.

(2) There is, of course, overlap between (1 + 2) and (3 + 4) and the rest (except COP).

(b) Measures of Profit in terms of above components

Profit Measure	Components	Balance Sheet Valuations
Accounting Profit	(COP+7+8+11+12)+(5+6)	Historical Cost
Adjusted Accounting Profit	(COP+7+11)+5-15	Adjusted (price index) Historical Cost
Money Profit (Realisable Profit)	COP+(1+2)+(3+4)	Current Values
Real Money Profit	COP+1+3-k5	,, ,,
Real Profit	COP+(5-16)-15	,, ,,

Note: 9, 10, 13 and 14 are not included in any of the measures except Money Profit (all of them) and Real Money Profit (9 and 13) on a cumulative basis.

Similarly, adjusted accounting profit (i.e. adjusted for changes in the general price level) is composed of current operating profit, together with the real portion of realised cost savings and inventory holding gains, plus real realised capital gains, less any loss arising from holding monetary assets during the current accounting period. Monetary gains and losses arising in previous periods will already have been absorbed in the retained profits account.

It might be thought, from most of what has been said above, that the "best" measure of profit is that of the economist, adjusted for changes in the general price level, i.e. real money profit as outlined above. However, it will be recalled that we have not yet settled the question of whether holding gains[24] ought to be included in a measure of income. Before we try to settle this question, we should note that in the long run real money profit and adjusted accounting profit amount to very much the same thing. Real money profit recognises holding gains in the years in which they accrue, whereas adjusted accounting profit recognises holding gains in the years in which they are realised.[25] In the long run, when all gains have been realised, the accumulation of profits on either basis will amount to the same thing. In the short or in the medium run, the accumulated difference between the two will be equal to accumulated unrealised real inventory holding gains and cost savings. In any given year the difference between income for the year measured on the two bases will be the difference between the real portion of inventory holding gains and cost savings realised in the current period but accruing in previous periods (which will be included in accounting profit) and the real portion of inventory holding gains and cost savings accruing in the current period but not realised by the end of that period (which will be included in real money profit).

The reason why, in the long run, adjusted accounting profit and real money profit amount to the same thing is that they are both trying to do the same thing. They are both attempting to maintain intact the general purchasing power originally invested in the enterprise (plus any further net investment since incorporation). The short and medium term differences (which are of course of paramount importance) arise because real money profit recognises unrealised changes, whereas adjusted accounting income does not. In the long run all changes are realised.[26]

Conceptually, the important thing to note is that both ideas of profit involve the same notion of capital maintenance. In a similar way one can draw parallels between historical cost measures of profit and money (or realisable) profit.

In the long run they will amount to the same thing because they each are attempting to maintain the original invested money capital intact. As before, the differences in the short and medium term arise because realisable profit recognises unrealised gains, whereas accounting or historical cost profit does not.

Now I think it is clear that, if one regards the firm essentially as a venture which will ultimately be liquidated, with the proceeds being turned over to the shareholders, a concept of profit which aims to maintain original invested money capital intact will be satisfactory provided that there is no change in the general purchasing power. In the real world, of course, we have to live with inflation and so in the real world it is clear that we will have a better measure of profit if we take purchasing power changes into account, and a profit concept which aims to maintain the original invested purchasing power intact will be more satisfactory when general price levels are changing.

The Relevance of Concepts of Capital Maintenance

However, it is highly questionable whether we can in fact regard the modern business corporation as a "venture" in the sense in which I have used that term above. In a modern capitalist economy, one simply does not regard an investment in shares of a corporation as something which will only be liquidated as a result of the liquidation of the corporation. Corporations (pace Rolls-Royce) are thought of as having an unlimited life, and shareholdings are normally realised by the shareholder selling the holding to a third party through the medium of the securities market. The investor is thus not really interested in changes in the general purchasing power of the original invested capital, since he does not contemplate receiving his share of it in the form of a distribution. If he wishes to liquidate his interest in the corporation he sells his shares and he will make his own correlation between the price at which he sells them and changes in the index of general purchasing power. Moreover, even if the shareholder did receive a liquidating distribution from the corporation, he may very well decide to invest the proceeds in shares of another company rather than spend them in a way to which the index of general purchasing power would be relevant.

Similar conclusions will be reached if one looks at the matter from the point of view of the directors and the management. They are not normally concerned with applying the resources of the corporation to the purchase of assets whose prices correlate with changes in the general purchasing power. On the contrary, they are much more concerned with changes in specific price levels of the assets which the enterprise deals with in its normal course of business, whether they be fixed assets or current assets. Indeed, the only way in which shareholders and directors come together in this area is over the question of dividends, where presumably changes in the purchasing power of money are relevant. However, in this respect shareholders are quite capable of making their own calculations as to the change in the real value of the dividends which they receive periodically from their investments.

In fact, the accountant's concept of the going concern implies that it is the wish and intention of both shareholders and management (to say nothing of employees, creditors, etc.) that the corporation should maintain itself. This, of course, by no means implies that it will maintain itself in the same form. Clearly its substance will change as assets are sold and wear out, and in the short run the replacements (inventories, machinery, etc.) will probably be similar in form to that which is being replaced. But over the medium term it is likely that style changes, product changes, technological improcements, changes in demand, etc. will result in changes in the company's marketing and production planning, and as a result the corporation will slowly evolve into an organism which is materially different in form, substance, and lifestyle from what it used to be.

What all this adds up to is that, whilst a maintenance of capital concept based upon original invested money capital, or upon original invested general purchasing power, is unlikely to be satisfactory, it is difficult to argue that a concept based upon maintenance of real tangible physical assets is superior.

Nevertheless, I believe that it is possible for the accountant to select an appropriate maintenance concept which still takes account of the long-term need for the corporation to maintain flexibility and adaptability. I think it can be done (in the adsence of very rapid technological change) by taking advantage of the fact that change is an evolutionary process and in the case of corporations it occurs with tolerable slowness. Over a long period of time the corporation may change unrecognisably, but over short periods changes, including changes in the nature of the assets (inventories, fixed assets, etc.) in which the company deals, will be perceptible and readily measurable. Thus I think it is possible to develop a concept of maintenance of real physical tangible capital which will have relevance between the beginning and the end of any given accounting period. Indeed, if this were not possible the process of budgeting would not be possible.

As an analogy I might suggest the process of driving a car through the countryside. There will be considerable differences in surroundings between the beginning of the journey and the destination, but provided the road does not contain major discontinuities, and provided one is not driving at night without lights, it is normally possible to see where one is going and to keep on the road.[27]

If all of this is accepted, then I think we end up with a concept of capital maintenance which aims to preserve the entity's capacity to reproduce itself. If it can do this, then by the slow processes of evolution it will be able to adapt and survive and change its form, as well as, through the process of renewal, its substance.

Holding Gains not a part of Income

If we now direct our attention back to the problem of deciding whether holding gains form a part of income it seems to me that the answer is fairly clear. (For simplicity I will use the generic term "holding gains" to denote inventory holdings gains and cost savings). I think it is clear that the fictional element of both realised and unrealised holding gains must be excluded. Moreover, whilst the important distinction between realised and unrealised gains should be preserved, this should be done in the capital reserve section of the balance sheet since neither constitutes a part of income. On the contrary, they represent the amount by which the value[28] of what it is that has to be maintained has increased during the period of the firm's ownership of its assets. Provided the offsetting debits are recovered from realised revenues the firm will be able to maintain itself.[29]

Thus, it seems to me, we come to the conclusion that the "best" measure of profit that we are likely to obtain for the going concern corporation is made up (see the Exhibit on page 233) of current operating profit plus the windfall element of realised capital gains[30] less any loss in the current period attributable to holding monetary assets.[31]

I would also argue that the most informative set of financial statements would include computations of profit according to all of the concepts described in the Exhibit. Furthermore, as I have argued elsewhere,[32] I would like to see, parenthetically or otherwise, a notation of the estimated margins of errors in the various measurements included in the financial statements.

I have not dealt with the location and classification on the balance sheet of the credits arising from the incorporation of replacement costs. The realised and unrealised portions would of course be segregated and shown separately. But should the credits be shown as a part of proprietorship equity, or as a non-proprietorship item (as is often done in the case of "tax-allocation reserves" for example)? This issue can really only be decided after one has settled one's views on the nature of the accounting entity, and this matter is beyond the scope of this paper.[33]

However, one should note that the way the entity is financed will generally not be relevant in deciding the issue. The fact that a company is very highly geared, so that most of the asset financing comes from debt, does not preclude treating unrealised and realised holding gains as increments to equity (without, of course, passing them through the income account). Indeed a public utility financed entirely out of debt capital, might well treat holding gains as a form a equity reserve!

Finally, it is perhaps necessary to emphasise that a decline in replacement cost would be debited to the holding gain "reserve" and would not be charged against income. The reasoning behind this is similar, mutatis mutandis, to that given above when replacement costs are increasing.

Two Objections to Change

Let me deal, finally, with a couple of objections which might be advanced against these proposals. The first concerns the objectivity and practicality of the measurement changes which are implied, and the second relates to the supposed damage which might be caused if the suggested changes were to be made.

All objections which rest on the ground of practicality or objectivity are, of course, directed against the recognition in the accounts of unrealised value changes. As I have already pointed out, the historical cost basis (against which unrealised changes are computed) is itself lacking in objectivity, and as Professor Hatfield said many years ago "the objection to recording appreciation because it is a vague estimate applies just as truly to depreciation". It really all boils down to the question of whether the accountant is capable of developing measurement techniques to enable him to compute replacement costs and net realisable values for tangible assets. I have spent a dozen years in practice and

I do not have to be told that this is often a difficult problem. It ought to be regarded as soluble in the case of inventories, since if auditors really attempt to determine whether inventories are being properly valued, at the lower of cost and market value, they are supposed to make some effort, now, to determine replacement costs and net realisable values. It can be done, and I think it frequently is done quite successfully in practice. In the case of fixed assets it is possible to use specific and industry-wide price indices in the case of many categories. There will no doubt be a small residuum of assets for which it is impossible to make any kind of objective and reliable estimate of value to the firm. In these cases I would be perfectly happy to see a general price index applied against them, in much the same way as is done in price-level accounting. Such a procedure might not produce the whole truth, but it will certainly be a closer approximation to the truth in most cases than historical cost.[35]

Doubts about the practicalities do exist in powerful quarters, however, and in an interview with Robert Jones (printed in THE TIMES on November 11, 1970 on page 27) Sir Henry Benson made the following statement:-

> "The most difficult subject of course is how to deal with proper presentation of accounts in an inflationary society. And unhappily nobody so far has arrived at a practical solution."

This is a very surprising comment since Sir Henry's firm, Cooper Bros., are the auditors of the British affiliates of the Dutch enterprise N.V. Philips' Gloeilampenfabrieken. Philips have not only pioneered a system of replacement value accounting but have demonstrated, quite conclusively, that it is a practical system which can be used effectively by a large multi-national industrial enterprise with affiliates scattered throughout the world. If the Philips system is practical, as it clearly is, how much more practical is the system described in the English Institute's booklet Accounting for Stewardship in a Period of Inflation, referred to earlier. Indeed, by comparison with the Philips system, the English Institute proposals are child's play. As I hope this Paper demonstrates, the real problems are the theoretical ones, and it is really not possible to argue any more that a practical solution cannot be found.

The second objection concerns the possible inflationary effect of reporting information such as that which I have described. Thus it is argued that in a time of rising prices, reporting price-level adjusted figures (for example) would have the effect of lowering reported company earnings. Management would then feel impelled to raise prices, with a resultant snowballing inflation.

It is clearly impossible to produce a conclusive refutation of an assertion of this kind without empirical evidence. (It is similarly impossible to prove the assertion!) But I suggest that there are other alternatives open to management. They might, for example, try reducing dividends, and they might have a shot at reducing some of their costs, particularly their labour costs, by improving productivity, eliminating feather-bedding, and possibly even compelling the unions to accept wage reductions.

Clearly, in any individual case it will depend upon the forces operating in the market. In some circumstances it might be just as difficult to raise prices as it would be to force down labour costs. Reducing dividends will ultimately raise the cost of capital, and there is no doubt that lower reported earnings will make it more difficult for companies to raise new capital. But surely the point of the whole exercise which I have described in this paper is to reveal the truth as it really is. I can see little merit in living in a fool's paradise, and it is encouraging to see leaders of the business community, like Mr. Alex McDonald, the Chairman of Distillers, beginning to speak out on this subject.[36]

Conclusion

In this paper I have been dealing with an area of what academics generally describe as accounting theory. It is an area which is growing in importance, and it is certainly very much more important today than it was even twenty years ago when I started learning about accounting. It is a truism that the more one learns the more one realises how much more there is still to be learnt, but it is a truism which I think applies with especial force to the modern accountant. I would certainly be the last to suggest that we will find all our answers from studying and developing accounting theory. In fact, as I hope I have been able to demonstrate in this paper, the role of accounting theory is not so much to provide answers as to make sure that we ask all the right questions. It is only experience that will finally give us the answers.

FOOTNOTES

(1) J.R. Hicks: Value and Capital (second edition) (Oxford; Clarendon; 1946), page 172.

(2) N. Kaldor: An Expenditure Tax (London; Allen & Unwin; 1955), page 65.

(3) Op. cit., pages 178-179.

(4) A similar approach to opportunity value with different conclusions is used by Professor Wright. See "A Theory of Financial Accounting", JOURNAL OF BUSINESS FINANCE, Vol. 2, No. 3 (Autumn 1970), pages 57-69.

(5) J.C. Bonbright: The Valuation of Property (New York; McGraw-Hill; 1937), page 71.

(6) I apologise for adding to an already burdensome list of accounting jargon. But some identification is necessary here, and "netback" is a term which is very widely used in the petroleum industry and seems relevant to our present purpose.

(7) The case of non-vendible durables is a special problem and is dealt with below. But it should be noted that in profitable enterprises they fall into the second column, not the third.

(8) Thus, "Assets represent expected future economic benefits, rights to which have been acquired by the enterprise as a result of some current or past transaction". R.T. Sprouse and M. Moonitz: A Tentaive Set of Broad Accounting Principles for Business Enterprises. (New York; AICPA; 1962), page 20.

(9) Although I cannot accept the central thesis of his theoretical analysis I regard Chambers as one of the leading thinkers in the field of financial accounting theory. The book referred to above is published by Prentice Hall.

(10) See, for example, his latest article in Abacus, Vol. 6, No.1 (September 1970), entitled "Second Thoughts on Continuously Contemporary Accounting".

(11) See also footnote 15. It means an abandonment of historical cost, but unless value increments are reported as income the realisation principle-insofar

as it relates to revenue - will not be violated. In fact, as I explain in detail below, I believe that in most cases such increments (whether realised or not) are not income. However, the debit side of the increment should be charged against income (as depreciation, cost of sales, etc.), so the realisation principle is involved.

(12) Indeed, in the period of realisation the value increment may be zero - or even negative!

(13) "Holding gain" (or, of course, loss) is here used in a generis sense. A distinction is made later between "inventory holding gains", and holding gains on fixed assets (which will be denoted as "cost savings") being used in the business.

(14) The problem of choosing the most appropriate index is by no means as simple as it may appear. See, for example, E.S. Hendrikson "Purchasing Power and Replacement Cost concepts - are they related?" Accounting Review, July 1963, pages 483-491. Nevertheless, I suggest that satisfactory, objective and verifiable adjustments can be made in the U.K. using the basis (and the index) illustrated in the English Institute's booklet, Accounting for Stewardship in a Period of Inflation.

(15) The proceeds are the net realisable value. For present purposes this is assumed to be equal to replacement cost. It it exceeds replacement cost the excess can be regarded as a windfall profit. See below.

(16) Quoted in R.H. Parker and G.C. Harcourt (eds.): Readings in the Concept and Measurement of Income (Cambridge; C.U.P.; 1969), page 40. Note that Fisher thinks of income as consumption, and excludes saving (in contrast to Hicks). But this does not vitiate the point he is making here.

(17) This term, and a number of others, follow the usage of E.O. Edwards and P.W. Bell: The Theory and Measurement of Business Income (Berkeley; California University Press; 1961), passim. This pioneering work should be on the bookshelf of every thinking accountant. The conclusions of the analysis in this paper differ considerably from those of Edwards and Bell, particularly in regard to the treatment of holding gains, and some modification of their terminology has therefore been inevitable in order to clarify my argument.

(18) Post-realisation assets, such as receivable and cash, will of course be shown at net realisable value.

(19) The importance of the "quality" of the constituents of even conventional accounts was stressed by J.D. Slater in his address to the English Institute Cambridge Summer Course in 1970. See the Proceedings thereof, What is Profit? (London; I.C.A.E.W.; 1970), pages 58-73, especially page 64.

(20) Note that the excess of net depreciated current cost over net depreciated historical cost is a realised (real and fictional) holding gain. Normal accounting terminology classifies this plus the windfall as a "capital profit" (in one figure).

(21) "Holding gain", as a generic term, applies only to the first two.

(22) "Realisable" is a useful way of describing this important element; the term was coined by Edwards and Bell (op. cit.).

(23) Using "capital gain" in its conventional sense which equals realised holding gans on fixed assets sold (excess of net current cost over net historical cost at time of sale) plus "windfalls" as defined above.

(24) In the generic sense, including cost savings. Since I do not regard holding gians as part of income I would really prefer to give them a new title. But on balance it seems better to use a term which will be familiar to most accountants who are familiar with the literature.

(25) A similar comparison is of course possible between conventional accounting profit and Realisable Profit.

(26) But, as Keynes observed, in the long run we are all dead!

(27) In the calculus one uses a similar approach to the one I am describing, in the process of integration.

(28) i.e. Value to the Firm.

(29) In a sense even this is a long-run concept since in the absence of "backlog depreciation" there may be temporary financing problems unless the firm is in a state of dynamic equlibrium.

Note also that unrealised holding gains relate to assets currently owned or in use, whereas realised gains relate to the increase in value of assets consumed and/or replaced.

(30) The "windfall" is not required for capital maintenance. This is why I deem it to be a part of income.

(31) Such losses, if one reverts to a venture approach, can be thought of as unrealised until the cycle has been completed by replacement.

(32) In "Accounting Principles and Management Accounts", and Address to the I.C.W.A. Conference held in the University of Lancaster. Reprinted in MANAGEMENT ACCOUNTING, May 1971, page 141.

(33) For a good discussion of various alternatives see E.S. Hendriksen: Accounting Theory (second edition) (Homewood; Irwin, 1970), Chapter 17.

(34) "A Symposium on Appreciation", ACCOUNTING REVIEW, March 1930, page 33.

(35) Unless there is clear (even if unquantifiable) evidence that the specific price change is manifestly not represented even approximately by the change in the general index. Such cases should be explained in a footnote to the financial statements.

(36) In a widely reported comment in the company's annual report published in 1970.

15 Value to the Firm and the Asset Measurement Problem

Hiroshi Yoshida

Professor Edward Stamp's paper, 'Income and Value Determination and Changing Price-Levels' is directed towards clarifying a theoretical basis of replacement cost accounting.[1] For the purpose, he has adopted the concepts of value to the firm (p. 285). The concept, as he says, was framed by Professor Bonbright. Stamp also made use of the concept of opportunity value (p. 285) which was originally introduced by Professor Wright.[2] The opportunity value, defined as the least costly sacrifice avoided by owning an asset, is introduced as the measure of the value to the firm of an asset. To examine whether Stamp has succeeded in developing a proper concept of asset measurement will be the object of this paper.

The Role of the Concept of Value to the Firm

This concept is used by Stamp to show the essential role of value in income determination. He has carefully examined the nature of the historical-cost/realized-revenue system: he found it to be characterized by (1) a venture approach to income measurement and (2) the maintenance intact of the original money capital invested.[3] His use of the concept of value to the firm signifies his departure from historical cost accounting to a form of value theory for the determination of income.

Stamp affirmed the necessity of basing corporate accounting on a going concern approach which, in his view, means that the value of an asset owned by a firm should be measured in terms of replacement cost in principle. The concept of value to the firm is considered to be the keystone of an entire system of replacement cost accounting.

He analyzed the significance of replacement cost, net

realizable value, and economic value with respect to the concept of value to the firm. His conclusion was that 'the value of an asset to the firm is equal to the lower of its netback value and its replacement cost' (p.285). Net back value is defined as the higher of economic value and net realizable value. And it is said that 'if the firm is suddenly deprived of an asset, the maximum loss which it will sustain as a result will be the lower of the replacement cost of the asset and its netback value' (p. 285). Thus value to the firm is synonymous with the maximum value of the loss sustained by a firm through sudden deprivation of an asset owned by it. And it is expected that a firm will manage its investment action to minimize the maximum value of the loss. The managed value of the loss is defined as the opportunity value. This managed maximum value of the loss, that is, the mini-max value of the loss, is adopted as the criterion of asset measurement.

The least-costly-sacrifice notion of asset value is combined with the consideration of whether a firm is a profitable going concern to reach a conclusion on the rule for the valuation of the asset. Stamp says: 'We can feel reasonably sure that in most cases, in profitable enterprises, this will turn out to be replacement cost' (pp. 285-6). Thus the least costly sacrifice is taken to be represented by replacement cost.

Stamp shows six possible combinations of replacement cost, net realizable value, and economic value which are arranged in order of size. Those six combinations are divided into two groups, the first of which is composed of cases where the netback value is equal to economic value, while the second group is the set of cases where netback value is equal to net realizable value. The groups are as follows:

EV	EV	RC	‖	NRV	NRV	RC
NRV	RC	EV	‖	EV	RC	NRV
RC	NRV	NRV	‖	RC	EV	EV

This grouping is preceded by the observation that 'if they estimate economic value to be lower than net realizable value, it does not make sense to retain the asset and they will dispose of it'. In other words, 'if net realizable value is the higher, it will pay the firm to dispose of the asset' (p. 285).

As for the relation of netback value to replacement cost, Stamp gives the following explanation: 'if netback value is higher than replacement cost, it will pay the firm to replace the asset'; and 'if, on the other hand, netback value is lower than replacement cost, then it would not pay the firm to replace the asset if it was lost' (p. 285).

Following this line of thought, we can reclassify the six cases as follows:

EV	NRV	EV	NRV		RC	RC
NRV	EV	RC	RC		EV	NRV
RC	RC	NRV	EV		NRV	EV

The first group comprises cases in which it would be worth while to replace the asset if it were lost, and the second group consists of cases in which it would not be worth while to replace the asset if it were lost. The maximum value of the loss which the firm sustains in the cases of the first group is replacement cost and that in the cases of the second group is netback value. But this grouping will lose its effectiveness if, following Stamp, we take account of the relative sizes of economic value and net realizable value. The revised grouping will be as follows:

EV	EV		NRV	NRV		RC	RC
NRV	RC		EV	RC		EV	NRV
RC	NRV		RC	EV		NRV	EV

In the cases of the first group, it would pay the firm to replace the asset if it were lost. In the cases of the second group, it would not pay the firm to replace the asset for use if it were lost since economic value is lower than net realizable value. These second cases should be distinguished from the first two cases. As Stamp says, it will not pay the firm to retain the asset for use in the second group of cases; the firm should dispose of the asset. This would mean that, if the firm were deprived of the asset, it will not pay the firm to replace it for use, though it would pay the firm to replace it for resale. In the cases of the third group, it would not pay the firm to replace the asset if it were lost.

It is now possible for us to show a final grouping of the six cases, as follows:

EV	EV		NRV	NRV	RC		RC
NRV	RC		EV	RC	NRV		EV
RC	NRV		RC	EV	EV		NRV

In the first two cases, the value of an asset to the firm will be equal to replacement cost since it will pay the firm to replace the asset; in the second cases, the value to the firm of an asset will be net realizable value since it will pay the firm to dispose of the asset; and in the case of the third class value to the firm will be economic value.

Stamp has excluded two cases where replacement cost is highest (i.e., the last case of the second group shown above and the case in group three) from his consideration of the value of an asset to the firm when he reaches the conclusion that 'we can feel reasonably sure that in most cases, in profitable enterprises, this will turn out to be replacement cost' (pp. 285-6). His inclination to replacement cost accounting is further evidenced by the statement that 'Over a long period of time the corporation may change unrecognizably, but over short periods changes, including changes in the nature of the assets (inventories, fixed assets, etc.) in which the company deals, will be perceptible and readily measurable' (p.291)

Replacement Cost as Value to the Firm

Thus, in general and at a practical level, Stamp has treated replacement cost as the representative of value of an asset to the firm. In other words, theoretically he has recognized there are cases where either replacement cost or net-back value may be the value of the asset to the firm; but he has felt reasonably sure that these are not crucial cases, since 'it is obvious that, although the net realizable value may be low, the economic value is presumably high, otherwise the firm would not have invested in the assets, and the presumption is that economic value is higher than replacement cost' (p. 286).

If we follow Stamp's argument, the cases in which a firm would hold an asset will be restricted to the first two cases classified above, in which economic value is the highest; in those cases it would be worthwhile replacing the asset if it were lost.

We can now see the result of Stamp's analysis of value to the firm. We obtain a valuation rule of an asset which is applicable only to the cases where a firm's investment decision is well managed, i.e., the firm remains profitable. His exposition of value to the firm is thus conditional.

On the occasion of defining the value of an asset to the firm, Stamp presupposed that the firm can always and does always adapt its behaviour to remain profitable. 'Change is an evolutionary process and in the case of corporations it occurs with tolerable slowness' (p. 291). But he provides no discussion of the kind of circumstance (credit restriction, crippling competition or sudden obsolescence) which may make net realizable value the only value of real consequence to the firm, and replacement cost of no consequence whatever.

Stamp's theoretical analysis thus yielded three possible representations of value to the firm, economic value, net realizable value, and replacement cost. From these economic value was expelled because it is not objectively measurable; 'the subjectivity of the concept makes it useless for objective accounting purposes' (p. 284). In the case where economic value would, according to Stamp's analysis, be the appropriate value to the firm, he suggested the use of net realizable value in lieu of economic value; 'I suggest that since this is a subjective and non-measurable quantity we would not go very far wrong in most instances if we treated Value to the Firm as net realizable value in this case' (p. 285). The consequence is that 'the two current objective values which can be attached to an asset are its replacement cost and its net realizable value' (p. 284). The objective of Stamp's paper is 'to decide which of these two is the relevant measure of value for use in the determination of income' (p. 284). And as we have seen, Stamp rejected net realizable value on the ground of practical reason. The reason is conditional on a particular assumption about the slowness of change and adaptation; it cannot cover all of the cases of asset holdings which fall within the scope of the asset measurement problem.

Asset Measurement

Stamp holds that the concept of value to the firm is not only useful for asset measurement but also for income determination. The value of an asset to the firm is synonymous with its opportunity value, as Stamp uses the term. It means the least costly sacrifice avoided by owning an asset. In other words, the condition, 'if it were lost', is presumed for valuing an asset of a firm which is in possession of it. This presumption is criticized in another context by Chambers: "This seems to suggest that value to the owner is a special term, devised for the purpose of resolving litigated claims'.[4]

The notion of 'least costly sacrifice' introduced by Stamp is constructed in three steps: find the net present value of the expected stream of future net receipts attributable to owning the asset in question, the net realizable value of it, and its replacement cost; find the higher of the net present value and net realizable value, i.e., netback value; and find the lower of replacement cost and netback value. Thus the least costly may be any one of three values of the same asset.

But if we think about the value of an asset to the firm, we cannot help but consider the subjective capitalized value of its future net earnings, i.e., present value, as a significant meaning of value to the firm. It is specific to the firm, as it depends on the specific setting of the firm and the specific use of the asset by the firm. Of this value Chambers says, using Bonbright's form of words: "The value of a property to its owner is the amount of the entire gain, direct and indirect, that the owner might expect to accrue from possession of the property' (p. 64). It is not a market price observed directly, but a subjective estimation. It has, therefore, no relation with measurement. To measure something we must have a fact observable as an object for measuring. Replacement cost and net realizable value, i.e., selling price, are facts observable in markets.

This is known to Stamp too; that is why he excluded economic value from concepts appropriate to asset measurement. But the development of his exposition depends on the concept of economic value to decide the maximum value of the loss the firm would sustain if it were to lose the asset in question.

Thus, to measure the asset, according to Stamp, one must first know its economic value. Otherwise he cannot determine the lower of replacement cost and netback value; and consequently, he will be unable to measure the asset by replacement cost, following the stipulated rule for asset valuation. This seems to me to contradict Stamp's own standpoint, since he rejected the concept of economic value for asset valuation because 'the subjectivity of the concept makes it useless for objective accounting purposes' (p. 284).

Apparently he has denied the usability of the concept of economic value for asset valuation, but his rejection of it is limited to a direct use of it for asset valuation; for without relying on the concept he cannot determine value of an asset to the firm. This means that an objective measurement of an asset cannot be obtained without making use of a subjective valuation of it. If we want to get rid of this irrational conclusion, we must base the value of an asset to the firm on independent evidence 'which an independent assessor might be prepared to take into account' (Chambers, p. 65). And if we do so, the concept of value to the firm will be no use for asset measurement because it is an expectation of the value of an asset to a firm.

On the other hand, Stamp's concept of value to the firm was used by Stamp to define the least costly sacrifice avoided by owning an asset. This, he claims, establishes the validity of replacement cost as a measure of the asset. This least-costly-sacrifice approach means that the asset should be measured by the amount of the sacrifice which is expected to be necessary to reinstate the firm by replacement of the asset if it were lost. The hypothetical amount of this sacrifice, however, is not the value of an existing asset itself. Strictly it is nothing more than the hypothetical amount of a hypothetical outlay. The value which an asset will bring to a firm must be quantified by the net gains expected to be obtained from the utilization of the asset. So that, if we want to quantify the value of an asset to the firm, we must estimate the present value of an asset in question. In short, the concepts of replacement cost and value to the firm belong to different classes of quantification.

Conclusion

The notion of value to the firm was introduced by Stamp to establish a theory of replacement cost accounting. But, in spite of his energetic endeavour, this concept cannot be a basis of asset measurement in accounting. The function of accounting, in relation to statements of financial position and income, is to measure events which have affected a firm and not to evaluate future things. The concept of value to the firm is concerned with the expectation of future outcomes of events, of which the specific circumstance of a lost asset is only one kind of event, and relatively rare kind at that.

FOOTNOTES

(1) The Accountant's Magazine, June 1971, pp.277-92 esp. p. 291. (pp. 284-92 are reproduced as Reading 19. Eds.)

(2) F. K. Wright, 'Capacity for Adaptation and the Asset Measurement Problem', Abacus, Vol. 3, No 1, August 1967. 'The opportunity value to a firm of an asset owned by it. is the cost, loss or sacrifice which the firm would have to incur it it did not already own that asset; it is measured by the least costly of the alternatives avoided through owning the asset' (p. 76).

(3) As evidence of (1): 'This illustration underlines the fact that the realization principle really imples a venture approach to income measurement by a corporation; the acquisition of every asset is regarded as a separate venture, and no profit can be shown until the cash cycle has been completed for that asset, i.e., until realization has taken place' (p. 280). As evidence of (2): "Thus a moment's reflection enables us to see that the historical cost/realized revenue system implies a concept of income which ensures the maintenance intact of the original money capital invested in the enterprise' (p. 281).

(4) R. J. Chambers, 'Value to the Owner', Abacus, Vol. 7, No. 1, June, 1971, p. 65.

16 Comparative Analysis of Net Realizable Value and Replacement Costing

Norton M. Bedford and James C. McKeown

Recent proposals for financial accounting models based on net realizable value or current replacement cost have resulted in a conflict among financial accounting theorists.[1] This controversy has not been examined precisely yet such an analysis is needed to provide a basis for future discussion of this issue and development of a solution.

Basically, the issue is whether or not society is better served by the valuation of assets for public reporting at the cash they command upon sale (current exit value) or at the cash required to have them available for use by the firm (current entry value). It might appear that under pure and perfect competition, with equally well informed actors, the gap between the net realizable value and the replacement cost would be minimal and could be ignored. This is not the case due to the existence of frictions in the market place, such as commissions, transportation costs and the like. Frictions are not minor elements in our society. Even on the stock exchange, entry and exit values differ between a buyer and a seller by the total amount of commissions.[2] That is, the net receipts to a seller of stock differ from the cash payments made by the buyer. Because this gap exists in most markets and is frequently significant,[3] the conflict between net realizable value and current replacement cost as valuation bases should be investigated.

In order to provide perspective for this issue, it may be appropriate to set forth illustrative statements in support of each of the alternatives.

SUPPORT FOR NET REALIZABLE VALUE

The net realizable value of an asset is defined as the maximum net amount which can be realized from the disposal of that asset within a short period of time (not a forced sale situation, but not long enough to allow disposal of fixed assets through ordinary use of services). Net amount is defined as the selling price less disposition costs including tax effects discounted to the point of measurement.

From the point of view of an external user, the accountant, by measuring assets, serves two primary functions:

1. The presentation of the financial position of the entity.
2. The determination of nontransaction changes in the value of assets (for measuring net income).

In the case of financial position, the valuation of fixed assets at current cost of replacement seems to answer the question: "What would be the cost today of purchasing assets, having services equivalent to those now held and expected to be used, in the least costly form in the markets in which the entity normally trades?" On the other hand a valuation at current net realizable value tends to answer the question: "What generalized command over resources, in monetary terms, could be attained by selling one or more assets?"[4] In part the decision as to which valuation basis is preferred depends upon which question the statement user wants answered. If the questions refer to assets held by an individual with a variety of wants some of which can be satisfied through the expenditure of money, an answer to the second question would appear to be more relevant, since it would indicate the amount of money which could be made available immediately to aid in the satisfaction of wants. An answer to the first question normally would not be relevant in such a situation. While a corporation does not have human wants, it may be thought of as an extension of the stock-holders' interests and therefore having objectives representative of a variety of human wants. Thus one could contend that net realizable value would be more appropriate for a corporation because stock-holders would want to know the amount that could be realized by the corporation and distributed to them through sale of particular assets.

A stronger argument favoring net realizable value is based upon the frequent reference by statement users to a rate of return computation. The measurement of assets influences both elements of this computation since this measurement affects the denominator directly and the numerator through the depreciation charge. The amount to be included in the denominator would appear to be the amount for which the assets could be exchanged, not the cost of acquiring equivalent assets, because at any point in time the only externally visible alternatives open to management are to sell or not sell those assets which the corporation already owns. Net realizable value is the implicit current investment. The option of not buying these assets is no longer available. Since the option not to buy is not available, it is not meaningful to attempt to evaluate management by expecting them to earn a particular return on an investment they might now refuse. On the other hand it is reasonable to expect a certain return on net realizable value - the amount which management refuses to accept in exchange for the assets.

Net income, the numerator in the return on investment computation, should also, by the same line of reasoning, be computed using net realizable value measurements of assets. Depreciation would be the difference between beginning and ending net realizable values.[5] Corporation income would exist only if net income before depreciation exceeded the decline in the net realizable value of the fixed assets over the period. An income would indicate that management made a correct decision at the beginning of the period by holding the assets since the proceeds from the use of the assets were greater than their decline in value. Stated alternatively, if management were to sell the asset at the end of the period, the net amount realized from the sale plus the net revenue of the period would be greater than the proceeds fore-gone at the beginning of the period.[6] This concept of income results in a comparison of the net revenue of the period with the necessary decline in value of the fixed assets due to their use and retention during the period.

If depreciation is based on replacement cost (beginning current replacement cost minus ending current replacement cost), management is charged with refusing an option they did not have; that of taking the current replacement cost in exchange for the asset at the beginning of the period. This could result in a loss from a correct management decision to hold an asset, as the following example illustrates. Assume an asset with the following values:

	Time end of period	
	2	3
Current replacement cost	$1,300	$600
Net realizable value	1,050	500

If income before depreciation in period three is $650, income under net realizable value would be $100 ($650 - ($1,050 - $500)). The current replacement cost income would be a $50 loss ($650 - ($1,300 - $600)).. In such a situation, the corporation would be better off by holding the assets and selling at the end of period three, yet the income determined by current replacement cost would be a loss.

SUPPORT FOR CURRENT REPLACEMENT COST

The current replacement cost of an asset is defined as the cash or cash equivalent that would have to be paid now to acquire resources capable of providing services equivalent to those currently expected to be extracted from the asset.

The case for current replacement costing assumes that survival is a basic need of the entity. A report of income ought to be positive if, and only if, provision has been made for the survival of the firm as a going concern. Survival implies that the firm has the capacity to replace used services. This would require that expense be measured by the current replacement cost of those services. This means income is not necessarily the excess of one balance sheet over another since only part of the increase would qualify as income.[7]

As to balance sheet valuations for those user decisions which start with the assumption that the entity is a going concern, it appears that the correct valuation of the assets and equities would be in terms of the cost of getting the firm into its current state if the effort to do so were undertaken at the balance sheet date. This valuation basis would assure comparability among entities, one of the major demands of report users, and would reveal the type of resources which the entity expects to use in its future activities.

It is the future with which most users are concerned, and they would find any valuation which purports to reveal the cash market value of the entity assets at a particular point in time as a rather "iffy" valuation and of current interest only as a reflection of the firm's flexibility, which requires the valuation of the assets in their second or third best use. To most users for most decisions, the tradeoff between information on firm flexibility and firm intention for the future appears to give the advantage to replacement costing. Especially is this so when the costs involved in disposing of the asset through sale might be so great that a negative net realizable value could exist, as might be the case for fixed assets with high removal and disposition costs.

THE ANALYSIS

In order to synthesize the foregoing two points of view, an evaluation of the two positions is necessary. Although survival is stated to be a basic need of the entity, it would appear that the desirability of survival should be affected by the efficiency of its use of assets. If the entity cannot achieve a return, from the use of an asset, which is greater than the decline in net realizable value, both society and owners could be informed of this fact by means of reports prepared using measurements based on net realizable values of assets. The owners should be informed because they may wish to terminate the management or the entity.

Net realizable value is considered significant because it purports to reveal an alternative available to a firm in which the firm, as a periodic (year end) opportunistic calculator, ever seeks to exploit by selling the assets. However valid this might be in the minds of many profit seekers, it tends to misdirect the energies of management from production and the creation of values to the trading function alone. Such misdirection could well result in limited production and thus a lower standard of living.

Net realizable value is widely used in practice. Accounts receivable, for example, are valued at realizable value rather than the cost of replacing them. The lower of cost or market valuation of inventories frequently relies on net realizable value in computing market value. Even the estimation of salvage value in computing historical cost depreciation purports to be a realizable value. On the other hand, most of the literature discussions of fixed asset valuations tend to consider primarily replacement cost as the alternative to acquisition or historical cost. This is now challenged with the net realizable value proposal.

It may be observed that the arguments supporting net realizable value are pitched at a micro level while those supporting current replacement cost take a broader view. Perhaps a common ground for comparisons can be found by considering the decisions of replacement of an existing asset with another which will provide the services expected to be extracted from the existing asset. Although the asset replacement decision is not of direct concern to an individual outside shareholder, such a shareholder would want to receive information which would allow him to determine whether or not management has taken advantage of appropriate replacement opportunities. Thus the asset replacement decision may be used as a benchmark for evaluating the alternative valuation methods. While other benchmarks may be used, there is much to suggest that the asset acquisition or replacement decisions represents a rather basic test particularly since asset replacement considerations may be a continuous concern of managers and shareholders in a period of rapid change.

Assuming a company is using the services in its assets in their best or most valuable internal use, a decision to replace should be made if the current replacement cost of the services being used is less than the net realizable value of the asset held. This situation should occur, in perfect markets, only when the asset held can provide more than one service. If the asset provides only one type of service, replacement cost of the service will not be less than net realizable value since firms would immediately replace and sell until the values were realigned. There are at least two ways in which current replacement cost can be less than net realizable value for a multi-service asset:

1. A new asset which will provide the desired services more cheaply may become available.
2. One or more of the alternative services contained in the existing asset may become more valuable.[8]

To cope with either case management needs to be aware continually of both net realizable value and current replacement cost of each asset held. This conclusion would support preparation of reports using measurements based on both net realizable value and current replacement cost.

The micro argument for net realizable value was based in part on the principle of goal congruence in the construction of evaluation systems. One objective of such a system is that the actions which result in the highest or best evaluation are those actions most desired by the evaluators, the owners and society.

In the example cited to support net realizable value, an evaluation system based on current replacement cost would tend to cause the management to sell the asset at the beginning of the period rather than accept responsibility for the loss which would be reported. An evaluation based on net realizable value would tend to cause management to hold the asset at least to the end of the period. This would seem to be the action most beneficial to owners and society because the decision to sell at the end of the period should be based on an examination of projected returns and net realizable value in the next period. The discrepancy which might result under replacement cost, between the action which management might take and the action desired by owners and society, would be caused by the implication that management has the alternative of not purchasing the asset. Since this alternative does not exist for an asset already held, replacement costing should not be used because any evaluation system should imply only available alternatives. By use of net realizable value management can be motivated to make the most desirable choice among the alternatives currently available.

The preceding conclusion would apply only in periods after the first period of an asset's life because the alternative of not buying the asset is available to management at the time of initial purchase. Obviously, if an asset were purchased the returns should be greater than the decline in its current replacement cost. If the asset is valuable enough for later periods, it could be purchased for the replacement cost prevailing at the end of the first period, so the cost of the services used in the first period would be the difference between the beginning and ending current replacement costs. Here the principle of available alternatives indicates that the proper reporting basis would be current replacement cost.

The appropriate reporting basis, assuming dependable measures of each are available, seems to be current replacement cost for the first period and net realizable value for succeeding periods of an asset's life. This inconsistency raises an obvious question: What is the appropriate disposition of the difference between current replacement cost and net realizable value at the end of the first period?

Before presenting possible answers to this question, note that whatever choice or combination of the two methods is selected, the discrepancy between the replacement cost and net realizable value must be dealt with at some point in time.

1. If net realizable value is used exclusively, the discrepancy must be handled at the time of purchase since assets whose measurement equals the current replacement cost will be given up and the purchased asset will be measured at the net realizable value.
2. If current replacement cost is used exclusively, the discrepancy must be handled at the time of disposal of the asset since the assets received will be measured as equal to the net realizable value. This choice has the advantage that the discrepancy will probably be smallest at the time of disposal since the frictions in most markets are related to the value of the asset, which in most cases should be least at the time of disposal.
3. If any combination of these two methods is chosen, the discrepancy must be dealt with each time a change in method occurs. In particular, the combination suggested above would require that the discrepancy be recognized at the end of the first period.

There are at least two possible solutions to the question arising when the proposed combination of net realizable value and current replacement cost is suggested.

1. Allocate the discrepancy based on change in replacement cost, net realizable value or equal rate of return. This suggestion has many forms which in several ways remind one of the problems of allocating historical cost.

2. Ignore the discrepancy when evaluating performance in individual periods. Evaluate performance in each period by use of a report based on the measurement method which implies the available alternatives. The discrepancy will be handled when the project (life of the asset) is evaluated. At that time the returns generated by the assets will be compared to the net cost of the asset (current replacement cost at time of purchase minus net realizable value at time of disposal).

The preceding analysis was based on the assumption that income is a measure of "value" increase between two balance sheets. Such thinking is in line with the reemphasis being placed on the balance sheet in recent years. In determining income under the matching concept, or for any operational cause and effect disclosure endeavor, current replacement costs in the expense accounts tend to eliminate certain external fortituous events, such as an increase in frictions on the selling side of the market, from the operating income or success indicator measurement. Net realizable value tends to place greater weight on these external happenings.

On balance, it seems to the authors that advantages accrue to both net realizable value and current replacement cost valuations. It is our conclusion that the complexities of modern economic life require both calculations. We contend that attempts to find simple unequivocal answers to complex problems are bound to fail. Complex problems require complex solutions. Clearly the accounting profession must start presenting multiple valuations and make multiple disclosures in their annual public report. Simple income statements and balance sheets of the past were designed for a much simpler society. This analysis of the nontrivial valuation issue (net realizable value vs. current replacement cost) indicates that multiple and complex, but precise, annual reports are now required if the accounting profession is to comply with its ethical requirements to provide useful information.

FOOTNOTES

(1) For example, see R.R. Sterling, ed., Asset Valuation and Income Determination (Scholars Book Co., 1971).

(2) The effect on the seller's income tax liability normally would increase this difference.

(3) For evidence on the extent of the variation in one case, see James C. McKeown, "Comparative Application of Market and Cost Based Accounting Model" (unpublished paper).

(4) See James C. McKeown, "Additivity of Net Realizable Values" (unpublished paper).

(5) If a change in the general price level has occurred, an adjustment of the beginning amount would be appropriate.

(6) Although an interest adjustment to the beginning net realizable value would seem appropriate, current net realizable value models do not provide for it.

(7) The income would be equal to the increase in the owner's equity reduced by the implicit interest charge.

(8) Even though a perfect market exists, a particular firm may not be able or may not choose to alter its mode of operation to use the more valuable alternative services. The existence of a higher net realizable value would merely indicate that some firms are able and willing to make use of the more valuable services.

17 Continuously Contemporary Accounting

R. J. Chambers

The 'varieties' of accounting we have considered are all based on one or two reasonable or plausible grounds. Historical cost accounting is held to give an account of what has been done with the funds which became available to a firm or its managers. Price level adjusted accounting, it is claimed, takes account of the necessity, if money sums are to be added, of expressing all those sums in units of similar purchasing power. Replacement price accounting, it is claimed, takes account of current prices and of the desirability of calculating income by reference to the maintenance of capital in some sense. Present (or discounted) value accounting, it is said, is forward-looking and for that reason is closely related to decision-making.

These claims, as we said, are all plausible. But if we accept them all as plausible, then none of the varieties of accounting meets all the criteria. Historical cost accounting, for example, entails the addition of sums of money paid or received at different times when the purchasing power of the pound was not the same. Replacement price accounting does not give stewardship accounts in the same sense as historical cost accounting; neither does present value accounting. The reader may make other such contrasts.

It would be valuable to have a variety of accounting which is both backward-looking and forward-looking; which yields a basis for judgements of stewardship (and generally of past performance), and for judgements about future prospects; which avoids, or somehow copes with, the problems both of changing prices and changes in the purchasing power of money; which represents results and financial position in a way which is fair to all readers of financial statements. We claim that a variety of accounting which we have called continuously contemporary accounting meets all these requirements as far as they can be met.

FEATURES OF THE SYSTEM

Monetary Accounts

Over a very large range of accounting entries this system is no different from conventional accounting. All transactions of which at least one-half of the double entry relates to cash, amounts payable or amounts receivable, will be recorded initially in the same way. This covers all usual transactions between the firm as such and the outside world. All operations on cash accounts, debtors' accounts and creditors' accounts (long- or short-term) will be exactly the same as they are now. The propriety of this will be obvious, for in relation to outsiders the firm is bound to the monetary amounts, payable or receivable, for which it has contracted. Whether prices or price-levels subsequently go up or down, the money amount of a debt or claim is fixed in the ordinary course of events.

Inventories

For inventory or goods accounts the initial entries will be the prices paid. These entries will be the 'other' halves of entries in cash-book or creditors' accounts. Now, whenever the price of a good or service used by a firm rises or falls, its management must do its reckoning in terms of the new price. It must do so whether rises in selling prices, switches in factor inputs, changes in product composition or any other possibility is being considered. And it must do so because it cannot know how soon its competitors will respond to the same change in input prices which it has experienced. If a firm's management must do its reckoning in this way, its accounts should contain figures which are appropriate to this reckoning. To bring about this effect, the recorded unit price of any goods on hand will be changed whenever a change occurs in the purchase price. The value of the balance of the goods account will be increased if the unit price has risen; there will be a corresponding credit to a price variation account. Downwards movement in prices will give rise to similar but opposite kinds of entries.

The entries may be illustrated. Suppose the balance of a certain material in stock consists of 100 units at £1 each, and that the firm buys another 50 units at 22s each. The value of the 100 units in stock will be raised to 22s per unit. The balance of the materials account will be 150 units at 22s per unit. And the credit to the price variation account will be £10 (100 units at 2s each). Notice that all units of stock are then at the same price, an actual current price; and that this is more sensible than carrying the materials at two different prices when they are the same materials.

At the end of the year we want to know how the firm stands financially in relation to the rest of the community. How a firm stands is given by the equivalent in money of what it holds, that is, the selling prices of its assets separately. We must therefore find the selling prices of its stock of goods. For those goods which can be sold the firm already has a price list. Some may be unsaleable, particularly some work in progress; but for any goods for which a market price can be found, that price will be the present money equivalent per unit. A schedule of all goods on hand giving their resale prices in their present condition will be compiled. If the sum of these prices exceeds the total book value of the stock at current purchase prices (see previous paragraph) the excess will be credited to the price variation account, and the amount shown in the schedule at resale prices will be shown as the amount of the assets. If the book value exceeds the amount of the resale price schedule, the latter will still be shown as the amount of the assets. but the price variation account will be debited the difference.

A refinement of the process is possible. An account styled purchase price variation account may be used to carry the adjustments due to changes in purchase prices. The closing adjustment mentioned in the previous paragraph may be shown in a resale price valuation account. The refinement identifies the two kinds of adjustment. It may be useful, for the two adjustments arise from quite different kinds of cause.

Profit and Loss Account

During the year the goods account will have been credited with the current recorded cost of the goods sold; the profit and loss account will have been debited like amounts. The profit and loss account will have been credited the amounts charged to customers or the cash received from sales. The balances of the price variation account or accounts will also be brought into the profit and loss account. The balance of the account at this stage we will simply call 'increment'.

One other thing will have been happening during the year. The purchasing power of the pound will have been changing. We cannot take account of this from day to day, or even monthly. And as daily business is done in terms of prices as they are quoted, it is not necessary to take account of changes in purchasing power very often. But at the end of the year account should be taken of it. Otherwise we may suppose that the firm has become better off in terms of what can be bought generally, than in fact it has become.

We can make allowance for the change in purchasing power very easily, provided that the opening and closing prices used in valuing assets (other than monetary assets) are prices ruling at opening and closing dates. Suppose a general price index stood at 100 on January 1st (t_o) and 110 on December 31st (t_1). Every pound ($£_o$) represented in the balance sheet at January 1st is equal in purchasing power to 1.10 of the pounds used in the balance sheet at December 31st. Using the notation we introduced in the first article of this series (February 26th issue), $£_o1 = £_11.10$. The profit of a year is the amount be which the firm is better off at the end than it was at the beginning of the year. But we cannot discover this if the opening and closing amounts of the owners' equity are expressed in pounds of different purchasing power. Suppose we express the opening equity in pounds of the closing date; that is to say, we add, to the original number, 10 per cent of it in the present case. Deducting the amount of this 10 per cent from the balance of the profit and loss account (the increment) so far calculated, we will obtain the net income in $£_1$. And crediting the same amount to a capital maintenance adjustment, which will be part of the owners' equity accounts, we will have an amount for owners' equity, expressed in $£_1$, which is equal in purchasing power to the original owners' equity expressed in $£_o$. The balance of net income and all other balances in the balance sheet will be in $£_1$, and it is therefore quite proper to add, subtract or calculate ratios or percentages for any of them.

SYMBOLIC DEMONSTRATION

We may represent the system symbolically as follows:

Let $£_o$ and $£_1$ represent pounds of the purchasing power of the pound at the dates t_o and t_1 respectively, the opening and closing dates of an accounting period.

Let $£_oM_o$ and $£_1M_1$ represent the amounts of the net monetary assets of the firm at the two dates. Net monetary assets are cash balances and accounts receivable, net of accounts payable. M_o and M_1 are two different numbers in the usual case.

Let $£_oN_o$ and $£_1N_1$ represent the amounts of the non-monetary assets of the two dates. They are the sums of the resale prices of all assets other than monetary assets.

Let $£_oR_o$ and $£_1R_1$ be the amounts of the owners' or shareholders' equity in the net assets of the firm at the two dates.

Now, the balance sheets of the firm at the two dates may be shown thus:

at t_o, $£_oM_o+£_oN_o=£_oR_o$

at t_1, $£_1M_1+£_1N_1=£_1R_1$

The amounts on the left-hand sides of these equations are derived by actually checking the quantities of assets and liabilities, and using the resale prices of non-monetary assets. They are factual statements at the dates to which they relate. We want to find what the profit of the year is.

Let p be the proportionate change in the general level of prices during the year, expressed as a decimal fraction (such as .10, where the price index has risen by 10 per cent).

We may then write $£_o1 = £_1(1+p)$

At the end of the year the only pounds in circulation and the only pounds in which prices are then expressed are $£_1$. We can write the balance sheet at t_o in terms of $£_1$ by using the relationship $£_o1 = £_1(1 + p)$, thus,

at t_o $£_1M_o$ $(1+p)+£_1N_o(L+p)=£_1R_o(1+p)$

And as we have said above

at t_1 $£_1M_1+£_1N_1=£_1R_1$

These two equations are all in terms of $£_1$. We can therefore subtract the right-hand sides, at t_o from t_1, to obtain the net profit, thus:

Net profit $= £_1R_1-£_1R_o(1+p)$

$= £_1(R_1-R_o-R_op)$

And we can represent the owners' equity at t_1 thus:

Opening balance	R_o	i.e.
Capital maintenance adjustment	$R_o p$	$£_1 R_o(1+p)$
Profit of the year	$£_1(R_1-R_o-R_o p)$	
Total closing owners' equity	$£_1 R_1$	

Now what should happen if we accumulate entries of transactions in the books of account during a year, if we incorporate the price variations in the manner described earlier and if changes in the purchasing power of the £ are occurring slowly during the year? We cannot keep track of £s with a whole series of different purchasing powers. We keep the daily records only in terms of numbers of £s regardless of their purchasing power. We could keep the whole year's records in the same way as they are now kept, if we wished, provided only that the opening and closing balances were correct in terms both of quantities and the unit prices were then prevailing. But in this case the account balances would not be continuously consistent with current prices during the year. We mention the possibility, however, simply to show that if we know the kinds of figures we need at the year's end, and if we obtain them from observations independently of the book balances (correcting the book balances where necessary), no major change need be made in day-to-day book-keeping. The critical differences between this system and traditional accounting are the unit selling prices used at balance dates and the simple calculation of the capital maintenance adjustment.

DURABLES AND DEPRECIATION

We have spoken of 'goods' throughout, making no reference to durable goods such as plant which depreciates. In essence. depreciation is just another kind of price variation. If the resale price of a machine falls in a period through its use and obsolescence, the amount of the fall is the depreciation. It seems to some people that this is a curious idea of depreciation; especially to those who think depreciation occurs in some regular fashion such as may be represented by a straight line or a curve. But depreciation does not occur in regular fashion; the most obvious evidence is the frequency with which 'book' surpluses or deficits occur on the sale of plant, and the frequency with which assets survive long after the asset has been written off according to a 'regular' pattern. Some may object, on the other hand, on the ground that prices are not available for all assets in all conditions. But there are many more sources of information on second-hand prices than those people imagine. And if a good is not saleable, it has no present financial characteristic, even though it is expected to assist in the earning of future income.

There may be some difficulties in respect of some assets. But if the system meets many of the tests which an accounting system is required to meet, we do have a clear idea of the kinds of figures which it must yield. Accountants may then quite properly use their judgements in approximating resale prices from other price information. To attempt to do what yields a useful and usable result is far better than producing, by routine, figures which are nothing like what is useful and usable.

SOME OBJECTIONS ANSWERED

Some object to the system on the ground that, to use current resale prices in respect of durable assets, implies that it is intended to sell them. Of course it does not. A shareholder can look at the buyer's quotation for his shares day after day without any intention of selling them on a particular day. He simply wants to know how his investment stands. A car owner or home owner may do likewise for the same reason. If any of these persons concludes at some time that he will be better off by taking the price offered and doing something else with it, he will do so then. But watching one's position, like watching the financial position of a firm, is preparing oneself for what one might do when better opportunities arise. No other kind of information is equally serviceable for this purpose.

Others may object on the ground that the mere discovery of a resale price does not guarantee that that price will be obtained if the good is sold at the time. It is not the intention of the system to predict with a high degree of accuracy what would be obtained if any good were sold. The intended function of the balance sheet is to provide an indication of the current financial relationship of the firm with the rest of the world. Quoted prices, or the best approximations to them, are used because they are the prices which indicate the extent of the firm's claims against all other goods and services. Resale prices are not the opinions of the firm or its officers alone, as many figures in traditional balance sheets are admitted to be. They are prices or approximations to prices which others in the community are prepared to pay or are currently paying.

This quality of the system is particularly important as far as outsiders are concerned. If the management of a firm, or its accountant, reports in its financial statements what is thought, inside the firm, to be the values of its assets, there can be no assurance that the resulting statements of position and results fairly represent the firm's real situation. Insiders may be pessimistic or optimistic; in either case the reported figures may diverge materially from the judgements which outsiders would make of their components. Because traditional accounting is not firmly tied to currently quoted prices, there are many cases in which glowing impressions have been given of failing companies, and modest impressions have been given of companies which really control far greater asset values than those reported. This puts outsiders at the mercy of insiders, unless outsiders have the money, time, patience and ingenuity to find out the facts for themselves.

EXAMPLE

We may now give a slightly more complex example of the method used in Case 11 of the first article in this series (February 26th issue), for that case gave an example of continuously contemporary accounting. The full details of the positions and transactions of a firm are given in tabular form in the work sheet following. The key letters in the 'Transactions and events' column are given to aid the tracing of the double entries. It is assumed that in the year the index of changes in the general level of prices rose by 10 per cent. The cash, debtors and creditors balances and movements need no explanation; they are obtained in the same way as under present forms of accounting.

The goods, plant and land will have been valued at resale prices at January 1st, 19X1. The balances of goods, plant and land at December 31st, 19X1 will have been obtained in the same way, by evidence of possession and quantity and by the use of resale prices. The price variation adjustment for goods (C) will be the sum of adjustments made during the year, as goods held were repriced consequent upon price movements, and of adjustments at the end of the year for variations between book and actual quantities and repricing at resale prices. The cost of goods sold (F) is the adjusted cost at the time of sale; that is the original price paid plus any variations due to changes in the particular prices of the goods between purchase and selling dates. Running expenses (G) are net cash outlays for all annual costs of operation. The price variation adjustments for plant (H) and land (J) are obtained by inference from opening and closing values.

	At January 1st, 19XI.		Transactions and events		At December 31st, 19XI	
	Dr.	Cr.	Dr.	Cr.	Dr.	Cr.
Assets						
Cash	20		390D	230E	125	
				55G		
Debtors	40		400A	390D	50	
Goods	120		250B	260F	140	
			30C			
Plant	80			20H	60	
Land	40		10J		50	
Equities						
Creditors		50	230E	250B		70
Owners:						
paid in		150				150
capital maintenance adjustment		30		18K		48
undistributed profit		70		7L		77
profit of year				80M		80
Profit and Loss Account						
Sales				400A		
Cost of goods sold (adjusted to cost at time of sale)			260F			
Price variation adjustment:						
goods				30C		
plant (depreciation)			20H			
land..				10J		
Running expenses			55G			
Capital maintenance adjustment:						
on opening balance			18K			
on undistributed profit			7L			
Net profit			80M			
	£300	£300	£1,750	£1,750	£425	£425

The opening balance of the capital maintenance adjustment is the accumulated adjustment, for changes in the general level of prices (or the purchasing power of money), in respect of the amount paid in by owners some time previously. The sum (£180) of the amount paid in and the capital maintenance adjustment is the equivalent in purchasing power at January 1st, 19XI of the amounts previously paid in. The adjustment (K) of £18 during the year is to take account of the rise of 10 per cent in the general level of prices during 19XI, in respect of this opening balance of £180. There is a similar adjustment (L) in respect of the opening balance of undistributed profit. Both adjustments are necessary because the total amount of the opening net owners' equity (or net assets) is subject to the fall in the purchasing power of money in the year.

Although, in the formal demonstration, we identified the different £s by different subscripts, there is no need to complicate the accounts in this way. At the end of the year, as we have said, all the sums expressed in £s are in £s of the then prevailing purchasing power. No one can possibly interpret them at the time in any other way. And the devices we have used have the effect of representing tham all in £s of the same kind. A profit and loss account and balance sheet can easily be drawn up from the work sheet.

APPRAISAL

We will appraise the system by reference to the points mentioned at the beginning of this article and held to be the grounds for adopting one or other of the methods discussed in previous articles in this series.

First, the accounts contain the original entries of transactions exactly as they occurred. The final financial summaries do not contain the unmodified results of manipulating those entries; for the events of the year will have necessitated modification of many of them. But the accounting system does contain them, and they may be checked in their original form in the course of any audit of the accounts. Auditors are able to give assurance that no unauthorised or improper usage of the firm's funds has occurred, to give a warrant of good stewardship in that sense. Historical cost accounting is justified on all these grounds. The proposed system satisfies them.

Second, price level adjusted accounting is justified on the grounds that it avoids the addition of quantities of unlike £s, and that it takes into account the effects on income of changes in the purchasing power of money. The proposed system also satisfies both of these specifications. In the course of deriving the final figures there are additions and subtractions of different £s. But the overall corrections, the price variation adjustments and the capital maintenance adjustment, and the use of current prices at the close of the year, have the effect of making the final statements into statements in homogeneous pounds.

Third, price level adjusted accounting does not give final statements in terms of current prices; for original prices are merely corrected by an overall price index. The use of current prices is one of the advantages claimed for replacement price accounting. The system proposed also uses current prices - in making the price variation adjustments and in deriving the financial position at the year's end by reference to current prices. Though the proposed system uses different current prices (selling prices) from those of the replacement price proposal, it does use current prices.

Fourth, present (discounted) value accounting is said to be necessary for forward-looking estimation. But it presupposes that the reported present values are reliable. The system here proposed requires no such assumption, on the ground that no future estimates are free of the biases and guesswork of those who make them. The system goes as far as it is possible to go, by seeking to give the best indication that can be given of the actual state of a firm as it faces the future at each reporting date. It therefore meets the principle that the information be useful for forward-looking estimation, without committing readers of financial statements to the optimistic or pessimistic outlook, as the case may be, of managers or accountants of firms.

In meeting all these tests in its own special way, the system has other important practical consequences. One can proceed to analyse the financial statements of a firm at any date without committing the solecism of relating figures in unlike pounds. The figures in the balance sheet and the net income figure are all in £s of the closing date. If all firms used the same system, as they would if it were generally adopted,interfirm comparisons of ratios and relationships would be realistic and mathematically valid. They are not under present accounting. Interperiod comparisons of ratios would also be valid; for although successive financial statements are in different £s, the ratios of any particular year are pure numbers or percentages and are thus comparable with like numbers or percentages of other years. Above all, the figures would be readily interpretable because they are all in reasonably up-to-date purchasing power units, year by year.

CONCLUSION

We have sketched only briefly the reasons for, and the characteristics of, the system. These are developed more fully in the writer's "Accounting, Evaluation and Economic Behaviour" (Prentice Hall). But, in concluding this series, we may simply observe that continuously contemporary accounting meets most, if not all, of the requirements of users and the general tests of logic and mathematical propriety, whereas other proposals meet few of them. The number of criteria met by any system is a test used in appraising all kinds of product and device. On this ground, the system proposed has marked superiority over all others.

VI On Dutch Replacement Value Accounting

18 Theodore Limperg and his Theory of Values and Costs

Abram Mey

1. GENERAL SURVEY

(Biographical and historical background omitted).

Sketch of Limperg's System

Cost and value.

Under modern industrial conditions, cost is an entirely different concept from expenditure. Expenditures are outlays made for the acquisition of producers' goods. The concept is derived from cash-based accounting. Costs, on the other hand, are the sacrifices technically required and economically unavoidable in the production of a certain product. Sacrifices technically required are the minimum sacrifices under optimal conditions; sacrifices economically unavoidable include allowances, additional to factors entering the product, which are unavoidable under optimal conditions.

The required sacrifices can be measured in physical or conventional units - quantities of materials, man-hours of labour, machine hours. These quantities multiplied by their several current values or replacement-values give the aggregate value of the product. The unit values of all services embodied in a product are to include pro-rata parts of the costs of all ancillary services. Thus, the value of a man-hour necessarily spent will include necessary supplements for the costs of providing instruction, supervision, administration, amenities, as well as the wage or salary component itself. Materials and machine-hour costs would be similarly augmented. The whole organization requires to be analyzed so that costs per unit of service can be obtained which will be the basis of price, product and sales policies, and which will provide critical norms for judging the efficiency and accountability of middle and higher management.

The product costs calculated on the basis of these unit values are described by the Limpergean terms 'integral unit cost' and 'integral periodic cost', the former for materials and labour and the latter for plant capacity. The distinction is comparable with Keynes' components of prime-cost, namely factor costs (for materials and labour) and user costs (for the necessary usage of plant). Outlays made for unused labour and machine time and for lost or wasted materials have no value under such a scheme. The distinction between integral and full costs should be clearly understood. Integral costs only include the sacrifices that are technically required and, or, economically unavoidable. Integral unit cost measures the replacement value of a product to its producer.

Taking cognizance of technological change, changes in economic conditions, and changes in the flows of goods within an economy, Limperg was led to a double concept of value, replacement-value and proceeds-value or sales-value,[1] the lower of which is the critical measure of the significance of a good to its owner.

The Theory of Costs and Returns

This notion of value is applied to the analysis of costs and returns. We speak of returns, rather than of profits and losses, to avoid the supposition that governmental enterprises (postal, telephone and telegraph services, railways, and so on) may be exempt from the necessity of calculating in terms of contemporary values. The distinction between expenses and costs is as important in relation to the administration of social and governmental services as in private business enterprises.

The theory of value is applied to the analysis of the internal operations of business organizations. Taking account of all necessary sacrifices at each production centre, it is possible to obtain an analytic representation which is normative in character. If the actual sacrifices made are compared with the normative costs, the whole system assumes the character of a signalling system, indicating efficiency, inefficiency or excess capacity in production, marketing, administrative and other centres. Normative costing in this manner is indispensable as an aid in choosing between alternative actions of every kind, and for planning and budgeting. It is no less valuable to the auditor, if the auditor's function is conceived as satisfying himself that the affairs of an enterprise are properly represented and reported.

So that the necessary comparisons may be made, accounting must be based not on old-fashioned generally accepted rules but on contemporary values; in most cases, on replacement-values. Accounting will then be more than a mere instrument for controlling payments and receipts. Double-entry accounting in conjunction with normative costing will be the best-equipped instrument for calculations preparatory to policy-making for controlling the execution of policies and for assessing the results of policies adopted. This is how Limperg conceived its function.

Costs and the Theory of Finance

Business calculations are concerned not only with the internal efficiency of business organizations. They are concerned also with the financing of business activity; with the investment, borrowing and lending policies of the firm; with the relation between the costs of active and passive financing of assets acquired for longer and shorter periods. Limperg became aware of the relatioship between the internal characteristics of the firm and the circumstances of the markets in which it had to operate. His notion of financial policy was related to the idea of maintaining a financial position which would be continuously consistent with the changing exigencies of the firm as a permanent instrument in the productive apparatus of society. This forced him to consider the factors which influenced swings in business conditions, and the effects these may have on the financial policies of firms from time to time.

The Theory of Labour Conditions

Similarly, the continuity of production requires a continuous labour supply; and like the problems of finance this is in part a macro-economic problem. Among its facets are fluctuations in the demand for labour, overemployment and underemployment, and the worker's place and status in the industrial organization of society. Limperg proposed an economic theory of labour conditions, of employer-employee relations, of profit-sharing and co-partnership, of communication in industry: and this on the basis of his unitary conception of the interdependence of factors. As developments occurred in this field, I was able, when I succeeded him, to graft on to these fundamentals modern ideas of personnel management business psychology and industrial sociology. The integrating notion, of course, was the idea of costs as sacrifices, costs to the firm being the costs of reproducing and expanding the working capacity of society at large.

The Theory of Organization

Limperg found it necessary, as auditor, to visualize the role of administration and management in the organizations with which he was concerned; and, generalizing from this, to form a conception of the role of management in the social process of production as a whole. His conclusions emerged from his observations of the flows of goods and services in factories, where the foundation of his audit programmes were the physical processes and flows by which naturally differentiated goods were brought together to produce differentiated products. That this was simply the process, on a microscopic scale, of what was going on in the whole society, indicated that the same principles were at work, namely the specialization of functions and the division of labour in pursuit of economic advantage. The role of management is therefore subservient to these principles, and the pursuit of efficiency within the firm is explicable in terms of them. The relationship between this view and Limperg's suggestions for showing up inefficiencies and idlenesses through the accounting processes will be obvious.

Social Income and Production

His years of association with and observation of individual organizations brought under Limperg's notice the effects on firms of swings in the general level of business activity and the effects on these swings of the methods used in calculating the incomes of firms. The total production of a society in any interval consists of production for consumption, production for replacement of goods currently consumed in production, and production for expansion (or new investment out of savings). Specialization of firms and the individual pursuit of profits by firms gives rise to excess investments in producers' durable goods and stocks from time to time, disturbing the even flow of production. This disturbance is accentuated by calculating costs on the basis of the historical values of producers' goods (stocks and durables). As prices rise, the purchasing power of profits as traditionally calculated falls.

Firms resort to bank credit and other sources of finance to maintain production and to expand to take advantage of the rise in the level of business. And this credit is easily obtainable because reported profits are inflated by the amount of disinvestment ignored in forms of profit calculation which disregard changes in purchasing power. The consequence is stimulation of the tendency for prices to rise and for firms to over-invest. On the downswing similarly, the lag in recognizing falling prices delays the reporting of improved profits and tends to force recession to a deeper level than would occur if a more realistic form of accounting were adopted. Limperg's theory of replacement-value as a basis of income calculation avoids the error inherent in the traditional methods. (.....)

Traditional theory deals with the problems of cost and profit calculation as if initial purchase prices measure for all time the significance of the purchased goods to the user. But as purchases of raw materials may occur months in advance of their use and purchases of equipment may occur years in advance of use, and as prices are constantly subject to change, initial purchase prices cannot be said to express the magnitude of subsequent sacrifices or uses of those goods in production.

The financing of investments in producers' goods and the consumption of those goods in the course of production are just as different as are the production and selling of finished goods. The separation of these functions by the passage of time subjects the goods in question to changes in value. Consequently what is consumed at the point of production is not the amount of the expense originally incurred, but the amount of the value of the goods consumed at the time of production.

Consider a further point. That marginal cost is one of the criteria for choosing a production volume given the selling price seems to be incontestable. But the extent of its usefulness may be overstated. Some economists and accountants so define constant and variable costs that they reckon as direct costs per unit of output only the costs of material and labour, and treat all other costs as sums to be charged to the income account in total at the end of a period, commonly at the end of the year. Such a view overlooks the fact that a manager needs to know, day by day, the value of each of his products in its entirety and its specific composition. Only thus can he judge whether to accept at any time an order at a price below the integral cost, which is, to use the words of Keynes, the sum of factor costs and user costs. If he has to sell below integral cost he must be aware of the extent to which selling price falls short of integral cost, the extent of his loss per unit. He must be aware of this even though the proceeds of the additional output exceeds its specific costs, and the additional output therefore contributes to the profits, or to the reduction of the amount of losses, over a period.

Therefore, although marginalism is an appropriate principle for the selection of a course of action, it is not a general normative rule for management. Machlup, though in principle marginalist, concludes that, in normal times when things go on as they have done before, the average cost theory of choice seems to work well. But 'the marginalist theory gives good results in time of change'.[2] Machlup's remark is quite right in respect of change from the upswing to the downswing in business conditions, but not in the reverse case. Dependence on marginal costing may, in periods of expansion, lead to excessive optimism. As Keynes pointed out, in long-term planning account must be taken not only of full costs but also of risk factors. In any case average cost is not a measure of the value of a product; it is only a rough expression of accountability.

Patently, goods of the same kind, in the same place and in the hands of the same owner cannot have different values. But in fact in many enterprises the book value of a given item of stock is the sum of different values ascertained at different times. Again, in the balance sheet of any company may be found valuations of 50 years ago (in respect of land and buildings), 20, 10 and five years ago (in respect of plant and machinery), added to values of raw materials ascertained quite recently, as if standards of value were invariable in a dynamic world. The ordinary balance sheet does not correspond with what it purports to be, a statement of the economic position of an enterprise. It is nothing more than a statement of the remainders of items which have passed through the cash book over a number of years. The statement itself and the account balances which it comprises have nothing to do with the contemporary economic position of a firm from time to time, nor with rational management, nor with the efficient exploitation of economic services.

Social Value and Enterprise Value

Value may be defined as the importance which a good or service has in relation to its owner's welfare, whether the owner is a producer or a consumer. Value in this sense is a measure of the sacrifices made by a producer in selling his products or in using his assets in the course of production. The time of valuation, the location of the good and the then state of the owner's wealth are essential elements of value. At any moment of valuation, therefore, a contemporary measure of value is necessary; outlays made at the time of acquisition will not serve as measures of value, nor will any aggregations of such outlays or parts of them serve as measures of the values of goods produced.

According to a well-known theory, value is measured by marginal utility. Most of the economists of this persuasion (Marshall, Edgeworth, Walker, Bohm Bawerk, Wieser and others) affirm, without further explanation, that the value of a good, for which there is available in the market any substitute good, cannot exceed the market price at the time of valuation. Thus, for example, Wieser suggests that no housewife will judge the last slice of bread in the bin to be a life-saving treasure - as probably did the purser of Columbus' Santa Maria - because the baker at the street corner sells new bread every morning for a few pence. But this is a statement, not an explanation of the influence on an owner's judgment of the value of a good which can readily be replaced.

Limperg's theory of value provides such an explantion. The theory deals with value in social intercourse; Limperg and his followers described it as a social concept; others since have called it a macro-economic concept. The constancy of the wants of a society as a whole gives rise to continuity of the differentiated output of goods. The production processes of society proceed from raw materials and labour which are naturally differentiated. The production processes themselves are specialized; any one class of homogeneous factor services may enter many of the different branches of production, yielding different kinds of output. The whole complex of differentiated original factors, differentiated processes and differentiated products is tied together by markets. These flows within the community as a whole have counterparts in similar flows within each firm; indeed the flows of goods and services through the industrial apparatus of a society are simply the aggregates of the flows through individual firms.

If the consumer wants of the society are continually to be satisfied the supply of the original input factors must be maintained. All factors consumed - human labour, materials, durable producers' goods - must be reproduced. There is a continuous circulation of factors, products flowing to consumers so that their services may flow back into the process of creating the same or other products. There is, correspondingly, a circulation of the values of factors applied to production, through the finished goods to the point of consumption, and finally as new factor inputs.

There are some normal interruptions to this flow. Institutional factors, such as the nature of the working week, cause some bunching of outputs. Seasonal fluctuations in the supply of raw materials which are required throughout the year require that stocks be held. Techniques of production and the indivisibilities of producers' goods may necessitate the production of some products in discrete batches and the consequential carrying of stocks. The costs of these interruptions must be considered as costs of the product outputs because they are technically or economically inevitable. In a given state of economic organization they have significance for the satisfaction of wants.

However, there are also abnormal interruptions. Changes in technology and in consumers' wants will give rise to economic losses in the interval in which factors are being diverted from one product or process or industry to another. Similarly, cyclical swings in business activity will cause some products to have different values during the upswing than during the downswing, their economic utility, as it is contemporarily judged, rising and falling. Again, excess capacity arising from mistaken projections of growth in an industry or in trade generally cannot be considered as a constructive part of the production process. It is a source of loss, not of accretions to the value of any product. (.....)

The Problem of Costs and Costing

As we have said, in Limpergean theory only sacrifices which are necessarily made for the production of a good can be considered as costs. Cost calculation, therefore, begins with the technical data of production, from designs and specifications, time and motion study and so on. Unit cost of production is given by the formula:

$$(1) \quad C = Q \times V \times \left(1 + \frac{P}{100}\right)t$$

where C = cost per unit;
Q = quantity of factor inputs technically required and economically unavoidable;
V = replacement value per unit, at the time, of factor inputs;
p = contemporary rate of interest in the capital market;
t = time factor.

The unit value of factor inputs is the contemporary replacement value at the point of production. The unit value of materials thus includes the costs of purchasing, storage and stock control. The unit value of labour includes the costs of training, personnel administration, amenities and similar services. The value of a machine-hour includes costs of housing, maintenance and interest. These calculations imply a critical analysis of the organization and the discovery of the relationships between direct costs and their associated indirect costs. Such an analysis is, in any case, necessary for effective administration. Because the analysis is not based on cash outlays and does not include deviations from normative data, the results can be used over long periods.

On this basis it is possible to work out the cost of the work flowing through each department, and to build up a unit cost of each product by following the steps in production. It is also possible from the direct and indirect cost components to budget the required costs of a future period, given the expected volume of production.

As long as goods or services are produced in a regular and systematic flow, no good or service can have a higher value to its owner than the cost of replacement, whether by production or by purchase in the market. Replacement value is not, however, to be confused with replacement price. Replacement price is to be understood as the price of an actual purchase. Purchase for replacement is based on rather different considerations than the use of goods actually in hand, and the distribution through time of replacement activity is not the same as that of consumption through use.

The cost per unit obtained in the above way is the basis of price determination and of unit profit; and the required quantities of inputs and their values are the norms on which judgments will be made as to the efficiency of the production process.

Value of Products Produced at Less than Full Capacity

Keynes affirmed that the classical economic theory of value was tenable under conditions of full employment of all factors of production. The allegiance of accountants to the calculation of average total costs also is reasonable given full employment and the absence of wastes, provided we disregard the possibility of purchase prices being different from values at the time of use.

Limperg affirmed that the integral cost of a product, its economically and technically necessary cost, is the proper basis of price policy, under conditions of imperfect, as well as perfact, competition. But he did not consider unit cost as the only factor in the formation of price and sales policies. As a general rule the firm will sell at a price higher than the value of the good to the firm; this is a consequence of pursuing its normal economic objective. Limperg recognized that there were times when goods could not be sold at or above cost, though he treated these occasions as anomalous. However, under any conditions, he asserted, the producer must know the value of his product, so that he will know the outcome of any transaction, whether it yields a profit or a loss; and he must know this continuously, even when prices are determined in the market independently of his own volition.

Some remarks of Keynes may be recalled:

> In the modern theory of value it has been a usual practice to equate the short-period supply price to the marginal factor cost alone. It is obvious, however, that this is only legitimate if marginal user cost is zero or if the supply price is specially defined as to be net of marginal user cost .... Even if all production is carried on by a completely integrated firm it is still illegitimate to suppose that the marginal user cost is zero.

Keynes' prime cost is of course 'the sum of the factor cost and the user cost'.[3] He distinguishes user costs (costs of production voluntarily undertaken when the entrepreneur decides on his scale of operation) from supplementary costs (the expected depreciation and obsolescence not included in user cost).

On long-term costs (recall Limperg's basic assumption of the continuous flow of goods and services) Keynes observed:

> Long-period cost must obviously include an amount to cover the basic supplementary cost as well as the expected prime cost approximately averaged over the life of the equipment ... the long-period cost of the output is equal to the expected sum of the prime cost and the supplementary cost; and, furthermore, in order to yield a normal profit, the long-period supply price must exceed the long-period cost thus calculated by an amount determined by the current rate of interest on loans of comparable term and risk, reckoned as a percentage of the cost of the equipment.

The reader will observe the parallel between the views of Limperg and Keynes; clearly the theories of macro-economics and industrial economics can be integrated. But, by comparison with the accountant's traditional definition of costs as equal in amount to outlays, consideration of the special characteristics of supplementary cost is revolutionary.

Now, we live in a dynamic society, in which the regularity of the flow of production is interrupted by changes in techniques and tastes. While the flow is continuous, as we have said, the value of any good or service can never be higher than the sacrifice required to replace it at the time and place where it then is. But if the flow is interrupted, replacement-value can no longer express the significance of the good for its owner's welfare. Then the producer can only value his marketable goods at the amount of money they will command in the market, their proceeds value or sales value.

There exists, therefore, at the same time, two alternative and co-ordinated notions of value, a replacement-value and proceeds-value or sales-value, of which the lowest is the critical one, expressing the value of a good at a certain time and place. This formulation of the notion of value meets the requirements of every situation and circumstance in a dynamic economy.

Given this conclusion, any reference to a producer's valuation of goods he holds at a certain time must be understood not as an act of subjective valuation. The value is for all firms a datum at a given time. Neither the producer nor his accountant has to place a subjective value on stocks or other assets; he has only to look for the contemporary value in the replacement market.

The prospective buyer of a good, of course, will make some subjective judgment of the worthwhileness of buying and using. But this is not the value of the good as we have defined it; this judgment is concerned with the possible or probable revenue which may arise from possession and use of the good. Necessarily the replacement-value will be less than the present value of the expected proceeds if the firm decides to buy. (.....)

In Limperg's theory there is no uncertainty about the unit cost of outputs; neither in respect of quantities, which can be technically determined and converted to standards by making allowances for technically unavoidable variations; nor in respect of prices which have been held to be data. In respect of prices there are usually available current market quotations, price lists, offers from suppliers and so on.

In general, and on the average, if selling prices are based on replacement-values, there will be a sufficient inflow of cash to finance the replenishment of stocks. It may happen, of course, that fluctuations in prices are unequal, so that occasional cash shortages or cash surpluses occur and recourse to bank credit is necessary. But during a year in which stock levels vary from maximum to minimum it is probable that the cost of cash deficiencies may be compensated by the gains from re-investment of cash surpluses. (.....)

The use of proceeds-value and the alternative resale value in business calculations is not a matter of choice. It is the only form of calculation which is logical and consistent with economical administration. The traditional methods were satisfactory enough before the industrial revolution, when changes in market conditions and production techniques were slow, and the identification of outlays with costs of production could not lead to mistakes in cost and profit calculations. But since then conditions have changed and costing methods must change with them.

The Theory applied to Durable Producers' Goods

Durable goods are acquired for a certain expected lifetime. That lifetime is sometimes dependent on technical factors (wear and tear only), in which case capacity unused in certain periods can be used in later periods. In other cases the lifetime is dependent on obsolescence as a consequence of technological developments. In the latter case the economic lifetime of the good for the firm ends before its technical capacity is used up. It is therefore difficult to estimate the economic life in advance, but it might be supposed that rational managers try themselves or through technical specialists to follow the progress of technology in their fields.

Limperg considered the economic character of durable goods as a stock of work units. These units are measured in terms of hours of capacity. Given the work programme for a firm (say a 40-hour week, for 52 weeks, and excluding holidays, giving about 2,000 hours per annum per shift) we may calculate the tariff per machine per working hour. The calculation will include depreciation, cleaning, maintenance, replacement of parts, interest on the investment and power consumed. The time taken for each operation on each product may be determined by time studies. Time lost in unavoidable idleness must be considered as part of the value of each effective machine hour.

If we calculate and enter in the accounts an amount for 'sacrifices of available capacity', representing the available working time at full employment of capacity for a given work programme, and credit the account with the number of units actually used in production, the balance will show the loss through idle capacity by comparing the causally estwblished norm with the experienced reality, in the same way as when accounting for materials.

When, during its lifetime, the value of any durable good has fallen, we must recognize that, although previous calculations of the value of a work unit were then correct, there has been a loss on the work units used in previous years. That loss has nothing to do with the products of future periods. Its amount has to be deducted from the income account of the year in which the change in value occurs, or has to be deducted from existing reserves on the ground that profits of previous years have turned out to be less than was then calculated. (.....)

At the same time, it seems to be nonsense to assert that the 'costs' of machine usage vary inversely with the volume of production. Certainly modern methods of production entail producing for stock, for future markets, with imperfect foresight, and estimating future demand on the basis of present market analyses and imperfect knowledge of the future. But it cannot be said that imperfect foresight causes variations in costs of production. The costs of idle capacity due to errors of anticipation have to be taken separately from the costs of production to the profit and loss account.

Consequently, what have traditionally been called 'fixed expenses' have to be divided into two items, both of which vary with the volume of output:

(a) the cost incorporated in the value of the number of work-units necessary for actual output; and

(b) the loss incorporated in the value of the number of work-units 'lost' by reason of unfavourable business conditions or wrong projections of the level of output. (.....)

The Replacement-Value of Work-Units of Durables

The value of a producer's durable good is at any time the present discounted value of the replacement values of the work units available in each year of its remaining life. Thus,

$$Va = \frac{v_1 q_1}{(1 + i)} + \frac{v_2 q_2}{(1 + i)^2} + \ldots\ldots + \frac{v_n q_n}{(1 + i)^n} + \frac{R}{(1 + i)^n}$$

where

Va = the value of the good at point of acquisition or at any other time;
v = the value of a work unit in each of the remaining years of life. This value will change from time to time as the technology or structure of the industry changes;
q = the number of work units available in each of the remaining years of the good's life;
n = number of years of life remaining at the time of valuation;
R = scrap or resale-value if any after n years.

This formula represents a calculation of the same kind as a budget. It gives a hypothetical value, but it is the result of the best judgments and forecasts of the market personnel and is as objective as forecasts can be. Although it is undeniable that, logically, the real character of the value of a good at the moment of acquisition is a derivative of the probable future values of the work units, obtained in the above manner, the only way to bring these future values to quantitative presentation is by taking the replacement-value at any given time. Changes in technique of every kind will thus be brought into account as they occur.

It is necessary, therefore, to adjust the values which appear in the accounts at least every year at balancing date and more frequently if material changes in replacement-values occur. The balance sheets and accounts which result will be aggregations of comparable or similar values and all work units used in production will be changed on the basis of their contemporary replacement-values in the cost accounts.

The effect of this procedure on the accounting for durables is to make it consistent with observable movements in prices beyond the firm. It is known that in periods when prices tend to rise or fall, fluctuations in prices are much stronger in the durable producers' goods market than in the market for finished goods. But under traditional methods of accounting, just when producers' goods prices are falling (rising), the unit costs of using producers' goods rise (fall) under the influence of falling (rising) output. Our theory avoids this error, because as the prices of durable goods fall their replacement-values fall and the change in the level of output is reflected in the separate cost of idle capacity.

Accounting for Replacement-Value

We are accustomed to making entries in the accounts at the time of acquisition of goods and services at the prices then ruling. And we make entries at the times when goods are delivered to manufacturing and selling divisions. The only change necessary to give effect to replacement-value accounting is to make entries also at times when the values of goods on hand change. At the time of any such change, special entries would be made in the stock ledgers and corresponding general ledger account for the mathematicl product of the quantity in stock and the difference between old and new values. Producers' durable goods would be dealt with similarly.

In practice, these entries are made when changes in values are of sufficient importance, or at the end of each accounting period for all small changes which have occurred during the period. The amount of work may be minimized by using standard values (rounded replacement-values) instead of actual values. By comparison with the number of entries necessary in any day or week to record stock movements inwards and outwards, the number of entries necessary to record changes in values is inconsiderable. In any case the necessary calculations and entries are made usually by machines, speedily and at little cost. (.....)

Economic Unit Cost the Scientific Basis for Standard Costs and Variable Budgeting

The 'cost price' of a product is built up by a great number of 'C's' of the kind referred to in equation 1 above. It will be recalled that the quantities Q in respect of each C are the required quantities only, and the C's will therefore include the cost of materials per unit of output, the required costs of labour, and the required costs of machines in each of the required centres of responsibility of the firm. There will be as many C's as there are centres of responsibility successively required to produce the product, and as are necessary indirectly to facilitate production (finance, buying, selling departments, etc.).

The idea of costing by centres of production appeared in the American literature, notably the work of Hamilton Church, about 1907. In the Limpergean system the term 'centre of responsibility' is used, to indicate the quasi-independent functioning of the various departments of a firm. The costs incurred in every centre of responsibility are to be brought into account. Every such cost has a causal relation to the output. But in the Limpergean system this relation is made to run through one of the direct factors: e.g. the buying, storage and handling costs are applied through material costs, and so on, in the manner described in an earlier section. Such a causal relation may be established for the costs of top-management; it may be a third or fourth degree relation in some cases as top-management costs may be necessarily incurred for divisions intermediate between the top and operating divisions. (.....)

Consider also the problem of cost calculation as a basis for expansion. It is quite in order to base decisions on marginal costs when a firm's capacity is not fully employed. But it is dangerous to expand the capacity on the basis of the same cost information. The work-units embodied in any new durable goods must themselves be replaced when those goods are worn out. The cost to be compared with expected selling prices in this case is not the marginal cost, but the integral cost. Marginal costs may not be used for creating new conditions; they may be used only in the process of adapting the firm, with a given productive capacity, to external market conditions. The long-run policy of a firm must be directed to its continuity as a productive instrument, even though conditions may vary in the short run. The firm therefore, must endeavour to maintain, by replacement, its durable means of production.

As it seems to me, the normal procedure of any entrepreneur is to view each transaction, first as one incident in a sequence of incidents in the life of a business, and then, if there is sufficient reason, as a specific transaction peculiar to the firm's circumstances at the time. This is how, in Limpergean theory, Keynes' distinction between long period and short period costs may be understood.

Footnotes

1. 'Proceeds - value' is used to denote tht proceeds of sale other than sale in the ordinary course of business e.g. prices which, in recessions, are lower than replacement values, or sales made at different prices lower than prices in the ordinary course of business.

2. The Economics of Seller's Competitions, Baltimore, John Hopkins Press 1952, p. 75.

3. Keynes, The General Theory of Employment, Interest and Money, p. 53, 67.

19 The Practice of Current Value Accounting in the Netherlands

J. Klaasen

1. Introduction

The practice of current replacement value accounting in the Netherlands has a relatively long history. Especially since about 1950 a number of the bigger corporation has applied this system for financial reporting purposes. At that time there were no legal requirements concerning the valuation bases to be used in Annual Accounts, so corporations introducing this valuation method were free to do so. Before the introduction in published Annual Accounts, in academic circles current replacement value accounting had been developed and discussed for at least two decades. In the Netherlands Limperg was the pioneer who developed the large part of the underlying theoretical framework.

Since the early fifties some companies have very much contributed to the distribution of knowledge about this approach. But none the less, only a minority of the companies listed at the Amsterdam stock exchange applied current replacement value accounting, whereas the majority used the conventional basis for reporting based on historical cost. Unlike the situation in other countries, in the Netherlands the influence of Stock Exchange Authorities on financial reporting is negligible. The accounting profession did not issue any detailed prescriptions either. The main regulations are laid down in the New Civil Code. (This is an amalgamation of the Commercial Code and Civil Code.)

In 1971, the Act of Annual Accounts of Enterprises became effective. Since 1976 this Act is included in the New Civil Code.

The main elements of this Act include:

- Detailed prescriptions concerning the disclosure of certain items.
- Some general rules concerning valuation issues e.g.

  Section 2: The annual accounts provide such information that a sound judgement can be formed on the financial position and result of the enterprise and, to the extent to which annual accounts permit, on its solvency and liquidity.

  Section 5: The bases underlying the valuation of the assets and the liabilities and the determination of the result comply with standards that are regarded as being acceptable in economic and social life.

- A Chamber of the Amsterdam Court of Justice is given the task to supervise the financial reporting practices by judging on the basis of appeals of interested parties.

- All companies with limited liability (N.V. and B.V.) are subject to these rules, although only the bigger companies are obliged to give full disclosure in their published financial reports. The smaller companies are allowed to publish only a condensed version of their financial statements.

Since the Act does not specify strict valuation rules, but restricts itself to the general requirement of acceptability of the valuation based used, a Study group was formed, representing Employers, Employees and Registered Accountants. This Studygroup issues Accounting Recommendations concerning replacement value accounting: the Studygroup stated that both Historic Cost Accounting and Current Replacement Value Accounting are acceptable valuation bases. Although if results and/or equity capital are materially different (compared with the outcome on the basis which is not used) additional information should be given about these differences. The Studygroup is preparing prescriptions on the procedures that should be used to estimate current values.

Concerning the details of the application of Current Replacement Value Accounting, there are no strict rules. So it could be said that C.R.V.A. has been developed the way management and auditors considered to be the best. Of course, the replacement-value theory, as advocated by Limberg and others has clearly influenced the methods applied.

In order to make a comparison between theory and practice the author did some research on the application of C.R.V.A.

during 1973 and 1974. Since only a couple of firms included in this research have changed their valuation system, and since there is no indication that the other firms have changed their practice or their attitude, the information given in the following section which is based on that research, is largely still valid. From some recent surveys it might however be concluded that a few of the bigger Dutch firms have (after 1972) adopted some form of C.R.V.A. in addition to their conventional historical cost accounts.[1]

2. The Practice of Current Replacement Value Accounting (C.R.V.A.)[2]

Approximately 16% of the companies listed at the Amsterdam Stock Exchange valued their fixed assets at replacement value, in 1972, whereas only 5% used this method for the valuation of inventories (see tables I and II).

Table I

Valuation methods used for fixed assets (according to published financial statements)

Method	Number of Companies	Percentage
A. Historical cost	93	45%
B. Replacement value	34	16%
C. Balance Sheet: Historical cost		
Depreciation: Replacement value	11	5%
D. Various methods	71	34%
TOTAL	209	100%

Table II

Valuation methods used for inventories

Method	Number of Companies	Percentage
A. Replacement value	10	5%
B. Various methods	194	95%
	204	100%
No inventories	5	
	209	

On the bases of these data we requested 37 companies to discuss with them their method of valuation. 31 Companies were willing to be interviewed.

The two main topics of these interviews were:

- the reasons for the application of C.R.V.A.
- the applied techniques to estimate replacement values, and to determine profit.

2.1 Reasons for the Application of C.R.V.A

It should be pointed out that the interviewed officials generally gave only their personal opinions, although they were in most cases members of the Board of Directors or the company's internal auditors.

Table III

Motivation in favour of application of C.R.V.A.

Reason	IMPORTANT Number of companies	%	UNIMPORTANT Number of companies	%
A. Balance sheet valuation of physical assets	24	77%	7	23%
B. Accordance with product costing method	12	39%	19	61%
C. Effect on profit-Magnitude	19	61%	12	39%

As is shown in Table III twenty-four out of thirty-one of the interviewed companies considered the valuation of assets for balance sheet purposes to be an important argument in favor of the adoption or application of C.R.V.A. in their company. A few of these companies adopted this system at the moment of the introduction of the Dutch law on Financial statements in 1971. Eight companies indicated that the presentation of realistic asset values was the only reason to apply this system.

The large majority (22) of the companies interviewed, did not value the inventories at replacement value for balance sheet purposes (See Table IV) because they had only

Table IV

Parts of physical assets valued at replacement value on balance sheet.

Item	Replacement Value Number of companies	%	Other Valuation Basis Number of companies	%
Land	14	45%	17	55%
Buildings	29	94%	2	6%
Machinery	26	84%	5	16%
Inventories	9	29%	22	71%

minor stocks of inventories. Five mentioned that it was too difficult for them to determine replacement values. Most of these officials believed that their method of inventory-valuation was consistent with their opinion that the current value of assets should be shown, since turnover of their inventories was fairly quick. Three companies were not willing to disclose the current value of their inventories because they had large stock and experienced large price fluctuations. Therefore, large yearly capital adjustments would frustrate the calculation of meaningful rate of return on capital employed. Also, in their opinion, stockholders did not understand the reason for these fluctuations in the revaluation reserve account.

The desired relationship between product-costing and other features of the management information system on a C.R.V.A. basis and the application of C.R.V.A. for profit determination purposes was an important reason for twelve companies. These participants think that it is desirable to calculate product costs on a replacement cost basis, since management should know the profitability of products on this basis. Most of these companies had the opinion that the calculation of results for internal, as well as external, purposes should be the same.

Concerning Philips Company, Goudeket[3] wrote in this respect: "In accordance with the principles of 'accounting for management' the responsible managers of all levels must know periodically the income and the capital employed, both in total and in detail. For this purpose the replacement value is applied... For external purposes, the management renders an account of stewardship and supplies any other information on the operation and prospects of the enterprise which may be considered useful. This implies that the method of calculation of the income and capital must be the same for both purposes and that the reports for both purposes may vary as to the details of information and frequency of issuance. There is, therefore, no reason to make any further distinction between internal and external requirements."

All twelve companies stated, in addition to this reason, other reasons for their application of C.R.V.A. Most of the nineteen companies, which considered this argument to be important, nevertheless calculated their product costs at current prices.

Effects of C.R.V.A. on profits shown was an important reason for nineteen of the participating companies to apply the method of profit determination. Eight of these companies had the opinion, that only if they show relatively low profits, can they retain enough cash flow to finance the assets needed for the desired volume of the company's production. The officers of these companies feared dividend and wage claims if the shown profits were "too high."

Some other companies stated that their stockholders would not oppose C.R.V.A., as stockholders appreciate a prudent financial management, and would not object to the automatic retention of the cash flow which is needed for that purpose. This policy would, in their opinion, enhance the firm to maintain its level of employment.

Some companies stated that the firm, having an obligation to replace its assets, only gives correct information to the outside world if it calculates its profit on a replacement cost basis.

Six companies were afraid that the automatic revaluation of fixed assets as a consequence of price rises, might cause too much pressure on profits: because of this, four of them had limited the percentage of revaluation.

Although it is impossible to quantify the relative importance of the reasons stated, tentatively, the companies can be divided in two groups:

- Companies which consider the presentation of their physical assets on the balance sheet at current values to be the most important feature of C.R.V.A. These companies consider the calculation of profit as a consequence of their approach to balance sheet valuation.

- Companies which are primarily concerned with the profit determination on a C.R.V.A. basis; as a consequence of that (partly due to the influence of their public accountant) they present the physical assets in the balance sheet at current values. Many companies didn't value all their physical assets at current prices (see Table IV).

To get an impression of the motivation stated in the footnotes to the financial statements published in the year of adoption of the C.R.V.A. system, we investigate those statements.

Table V

Motivation for application of C.V.R.A. as stated in financial statements.

Motivation	Number of Companies	%
A. Information about asset values	10	34%
B. Information about asset values and return on capital employed	7	26%
C. Other	2	7%
D. No motivation stated	8	30%
	27	100%
Financial statements not available	4	
	31	

Table V shows that the companies emphasized the effects of this system on the book values of their assets, and paid little attention to the effects of C.R.V.A. on profits shown.

2.2 The Determination of Replacement Values

As shown in Table IV, many companies only valued part of their physical assets at replacement cost.

An important reason for some companies to make exceptions, was that, in their opinion, the value to the business of certain assets was lower than their current replacement cost.

Six companies valued certain groups of fixed assets at an approximated net realizable value, since they did not plan to replace these assets. In addition, seven companies stopped revaluation at some time because the company, or certain parts of it, incurred losses. They did not try to calculate an economic value of their assets.

Five companies did not value the assets or one or more foreign subsidiaries at current cost in the consolidated statements, mainly because these subsidiaries had an independant position and used their own accounting standards.

Seven companies valued their land at historical cost and eight used a fixed amount per m^2 land as a valuation basis. A reason given was that the value attached to land is not important for profit determination and they have no intention to sell the land. Others state that, since there is no obligation to replace the land, replacement value is not relevant.

The fourteen companies that periodically determine the replacement value of their land use various estimation methods. Most companies refer to the prices of land for industrial purposes. (In the Netherlands, the local government is the only seller of land in industrial areas). Some companies revalue their land with the same percentage they use for buildings.

The estimation of replacement values for buildings and machinery causes some problems, because of technolgical changes and the various sources for current prices. We separately investigated the sources from which the valuations were derived and the adjustments accounting for those technological changes.

Table VI shows the sources from which the valuations were derived. It is important to note that many companies (9) used reports of independent valuers, who estimate the value of fixed assets for fire insurance purposes once every two and a half years. Eight companies used their own estimates and, in general, they applied a percentage write up for all buildings and machinery. Decisions on these percentages were, in some cases, based on investigations of price rises for certain assets. Six companies derived the valuation of their machinery to a large extent from the information of suppliers.

Six companies had not revalued their fixed assets (or a large part of it) either because of losses or because they contended that their technological improvements made it unnecessary to raise the book value.

Table VI

Sources for determination of replacement values

Source	Buildings Number of companies	%	Machinery Number of companies	%
A. Index number	6	21%	3	12%
B. Appraisal for insurance purposes	9	31%	9	35%
C. Company's estimates	8	27%	4	15%
D. Information from suppliers	-	-	5	24%
E. No revaluation	6	21%	5	24%
	29	100%	26	100%

One company (a large steel factory) was going to return to historical cost accounting since the application of C.R.V.A. would cause a bad picture of its earnings, and, in its opinion, make it more difficult to borrow money on international capital markets.

The incorporation of technological changes in the estimation of replacment values for buildings and machinery is described in Table VII.

The need for an adjustment of price indices to account for technolgical changes depends upon the method of calculating these indices.

The Dutch Bureau of Statistics calculates no separate indices for business buildings, but only provides index numbers on the building cost of houses. The bureau incorporates technological changes and improvements of productivity only as far as these influence the building costs of houses of a certain type.

The bureau does not incorporate the changes in value which arise as a consequence of improved lay-out, etc. The price indices for machines are intended to measure the price rise (or fall) of groups of identical machines. If old machines are replaced by new types, the price rise is calculated by measurement of the prices of input factors, i.e. if a new machine has a larger capacity, but has the same price as an old machine, no price rise nor price fall is calculated.

It can be concluded that the price indices only take into account technological changes that affect the sales prices of machines. They do not take into account the advantages that companies can derive from the lower product costs resulting from a higher degree of automatization, better use of raw materials, longer useful life, higher capacity per hour, etc. The bureau does not publish detailed statistics on the price behavior of imported machinery and other equipment.

The appraisers estimating the value of buildings and machinery make their decisions assuming that the buildings, in case of fire, are to be rebuilt in their original state. They do not account for technological changes. The same policy is applied for machinery.

Since valuation takes place only once every two or three years, the estimates are relatively high. Another reason for high estimates is that, in cases of partial damage of the fixed asset by fire, the payment by the insurance companies should cover the (high) cost of parial renewal.

Because of these factors, it is safe to assume that the application of indices and valuations for insurance purposes without adjustment, results in high valuations.

Table VII

Approximation of influence of technolgical changes on replacement values

Method	Number of Companies all buildings and machinery		Number of Companies part of buildings and machinery
A. No deviations from external data	6		3*
B. Lower percentage of revaluation	8		1*
C. Individual estimates of required investment costs	4		3**
D. Estimation by means of cost comparisons	3		1**
	21	+	4 = 25***

* Mainly buildings

** Mainly machinery

*** Four companies are not included, since they did not revalue their fixed assets during a long period.

As indicated in Table VII, nine companies applied either valuations or index numbers without any adjustments for technological changes. Most of these companies stated that they experienced only slight technological changes.

A few stated that they did not make adjustments in order to prevent subjective valuations.

Eight companies adjusted external data by some percentage, or used their own estimates to account for technological improvements. Four companies estimated the current investment needed to replace their fixed assets at hand. (Three companies applied this method for machines only.)

Finally, three companies revalued their fixed assets (exclusive of land) on an individual basis, taking into account the product cost using the best assets available. The inferiority of assets at hand compensates the price increase which would have arisen if there were no technological changes.

Table VIII

Frequency of revaluation of fixed assets

Frequency		Number of Companies	%
Once per:	1 year	13	45%
	2 years	2	7%
	3 years	4	14%
	4 years or more	1	3%
	no fixed period	5	17%
	no revaluation	4	14%
	TOTAL	29	100%

Table VIII shows that approximately half of the interviewed companies revalue their fixed assets once a year. (All companies which use index numbers are among this group). The rest does not revalue the assets each year, especially companies using appraisals only do revalue their fixed assets once every two or three years. Companies which do not have a fixed term, revalue their assets only "if circumstances require it."

Concerning the presentation of inventories at current values, the companies interviewed stated that they could easily determine the current prices of inventories from recent invoices or market quotations.

Nonidentical replacement, in the sense of replacement by

machines used for the production of new products, or the introduction of new products by merchandising companies was not considered to be replacement at all. If companies closed old facilities they generally did not subtract any amount from the revaluation reserve account.

To get an impression of the magnitude of the yearly revaluations of fixed assets, we examined the published financial statements of the interviewed firms for the period 1967-1972. Only 15 companies (out of 29) provided sufficient information to calculate a yearly revaluation percentage. The results are shown in Table IX.

Table IX

Average revaluation per year as a percentage of book value (1968-1972)

Percentage	Number of Companies
2%	5
2-4%	4
4-6%	5
6-8%	1
TOTAL	15

They indicate the average percentage of yearly revaluation during the period varied between 0% and 8%. These revaluations have direct consequences for the magnitude of depreciation as compared to historical cost, although it cannot be concluded that firms with a higher percentage for revaluation show a higher depreciation (in relation to historical cost depreciation) since the average age of the fixed assets on hand might be different per company.

2.3 Profit Calculation

In all cases except one, the depreciation of the interviewed companies was based on the new replacement value of the fixed assets. The companies use straight line depreciation, and some even continue the depreciation if the book value of the assets is zero, because they underestimated the useful life of certain fixed assets. (In those cases the depreciation is credited to the Revaluation Reserve Account, or to an equalisation account from which amounts are deducted if the useful life of some assets proves to be less than estimated).

Only one company deducted back-log depreciation from profits. The other twenty-eight companies did not apply back-log depreciation, considering it unnecessary. Some companies stated that profits would be too low if back-log depreciation was adopted, others contended that, because of the diversity in useful lives of their assets, back-log depreciation was not needed. This causes the companies to only revalue the book value of their fixed assets on hand with the estimated percentage of price rises. The resulting write up is credited to a Revaluation Reserve Account published (in total) separately on the balance sheet.

The determination of costs of sales was based (for the companies presenting their inventories at replacement value) on the replacement values effective during the year.

Only one company used a concept of normal stock level to calculate the cost of sales, and the revaluation of inventories. This was mainly done to identify speculative positions on inventories. The other companies advanced the opinion that they did not speculate in inventories.

As stated earlier, some of the companies did not present their inventories on the balance sheet at their current replacement cost. However, ten of them calculated their profits, using a method very similar to C.R.V.A. with some applying the base stock methods and others calculating the price rise of inventories during a period separately and deducting this amount from their profits.

No companies took the financial structure into account when calculating profits. Thus, no part of the revaluation reserve was considered to be profit. Four companies, however, showed as additional information in their income statement (or in the footnotes) the profit on an historical cost basis.

We tried to calculate from the published statements the differences in depreciation between C.R.V.A. and historical cost accounting. The results are depicted in Table X; we also calculated the influence of these differences in depreciation on the profit after taxes (see Table XI)

The companies showing a higher replacement cost depreciation compared to historical cost depreciation, do not necessarily show much lower profit (after taxes) on a replacement cost basis compared to their historical cost based profit. The reason for this devergence is that the profit levels are different; the relation of depreciation with total cost is different; and companies use different methods to calculate their income tax. Some of them show the taxes they have to pay while others show the tax rate (48%) over the replacement cost based profit.

Table X

Difference between replacement - value depreciation and historical cost depreciation.

Percentage of Difference	Number of Companies
5%	1
5-10%	4
10-15%	1
15-20%	4
20-26%	4
Total	14

Table XI

Influence of C.R.V.A. system applied to fixed assets on profits after taxes (compared with profit determination on a historical cost basis)

Difference in Profit after Taxes as a Percentage of C.R.V.A. Profit	Number of Companies
5%	2
5-10%	4
10-15%	1
15-20%	1
20-25%	4
Total	12

3. Conclusion

From the preceeding it is clear that the motivation for the application of C.R.V.A. is quite pragmatic for most companies.

In the application of C.R.V.A. especially the determination of replacement values for fixed assets is a problem. Different methods are used to estimate these values, and the same applies for the approximation of the influence of technological changes on these values. Also the frequency of revaluation varied. Clearly this variety of approaches has influenced the magnitude of the revaluations. It is however impossible to measure these influences. Finally, this variety of approaches is a consequence of the attitude towards financial accounting in the Netherlands, in which strict rules are not considered as important as in other countries. Consequently reporting practices are flexible and ready to adapt to circumstances.

However, it is conceivable that part of the variety in practices is not justified by the circumstances.

FOOTNOTES

(1) Especially Unilever and AKZO recently introduced extensive additional information in their Annual Reports.

(2) The information in this section is based on research for the authors dissertation, published in Dutch in 1975. An extensive summary of this research was published by the Accounting Department of the Oklahoma State University, Stillwater U.S.A., Current Replacement Value Accounting in Western Europe, 1976.

(3) A. Goudeket, An Application of Replacement Value Theory, the Journal of Accountancy, July, 1960.

20 Reservations about Replacement Value Accounting in the Netherlands

R. Burgert

1. LIMPERG'S THEORY OF REPLACEMENT VALUE

When Limperg started lecturing as a professor at Amsterdam University in the 1920s, the breakthrough of the marginal utility school in economic theory was complete. Limperg had such serious objections to this theory, however, that he deemed it necessary to formulate a theory of value of his own. (.....) Limperg's own value theory is summarised below; it culminated in the following valuation-rule:

> The value of a commodity is its realizable value or its replacement value, but always the lower of the two. As to the realizable value, a distinction should be made with regard to factors of production between the direct and the indirect realizable value; of these two the higher is always relevant.

From the producer's point of view, the direct realizable value corresponds to the proceeds by immediate sale, whereas the indirect realizable value should be understood as the proceeds to be realized in the normal course of business. Although it is not clear whether Limperg thought of calculating the indirect realizable value as the present value of future proceeds less associated costs, other authors have indeed taken this view. The difficulty of the allocation of total proceeds and costs to individual means of production inherent in this concept, is after severe but in my opinion unsound criticism of the Austrian theory, eliminated by the thesis, that

> usually, the indirect realizable value of the combined means of production, governed by the sales price of their products is higher than their

> combined replacement costs. Usually, that is to say for the profit-showing company, the combined replacement costs assess a specific contribution to the proceeds and to the income; from this it follows logically that the value of each means of production is assessed as its cost of replacement.[1]

Because

> in practice the matter is in most cases decided upon in favour of the replacement value, the concept of replacement value becomes extremely important for the problem of production, for which the judgement of value plays a role: it plays therein a role which greatly exceeds the role attributed to it by the theory of marginal utility; this is not just for practical reasons but on the foundation of a consistent elaboration of the concept of utility that is the basis for the theory of marginal utility as well.[2]

It follows that, for the profit-showing company, the entire rule of evaluation given above is reduced to the simple maxim that value is governed by replacement cost. Limperg thus achieved his aim - 'to give the concept of cost as the basis for value the role it deserved'.

To amplify the above information about Limperg's theory of value I refer to an article in English, published in 1966 by the late Abram May, who had always energetically disseminated the Limperg ideas.[3] Here the reader can find two arguments for the central evaluation rule, one taken from the marginal utility school and one based on the doctrine of continuity of production in society as a whole.

The first argument is, that the economists belonging to the marginal utility school 'affirm, ... that the value of a good, for which there is available in the market any substitute good, cannot exceed the market price at the time of valuation'.[4] Though not in conformity with his need to fortify this affirmation as much as possible, he goes on to say that the marginal utility school gives this affirmation 'without further explanation'.[5] In doing so Mey implicitly claims that this explanation is offered by Limperg's theory. In part III, 1 below it will appear that this explanation is far from convincing.

The second argument states that to satisfy consumer wants in society continually, the supply of all input factors must be maintained or reproduced. This aim can be realized by using 'integral unit cost' as a basis for pricing. Integral unit cost is to be understood as the sum total of a number of multiplications of economically unavoidable quantities of input factors by their current replacement values. This reasoning ends with the conclusion:

> As long as goods or services are produced in a regular and systematic flow, no goods or service can have a higher value to its owner than the cost of replacement, whether by production or by purchases in the market.[6]

This conclusion comes to the same as Limperg's saying, quoted above, that usually ... the value of each means of production is assessed at its cost of replacement. As did Limperg himself, Mey considered realizable value only as an exception to the general rule:

> if the flow is interrupted, replacement value can no longer express the significance of the good for its owner's welfare. Then the producer can only value his marketable goods as the amount of money they will command in the market.[7]

The question may be asked: What valuation rule should be used for goods which are not so readily marketable?

So much for Limperg's theory of value. In Part III I shall give some critical remarks on it. Now I turn to his theory of income measurement which is based on the theory of value.

II. LIMPERG'S THEORY OF INCOME REPLACEMENT

The theory of value contains the foundations of the theory of income measurement for, 'there is, in principle, no difference ... between the problems of valuation and the problem of income measurement at the moment of sale and in composing annual financial statements'.[8] At both instants of time Limperg considers the theory of value of decisive importance. However, the annual financial statements give rise to an additional problem with regard to the meaning of the difference between replacement value and historic cost. In answering this problem the purpose of income calculation must be borne in mind; this purpose is formulated by Limperg in his concept of profit; the aim is the determination of consumable income for the suppliers of equity capital, that is, the increase in capital which can be consumed on the condition that the source of income is maintained intact.

The means to this end are quite simple in nature, although they require much work when put into practice in complex circumstances. Moreover, the proper ascertainment of replacement values is sometimes less easy than it looks at first sight. This is especially true with regard to fixed assets. The necessary accounting techniques for implementing this theory will not be dicussed in detail here, because they have already been explained by Goudeket with respect to a large enterprise, although not entirely in harmony with the theory.[9] The rules given in Limperg's theory are the following:

- there can never be a profit without a sale, so that the realization principle is consistently adhered to;
- the favourable difference between replacement value and historic cost cannot be profit, either for goods sold or for goods not yet sold;
- the favourable difference between historic cost and replacement value is always a loss.

The most frequently used application is broadly the revaluation of fixed assets and stocks of goods in the accounts after every material price change; the difference in value is credited or debited to a 'revaluation account' which belongs to the equity capital group. If the credit balance of this account becomes zero by debiting price falls, any further price falls leads to the entrance of corresponding losses in the income statement. In ideal circumstances the latter account would show only so-called 'transaction' profits or losses being the difference at the moment of sale between the sales price and cost on the basis of replacement value.[10] (....)

In order to bridge the gap between the theoretically ideal situation and reality, the theory has been extended by recourse to the concept of 'normal stock', that is, a stock of goods of such quantity that the company can be sure of being able to continue its production process without disturbance. Speculation occurs when real stock differs from normal stock.

The rule about the importance of price variations is now changed in such a way that only alterations in the value of normal stock are credited or debited to the 'revaluation account'. Price changes on a surplus or shortage or stock give rise to profits or losses from speculation, which are entered directly in the income statement.

In this respect, fixed assets create a special problem because of their indivisibility and their usability for a whole series of production processes. It is implicitly assumed that the normal stock of a certain fixed asset, e.g., machinery, consists of a number of entirely new machines. As soon as a machine has been used for a certain period, e.g., a year, then there is a shortage of normal stock. Assuming that for depreciation purposes, the economic lifetime is considered to be ten years, this shortage will amount to one-tenth of a whole machine, and so on. In periods of rising prices, such a shortage of normal stock leads to consequence comparable with a 'loss by speculation'. This loss is taken as such in the income statement under 'additional (make-up) depreciation'. (.......)

By applying these rules, Limperg states that consumable income, under the condition of maintaining the source of income intact, can be calculated 'unambiguously and with certitude'.[11] Before discussing the criticisms of this theory, I wish to draw attention to the considerable correspondence between Limperg's concept of income - indubitably an ex-post concept - and the economic concept of income aiming at the maintenance of economic capital as presented by writers such as Lindahl, Hicks and Palle Hansen. The latter consider that maintaining economic capital intact is only theoretically feasible as an ex-ante calculation on the supposition of perfect foresight. Once this assumption has to be discarded, as when making actual ex-post calculations of income, great difficulties arise. The concept of income then becomes, as Hicks says, 'rough approximation(s), used by the businessman to steer himself through the bewildering changes of situation which confront him'.[12] The measurement of income is such a difficult task that it hardly seems possible that consumable income can be calculated 'unambiguously and with certitude' by the techniques advocated by Limperg, with the source of income maintained intact.

III. THE CRITICISMS OF LIMPERG'S THEORY

In this section we shall review the criticisms brought forward in the Netherlands against Limperg's theory of value and income measurement based on replacement values.

1. The Theory of Value

> In this world therefore every plain and simple doctrine as to the relations between cost of production, demand and value is necessarily false: and the greater the appearance of lucidity which is given to it by skilful exposition, the more mischievous it is. (Alfred Marshall, Principles of Economics (8th printing, Book V. Ch. V, p. 306).

As we have stated previously, the theory of value is the foundation of the theory of income measurement: rejection of the former automatically implies rejection of the latter. In this respect, it is interesting that Limperg sees his theory as a 'normative theory' that is to say, that the theory not only offers a causal explanation of events in reality, but also gives a rule of conduct.

In all fairness to the critics, it must be noted that not until after Limperg's death was an authorised presentation of his thoughts made available in 1964.

In 1967 I tried to demonstrate the fundamental weakness of Limperg's valuation rule, the central question being, why the value of a good is governed by its replacement value or its realizable value, but always the lower of the two. In my opinion this rule is an apriorism for which no explanation is offered. This becomes clear from the way in which Limperg explains the relation between the two concepts: Replacement value and realizable value, on the one hand, and the concept of value in general, on the other hand.

So runs Limperg's argument,

> Immediately we can ascertain that it is impossible, that both quantitative presentations can express at the same time the value. If the figures of two measurements differ- and only for that case does the question have sense - then only one of them can express the importance of the object to be valued; it is logically impossible that the availability of an object for a person's wealth depends on two different amounts of money. Therefore the question remains, which of the two expresses that dependence.
>
> It is not difficult to find the answer to that question; it is easy to see that the value is governed by the lower of the two quantitative presentations.[13]

This apriorism is the ultimate theoretical basis of Limperg's rule of valuation.

In Part 1 above, I pointed out that Limperg rejected the then prevailing marginal utility theory of value; therefore he engaged himself in a hard fight with the Austrians. The reader cannot escape the impression that Limperg somehow was nostalgically longing for the times during which economists thought that value is governed by cost only. I have mentioned that he wanted to give the concept of cost, as the basis for value, the role it deserves. In my opinion, a value theory that does not thoroughly consider the possibility that there may be irreplaceable goods or that there may be goods which are more or less difficult to replace (e.g. because some time has to elapse before replacement is complete) and that those more or less irreplaceable goods can sometimes be used in different directions and may yield in each of them different (marginal) utilities, cannot be very helpful in making managerial decisions. Unless ... these decisions are no more difficult than making replacements all the time, in order to maintain continuity in the flow of goods and cost-factors in society as a whole. A striking point is the obviously great difficulty of reconciling the theory with the concept of opportunity cost, so important in managerial economics.

It would be incorrect to think that professional literature in the Netherlands always agreed with Limperg as to the value of production factors for a company. In 1924, Professor Polak of the Netherlands School of Economics offered a further elaboration of the ideas on production of Bohm-Bawerk and Marshall. His appreciation of replacement values is clear from the following. 'That nobody would valuate any commodity higher than the cost for which he can acquire or replace this commodity' is a 'seeming axiom that has already given rise to many misunderstandings in the theory of value'.[14] Polak derives the values of a commodity for the producer from the expected future proceeds and the costs to be incurred. He explains the possible coincidence between this value and replacement value as follows for goods and services capable of serving only one process of production: 'the value the company attaches to such goods in its possession can, statically considered, equal the replacement value'. However, the value, 'which such a commodity has for the company is derived from the future proceeds and the cost to be incurred in realizing them; only under certain rather rare conditions does this value equal the replacement value'. Under static conditions, the value of durable factors of production shows the same tendency to correspond to the replacement value. However, on the basis of Marshall's analysis, distinguishing between short and long periods and leading to the concept of 'quasi-rents', Polak concludes that for 'performances of durable factors of production the value to the company can differ considerably from the replacement value'.[15]

This opinion seems to be more in harmony with contemporary economic theory than with Limperg's reasoning, and proves that not everyone in the Netherlands can be considered to advocate replacement value theory.

The criticism leaves the impression that there may be one theoretical situation in which it may be true that value or utility equals replacement cost. That is a situation of complete equilibrium in which no entrepreneur sees opportunities for innovation and new production processes and in which no consumer is induced to correct or change his scale of preferences, including his preference for saving or consumption. That would be the condition of a stationary economy.

I shall now attempt to evaluate Limperg's theory of income measurement on its own merits without further reference to the theory of value. Dealing with the whole structure in this manner can be considered permissible since, as a reaction to my 1967 paper, an authoritive advocate of the replacement value theory, Professor van der Schroeff, drew the conclusion that it is better not to tie the theory of income measurement explicitly to the theory of value.[16]

2. The Theory of Income Measurement

In considering the criticisms of Limperg's theory, it is important to be well aware of its aim and the means advocated.

Aim: to calculate unambiguously and correctly the income that can be consumed under the condition of maintaining intact the source of income.

Means: rises in replacement value never constitute income; declines in replacement value always constitute a loss unless they can be debited to a revaluation account showing a credit balance.

a. Do rises in value of normal stocks never constitute income? This question must be answered in the negative. The disadvantage of the theory is that it does not consider what is going to happen on the sales market once the replacement value of one or more production factors has risen. The source of income would be maintained intact only if it could be taken for granted that the future total absolute margin of profit on total production would remain unchanged. In general economics, price theory explains without further ado that this situation will only occur improbably. If the absolute margin of profit increases, the rise in value can be considered wholly or partly as income; in order to arrive at the same income as before it is not essential to have the same production capacity available. Full replacement of present assets is not strictly necessary. If the absolute margin of profit decreases, withholding the rise in value of assets will not suffice to maintain the source of income intact. In that case, a greater production capacity, requiring more assets, is essential in order to reach this aim. The conclusion must be drawn that the advocated treatment of rises in value in most cases either falls short of what is necessary or overshoots its mark.

To put it in another way, the theory works well only in the case of a purely monetary rise in the general price level. Purely monetary price changes should be such that the proportion between all prices remains the same. In our dynamic and complicated society, however such equiproportionate price changes, even when triggered off by a monetary cause, do not occur. The theory itself does not distinguish between monetary price changes and specific real price changes. Presumably the theory is intended for the latter, but after the devaluation of the Dutch guilder in 1936 Limperg wrote: 'The circumstances whereby the guilder is the cause of the rise in replacement cost in itself does not change the reasoning.'[17] The field of application of the theory seems to have been extended in 1937, with the remarkable consequence that the effectiveness of calculation techniques has a better chance of succeeding in the new field than in the old.

If it is intended to keep the source of income intact, the theory on the economic concept of profit should be further explored, present quantities and prices being ineffective guides. It should be noted, however, that profit calculations would then become much more subjective.

Withholding increases in value from income could be defended by an entirely different argument, viz., that increases in value have to be financed without the acquisition of new capital, either loan or equity-capital. The theory should then refute the argument that financing by new capital is acceptable. It is difficult to see, however, that this argument is really unacceptable when it can be ascertained that the given allocation of production factors is still rational after the price rise. In such a case all costs, including the cost of the additional capital, will be recovered.

b. Do increases in value of normal stocks always constitute a loss? To prove this thesis, the theory should explain that replenishment of capital equal to the decrease in value of assets is an inevitable condition for keeping the source of income intact. However, it does not do so. This thesis can only be accepted if the aim of the theory is extended to include maintaining nominal capital. It should then be realised that the theory does not lead to the actual nominal capital being kept intact but the amount of capital that has been historically invested in the company. This becomes clear from the fact that decreases in value are to be debited to the revaluation account as long as this shows a positive balance. If actual nominal capital is to be maintained, every decrease in value should be immediately entered in the income statement.

c. Non-identical replacement. In our dynamic society non-identical replacements occur so frequently, especially in regard to fixed assets, that it is unacceptable to think only of more or less automatic pure replacement purchases which are known beforehand. In actual fact, management is continually confronted with the problem of selecting capital investment projects. Sometimes management buys a copy of an existing asset; more often, the purchase of an identical production factor will not be among the available alternatives. (.....)

This argument concerning the difficulties of non-identical replacement has been countered by the statement that the theory aims at an objective ex-post income calculation and that, as a consequence it should be restricted to the valuation of production factors that are actually in the possession of the company. No attention should be given to production factors by which the former could or should be replaced. It is admitted that it then becomes very doubtful whether the aim of maintaining the source of income will be realized under dynamic circumstances. According to this reasoning, any shortcomings should be allowed for in the income distribution phase. No solution, however, is offered to the problem of finding values for production factors which will no longer be replaced in kind.

The theory appears to be rather too optimistic about the replaceability of production factors; this can be traced back to the exposition of the replacement value theory, especially Limperg's remarks on the theory of Bohm-Bawerk.

d. The concept of normal stock. The role of this concept has been explained previously. As far as the qualitative aspect is concerned, its precise definition is linked with what has been stated under (c) above. We shall therefore now consider the quantitative aspect only. Assuming that we are certain that there will only be identical replacement: what should be the volume of normal stocks of goods? (.....)

In the beginning there was little concern about the problem of the volume of normal stock. Later, it was realized that management was unable to control all factors influencing the volume of real stock effectively; this resulted in the appearance of a greater or lesser amount of speculative profit or loss on the income statement without genuine speculation on the part of management. To mitigate this, the notion was put forward by other writers of distinguishing a zone within which stocks fluctuate without their surplus or shortage on normal stock giving rise to a speculative position. This development was in recognition of the fact that the crucial problem is not to find an acceptable figure for the volume of normal stock, but to assess whether and to what extent a shortage must be provided for in order to maintain the source of income. In dynamic circumstances this question can only be answered with regard to the future, by a managerial decision comparable with that needed in the case of non-identical replacement. Again, the objectivity of the income calculation is greatly endangered.

Another problem is: what should happen to previously retained increases in value in the revaluation account when the volume of normal stock is reduced? Limperg's theory does not answer this question. An opinion frequently voiced is that amounts that have once been added to the revaluation account can never return to income except, of course, in the case of decrease in value.

e. Addition of past depreciation. The procedure concerning additional past depreciation on the revaluation of performance of durable production factors used in the past has been dealt with earlier. The essential element is that a rise in the replacement value of fixed assets leads at the same time to a non-consumable increase in capital and also to a loss by way of a correction of past depreciation.

'Go to the margin and find the truth' is a maxim well known to economists. Assume that the value of a building increases considerably during its last year of service. The building has been financed to a great extent by a mortgage loan and the company is certain that such a loan will again be made for the acquisition of a new building. It is then difficult to understand why, in order to keep the source of income intact, we should be obliged to charge the income statement with an amount practically equal to the entire rise in replacement cost of the building. This procedure can only be defended by an aprioristic argument, viz., that the rise in value has to be financed with equity capital which in fact is acquired by retaining profit in the business. Whether financing by new capital or even by loan capital is feasible is not even considered.

f. Lack of interest in assets other than durable production factors and stocks of goods. It is not easy to understand how the source of income can be maintained by paying attention to non-monetary assets only. Rising prices, for instance, also affect monetary assets. It is quite logical, therefore, that the Philips concern has extended its application of replacement value by taking measures with respect to monetary items. The company calculates that part of equity capital that is invested in net monetary assets by comparing total monetary assets with total liabilities. If this comparison shows a debit balance, part of the equity capital is then considered to be invested in monetary assets. On the basis of an index number expressing the changes in the purchasing power of money, a charge in the income statement is made to make up for the corresponding loss of purchasing power. This is an interesting amplification of the theory. It should be noted that Philips does not strive to maintain the source of income. Its system may perhaps be best defined as aiming at maintaining the specific purchasing power of that part of equity capital that is invested in non-monetary assets and also the general purchasing power of that part of equity capital, if any, that is invested in monetary assets.

g. Special problems in times of price falls and recession. Taking for granted that the indirect realizable value of individual factors or production is unfit for practical objective calculation, an enormous new problem comes up. Then the evaluation rule is reduced practically to the rule that value equals the lower of replacement cost and direct realizable value, the latter being extremely low in many cases. The lower of the two being relevant, the number of cases in which the replacement value is decisive, will be reduced enormously. (.....)

The theory is confronted with an unexpected new situation under conditions currently described as "stagflation', the combination of recession and inflation. In traditional recessions, replacement values showed a tendency to fall; nut nowadays they continue to rise in a situation for many companies in which stocks increase, while turnover and contribution-margins decrease. Then the use of replacement values in income calculations puts a heavy burden on profit figures.

We thus have seven rather severe criticisms of Limperg's theory which, in our opinion, does not represent the last word on the problem of income measurement, even in the Netherlands.

IV. SUMMARY AND CONCLUSION

In this article, we have brought forward the more important critical observations made in the Netherlands against replacement value accounting according to Limperg's theory. The main points may be summarised as follows:

a. The theory shows inconsistency between ends and means. The valuation methods and accounting techniques together are unable to yield objectively the income that can be consumed without endangering the source of income.

b. It is an exaggeration to say that favourable increases in value can never constitute a profit, with the exception of 'speculative' stock positions.

c. Similarly, to say that unfavourable changes in value always constitute a loss is going too far, unless a second aim is introduced, viz., maintenance of nominal capital.

d. The problem of the inevitable time lags between purchases and sales has been solved by introducing the concept of normal stocks, but it is extremely difficult to assess their volume 'unambiguously and with certainty'.

e. This argument is more important for fixed assets than for stocks of goods. For the former it raises the question of 'additional depreciation', which is esentially a loss in times of rising prices on a shortage of normal stocks. Its necessity seems to be based on an aprioristic thesis in the field of finance.

f. The theory has never offered a solution to the problem of non-identical replacement. This, too, is more important for durable production factors than for stocks of goods. Moreover, in many situations, it is more difficult especially for the former to find replacement values than it seems at first sight.

g. There is serious doubt about the validity of Limperg's theory of value.

h. The theory wrongly disregards monetary assets; the Philips application provides a solution to this problem.

i. From the appendix (omitted - eds.) it appears that Dutch companies which really apply replacement values are in the minority.

It should be remembered, however, that the means advocated by the theory might in themselves be important if the aim of calculating the consumable income while keeping the source of income intact is done away with. In doing so, a bridge might be built between Limperg's ideas and those of recent American writers, such as Edwards and Bell, and Sprouse and Moonitz. Perhaps it would be worthwhile to consider whether any similarity exists between, on the one hand, Limperg's saying that 'normally, that is, for the profit showing company, values are governed by replacement costs' and his obvious preference for transaction profits and, on the other hand, Edwards and Bell's saying that 'current operating profit ... is essentially the long-run profit associated with the existing process of production carried on under existing conditions'.[17]

I am inclined to seek a solution for the problem of income measurement by way of 'different concepts of profit for different purposes'.

FOOTNOTES

(1) Limperg, Bedriffseconomie, p. 209.

(2) Limperg, Bedriffseconomie, p. 210.

(3) Abram Mey, 'Theodore Limperg and his Theory of Value and Costs', Abacus, Vol. 2. No. 1, Sept. 1966. (here reproduced as Reading No. 18 Eds.)

(4) Mey, 'Theodore Limperg ....', p. 10.

(5) Mey, 'Theodore Limperg ....', p. 10.

(6) Mey, 'Theodore Limperg ....', p. 12.

(7) Mey, 'Theodore Limperg ....', p. 14.

(8) Th. Limperg, Bedriffseconomie, Part VI, p. 291.

(9) A. Goudeket, 'An Application of Replacement Value Theory', Journal of Accountancy, July 1960. Since the present article was written, it has been announced that, beginning with financial year 1971, the method used by the Philips company has been changed, in respect of the treatment of tax liabilities on the revaluation account and the treatment of price increases for stocks which for technological reasons fall short of the increase of prices in general.

(10) We shall not enter here into the problem of accurate calculation of the total unit cost of all articles sold. This figure is indispensable for the concept of transaction profit.

(11) Limperg, Bedriffseconomie, Part VI, p. 282.

(12) J.R. Hicks, Value and Capital, 2nd printing 1946, p. 171.

(13) Limperg, Bedriffseconomie, Part I, pp. 179-80. Emphasis added.

(14) N.J. Polak, 'Waarderings-en balansproblemen' ('Problems of Valuation and Balancing'), Verspreide Geschriften, 1924, p. 206.

(15) Polak, 'Waarderings ... ', pp. 203 and 207 respectively.

(16) H.J. van der Schroeff, Kosten en Kostprijs (Cost and Cost Price), 7th printing 197 p. xvi.

(17) Limperg, 'De gevolgen van de depreciatie van de gulden voor de berekening van waarde en winst' ('The consequences of the Depreciation of the Guilder for the Calculation of Value and Profit'), Maanblad voor Accountancy en Bedriffshuishoudkunde, January, 1937.

21 Replacement Value Accounting

Geoffrey Holmes

One glance at the accounts of Philips (sales over £1,6000 million in 1970, 359,000 employees at the end of 1970) is sufficient to show that they are different. The most obvious differences are, perhaps, the least important ones:

To a British reader the balance sheet is the wrong way round, assets on the left, liabilities on the right.

The consolidated balance sheet, termed a 'consolidated statement of financial position' is undated, though the auditors' report makes it clear that the position is that at 31 December 1970.

The normal grouping of assets into fixed, current and intangible is largely missing, and there are other unfamiliar factors, such as the appearance (not as a note of contingent liability but as a negative asset) of 'discounted bills', for these are what is normally understood by the term 'advance payments by customers'.

Profit available for distribution appears as a separate heading; 'retained profit' in the balance-sheet includes the transfer from net-profit of the current year.

Important words

But these are minor differences. The vital difference of principle in Philips accounting, almost hidden from the uninitiated, lies in four words, two on each side: 'replacement value' and 'revaluation account'.

For, while Britain has until recently shown little enthusiasm for inflation accounting, Holland, and Philips in partic-

COMBINED STATEMENT OF FINANCIAL POSITION (COMPARATIVE FIGURES ARE OMITTED) (DUTCH FLORIN)

		1970
Property, plant & equipment		
Replacement value	10,203,991,000	
Accumulated depreciation	-4,689,821,000	5,514,170,000
Intangible assets		—
Investments in nonconsolidated subsidiaries & affiliates		2,026,551,000
Sundry noncurrent assets		380,262,000
Inventories		
Factory inventories	2,823,582,000	
Advance payments by customers	- 308,987,000	
	2,514,595,000	
Commercial inventories	2,792,460,000	5,307,055,000
Accounts receivable		
Trade receivables	4,706,527,000	
Discounted bills	- 396,292,000	
	4,310,235,000	
Other receivables	499,941,000	
Prepaid expenses	307,270,000	5,117,446,000
Liquid assets		
Marketable securities	83,320,000	
Cash	660,400,000	742,720,000
		19,088,204,000

COMBINED STATEMENT OF FINANCIAL POSITION (COMPARATIVE FIGURES ARE OMITTED) (DUTCH FLORIN)

	1970	
Stockholders' equity		
Common capital stock	1,213,608,000	
6% Cum. part. pref. capital stock		
Additional paid-in capital	669,075.000	
Retained earnings	3,032,720,000	
Revaluation surplus	1,408,172,000	6,323,575,000
Minority interests		748,649,000
Sundry provisions		
Long-term	1,446,328,000	
Short-term	353,767,000	1,800,095,000
Noncurrent liabilities		
Current debentures	780,064,000	
Other debentures	497,436,000	
Other noncurrent liabilities	2,600,226,000	3,877,726,000
Current liabilities		
Bank credits	2,309,665,000	
Accounts payable	2,595,813,000	
Income taxes	350,215,000	
Accrued expenses	840,323,000	6,096,016,000
Income available for distribution		242,143,000
		19,088,204,000

COMBINED STATEMENT OF RESULTS

	Dutch Florins 1970		Dutch Florins 1969	
Sales		15,070,068,000		13,023,135,000
Costs and expenses:				
Cost of sales	10,425,269,000		8,749,716,000	
Selling and general expenses	3,364,378,000	13,789,647,000	2,919,787,000	11,669,503,000
Income from operations		1,280,421,000		1,353,632,000
Other income and charges:				
Interest paid	507,010,000		338,098,000	
Interest received	99,909,000		76,958,000	
	407,101,000		261,140,000	
Miscellaneous	-17,326,000	389,775,000	38,555,000	299,695,000
Income before taxes		890,646,000		1,053,937,000
Income taxes		444,773,000		526,059,000
Income after taxes		445,873,000		527,878,000
Equity in net income of nonconsolidated companies		28,348,000		49,764,000
		474,221,000		577,642,000
Minority interests		39,160,000		59,184,000
Net income		435,061,000		518,458,000

ular, have developed an entire system of accounting based on replacement values - not merely in published final accounts, but for internal management accounts as well.

Under British or American Accounting; fixed assets appear in the balance sheet at historical cost, less provision for depreciation based on historical cost; current assets appear in the balance sheet at (historical) cost or net realisable, whichever is the lower (though some companies state current assets such as stock at 'replacement price' where this is lower than either cost or net realisable value). Cost of sales appears in the profit and loss account at historical cost (both goods consumption and depreciation). In contrast, Philips adopt replacement value both as a basis for valuation of assets and calculation of cost of sales in the profit and loss account.

Consolidated subsidiaries follow the same principles as are adopted by the parent company. As regards other investments, Philips recommend that the companies keep accounts along similar lines, but where these principles are not applied investments are included in Philips accounts as nearly as possible in accordance with their normal principles, on the basis of the information obtained from them.

Investments Valuation

As a consequence, the valuation of the investments in non-consolidated subsidiaries (loans and long-term debts receivable - totalling Dfl. 838 million - excluded) is based upon replacement value accounting.

In its most simple form, the replacement value theory comprises two elements: assets are valued at replacement value; transaction profits are calculated on the basis of replacement value of goods consumed.

The differences between historical value and replacement value at the moment of sale, alternatively at the next balance sheet date - are not regarded as profits (or losses) of the period, but instead, are directly transferred to revaluation surplus (a component of stockholders equity).

Replacement value theory was developed as far back as the 1930s as a brain-child of Th. Limperg, a Dutch professor of business economics, and has been improved, refined and extended in more recent years, partly as a result of its practical application.

Nowadays the theory provides a basis for determining the

value in exchange and the balance sheet value of goods, and for calculation of capital increments and of distributions to shareholders.

In addition to 'replacement value' the theory has regard to return value, based upon future proceeds: realisable value (the actual price of a commodity on the selling market); economic value (the present value of future proceeds).

In the case of a current asset, realisable value and economic value are normally the same. In the case of a fixed price which it will fetch on the second-hand or scrap market; and economic value the present value of the difference between future revenues from the asset and the direct costs connected with its operation.

An apparent difficulty arises in determining the economic value of a single asset which forms part of a group of complementary assets, all of which are needed to make the product. But this difficulty is more apparent than real, for if an asset is indispensable to the production of a particular product its economic value is assumed to be higher than replacement value so long as production yields a profit (with costs including depreciation taken on the basis on replacement value).

Normally, valuation is done at replacement value. However, the return value is relevant if it is lower than replacement value. In that case, the highest return value (either realisable or economic) is used to value the assets, on the basis that it will be used in such a way that it yields maximum profits or minimal losses.

An Example

For instance, in Table 1, a ship cost £1,000,000 in 1970. The vessel could be replaced for the amount stated in column 1. It could be sold in the second-hand market for the amount stated in dolumn 2, and is assumed to have the economic value shown in column 3. (i.e. the present value of the net revenues is stated).

The logic behind these valuations is that in case A and B we may expect the vessel to be replaced at the end of its effective life; whereas in C and D it is unlikely to be. In case C the company would maximise profits by retaining the vessel; in case D the proceeds from immediate sale exceed the net present value of the vessel's continued use, and it should apparently be sold.

There is, of course, considerable opposition to replacement value accounting. Many reject it in principle, some regard it as impractical in application. Philips has shown otherwise, although they do not pretend to have the final answer.

Table 1

All figures in £000

	1			2	3	
Case	Replacement Value	Depreciation	Net	Market Value	Economic Value	Balance Sheet Value
A	1,200	120	1,080	800	2,000	1,080
B	1,200	120	1,080	1,100	2,000	1,080
C	1,200	120	1,080	400	800	800
D	1,200	120	1,080	600	400	600

The Philips accounting system:

1. Its object is to provide the management of each section of the concern with the information it requires for operating that section, and to provide the top management of the company with the information required for its central management.

2. The accounting system is based on a system of budgets and standard costs.

3. It is decentralised: each section of the organisation has its own accounting department which produces each month a profit and loss account and balance sheet for that section, employing uniform, company-wide accounting principles.

4. Philips hold the view that changes of stockholders equity resulting from changes of the replacement value of assets are not 'income'.

5. Responsible managers of all levels must be told periodically the income and the capital employed, both in total and detail.

Replacement value theory is not merely a calculation technique used in preparing the annual accounts of the entire organisation: it is integrated into the accounting system of each section of the concern at every stage. All information for management is compiled in accordance with the principle, and replacement value automatically enters into all management thinking.

Replacement value is determined on the basis of the trend of specific price levels, not that of the general level of prices. That is to say, the trend of prices is followed for:

First, factory and building and dwelling houses, revaluation being on the basis of index numbers computed by Philips for each type of building.

Second, machinery, either on the basis of market prices, or, if the machinery is of a type made in the company's own factories, on the basis of current costs.

Normally, assets are handled in homogeneous groups, Only where an individual machine cannot be classified in this way is the revaluation effected item by item.

Details Available

A department of Philips (allied to purchasing) has the duty of following the trend of price levels, and the accounting department sees to it that individual items are recorded in such a way that information needed for revaluation purposes is readily available.

Insignificant price fluctuations are ignored. Normally, larger fluctuations are put through when they arise, because of their effect upon budgets and standards, at the end of the year.

The accounting system involves the use of accounts for:

1. Fixed assets at replacement value;

2. Accumulated depreciation of fixed assets at replacement value;

3. Revaluation surplus on fixed assets;

4. Cost of depreciation of fixed assets.

Accounts of types 1 and 2 appear in the balance sheet under the heading 'property, plant and equipment'. Revaluation surplus 3 forms part of 'stockholders' equity' and accounts of type 4 form part of the charge for depreciation appearing in the profit and loss account.

If an increase in replacement value occurs the appropriate fixed asset account is debited to bring it up to current replacement value, the necessary contra entry being made to revaluation surplus. Future depreciation is then based upon the life of the asset and this revised replacement value. Past depreciation will, of course, have been based upon the earlier (and lower) replacement value, and seems to this extent inadequate.

For example, a machine was acquired on 1 January 1962 for £10,000 and had a life expectancy of ten years. At the end of 1970 (i.e. after nine years) replacement value was still £10,000; meanwhile depreciation of £9,000 had been charged to production and appeared in the balance sheet as accumulated depreciation.

At this point the replacement value increased by 50 per cent to £15,000. Depreciation for 1971 (based upon replacement value) is thus £1,500; and the total charge for the ten years £10,500.

Strict application of the theory demands that backlog depreciation of £15,000-£10,500 (i.e. £4,500) be charged in 1971 to ensure that £15,000 is available for replacement after the tenth year.

Philips do not do this because 'due to the size of the concern the composition of the total fixed assets as far as lives are concerned approximates an average. As a result, yearly replacements for all practical purposes are equal to the yearly depreciation'.

This may be seen more clearly with the help of another example. A company has ten identical machines bought at yearly intervals at the beginning of years one to ten. At the end of year ten this type of machine costs £12,000 (it cost £5,000 in year one), so the charge for depreciation in year ten (based on replacement value) would be

$$\frac{£12,000}{10} \times 10 = £12,000 \text{ (ignoring any scrap value)}$$

exactly the sum required to replace the machine on 1 January, year 11.

Where fixed asset price levels decline, the reverse procedure is followed. But it must first be established that the decrease is the result of a changed price level, and not the result of technological improvement. Any decrease due to technological improvement must be charged to profit and loss account.

Normal changes in price levels are first charged to the fixed asset revaluation account of the section concerned, and when that has been completely exhausted, to profit and loss account.

Each country in the business stands on its own. However for practical reasons no revaluation surplus (reserve) in any country may ever show a debit balance.

Standard prices are in operation for all types of raw materials, components, work in progress and finished goods. They are revised periodically, at yearly or shorter intervals, depending upon the need for adjustment.

In view of the volume of work involved, the decision to adjust standard prices requires careful consideration, particularly bearing in mind the large degree of integration which exists at Philips. But this does not mean that fluctuations in price levels are ignored; adjustments are made on a group basis by means of index numbers, that are published once per month by the estimating department.

Recorded Value

In order to compute the replacement value of the company's own production (i.e. of work in progress and finished goods), the estimating department keeps records of labour and expense price levels; but once again index numbers are not calculated for each individual article but by appropriate groups on the basis of one or more prototypes.

To sum up, the estimating department keeps data on the following:

standard prices and index numbers of all purchased articles; standard prices and index numbers of products produced by Philips; standard prices and rates per man and per machine hour for each production unit.

Four basic types of account are kept:

1. inventory accounts;

2. adjustment accounts, to reflect changes in index numbers;

3. price difference accounts;

4. revaluation surplus on inventory

Inventory accounts 1 are kept at standard prices. Any

interim revaluation is debited to account 2 and the corresponding credit made to revaluation surplus 4. After revaluation, any inventory movement is priced at standard price times the index, the relative being posted to accounts 1 and 2.

Thus if the standard price of an item is 100p and stocks have been revalued on the basis of an index of 106, a purchase of 108 would be debited 100p to an account 1, i.e. inventory at standard prices; 6p to the adjustment account 2, to reflect a change in index numbers; and 2p to the price difference account 3. As goods are consumed, accounts 1 and 2 will be credited and production debited with standard price times index number (in this case 106p).

Each division preparing an individual profit and loss account and balance sheet keeps separate accounts for the index adjustments on raw materials, work in progress and finished goods.

Contra Entry

Whenever standard prices are changed the appropriate contra entry is made to revaluation surplus on inventory account; and the balance on the adjustment account to reflect changes in index numbers, account 2, is transferred to the debit of the revaluation surplus on inventories account. If there is a large difference between the two entries to account 4, an analysis is made to investigate the matter.

Decreases in price level are handled in the same way as was explained under fixed assets. When Philips revalue their own manufactured products, they give consideration to the fact that the trend in prices may also be affected by changes in technology. Continuous improvements in efficiency tend to have a retarding effect on the increase in price level.

Any decrease in standard prices which is due to a higher rate of efficiency in the company's own factories is therefore charged to income account, and not to revaluation surplus. Inventories are never revalued above the amount at which they can be sold at a profit.

In its external reports, Philips includes intangible assets at no value, so that no problems of revaluation occur. In internal accounts expenditure in connection with the starting up of products is recovered over a period on the basis of a precalculated volume of production. For practical reasons this asset is valued at historical cost.

Philips contend that there can only be profits if, after the application of replacement value theory, the purchasing power of stockholders' equity has been maintained. In summary form the Philips balance sheet can be looked upon as consisting of four items:

Balance sheet at the beginning of the period

Inventories, fixed and intangible assets, and investments	a	Stockholders' equity	c
Monetary assets (as previously defined	b	Liabilities	d
	x		x

We have already discussed the treatment of inventories, fixed and intangible assets. But part of the stockholders' equity is invested in other, monetary, assets, and the purchasing power of that part will diminish if the value of money decreased. For this reason, Philips calculate, on the basis of the cost of living index, how many currency units represent the same purchasing power as the part of capital which at the beginning of the period was invested in monetary assets.

Using the symbolism of the balance sheet above, this amount equals (b-d). The amount (b-d) has to be obtained for each country in which Philips holds monetary assets.

For Philips as a whole, the liabilities exceed the nominal assets as can be seen in the consolidated statement of financial position (in millions of Dutch guilders):

Debtors	5.117	Long-term liabilities	3.878
Liquid assets	0.742	Current liabilities	6.096

Local Statistics

So in principle there seems to be no problem, as on a concern-wide basis no equity is invested in monetary assets. However, the situation may differ from country to country, and, for local management, information about inflation is essential.

The appropriate balance (b-d) for each country is multiplied by the inflation factor based on the cost of living index for that country, and as a result cost of inflation (the profit and loss account item) is debited (assuming that the cost of living has risen) and the reserve for diminished purchasing power of capital invested in monetary assets (a balance sheet account) is credited.

The necessary information is available at short notice; the calculations and adjustments are made at such intervals as seem appropriate, bearing in mind the pace at which the currency of the country is decreasing in value - the faster this pace, the shorter the intervals will be.

Many of those who reject replacement value theory do so on the grounds that it is not acceptable for tax purposes. Certainly, in most countries the income calculated according to replacement value theory will differ from taxable income. In periods of rising prices the taxable income will be higher than the income on the basis of replacement value. Since the amount provided for taxation must at least equal the amount actually to be paid, the burden of taxation, if expressed as a percentage rate on the economic profit, will appear higher than would otherwise be the case.

Latent Liability

The tax authorities do not, of course, assess to taxation the revaluations credited to net worth; but to maintain consistency net worth must be free of tax liability. So when making the entry to give effect to revaluation, revaluation account is credited. But it is also necessary to take account of the latent taxation on the revaluation; revaluation surplus is debited with this as taxation, and it appears as a latent liability under the heading 'sundry provisions'. To the extent that revalued assets are charged off to the profit and loss account (and thus brought within the tax sphere), the latent liability is transferred to revaluation surplus.

To return to the question of whether tax considerations should influence one against replacement value accounting: it is not usual for major differences to exist between a company's taxable profits and those in its published financial statements. Philips believe that if replacement value theory is accepted intellectually, then it must be conceded that to use historical costs in the accounts merely because they are used for tax purposes is to disclose knowingly an incorrect picture of income and capital, and one which might well lead to wrong impressions and wrong decisions.

If it is thought appropriate, the variation in taxation resulting in a difference between economic and taxable profits can be shown separately in the annual financial statements.

Back your Judgement

Another reason why those like Philips who are intellectually convinced of the merits of replacement value theory should not employ tax principle in their accounts is that they want the tax authorities to accept replacement value theory; and one cannot expect these authorities to do so if those who pretend to believe in the theory follow principles for information of the public which they are intellectually convinced are wrong.

Philips' belief in the appropriateness of replacement value accounting is emphasised by their conscious acceptance, year after year, of a less favourable position in their annual accounts than would have been shown by other enterprises adhering to a traditional method. During a long period of increasing prices the profits shown by Philips have been less favourable than they would have been under a traditional method. Their net worth is larger, as a result of which the ratio of profit to net worth has appeared much less favourable.

It is cold comfort that the ratio shareholders' equity/ total liabilities gives a more favourable (and certainly in Philips' opinion, a better) picture than would have been the case if traditional accounting principles would have been applied.

The system is not, of course, without its problems.

Philips find that financial analysts, when dealing with their annual report, deduct the revaluation surplus from the assets, rather than leaving it as part of shareholders' funds. This is basically incorrect. A very large part of the revaluation has already been absorbed in the profit and loss account by way of depreciation of fixed assets, and in the raw materials, etc., consumed.

As a result, in any other company's figures much of what appears as the revaluation surplus would have appeared as 'earned surplus'.

Thus, in the annual report under 'Information for American shareholders' it is reported that if the method of historical cost had been applied in the past, the item Revaluation, as shown in the Consolidated Statement of Financial Position at 31 December 1970 would have appeared as follows:

	US Dollars ('000)
Addition to retained profit	249,086
Deduction from property, plant and equipment and stocks	139,912
	388,998

VII Case Studies in Current Cost Accounting

22 Accounting Innovation

C. A. Tritschler

The History of an Accounting Innovation[1]

With the issuance of Statement 3 of the Accounting Principles Board, Financial Statements Restated for General Price Level Changes[2] and the current inflationary trends in the U.S. economy, the attention of accountants is once again turned to the why, how and when of adjusting financial statements for price changes. Though field studies[3] support the informativeness of price change adjusted statements, the historical fact is that this added dimension in financial reporting has not gained general acceptance in the United States.[4] The most obvious source of empirical evidence about adjusted statements - large-scale implementation in various foreign nations, has not led to any consensus in their favour either. The prevailing interpretation of the French experience with revaluation is exemplified in this statement by the leading United States authority on French taxation, Martin Norr:

> For merely ordinary price increases - creeping inflation, if you will - France finds the problems of revaluation not worth the price; she joins Italy and Japan, to say nothing of the countries that used a one-time post-war revaluation, in eliminating the device ... no advanced country now uses revaluation, although many have tried it.[5]

This paper uses French tax data and an accounting model to derive effects of the first order on financial reporting and tax levies from the omission of price change adjustments. This paper aims to use the coexistence of the adjusted financial reporting and tax benefits (specified subsequently) to simplify the research objective. That is, the tax benefit makes adoption of the accounting procedures economically rational. This hypothesis is used here to interpret the French experience with adjusted statements. Thus, given some excess of tax benefit over compliance cost, a firm would rationally maximise real profit and adopt adjusted statements to minimise taxes.[6]

Our interest is then focused on those firms who rejected the tax benefit.

The Mixed Pattern of Adoption of Revaluation

Revaluation was both a tax and accounting measure so that some part of the firms' reaction can be traced from comprehensive statistics given on tax returns. In broad context, it should be understood that corporate and personal income taxes are a much smaller source of revenue to the French government than the value added tax. Analysis here is confined to adjustments of fixed assets, since data are available in more detail on them and their effects are the most important.[7]

The revaluation of fixed assets was permitted beginning in 1946, when the rate on taxable income of "companies" (corporations and limited liability companies) was only 24 percent. Since the revaluation was optional, a lag in adoption of the account innovation might be expected. By 1954 the tax rate had risen to 36 percent and firms had had the time to adapt to the required accounting and to allay any fears as to the continuing benefits of the tax relief. As a result, the year 1954 provides an estimate of the extent of enterprises' acceptance of revaluation on a voluntary basis. It is the first year for which detailed data are available to the author. By 1958 the tax rate had risen to 50 percent thereby increasing the tax relief incentive for revaluation and that year was the last one in which the adoption of revaluation was voluntary. Since a final revaluation was made compulsary as of June 30, 1959, for firms with sales in excess of 5 million new francs, the extent of revaluation can again be measured in 1960 and subsequent years under that regulation.

1. Pattern of Adoption by Measure of Number of Firms with Revalued Assets. The data available extracted from Statistiques et Etudes Financieres[8] shows 43,422 firms revaluing in 1952, a peak of 47,020 in 1955 under voluntary adoption, and a peak of 51,470 in 1964 under the limited company basis after several extensions of the deadline for compliance.

EXHIBIT 1.

Statistics for Enterprises Taxed on Accounting Income (Le Benefice Reel): Number of Enterprises with Partial or Full Revaluation of Fixed Assets.

Classification by Legal Basis	Fiscal Year Ended 1954			Fiscal Year Ended 1958			Fiscal Year Ended 1954		
	Enterprises Eligible	Enterprises Revalued	Percent Revalued	Enterprises Eligible	Enterprises Revalued	Percent Revalued	Enterprises Eligible	Enterprises Revalued	Percent Revalued
Nationalized and Joint Public-Private Corporations	50	35	70	115	77	67	85	65	76
Private Corporations	23,577	8,369	35	36,719	11,910	32	51,479	16,257	31
Limited Liability Companies	133,438	17,224	13	117,357	16,715	14	106,474	14,702	13
Other Societies	7,925	943	11	8,187	1,028	13	8,64	1,171	13
Total Companies	164,990	26,571	16	162,378	29,730	18	166,680	32,195	19
Partnerships and Proprietorships	299,620	18,830	6	250,008	16,888	8	231,728	16,398	7
Grand Total	464,610	45,401	9	412,386	46,618	11	398,408	48,493	12

EXHIBIT 2.

Classification by Size	Fiscal Year Ended 1954			Fiscal Year Ended 1960			Fiscal Year Ended 1965		
	Eligible	Revalued	Percent	Eligible	Revalued	Percent	Eligible	Revalued	Percent
Sales - At Least F10 Million	2,371	1,694	71	5,389	4,049	75	9,151	6,547	71
Sales - Less than F10 Million	462,239	43,707	9	393,019	44,544	11	405,037	44,923	11

Sources: Ministere de L'Economie et des Finances, Statistiques et Etudes Financieres, May 1957. March 1961, February 1963, October 1963, February 1967

Exhibit 1 tabulates data in relationship to the varying base of eligible firms as first available for 1954, then in 1958 largely before the compulsory regulation, and in 1960 when most of the compulsory revaluation took place but before the base has been affected severely by the exit of firms eligible and the entry of firms not eligible for revaluation.

Only 12 percent of the eligible firms had adopted a revaluation by 1960, and the increase from 9 percent in 1954 is largely due to the decline in the number of eligible firms. As classified by form of organisation, the government controlled firms - utilities, transportation, and heavy industry - show the highest percentage of revaluation, reaching 76 percent in 1960. Even some of these firms rejected the option, as explained below. The percentage adoption for private corporations was next highest and actually declined from 35 per-- cent revaluing to 31 percent from 1954 to 1960 due to limited liability companies being reorganised as corporations. But the absolute number of corporations revaluing almost doubled. The totals of all companies' data provide the least fluctuation in the base and show an increase from 16 per cent to 19 percent in those revaluing in contrast with an increase from 6 percent to 7 percent for partnerships and proprietorships from 1954 to 1960. All of the data are based on exhaustive census and no estimation is involved.

The forms of organisation employed by large firms have higher percentages of firms adopting revaluation. For certain years data are available with classification into "large" firms (those with sales at least F 10 million) and "small" firms. The data in exhibit 2 establishes the fact that the large firms did revalue in a far greater proportion (75 percent in 1960) than did small firms (11 percent in the same year). These two populations are described subject only to error in the tabulation of the tax data. Statistical measures of the association between size of a firm's assets and adoption of revaluation cannot be inferred form only the two size classes nor is a caused relationship intended to be established, since other variables can be involved. The pattern of adoption is further delineated by another measure of the relation of size of firm to the decision on revaluation.

2. <u>Pattern of Adoption by Monetary Measure of Assets Revalued and Unrevalued</u>. The year 1960 is the first in which data of the value in Francs of fixed assets revalued and not revalued are available (see exhibit 3). Since the assets (net) are valued by different bases, the proportion of assets revalued is difficult to estimate. In 1960 net fixed assets of F 123,911 million were held by firms which adopted the revaluation

EXHIBIT 3.

Monetary Value of Fixed Assets of Enterprise on Historical Cost and on Revalued Bases for Eligible Assets, Fiscal Year Ended 1960 (Millions of Francs)

Classification		Net Fixed Assets of Enterprise: On Historical Cost Basis Only	Net Fixed Assets of Enterprise: On Revalued Basis As Eligible	Profit (Loss) Before Tax
Companies				
Profitable	F	24,734	98,301	12,270
Unprofitable		17,518	23,357	(2,239)
Total	F	42,252	121,658	10,031
Revaluation Writeup as of June Thirty, Nineteen Hundred-Fifty-Nine			53,266	
Partnerships and Proprietorships				
Profitable	F	7,294	1,980	4,950
Unprofitable		649	273	(240)
Total	F	7,943	2,253	4,710
Grand Total	F	50,195	123,911	14,741
All Profitable Enterprises	F	32,028	100,281	17,220

Source: Ministere de L'Economie et des Finances, Statistiques et Etudes Financiere;, February 1963

bases for eligible assets and F50,195 million by firms which rejected revaluation and remained on historical cost.

Data to adjust the historical cost of fixed assets to comparable values are not published, but even after allowing for a revaluation increase, the net fixed assets of firms employing some revaluation substantially exceeds those of firms wholly on historical cost. Again no criterion to determine what proportion of revaluation, in terms of assets, constitutes an adequate level of acceptance is available to us. The literal economic impact of revaluation on tax levies and firms' cash flow, however, is primarily a function of a measure of assets revalued rather than the number of firms.

Published tax data provides some indication of the effects on "companies" (equivalent to the U.S. corporate sector) arising from the revaluation. A 3 percent tax imposed on companies' revaluation reserves due to the increase of fixed assets, cumulative to June 30, 1959, and levied through 1966, is the only available source of data to estimate the magnitude of the revaluation adjustments. The tax amounted to F 1,598 million and thus places the reserve itself at 53,266 million.[9] Not all of the increases of net fixed assets as of June 30, 1959, corresponding to this reserve, would be reported in 1960 and shown in exhibit 3. By subtracting the cumulative increase a estimated historical cost F 68,392 million for the revalued basis class remains. The cumulative increase is 78 percent of this estimated historical cost, which included acquisitions after June 30, 1959.

A rough but conservative estimate of the equivalent increase on the books at June 30, 1959, for the firms not adopting revaluation might be 60 percent of the historical cost. This would place the net historical cost basis class of fixed assets adjusted to a revalued basis at F 80,000 million or approximately 40 percent of all fixed assets distributed among the 88 percent of the eligible firms (all forms of organisation) rejecting revaluation. While the estimates of the revaluation increase foregone may be criticised as crude, the materiality of the amount of fixed assets not revalued surely cannot be denied. More important to defining the motivations behind this pattern of adoption and rejection are two variables, the individual profitability and the management objectives of the eligible firms. A lack of taxable income eliminates or reduces the tax relief incentive. Absence of the profit maximisation objective, that is, an explicit profit satisfying objective, alters the firm's decision-making process.

3. <u>Effect of Profitability and Private Ownership on the Response to Revaluation.</u> Quite apart from whether private

firms in general attempt profit-maximisation or not, the firms controlled by the French government (nationalised or joint public-private operations in exhibit 1) are operated as an extension of government planning and many have the primary objective of providing essential services and products for economic growth. The government is in a position to impose its policies on accounting methods or allow exceptions for more complex motives of its own by administrative decision. In fact, the government itself allowed the rejection of revaluation for twenty of eighty-five corporations, which remained on historical cost. Most important of these is the French railroad system which operates at a loss and whose fixed assets constitute most of those government-owned assets remaining on historical cost.[10] The decision of such government firms should not be considered as part of the test of private firms' response to the accounting compliance with requirements for tax relief.

Firms owned entirely or partially by the government include nearly all of the electric power and gas utilities, the railroads, the airlines, the coal mines, the tobacco and petroleum industries, as well as a variety of other companies. To be sure, their taxable income is reduced by increased depreciation if fixed assets are revalued, but the coincidence of the private enterprises being the profitable ones is an historical fact in this time and place. Thus, the investment in fixed assets of government firms should be eliminated and considered separately in this analysis.

If the test of accounting compliance is measured in terms of revalued net fixed assets and restricted to private firms, after a conservative write-up of 60 percent applied to the fixed assets of private firms on an historical cost basis, the proportion of fixed assets held by the firms rejecting revaluation rises still further to F 70,000 million compared to approximately F 75,000 held by firms adopting revaluation.

The assumption of profit-maximisation would predict that the private firms on historical cost would have little taxable income and thus little potential tax relief. No data on revaluation strictly for profitable private firms exist. However, exhibit 3 reveals that firms holding F 32,028 million of net fixed assets at historical cost did have taxable income and can be inferred to be predominantly private firms. Thus, approximately 70 percent of the net fixed assets on historical cost are held by profitable private firms who reject current tax relief. These profitable private firms rejecting revaluation held net fixed assets estimated at F 51,245 million on a revalued basis for comparison, 41 percent of privately owned net fixed assets, which represents the most relevant, though admittedly crude measure of resistance to revaluation. Since depreciation can be deferred and deducted from taxable income under French law, all firms might potentially benefit from revaluation, but the rejection of current tax relief by profitable private firms provides a conservative estimate of the firms who judged the cost of accounting compliance to exceed the benefits of tax relief from revaluation. The materiality of these benefits is estimated next.

4. The Magnitude of Tax Relief Due to Revaluation. A corporate income tax rate of 50 percent prevailed during the last years that revaluation was possible and has continued since. This depreciation tax shield is offset by the 3 percent levy on the revaluation increase, when first placed on the books. The income tax rate for partnerships and proprietorships varies with the individual owner's tax status, but would be substantially lower than the corporate rate, the rate for "companies". Estimates of the tax shield foregone could be based on assumptions, which, though arbitrary, are justifiable within certain limits. Theoretically, a tax relief from F 10 to 15 billion applicable to profitable, private firms on historical cost appears reasonable. A crude gauge of the materiality of the tax shield is that the companies' income tax averaged F 5 billion per year from 1959 to 1963, after tax relief for those firms revaluing fixed assets. No provision for timing effects can be provided.

Though the reported profit is also reduced by the same amount and the tax benefit and compliance cost must be spread over the remaining life of the assets, the real net benefit to the companies is so substantial that some characteristics of the accounting prerequisite and/or the manner of implementation of the tax relief can explain this apparently "irrational" failure to minimise taxes. The hypothesis that the adoption or rejection of an accounting innovation is based simply on a criterion of profit maximisation is itself rejected.

What then is the source of such reaction against an accounting compliance that these tax rewards should be rejected? Apparently, revaluation was perceived as a burden, not a benefit by an overwhelming majority of the profitable firms controlling approximately 40 percent of the fixed assets in the private sector of the economy. Certainly, the lack of accounting assistance could not have been the only binding constraint on revaluation for fifteen years under the pressure of an active demand from businessmen.

Comparison with U.S. Tax Data on Adoption of Accelerated Depreciation and Lifo.

The importance of behavioural factors in changing established accounting practices can be more generally documented with evidence from other countries. U.S. tax records provide an insight into the adoption patterns of business firms in response to the accelerated depreciation and LIFO inventory options. Again the tax advantages available from an accelerated amortisation of asset cost is foregone for a substantial proportion of firms and assets, especially among medium to small-sized firms.

1. Pattern of Adoption of Accelerated Depreciation by Measure of Number of Firms. An analysis by Ture [11] of depreciation patterns used on tax returns surmised that a minimum of 86 percent of corporations rejected accelerated depreciation in 1954, the first year available. By 1960 the minimum percentage rejecting accelerated depreciation had declined to 70 percent. His calculations assume no firms use both sum-of-the-year's-digits and double-declining-balance methods, so that this minimum figure reflects an understatement of the percentage rejection of accelerated depreciation. With opposite effect, the calculations do not eliminate the firms without taxable income so that the figure reflects an overstatement of the percentage rejection of tax relief in this regard.

Ture's estimate of 70 percent of U.S. corporations rejecting accelerated depreciation compares with 81 percent of French companies rejecting revaluation in 1960 (exhibit 1). Using U.S. data available on number of returns classified by depreciation pattern and eight classes of total asset size, Ture found the Kendall coefficient of rank correlation to be - 1.0 with a standard error of 0.0 between the estimated minimum percentage of returns using only straight-line depreciation and the size of total assets for all industrial divisions. Predictably, U.S. data lend support to the pattern of rejection of accounting innovation being inversely correlated with size of the firm.

2. Pattern of Adoption of Accelerated Depreciation by Monetary Measure of Eligible Assets. For the year 1959 the Internal Revenue Service in 1965 conducted a detailed analysis of depreciation practices on corporate tax returns.[12] Exhibit 4 presents a summary of the adoption of the accelerated depreciation method by monetary measure of eligible gross depreciable assets classified by the asset size of firms. In the sixth year that the tax relief was available, "small" firms, those holding 67 percent of eligible assets owned by firms in that class, "medium" sized firms, those holding 55 percent, and "large" firms, those holding 43 percent, rejected depreciation for tax purposes. In total, firms holding over $48 billion or 47 percent of eligible assets rejected accelerated depreciation.

Exhibit 4. Corporations Claiming Depreciation for Tax Year 1959. Depreciable Assets Purchased from 1954 through 1959, by Industrial Division and Depreciation Method (Property Cost, Depreciation, and Asset Life, for Small, Medium, and Large Size Corporations)

Size of Total Corporation Assets and Depreciation Method	Amount (Thousand dollars) (1)	Percent (2)	Amount (Thousand dollars) (3)	Percent (4)	Depreciation accumulated prior to 1959 (Thousand dollars) (5)	Average asset life (Years) (6)
			All industrial divisions			
Total Assets Under $1,000,000						
All methods, Total	13,395,290	100.0	1,219,881	100.0	2,185,077	17.9
Depreciation methods based on years of						
life, Total	13,392,093	99.9	1,219,554	99.9	2,183,636	17.9
Straight line	9,007,570	67.2	779,428	63.9	1,450.847	17.2
Declining balance	3,627,003	27.1	358,718	29.4	553,420	19.3
Sum of the years-digits	743,276	5.5	80,103	6.6	178,046	19.5
Other life methods	14,244	0.1	1,305	0.1	1,323	17.2
Units of production and other nonlife methods	3,197		327		1,441	

Total Assets $1,000,000 Under $25,000,000						
All methods, Total	4,783,058	100.0	336,110	100.0	701,717	23.1
Depreciation methods based on years of						
life, Total	4,782,774	99.9	336,027	99.9	701,717	23.1
Straight line	2,642,074	55.2	169,776	50.0	385,486	22.0
Declining Balance	1,740,006	36.4	133,206	39.6	237,486	24.2
Sum of the years-digits	393,228	8.2	32,560	9.7	78,066	25.6
Other life methods	7,466	0.2	485	0.1	679	20.7
Units of production and other nonlife methods	284		83			
Total assets $25,000,000 or more						
All methods, Total	84,630,169	100.0	5,834,310	100.0	14,455,073	22.5
Depreciation methods based on years of						
life, Total	83,388,208	98.5	5,743,334	98.4	14,079,961	22.5
Straight line	34,006,310	40.2	1,833,028	31.4	5,224,490	22.2
Declining balance	26,875,843	31.8	1,996,268	34.2	4,626,469	22.2
Sum of the years-digits	20,979,641	24.8	1,839,635	31.5	3,974,950	22.7
Other life methods	1,526,414	1.3	74,403	1.3	254,022	21.6
Units of production and other nonlife methods	1,241,961	1.5	90,976	1.6	375,112	

Source: U.S. Treasury, Internal Revenue Service, Supplementary Depreciation Data from Corporation Tax Returns, 1959, Washington: Internal Revenue Service, 1965.

Though the form of accounting compliance, the degree of tax relief, and the data available are not strictly comparable to that from France, the same general pattern of response appears, where a substantial minority of assets are held by firms rejecting accounting compliance. While small and medium firms dominate this rejecting group in terms of numbers, large firms dominate it in terms of the monetary value of eligible assets. Approximately $36 billion or 75 percent of the eligible assets not on accelerated depreciation are held by "large" firms with total assets of $25 billion or more. The data from the United States does not provide the breakdown of the decision on depreciation pattern as between profitable and unprofitable firms as in the French data.

In comparison with revaluation, accelerated depreciation requires no initital utilisation of prior-period accounting records, less discontinuity and complexity in implementation, and no requirement that it be used for financial purposes with attendant reduction of reported earnings. Nonetheless, a parallel pattern of rejection of the tax shield by a majority of individual firms and for a sizable minority of the eligible assets is apparent. Unfortunately, conclusions are somewhat tentative due to lack of data of what proportion of firms using only straight-line depreciation also lack taxable income and thus forego no tax relief.

3. <u>Pattern of Adoption of LIFO by Number of Firms and Monetary Measure of Inventories</u>. The extensive rejection of the LIFO option by U.S. corporations is documented in a special survey of tax data.[13] In the year ending June 30, 1964, only 1.1 percent of manufacturing firms reporting an inventory valuation method utilized LIFO in full or part and only 0.43 percent of wholesale and retail firms did. Here too, larger firms more readily adopted this accounting innovation since 26 percent of total manufacturing inventory valuation and 5 percent of total merchandising inventory valuation is held by firms which use LIFO to some degree. The only industries where more than half the inventory valuation is held by firms using LIFO to some degree are petroleum (82 percent), primary metals (63 percent), and tobacco (60 percent). All of these industries carry large inventories of basic materials quantifiable in physical units for ease of LIFO computations, are characterized by economic concentration in a few large firms, and have historically been heavily involved with specialized tax provisions of one kind or another. Other data does not fulfill theoretical expectations so neatly.

Even within those industries (Standard Enterprise Classification of Major Groups) to which LIFO is more easily applied, the vast majority of firms do not utilize it. In petroleum, 97 percent of the individual firms do not use it all; in primary metals, 95 percent do not; in tobacco, 94 percent do not. LIFO is an accounting procedure taught religiously in accounting curricula, yet the accounting compliance requirements have limited its adoption to a mere 1,295 manufacturing and 1,129 merchandising firms as of 1964. Curiously enough, the number of firms adopting LIFO by industrial group range upward from nine in tobacco so that adoption of LIFO is widely dispersed and has been implemented to some degree in all manufacturing industries at the major group level of the Standard Enterprise Classification of the Bureau of the Budget. The potential extension of LIFO to a wide range of firms by way of the dollar value method is apparently rejected and the penetration of adoption is meager within all industries, whatever their operating characteristics.

Whatever the limitations of LIFO in a normative sense, this analysis initially assumes the tax benefit of LIFO foregone as a trade-off against its deficiencies in measurement, against its companion effect of reducing reported earnings, and its difficulties of implementation. Like the revaluation procedure in France, the LIFO cost flow assumption for inventory valuation, which is generally considered a tax relief measure in periods of rising prices, must be used for financial reporting if used for tax purposes in the United States. However, large publicly-traded corporations, which would be most affected by reduction of reported earnings due to use of LIFO, actually employ it in greater proportion than do all the taxpayers reporting inventory valuation method to the IRS. The evidence for this is that of the 600 large industrial and commercial companies tabulated in Accounting Trends and Techniques,[14] 179 (30 percent) employ LIFO to some extent in contrast with 0.64 percent of industrial and commercial taxpayers reporting inventory valuation methods. It is interesting to note that the number of companies to some extent employing LIFO tabulated in the AICPA survey peaked in 1957 at 205. The pattern of adoption of LIFO is as difficult to define and rationalise as those of the other tax accounting options. Another failure to confirm an hypothesis of general adoption of tax relief options emerges as a result.

The Function of the Change Agent in Accounting Innovation

Sociological research places heavy emphasis on identifying the change agent as a variable affecting the rate of adoption in relating and adapting the innovation itself, the potential adopters, and the socio-economic systems of which they are members. Because accounting acts as the information system not only for individual firms, but also for other interested parties, innovations usually have sponsoring organisations, such as the government (taxing and regulatory agencies), trade associations, professional accounting groups, and merchandisers of accounting services and equipment.

Ultimately, the change agent, the French government, was the decisive factor in the rejection of revaluation in the interest of its own policy objectives and only secondarily in deference to the individual firms which had already rejected it. These firms have been identified as smaller and as holding a minority of the relevant economic resources. The government came to recognise unintended consequences of the adoption of revaluation and switched to a system of accelerated depreciation provisions, when revaluation was terminated. Judging from the U.S. experience, there is little reason to think this new program is meeting with rapid adoption by the firms rejecting revaluation.

Ultimately, the rejection of revaluation did not come from "big business'; it came from the government and from small business.

1. The French government, committed to central planning, found the revaluation provided significant increases in the independence of the private enterprise from the central plan and governmental direction. An incompatibility between revaluation and the government's anti-inflation and growth objectives was perceived.

(a) Enterprises were all too well shielded from adverse effects of inflation. The de Gaulle government concluded that in order to contain inflation, the strategy to eliminate its origins precluded ameliorating its effects.

(b) Enterprises were provided with a cash flow from increased depreciation on assets "in place" that encouraged their use beyond optimal economic life and that facilitated self-financing where outside funds would optimally not be invested.

2. There was a notable failure of the government and small private enterprises to undertake the developmental programs necessary to implement fully the "laissez faire" compliance system.

The government took no integrated approach to the application of revaluation. Administration and implementation were inconsistent, extemporaneous, and without adequate theoretical and technical basis. Government controls over accounting expanded as these deficiencies engendered "reforms", revisions, and detailed procedures.

Perceptions of the Incompatibility of Revaluation and Socio-Economic Norms.

How did the government officials conclude that revaluation was not compatible with the nation's economic well being? The government position was reported as follows:

> The old tax system acted to protect by taxation the producers hampered by the economic instability of the nation and the multiple monetary depreciations. The return to economic and monetary stability made unjustifiable those privileges which often facilitated the survival of enterprises useless to the nation economy.

The deficiencies of revaluation in restraining inflation repeatedly were cited and its repeal had the aim: "To make (the economy) healthier by eliminating clauses of protection which weakened the resistance of entrepreneurs to the rise in the level of prices".

The basic flaw in fiscal policy was recognised as more fundamental than revaluation per se and it might be identified broadly as the array of "indexation" schemes employed in numerous areas of the economy. That is, as the government made available increasingly accurate, timely, and detailed indices of the effects of inflation, these were utilised to pace increases in wages, in supply costs, in depreciation charges, in inventory adjustments and in tax relief as discussed in this paper. These increases in turn led to higher prices to be reflected in the indices. In France even the national minimum industrial guaranteed wage (S.M.I.G.) was based on the consumer price index and the application of indices was commonly written into businesss agreements ranging from union contracts, to purchase contracts, to bond indentures.

The 1963 Organisation for Economic Cooperation and Development review of the French economy adds credibility to this outline of the behavioral pattern emerging from technical regulations "geared to inflation:

> Price stability no longer seems normal and there is no real resistance to price changes. Even vending machines are converted to new prices with startling ease, and no one is surprised at repeated price increases ... Buyers' resistance to a rise is very weak, and there is a similar process with regard to earnings ... To break this vicious circle it was

decided in 1958 to adopt a policy of "true prices" by abolishing subsidies and indexation schemes and by leaving the market as free as possible to determine prices......

Moreover, this pattern of a "legitimatised" inflation with the measures designed to measure and adjust for it contributing to its escalation was illustrated by taxation itself. As prices rose, revalued assets provided increased depreciation and lower taxes; as prices declined, the reverse, higher taxes. This is just the opposite of what economic theory calls for. Excessive accumulation of inventory as a hedge against inflation contributed to inflation and thereby justified itself with holding gains partially financed by the tax savings available from the increased inventory write-offs provided.

The tax benefits available from increased tax deductions were not interpreted as being passed along to the customer in pricing production, but rather as having "weakened the resistance of entrepreneurs to the rise in the level of prices". The government in repealing revaluation and outlawing indexation of bonds realized that these sophisticated procedures neither achieved their ends without adverse side effects nor contributed to the economic decisions appropriate to national planning objectives.

At the same time that the government aimed to contain inflation, it sought to plan for economic growth and to stimulate investment. To do so effectively, a program to channel investment into productive facilities and modernisation and to increase the mobility of capital for financing was initiated. Vergnaud characterises this phase of the program as follows:

Reform (i.e., the substitution of investment incentives for revaluation) favours the one that modernises his techniques, who increases his productivity and penalises the one that remains in the routine.

The key provision of the reform of 1959 was to replace revaluation with accelerated depreciation. That is, tax relief, previously available to the passive enterprise in varying degrees as long as it could keep fixed assets operable and the price level continued to rise, now was available only to the active enterprise inasmuch as it invested in new fixed assets presumably to its own best interest and that of the economy.

However, the assessment of investment incentives and revaluation tax relief has not fully run its course. For example, in the United States the investment tax credit, which is tax relief of the variety espoused by the French as noninflationary, is being criticised as inflationary by way of its procyclical effect and has been repealed by the Nixon administration. Consequently, the reported rationale of the French government for discontinuing the revaluation because of inflationary consequences now justifies discontinuing tax relief investment incentives of the type which the French substituted. Controversy not consensus is the result. While the revaluation accounting model surely has substantial limitations as a tax relief device, yet it may have its uses in providing equitable tax burdens between the more and less capital intensive firms in times of price fluctuations.

The significance of this rejection of revaluation would be incomplete if no mention of its effect on the proposed standardisation of accounting in the Common Market were made. The effect was to reduce the likelihood of revaluation being accepted as an accounting principle, since no member currently employed it on a national basis. Norr quotes Giscard d'Estaing to the effect that "harmonisation of depreciation would mark an important step toward the equalisation of competitive conditions in the Market". The necessity for compatibility of accounting innovation to systems of broad scope requires deliberate programs for achieving quick and wide adoption.

FOOTNOTES

(1) Accounting scholars may object to the term "innovation" applied to long familiar accounting concepts. See Everett Rogers, Diffusion of Innovations (New York: Free Press, 1962). Rogers defines " an innovation as an idea perceived as new by the individual. It really matters little, as far as human behavior is concerned whether or not an idea is 'objectively' new as measured by the amount of time elapsed since its first use or discovery. It is the newness of the idea to the individual that determines his reaction to it".

See also Edwin Mansfield, The Economics of Technological Change (New York: W.W. Norton, 1968), p. 99. Mansfield further clarifies the term as used here in saying, "economists have stressed the distinction between an invention and an innovation on the ground that an invention has little or no economic significance until it is applied".

(2) American Institute of Certified Public Accountants, Accounting Research Division, Statement of the Accounting Principles Board No. 3: Financial Statement Restated for General Price-Level Changes (New York : American Institute of Certified Public Accountants, 1969).

(3) See for example Ralph C. Jones, Price Level Changes and Financial Statements: Case Studies of Four Companies (Evanston: American Accounting Association, 1955), and Paul Rosenfield, "Accounting for Inflation: A Field Test", Journal of Accountancy (June 1969), pp. 45-50.

(4) This study does not weight the relative merits of general versus specific price change adjustments and uses "price change" as a generic term for the class of possible range of adjustments. The French regulations provided no operational definition consistent with specified theoretical objectives though some were claimed at one time or another.

(5) Martin Norr, "Depreciation Reform in France", Taxes (May 1961), p. 400.

(6) This is a focal hypothesis in the literature of innovation. "Taking account of uncertainty and the fact that the spread of knowledge is not instantaneous, farmers have behaved in a fashion consistent with the idea of profit maximisation. Where the evidence appears to indicate the contrary, I would predict that a closer examination of the relevant economic variables will show that the change was not profitable as it appears to be". Zvi Griliches, "Hybrid Corn: An Exploration in the Economics of Technological Change," Econometrica, October 1957, P. 522.

(7) See H. Peter Holzer and Hanns-Martin Schoenfeld, "The French Approach to the Post-War Price Level Problem: Accounting for Changes in Price Level in France," Accounting Review (April 1963), pp. 382-87, for description of the complex inventory adjustment regulations, which resemble a base stock method.

(8) Ministere de L'Economie et des Finances, Statistiques et Etudes Financierers (Paris: Imprimerie Nationale, 1964 and 1967).

(9) Ibid.

(10) Ibid.

(11) Norman B. Ture, Accelerated Depreciation in the United States, 1954-60. (New York: National Bureau of Economic Research, 1967).

(12) U.S. Treasury, Internal Revenue Service, Supplementary Depreciation Data from Corporation Tax Returns, 1959 (Washington: Internal Revenue Service, 1965).

(13) Statistics of Income, Corporation Income Tax Return, 1963 (Washington: U.S Government Printing Office, 1968).

(14) American Institute of Certified Public Accountants, Accounting Research Division, Accounting Trends and Techniques, 1968 (New York: American Institute of Certified Public Accountants, 1968), p. 54.

23 A Test Application of the Feasibility of Market-Based Measures in Accounting

Daniel L. McDonald

Objectives of the Study

Those who advocate the use of "current values"[1] in accounting seem almost exclusively concerned with basic concepts, that is, with the function, purpose, or objective of accounting. Of those opposed to the current value approach, some are opposed on conceptual grounds, but most opposition is based on the feasibility question, i.e., whether suitable measures of current value can actually be made.

The goal(s) of accounting and the attributes which ought to be measured and reported have been well discussed in the literature. The American Accounting Association[2] concludes that current values should be included as one kind of information presented in multi-valued general purpose financial statements. Edwards and Bell[3] advocate the use of present replacement cost as the basis for determining income and financial position. Chambers[4] advocates the market selling price of assets as the appropriate measure.

However, adoption of the current value proposals is unlikely until the proposals have been demonstrated to be feasible. It is toward such a demonstration that this paper is directed. To establish feasibility it is necessary to specify criteria and then make empirical tests which can be judged in terms of the criteria.

Feasibility Criteria

Feasibility is concerned with the practicality of making conceptually desired measures, and practicality is essentially a question of cost. Thus feasibility concerns costliness, and feasibility criteria are the standards for judging costliness. Four feasibility criteria are discussed below: 1) degree of dispersion, 2) degree of displacement, 3) costliness (out-of-pocket or opportunity costs), and 4) timeliness.

Costs are of two types: one is associated with making the measures; the other with the losses incurred in making wrong decisions because of incorrect or imprecise measures. The first presents no new problems to accounting; it is the direct out-of-pocket cost devoted to the measurement or the opportunity cost, the benefits foregone by devoting scarce resources to measurement rather than to the next best alternative. Determining the costs of wrong decisions presents new problems to accounting.

Decisions result from the analysis of input information which may be very scanty and may not be quantified. Moreover, the analysis may be formal or largely intuitive. The methods of analysis and the functional relationships employed by decision makers are beyond the responsibilities of the measurer. What then are the characteristics of input information which cause error in decisions? One source of decision error arises from input information which is disperse. A given measurement method may result in measures whose yields correct decisions when the analytic decision process is applied to it. Any one measure, however, is unlikely to be equal to the mean. The dispersion of the individual measures about their mean[5] is, therefore, a source of error. The more tightly clustered the individual measures are, the less likely are errors. There are many possible causes of dispersion: the attribute that is being measured, the skill and training of the measurers, the precision of the measurement rules which they follow, and the constraints imposed upon them. Because constraints are a source of dispersion, I hypothesize that as constraints are relaxed, the measures will become less disperse. For example, as more money is devoted to the measurement process for training measurers, constructing measuring devices, and specifying attributes and measurement rules more precisely, the measures become less disperse. Thus the first feasibility criterion is the degree of dispersion.

Decision error also arises from information that is displaced from the "true" measure. Although the "true" measure is appealing as an abstraction, it is unobtainable until all measurement error is eliminated. Its proxy is the mean of the obtainable measures, given no economic constraints on measurement procedures; call this the "ideal" measure. In a system of accounting which has as its objective the measurement of the net realizable value of each asset, each asset to be measured could be sold if there were no resource limitations on the measurement process. If done repeatedly, the mean sale price would be the ideal measure of the net re-lizable value of the asset. Repeatedly paying damages for failure to deliver or repeatedly repurchasing the asset (or purchasing an identical one) makes this measurement method extremely costly. It would be cheaper to conduct the experiment once, but such a single observation represents a lower order "ideal". Repurchasing the asset in order to have it available for use makes even this single observation method costly. Because of resource limitations, less costly methods seem desirable. For example, when an asset is sold, analyze the difference between the price realized and the price at which it was stated in the accounts. This difference would be the displacement of the measure of net realizable value; the degree of displacement[6] is the second feasibility criterion.

The last two recommended criteria are timeliness and the cost of measuring. Frequently there is either a direct or imputed cost to delays in making decisions. Given a choice between two measures which are equally feasible by the dispersion, displacement, and cost of measuring criteria, the one which is more timely is preferred. The cost of measuring includes the out-of-pocket or opportunity costs, and I hypothesize that there is a trade-off between the cost of measuring and the other three criteria (dispersion, displacement, and timeliness).

An Empirical Approach

Before measures can be empirically evaluated, the variables which affect them must be identified. The measurement model adopted here[7] treats measures as functions of the object, the attribute, the measurers, the measurement rules, and the constraints. In symbols:

$$X = f(O,A,M,R,C).$$

The object (O) whose properties are being measured may be physical (such as inventory) or relational (such as the relationship of debtor and creditor). The attribute (A) is the specified characteristic of the object which is being measured. The attribute may be "numerosity," "length of time the relationship has existed," or "the money payment required to sever the relationship." Typically, we will be thinking of accountants as the measurers (M).

The measurement rules (R) are the specified instructions which the measurers follow in expressing the magnitude of the attribute in numbers. The rules may be very general or very explicit. The constraints (C) are the limitations within which the measurers must work. Invariably, one of these is the money outlay to perform the measurements, and frequently there will be a time constraint. My test attempts to hold constant all variables except the attribute (A).

Two versions of a case-questionnaire were used to present accountants with a measurement problem. One version, the "net realizable value" version, asked the accountants to measure the net realizable value of a fleet of automobiles at the end of each of four years. The other version, the "present practice" version, asked the accountants to apply "generally accepted accounting principles" to select a depreciation pattern for the fleet and estimate the necessary parameters (useful life, salvage value, etc.). Although it is by no means clear that present practice measures any defined attribute, present practice does provide a basis of comparison against which alternative proposals can be evaluated. The object of the measurement process was a fleet of automobiles which was described in virtually identical terms in both versions of the questionnaire. The measurers were two randomly selected samples of Certified Public Accountants holding a license to practice in California. One sample group received by mail the net realizable value version of the questionnaire, the other the present practice version. It is difficult to hold measurement rules constant when different attributes are being measured. The closest approximation to holding measurement rules constant was to leave them virtually undefined. The only semblance of a measurement rule was implied - that the measure be expressed in dollar units. The constraints were those imposed by the measurers on themselves. Since the sample was randomly selected, it is reasonable to assume that the amount of time spent completing the questionnaire and the average opportunity cost of time did not vary significantly between the two groups.

The crucial difference between the two versions of the case-questionnaire was the supplementary information

	Net Realizable Value Version	Present Practice Version[(a)]						Simulated	
			Those Selecting						
		All Present Practice	Straight-Line	Dble.-Dec.	Syd.	Mileage	Other	Uniform Parameter (b)	Uniform Straight-Line Pattern (c)
Mean Depreciation									
Year 1	39,851	38,412	30,620	57,627	44,057	38,215	40,655	40,094	28,970
Year 2	20,908	31,624	30,620	29,536	32,538	37,061	28,345	33,574	28,970
Year 3	14,174	24,832	29,496	15,722	21,019	23,332	20,405	26,750	28,171
Year 4	15,318	16,464	26,679	8,646	11,876	14,389	15,177	8,666	25,451
Standard Deviation									
Year 1	7,757	13,305	6,735	12,968	6,654	7,617	10,026	10,044	6,605
Year 2	3,281	6,545	6,735	2,071	3,386	7,731	1,165	2,387	6,605
Year 3	3,549	7,320	4,054	2,699	2,717	8,927	3,913	7,305	4,696
Year 4	5,241	9,045	3,589	2,762	2,256	9,731	6,645	0	4,033
Number of Observations	(77 all years)	(87,87,81,44)	(46,46,44,16)	(17 all years)	(5,5,5,4)	(16,16,12,4)	(3 all years)	(84,84,84,17)	(68,68,66,35)
% of Present Practice Respondents Choosing the Particular Depreciation Pattern			53%	20%	6%	18%	3%		

(a) Zero depreciation (i.e. after end of estimated useful life) is not considered in the calculation of average depreciation. If it had been considered the average depreciation would tend to be lower and the dispersion higher in the later years.

(b) Depreciation calculated using the pattern selected by the respondent but imposing the following parameters: Life 3 years, scrap 494, estimated useful mileage 65,000, double-declining-balance per cent 47% (the three year life estimate was not used for those selecting double-declining-balance depreciation).

(c) Depreciation calculated using the parameters selected by the respondent but imposing the straight-line depreciation method. For those selecting double-declining-balance depreciation scrap estimates were supplied-life estimated 2 yrs \$263, 3 yrs \$602, 4 yrs \$292, 5 yrs \$525.

FIG. 1-1

provided. Each group of respondents was provided that information which is usually available for the same assignment in a real-life situation. The net realizable value version included appropriate extracts from two readily available used-car price books and from used-car auction prices as reported in a weekly trade newspaper.[8] The present practice version included some information on the depreciation practice and policies of other fleet operators[9] and a detailed capital budgeting analysis on which the decision to purchase the automobile fleet was based.

Automobile values were used in the experiment because vehicles are usually considered long-lived asset group[19] and because they are one of the easiest to measure within that group. Several sources of price quotations are published; also, the fairly constant margin between used-car wholesale and retail prices indicates that measuring "used replacement cost" is little different from measuring net realizable value. If the test can demonstrate that net realizable value is a more feasible measure than is cost less accumulated depreciation, then the test should be extended to other long-lived assets. "More feasible" means better on at least one of the feasibility criteria and no worse on the others. Conversely, if the test demonstrates that net realizable value cannot be measured more feasibly, serious doubt is cast on both the methodology and the possibility of similar measures for other types of long-lived assets.

Empirical Findings

Depreciation expense was calculated from the responses to the questionnaire. The results, which form the basis for the following analysis, are summarized in Figure 1-1. The most striking feature is that in each year the standard deviation of the present practice depreciation, which is the average resulting from using different depreciation methods, exceeds that of the net realizable value depreciation. Note that a similar comparison between the dispersion (as measured by standard deviation) of the depreciation resulting from the application of the straightline method and the dispersion of net realizable value depreciation does not yield such clear results.

The data are evaluated only with respect to the dispersion criterion. There is little reason to believe the cost of obtaining the two measures would be significantly different. In terms of timeliness, present practice gives measures of depreciation expense which are available as soon as the depreciation pattern has been selected and the parameters estimated. However, the time lag in determining net realizable value is not likely to be significant, especially for use in published annual financial statements. The displacement criterion is difficult to apply to "present practice" depreciation since the attribute being measured has not been specified. I assume timeliness and cost are the same for both measures.

An important reservation arises from the poor response rate to the questionnaire since the final usable response rate of 33% is too low to support generalizations.

The first test compares the dispersion of net realizable value depreciation and present practice depreciation and the data are graphically presented in Figure 1-2. For ease in comparing dispersion, all the data have been shifted to a zero mean to eliminate visual differences due to differences in mean. It is obvious that present practice depreciation is more disperse in each of the four years.[11] Taking year 1 as an example, the distribution of present practice depreciation was such that only 7 of the 87 measures of depreciation expense were within ± \$2,000 of the average present practice depreciation for year 1 (6 within - \$2,000 and 1 within + \$2,000). Two measures were more than \$42,000 greater than the average. In contrast, the distribution of net realizable value depreciation was such that 38 of the 77 measures of depreciation expense were within ± \$2,000 of the average net realizable value depreciation for year 1 (14 within - \$2,000 and 24 within + \$2,000). No measure was more than \$26,000 greater than the average.

It may be that there is one depreciation pattern widely accepted and used by fleet operators, and it may be that the mix of depreciation patterns used by my respondents was not the one used by fleet operators. Thus, lumping all present practice depreciation together would overstate dispersion, and other data suggest this is not the case.[12] The questionnaire responses show that straight-line is the most frequently used pattern, and this is consistent with other available data.

A more demanding comparison is that between net realizable value depreciation and the depreciation of respondents who selected the straight-line method. The observed differences in dispersion could occur by chance about 10 per cent of the time if the two

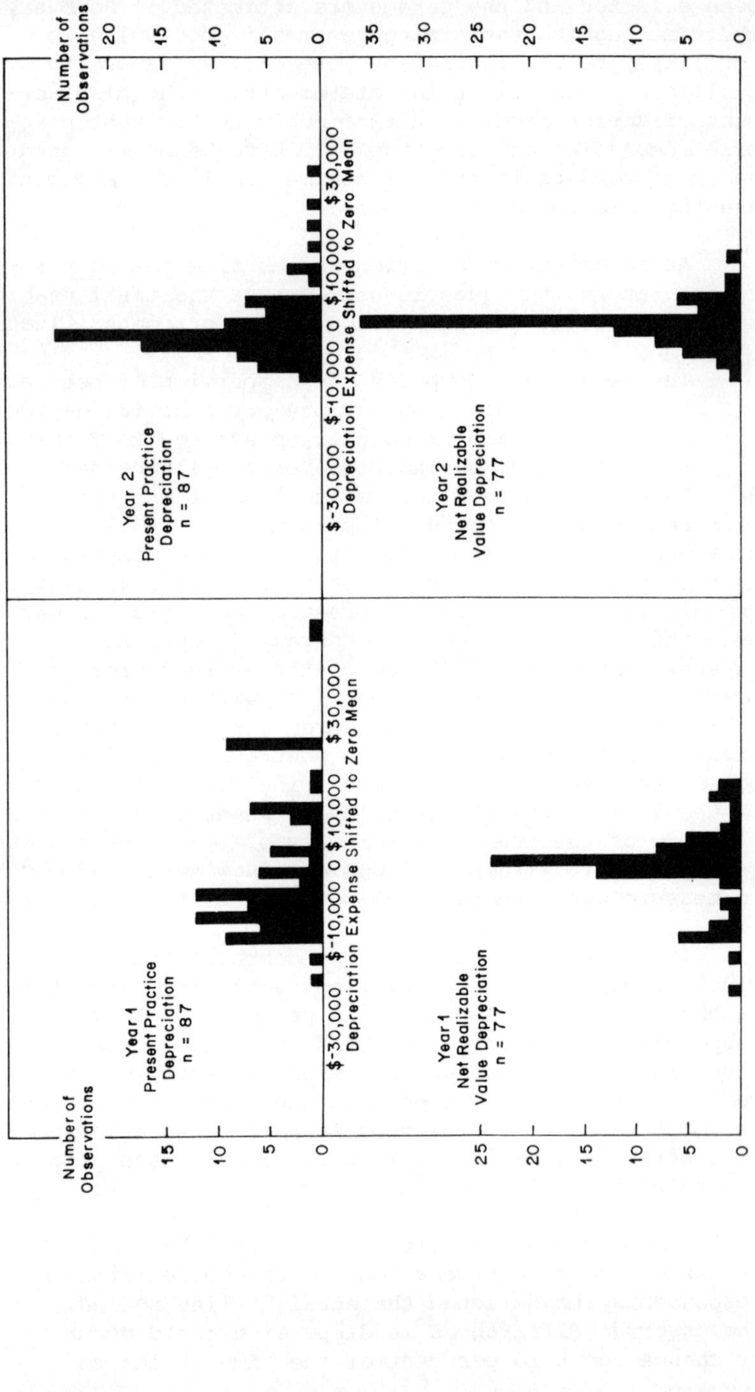

Year 1
Present Practice
Depreciation
n = 87
Year 2
Present Practice
Depreciation
n = 87
Year 1
Net Realizable
Value Depreciation
n = 77
Year 2
Net Realizable
Value Depreciation
n = 77
$-30,000 $-10,000 0 $10,000 $30,000
Depreciation Expense Shifted to Zero Mean
Number of Observations
15 10 5 0
25 20 15 10 5 0
20 15 10 5 0
35 30 25 20 15 10 5 0

Fig. 1 - 2

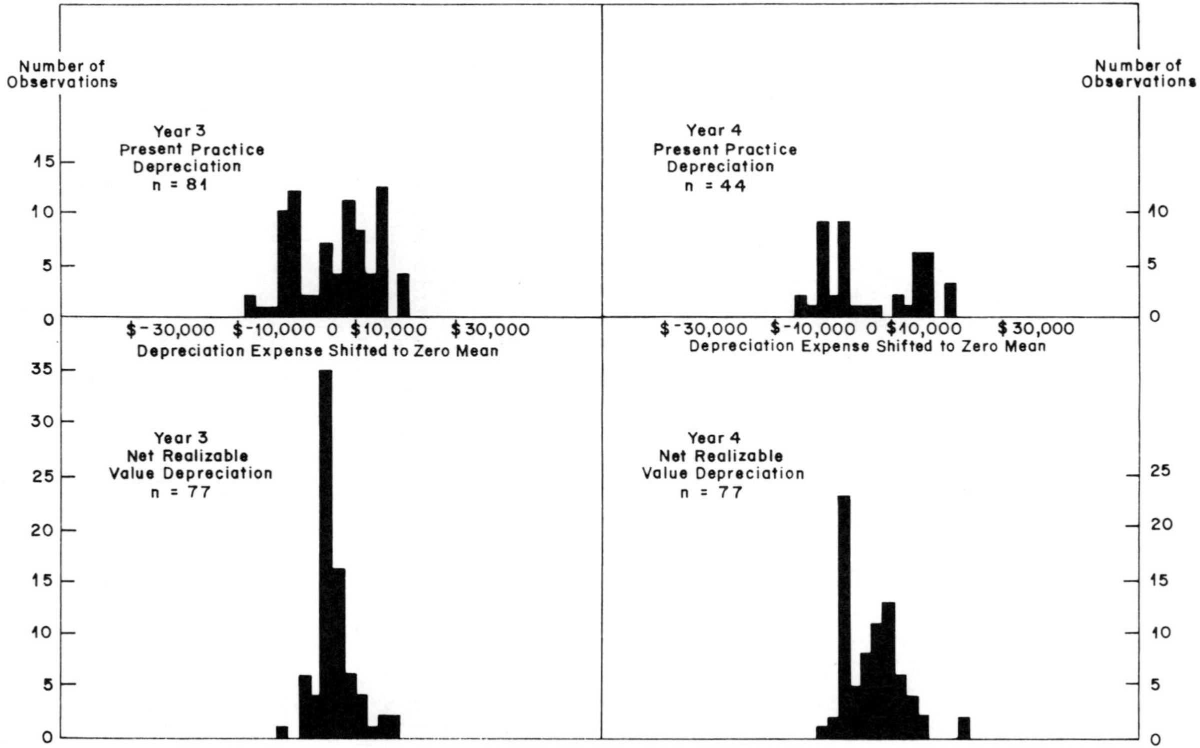

Fig. 1 - 2 Continued

sets are equal in dispersion.[13] This evidence is insufficient to reject the hypothesis that the two sets are equal with respect to dispersion. In other words, net realizable value depreciation is at least as good as straight-line depreciation when judged by the dispersion criterion.

Following the recent suggestion that accounting measures can be significantly improved if more uniformity can be achieved,[14] I analyzed the data in order to answer this question: if all accountants were to use straight-line depreciation and had only to estimate the parameters, would the dispersion of the resulting depreciation expense be less than that of the net realizable value depreciation? This was tested by programming the computer to calculate the depreciation on a straight-line basis for all those who had selected either straight-line, double-declining-balance, or sum-of-the-years-digits depreciation (see column headed "Uniform Straight-Line Pattern" in Figure 1-1). When the resulting depreciation expense was compared with the depreciation expense from the net realizable set, the differences in dispersion between them were not significant.[15] The effect of varying methods of depreciation was tested by eliminating differences in depreciation due to parameter estimates. When life and scrap estimates are held constant at the mean or modal estimate, with only the choice of pattern varying, the resulting depreciation expense was more disperse than net realizable value depreciation in two of the three years.[16] For automobiles, this evidence suggests that imposed uniformity is not a significant improvement over direct reference to market price unless the uniformity extends to specifying both pattern and parameters. None of the advocates of uniformity have suggested so extreme an imposition of uniformity.

Conclusions

Accounting needs a framework within which alternative proposals can be evaluated. The dispersion criterion is particularly useful since it conforms to at least one use of the term objectivity, i.e., verifiability. The displacement criterion cannot be applied until the attribute that is being measured is clearly specified. Both the cost and the timeliness criteria are sufficiently familiar to require no comment.

The empirical data reported for automobiles provide evidence that direct reference to available market price indicators results in less disperse measures than those now obtained under "generally accepted accounting principles." This is largely because of the variety of depreciation patterns now used. Even if the most frequently used pattern (straight-line) is employed, the resulting depreciation change is not clearly preferable in terms of dispersion.

It is sometimes argued that the measuring and reporting of market prices should not be undertaken until all assets can be so measured, but progress and change take place very slowly. Technological advances and changes in the socio-economic environment may gradually expand the feasibility horizon, and accountants should be prepared to take advantage of such developments.

FOOTNOTES

(1) "Current value" is used here as a generic term to include all specific valuation proposals which make reference to current market prices (new or used) of assets.

(2) American Accounting Association, A Statement of Basic Accounting Theory (Evanston: A.A.A., 1966), pp. 30-31; Committee on Concepts and Standards-Long-Lived Assets, "Accounting for Land, Buildings, and Equipment," The Accounting Review, 39 (July, 1964), p. 695.

(3) Edgar O. Edwards and Philip W. Bell, The Theory and Measurement of Business Income (Berkeley: University of California Press, 1961), pp. 144ff., pp. 185ff.

(4) Raymond J. Chambers, Accounting, Evaluation and Economic Behavior (Englewood Cliffs: Prentice-Hall, 1966), p. 92.

(5) Using the mean facilitates statistical techniques and is clearly appropriate if the measures are normally distributed. In accounting we may expect to encounter skewed distributions (e.g., resulting from conservatism) and bi-modal or multi-modal distributions (e.g., resulting from the application of alternative measurement procedures). If the only source of error is in the mechanics of the measurement process, the measures will be normally distributed. Choosing variance as the expression of dispersion assumes a quadratic loss function (the "importance" of errors is the square of the error rather than, say, its absolute size or its sign). For some decision makers this assumption may be inappropriate. However, the variety of statistical techniques based on this assumption, such as the F test, makes it extremely convenient in comparing the results of different measurement methods.

(6) The relation between what is here called dispersion and displacement and their relevance to accounting is from Yuji Ijiri and Robert K. Jaedicke, "Reliability and Objectivity of Accounting Measurement." The Accounting Review, 41: 3 (July, 1966), pp. 474-83. The relation is as follows:

$$\begin{Bmatrix}\text{variance of measures}\\ \text{about the true value}\end{Bmatrix} = \begin{Bmatrix}\text{variance of measures}\\ \text{about their mean}\end{Bmatrix} + (\text{mean-true})^2$$

In their terms: reliability = objectivity + bias.
In my terms: reliability = dispersion + (displacement)^2.

(7) Adapted from Iijiri and Jaedicke (1966), p. 436.

(8) Wholesale and retail quotations were from Kelley Blue Book Market Report (4 models quoted) and Red Book Official Used Car Valuations (6 models quoted). In each case the correct model of the fleet was included among the models quoted. Used car auction prices were from Automotive News. Model numbers are not quoted in the auction quotes; only the general model name (Chevrolet Biscayne), the number of cylinders, and number of doors are given to facilitate identification. The respondents combined these data in at least 14 different ways ranging from "Red Book retail only" to "lowest of Blue Book wholesale, Red Book wholesale, or auction." The complete questionnaires are reproduced in the author's unpublished dissertation, Feasibility Criteria for the Measurement of Long-Lived Assets with Test Application to Automobiles (Stanford University, 1967).

(9) Specifically, the examples in Business Car Allowances Practices and Controls (Chicago, The Dartnell Corporation, 1964, pp. 48-49) giving depreciation and trade-in policies of fleet operators who are wholesalers and distributors (as was the hypothetical firm in the questionnaire). Fourteen examples were given. Each included data on the number of cars in the fleet, average car miles per year, replacement schedule in both miles and years, and contributors' explanation of depreciation and/or trade-in methods and policies. From the explanations it was apparent that 2 used straight-line, 2 double-declining or diminishing-balance, 1 sum-of-years-digits, 2 were unclear, 2 used miscellaneous methods and 5 did not mention the depreciation pattern. See also footnote 12.

(10) The feasibility objections to the use of market values have generally related to long-lived rather than to current assets.

(11) H_o dispersion of net realizable value depreciation = dispersion of present practice depreciation. Using the Kolmogorov-Smirnov Two-Sample Test with data shifted to zero mean to eliminate differences in central tendency. Results of two-tailed test:

Year 1 Reject Ho at .001 level of significance.
Year 2 Reject Ho at .005 level of significance.
Year 3 Reject Ho at .001 level of significance.
Year 4 Reject Ho at .025 level of significance.

(12) Business Car Allowances Practices and Controls (Chicago, The Dartnell Corporation, 1964, pp. 45-51) cites examples of depreciation and trade-in policies of fleet operators. Of the 67 examples given, 39 make some mention of the depreciation pattern.

	No.	%
Straight-line	19	48.7
Double-declining-balance or diminishing-balance	5	12.8
Unclear-probably straight-line or double-declining	7	17.9
Sum-of-years-digits	3	7.7
Misc. methods (none were mileage)	5	12.8
	39	100.0

Those that were unclear quoted a depreciation percent without stating whether it was applied to cost, cost less estimated scrap or cost less accumulated depreciation. This mix of depreciation patterns is similar to that of the respondents to the present practice version of the questionnaire.

(13) Ho dispersion of net realizable value depreciation = dispersion of stright-line depreciation. Results of two-tailed F test:

Year 1 Cannot reject Ho at .10 level of significance.
Year 2 Can reject Ho at .02 level of significance. Direction indicates straight-line more disperse.
Year 3 Cannot reject Ho at .10 level of significance.
Year 4 Can reject Ho at .10 level of significance but not at .02. Direction indicates net realizable value depreciation more disperse.

(14) The entire Autumn, 1965 (30:4) issue of Law and Contemporary Problems is devoted to the topic "Uniformity in Financial Accounting."

(15) Ho dispersion of net realizable value depreciation = dispersion of present practice depreciation constrained to a uniform straight-line pattern. Results of two-tailed F test:

Year 1 Cannot reject Ho at .10 level of significance.
Year 2 Easily reject Ho at .02 level of significance. Direction indicates straight-line more disperse.
Year 3 Barely reject Ho at .02 level of significance. Direction indicates straight-line more disperse.
Year 4 Barely reject Ho at .10 level of significance. Direction indicates net realizable value depreciation more disperse.
The mixed results are insufficient to reject the hypothesis but do suggest that, if anything, present practice depreciation constrained to a uniform straight-line pattern is more disperse.

(16) Ho dispersion of net realizable value depreciation = dispersion of present practice depreciation constrained to uniform parameters. Using the Kolmogorov-Smirnov Two-Sample Test with data shifted to zero mean to eliminate differences in central tendency. Results of two-tailed test:

Years 1, 3 Reject Ho at .001 level of significance. Direction indicates net realizable value depreciation is less disperse.
Year 2 Reject Ho at .001 level of significance. Direction indicates net realizable value depreciation is more disperse. Note that it is in year 2 that accelerated depreciation methods "cross over" straight-line giving a depreciation expense approximately equal to straight-line.
Year 4 Not tested. The uniform life estimate was 3 years. Only the 17 observations reflecting double-declining-balance depreciation with a uniform rate of 47% remain.

24 An Application of Replacement Cost Accounting Theory

Edward J. Gress

The accounting literature abounds with discussions relating to the superiority of financial statements prepared on the basis of current replacement costs.[1] Despite the desirability of preparing such statements, the application of replacement costs in practice remains rare and not all too successful.[2] This article discusses one such application to a business firm with the object of demonstrating the practicality and objectivity[3] of accounting based on current replacement costs.

The term replacement cost as used in this article refers to the expenditure needed to replace an asset in use by an identical asset as of a given date. Such an expenditure includes the invoice price less any discount plus appropriate charges for freight, installation, taxes and other incidental acquisition costs. The replacement cost of assets that cannot be replaced by identical units due to technological innovations or other factors is the current cost of assets of equivalent productive capacity.

With the help of a national firm of chartered accountants, a company that was willing to provide the data necessary to undertake this study was located. The management of the company did not wish that the name of their company or the nature of their industry be identified; hence, this company will be referred to as Gress Co.

Gress Co. is a closely held forty-year old firm with assets of about $10 million. The historical-dollar[4] balance sheets as at 31st December 1969 and 1968, were to be adjusted to a replacement cost basis and the historical-dollar income statement for 1969 was to be restated on a maintenance-of-productive-capacity basis.[5] The comparative historical-dollar and replacement cost balance sheets as at 31 December 1969

Table 1

GRESS CO.
COMPARATIVE HISTORICAL-DOLLAR AND REPLACEMENT COST
BALANCE SHEETS
31 DECEMBER 1969 AND 1968

Assets

	1969		1968	
	Historical-Dollar $000	Replacement cost $000	Historical-Dollar $000	Replacement cost $000
Current assets:				
Cash	574	574	474	474
Accounts and notes receivable - net	436	436	420	420
Inventories	63	63	67	67
Prepaid expenses and other current assets	29	29	40	40
Total current assets	1,102	1,102	1,001	1,001
Plant and equipment:				
Land	180	822	180	783
Buildings and improvements	1,025	1,591	994	1,485
Machinery and equipment	1,676	2,255	1,662	2,119
Automobiles	48	52	35	38
Office furniture and equipment	117	127	110	121
Total	3,046	4,847	2,981	4,546
Less accumulated depreciation	1,609	2,259	1,410	1,894
Plant and equipment - net	1,437	2,588	1,571	2,652

Equities

	1969		1968	
	Histori-cal dollar $000	Replace-ment cost $000	Histor-cal dollar $000	Replace-ment cost $000
Current liabilities:				
Accounts payable and accrued expenses	336	336	379	379
Notes payable	16	16	14	14
Income taxes payable	(7)*	(7)*	169	169
Deferred revenue	41	41	42	42
Total current liabilities	386	386	604	604
Notes payable - long-term	13	13	29	29
Stockholders' equity:				
Contributed capital	524	524	524	524
Adjustment of stockholders' equity	-	1,814	-	1,573
Retained earnings	1,672	1,022	1,466	982
Total stockholders' equity	2,196	3,350	1,990	3,079
TOTAL EQUITIES	2,595	3,759	2,623	3,712
Other assets				
Sundry investments	1	14	1	9
Deposits and other assets	55	55	50	50
Total other assets	56	69	51	59
TOTAL ASSETS	2,595	3,759	2,623	3,712

*() signifies deduction

and 1968 appear in Table 1. The comparative income statements on a historical-dollar and maintenance of productive capacity bases for 1969 appear in Table 2. All figures were changed in accordance with the request of management but all relationships were maintained. The adjustment procedure is discussed below.

TABLE 2

GRESS CO.
COMPARATIVE INCOME STATEMENTS
ON A HISTORICAL-DOLLAR AND MAINTENANCE OF PRODUCTIVE CAPACITY BASES
FOR THE YEAR 1969

	Historical-dollar $000	Productive capacity $000
Revenue from operations	4,386	4,386
Expenses:		
Operating expenses (other than depreciation)	3,539	3,539
Administrative expenses (other than depreciation)	248	248
Depreciation expenses	200	366
Total expenses	3,987	4,153
Net income before income taxes	399	233
Provision for federal and state income taxes	193	193
NET INCOME	206	40

ADJUSTMENT PROCEDURE

Current assets

More than 90 percent of the current assets of Gress Co. consisted of monetary items that have no replacement cost per se. Inventories were kept on a first-in-first-out basis and had a rapid turnover. An examination of invoices received just prior to the end of the respective accounting periods produced figures that agreed with inventory costs on the books. Moreover, the change in acquisition cost during the two-year period was less than 1 per cent on the average and as such the adjustment of the cost of materials used on the income statement was not warranted.

The caption prepaid expenses and other current assets consisted of prepaid insurance, current deposits, and miscellaneous receivables. Since the renewal premium of insurance policies cannot be determined in advance and since deposits and receivables are monetary in nature, these assets required no adjustment.

Plant and equipment

The replacement cost of items of plant and equipment can be obtained by one of three methods: (1) an appraisal may be specific price indexes; and (3) current cost quotations may be obtained from manufacturers or agents.

Land

The determination of the replacement cost of land posed a problem as land is a unique asset that is not traded on an established market. An alternative to appraisal was to adjust the value of the land by means of "an index of land values as recommended in A Statement of Basic Accounting Theory (see p. 77). Unfortunately, no index of land values has been compiled for the city where Gress Co. is located.

The area of the particular plot of land is 20,556 square feet and is located in a major business sector in the city. Discussion with members of two firms of real estate appraisers, three real estate brokers and four assessors in the County Assessor's Office revealed that land in the vicinity of Gress Co.'s plant was selling anywhere between $35 and $45 per square foot at the end of 1969. The exact location of the land was not identified but from the identification of adjacent plots,, appraisers and brokers were more inclined to choose a valuation of $40 per square foot as of the end of 1969. The appraisers and brokers also indicated that land values in that particular location were on the average 5 per cent higher at the end of 1969 than they had been at the end of 1968. Accordingly, the $40 per square foot was selected as the best available measure of replacement cost of the land as of the end of 1969 and 1968 is computed below:

31 December 1969:	20,556 sq. ft. x $40	= $822,240
31 December 1968:	$822,240 ÷ 1.05	= $783,086

Buildings and improvements

Buildings and improvements are also unique assets without an established market. The replacement cost of a building cannot be easily determined since a building is rarely replaced by an identical structure.

In the absence of appraisals, the best alternative was to adjust the cost of the buildings and improvements by means of an index for building costs. Using the Engineering News Record Building Cost Index, the replacement cost of the buildings and improvements, were estimated at $1,590,717 at the end of 1969 - about $500,000 above cost - and at $1,484,933 - also about $500,000 above cost - at the end of 1968.

Machinery and equipment

The replacement cost of the machinery and equipment of Gress Co. was obtained through correspondence with manufacturers and agents. Such a task can be simple if a firm maintains detailed property records showing for each item the complete description of that item, its model and serial numbers, its original cost, and the name and address of the vendor. Where such details are available, the determination of the units acquired from a specific vendor can be easily determined. That vendor can then be asked to give current cost quotations for those items he has sold to the firm.

In the case of Gress Co. detailed property records were not maintained. The only record kept of machinery and equipment was a general ledger account with a scanty description of the items acquired. The matter was further complicated by the fact that many accessories were acquired at different dates and the general ledger account did not indicate whether such acquisitions were additions to existing units or represented independent units. Due to the condition of the property records, it was necessary to reconstruct the machinery and equipment account in terms of units with their additions in order to determine the original historical cost of each unit. The assistant production manager prepared a list of each of the units of machinery and equipment (including all additions) by model and serial number. His list also included the name and address of the manufacturer or agent. The next step was to reconcile the inventory list with the general ledger account to determine the original historical cost of each unit.

The reconciliation process was successful in matching 92 per cent of the historical cost of machinery and equipment as of 31 December 1968, with the inventory list prepared by the assistant production manager. The general ledger entries representing the 1969 acquisitions were all traced to the list of machinery and equipment without any discrepancy. The possibility of relating the unmatched 8 percent historical cost as of 31 December 1968 to the unchecked units on the list was rejected for four reasons: (1) the list may have contained units that were fully depreciated, written off from the books and retired from use, as was proved in the case of one unit; (2) the list may have omitted a few units; (3) the list may have contained units that were rented and not owned; and (4) the general ledger account may have contained some errors. Accordingly, the replacement cost of machinery and equipment equal to 8 per cent of the historical cost as of 31 December 1968 was obtained by applying the average ratio of historical cost to current replacement cost obtained for the other units comprising 92 per cent of the total.

The requests for current cost quotations were mailed early in 1970. These requests were prepared on the stationery of Gress Co. and were signed by the president and general manager. The strategy of mailing requests on the stationery of Gress Co. was adopted for two reasons: (1) a firm desiring to adopt replacement costing will have to request the data itself and not ask an outside party to do the job for them; and (2) the Dickerson and Dockweiler studies referred to in footnote 2 indicated that requests by a researcher are not given favourable consideration by vendors.

The letters of request included a form showing the details of the equipment with spaces for the respondents to write their quotations as of the dates requested. The form also contained a request that the vendor indicate the items that were no longer produced, and in that case he was asked to give current cost quotations for the items that represented the closest substitues and that had an equivalent productive capacity. It was felt that manufacturers and agents were in a better position to determine the units that supersede others than the personnel of the company. Gress Co. had several items that were superseded and in many cases the replacement cost of the equivalent capacity was less than the original cost. Twenty-four letters of request were mailed and a 100 per cent response was obtained.

The original cost and the replacement cost of machinery and equipment as of 31 December 1969 and 1968 are shown below.

	1969	1968
Original cost	$1,675,978	$1,661,600
Replacement cost	2,254,796	2,118,563

Automobiles

The replacement cost of automobiles was obtained through personal interviews with salesmen in six different automobile dealerships that sell to Gress Co. The salesmen were presented with copies of the original invoice and were asked to give price quotations for equivalent models with the same optional equipment as of 31 December 1969 (1970 models) and 31 December 1968 (1969 models).

The original cost of automobiles and their replacement cost as obtained from salesmen's quotations as of 31 December 1969 and 1968 appear below:

	1969	1968
Original cost	$48,134	$35,491
Replacement cost	52,094	37,740

Office furniture and equipment

Gress Co. had 569 items of office furniture and equipment as of 31 December 1968. These units ranged in original purchase cost from $6,53 to $19,141.70.

As in the case of machinery and equipment the ledger account of office furniture and equipment did not provide sufficient details. In many cases it was not possible to enumerate from the ledger account the identical units. The determination of the number of identical units would have rerequired the analysis of most of the vouchers and their supporting invoices. Such a project was rejected when a preliminary analysis of the invoices revealed that some of them were not sufficiently informative.

It was decided to estimate the current replacement cost at the end of 1969 and 1968 by means of a stratified random sample with an interpenetrating design. The units of furniture and equipment were stratified into 5 strata on the basis of their original cost. A stratified random sample of 86 units was drawn and current cost quotations of the 86 units were obtained as of 31 December 1969 and 1968. The replacement cost of the units acquired during 1969 was also obtained as of 31 December 1969, in order to arrive at the total current replacement cost estimate as of the end of 1969.

The current cost quotations were obtained through interviews with the suppliers of the various units of furniture and equipment. Most of the items were supported by original invoices.

In the case of many accounting and calculating machines, it was found that their replacement cost had declined substantially and in many cases they had been superseded by more efficient though less costly equipment. The suppliers were asked to estimate the ratio of the productive capacity of the units in the possession of Gress Co. with the new units in order to determine the replacement cost of an equivalent capacity.

The original cost of the office furniture and equipment and their replacement cost within ± $9,332 for 1969 and ± $9,078 for 1968 are shown below:

	1969	1968
Original cost	$117,023	$109,757
Estimated replacement cost	126,740	121,554

Accumulated depreciation

Accumulated depreciation based on the replacement cost of each unit of plant and equipment can be obtained by applying to the replacement cost the accrued depreciation percentage based on original cost. Unfortunately, accrued depreciation percentages on the original cost of the individual units of plant and equipment were not readily available. The problem was solved by applying the accumulated depreciation percentage on the total original cost of depreciable property to the total replacement cost of the depreciable property. Such a method does not give precise results since the change in replacement costs was not uniform for all items of plant and equipment.

Applying the accrued depreciation percentage on original cost to the total replacement cost of the depreciable items of plant and equipment gave the following accumulated depreciation figures:

31 December 1969	$2,259,268
31 December 1968	1,894,188

Sundry Investments

The sundry investments consist of 10 shares in the stock of a corporation. The investment is held at cost and the stock is not listed on any organised stock exchange. Accordingly the historical cost of the sundry investments was adjusted on the basis of the conventional book value of the stock of the issuing company.[6] This gives values of $14,453 and $8,933 on 31 December 1969 and 1968 respectively, as compared to a historical cost of $1,000.

Deposits and other assets

The deposits and other assets consisted mainly of a deposit with the Industrial Commission, deposits with a few major airlines, country club memberships and the cash surrender values of life insurance policies. These were left at their original amount.

Equities

In accordance with the classification of monetary and nonmonetary items in Statement of the Accounting Principles Board No.3 (pp. 28-9), all the liabilities of Gress Co. with the exception of deferred revenue are monetary in nature and are thus properly stated in current terms. Deferred revenue has no replacement per se and was therefore left unadjusted.

The account Adjustment of Stockholders' Equity represents the money adjustment of the historical-dollar stockholders' equity and its balance is equal to the advance in the replacement cost of assets. This account permits the presentation on a replacement cost balance sheet of the contributed capital at its original amount. The presentation of the original investment by stockholders may be desired for legal and historical purposes. Thus the original contributed capital of Gress Co. was left unadjusted.

Income statement accounts

Net income under the maintenance of productive capacity concept represents the maximum amount that can be severed without impairing the productive capacity of the firm as measured by the current replacement cost of such capacity. This is equal to the conventional revenue less the replacement cost of goods and services used during the accounting period. In the case of Gress Co., the historical-dollar income statement items with the exception of depreciation are properly expressed in current terms. Depreciation based on replacement cost for the year 1969 is the difference between accumulated depreciation based on replacement cost as of 31 December 1969 and 1958, after consideration of the replacement cost of assets retired from use during 1969. The adjusted net income figure came to about 20 per cent of the conventional income.

ANALYSIS OF THE ADJUSTED STATEMENTS

The adjustment of financial statements to a replacement cost basis must provide useful additional information not obtained from historical-dollar statements to justify undertaking the adjustment progress. A study of the historical-dollar statements and the adjusted statements in Tables 1 and 2 reveals significant changes in the two sets of statements. Net income on a maintenance of productive capacity basis is 19.63 per cent of the historical-dollar income for 1969. The total replacement cost of plant and equipment is 59.10 per cent and 52.51 per cent greater than historical cost as of 31 December 1969 and 1968 respectively. Also the adjusted stockholders' equity is greater than the unadjusted stockholders' equity by 52.98 per cent and 54.72 per cent as of the end of 1969 and 1968 respectively. These changes are bound to lead to marked differences in the ratios derived from the two sets of statements. Selected comparative ratios are presented in Table 3.

Table 3

SELECTED FINANCIAL RATIOS
DERIVED FROM THE FINANCIAL STATEMENTS OF GRESS CO.

	Conventional	Adjusted
Rate of return on average stockholders' equity	9.87%	1.26%
Earnings per share	$3.10	$0.61
Rate of return on total revenue	4.71%	0.92%
Asset turnover (number of times)	1.68	1.17
Rate of return on average assets	7.91%	1.09%
Rate of federal and state income taxes on income before taxes	48.26%	82.61%

CONCLUSION

The application of replacement costing of the financial statements of Gress Co. was successful and was done objectively. Current cost quotations on suppliers' stationery or on forms bearing the suppliers' stamps and signatures are objective and can be certified by an independent auditor. Also the use of specific price indices compiled by independent parties is verifiable, objective, and free from bias. It is hoped that more attempts will be made by accountants to experiment with replacement costs in order to test further the feasibility of such methods of reporting.

FOOTNOTES

(1) Among the most noted publications are: (1) Edgar O. Edwards and Philip W. Bell, The Theory and Measurement of Business Income, University of California Press, Berkeley and Los Angeles 1961; (2) Robert T. Sprouse and Maurice Moonitz, 'A Tentative Set of Broad Accounting Principles for Business Enterprises', Accounting Research Study No.3, AICPA, New York 1962; and (3) AAA Committee to Prepare a Statement of Basic Accounting Theory, A Statement of Basic Accounting Theory, AAA- Evanston, III. 1966.

(2) See for example Peter Dickerson, Business Income - A Critical Analysis, University of California Press, Berkeley 1965, and Raymond C. Dockweiler, The Practicability of Developing Multiple Financial Statements: A Case Study', The Accounting Review, XLIV (October, 1969), pp. 729-42.

(3) The term objective is used here in the sense that s competent investigator adopting the same approach should arrive at essentially identical results.

(4) The term historical-dollar is used in accordance with the recommendation in 'Financial Statements Restated for General Price-Level Changes', Statement of the Accounting Principles Board No.3, AICPA, New York 1969, p. 3.

(5) The concept of income underlying the application of current replacement costs in this article is that of the maintenance of productive capacity. This concept, unlike the concepts of income underlying many of the replacement cost studies, treats the entire advance in replacement costs as an adjustment of owners' equity rather than as an element of income or holding gain after adjustments for general price level changes. For a discussion of the maintenance of productive capacity concept, see the writer's Replacement Costing and the Maintenance of Productive Capacity Concept of Business Income - Theory and Application', unpublished PhD dissertation. The University of Arizona, 1970. The choice of income concept however does not interfere with the methods of obtaining current replacement costs.

(6) In the absence of market quotations for large blocks of stock held as a long-term investment, the AAA Committee to Prepare a Statement of Basic Accounting Theory recommends the use of book value figures after the accounts of the

issuing corporation have been adjusted to a current replacement cost basis. See A Statement of Basic Accounting Theory, pp. 75-5. The available financial statements of the issuing corporation were not adjusted for replacement costs and such an adjustment was outside the scope of this study.

25 Accounting for Price Changes

S. J. Gray

The emphasis of recent discussion and controversy in the U.K. over the problem of accounting for price changes seems to have been on the "replacement cost" and "current purchasing power" accounting systems as possible alternative solutions. But there is a third possibility which merits some consideration and that is the "continuously contemporary accounting" system devised by Professor R.J. Chambers (1); a system designed to account both for changes in relative prices and change in the general level of prices.

In this paper, the "continuously contemporary accounting" proposal is examined in an application to Richard Costain Ltd., a multinational company based in the U.K. The feasibility and effect of the proposal is determined over a four year period from 1969-73 and the impact on profits compared with the results of the "conventional" accounting system. The study focuses on the issue of measuring company profit achievements in a dynamic business environment with multinational dimensions[1] (2).

The "Continuously Contemporary" System

The main features of Chambers' Systems are (a) to retain the "conventional" historical recording system; (b) to periodically make adjustments to assets, as and when reports are required, so as to record changes in their current cash equivalents (usually indicated by current selling prices or market values); and (c) to periodically record the adjustment necessary to profits or losses which will maintain the shareholders equity in terms of purchasing power - this being a loss in a period of inflation. Both types of price changes are thus accounted for. Changes in relative prices, which affect the money value of assets held by the business, are recorded together with changes in the general level of prices, which affect the value of money itself in terms of general purchasing power.

The calculation of the profit result reflects this distinction. It represents the difference between the beginning and ending net assets or shareholders equity, stated at current market prices, adjusted by the amount appropriate to the maintenance of the purchasing power of the shareholders equity between the two points in time relevant to the report. The resultant amount effectively embodies "conventional" trading results together with (a) asset price change gains and losses not recorded in the "conventional" system and (b) general purchasing power gains or losses to equity capital.

These ideas can be stated symbolically, following Chambers (3), hereunder.

Let $£_o$ and $£_1$ represent pounds of purchasing power at the dates t_o and t_1 respectively, the beginning and ending dates of an accounting period. Let $£_oM_o$ and $£_1M_1$ represent the amounts of the net monetary assets of the business (excluding marketable securities) at the two dates. Let $£_oN_o$ and $£_1N_1$ represent the amounts of the non-monetary assets at the two dates. These are the totals of the current cash equivalents, or selling prices, of all assets other than monetary assets. Let $£_oR_o$ and $£_1R_1$ be the amounts of shareholders equity at the two dates.

The financial position of the business at the two dates can thus be shown as:

at t_o; $$£_oM_o + £_oN_o = £_oR_o \qquad (1)$$

at t_1; $$£_1M_1 + £_1N_1 = £_1R_1 \qquad (2)$$

The amounts on the left-hand sides of these equations are calculated by reference to the actual amounts of assets and liabilities and using selling prices in respect of non-monetary assets. They are statements of fact as regards current cash equivalents (which in turn represent current general purchasing power) at the dates concerned.

Now, in order to calculate the profit for the year it is also necessary to record the impact of changes in the general level of prices to the extent that there is an effect over time on the general purchasing power of the initial resources of the business.

Let p be the proportionate change in the general level of prices (inflation) during the year, expressed as a decimal fraction, (such as .20 where the price index has risen by 20 percent).

Thus it can be stated that:

$$£_o 1 = £_1 \ (1 + p) \tag{3}$$

Since at the end of the year the only pounds then in circulation and the only pounds in which prices are then expressed are $£_1$, the balance sheet at t_o in terms of $£_1$, can be restated by using the relationship $£_o \ 1 = £_1 \ (1 + p)$ as:

$$\text{at } t_o, \ £_1 M_o \ (1 + p) + £_1 N_o \ (1 + p) = £_1 \ R_o \ (1 + p) \tag{4}$$

and as stated above

$$\text{at } t_1, \ M_1 + £_1 N_1 = £_1 \ R_1 \tag{5}$$

Both of these equations are now in terms of $£_1$. The right hand sides can, therefore, be subtracted, at t_o from t_1, to obtain the net profit for the period, or net gain in shareholders equity, as follows:

$$\text{Net Profit} = £_1 \ R_1 - £_1 \ R_o \ (1 + p) \tag{6}$$

$$= £_1 \ (R_1 - R_o - R_o p) \tag{7}$$

The shareholders equity can now be shown as:

Opening balance	R_o	i.e. £ R (1 + p)
Add: Capital Maintenance (inflation) Adjustment	$R_o p$	
Add: Profit for the Year	$£_1 \ (R_1 - R_o - R_o p)$	
Total closing shareholders equity	$£_1 \ R_1$	

Impact of the System

The net effect on "conventional" profits will vary depending on the particular circumstances of the business. Its impact will be determined by the net size of the individual price gains and losses in respect of the company's assets, to the extent that they are not already recorded by the 'conventional' system, in relation to the size of gains or losses to the shareholders equity stake arising from changes in the purchasing power of money. A number of outcomes are possible but in the existing inflationary situation these are reduced to five general possibilities: (1) asset value gains are greater than purchasing power losses with the consequence that ' conventional' profit is increased or loss decreased, (2) asset value gains are equal to purchasing power losses with the consequence that results are unchanged, (3) asset value gains are less than purchasing power losses with the consequence that 'conventional' profit is decreased or loss increased, (4) asset value losses combine with purchasing power losses with the consequence that 'conventional' profit is decreased or loss increased, and, (5) there are no asset value gains and losses and so only purchasing power losses to account for with the consequence that 'conventional' profit is decreased or loss increased.

What then is the impact of the 'continuously contemporary' system when applied to the published profits of Richard Costain Ltd.? And what problems are there in the application process?

The System Applied to Richard Costain Ltd.,

Prerequisites for the application of the 'continuously contemporary accounting' system are access to (1) the market values or current selling prices of assets held by the business, and (2) the index of changes in the general level of prices. In this case, market value information was no problem being already uniquely provided by Richard Costain Ltd., in their published annual statement of assets on a market value basis. General price level information in the form of the general index of retail prices was also readily available from British Government publications such as the "Monthly Digest of Statistics".

Calculations and adjustments necessary to apply the "continuously contemporary' system and to arrive at adjusted profits on that basis are thus readily made. But before this is done the process of assessing the market values of assets must be considered and difficulties appraised.

The Assessment of Market Values

The main reason for choosing Richard Costain Ltd., as the basis for the study is that information about the market values (as an approximation to the current cas equivalents) of assets for the period 1969-73 is readily accessible to the outsider from their financial reports.[2] Additionally, however, the company is a significant multinational enterprise, and is currently ranked at 131 in "The Times 1000" for 1973-74. As stated in the 1973 report, "The Costain Group has a world-wide spread of varied construction and development activities. They include private housing, property development, building, civil engineering, dredging, mining, mechanical engineering, foundation engineering and construction, and the manufacture of concrete products".

The origins of Costain's unique publication of market values can perhaps be found in the takeover moves and ultimate bid by Hanson Trust Ltd., which was rejected by the shareholders early in 1972. This was responsible for the idea that information about market values was relevant to shareholders; an idea which first became manifest in the 1970 report and accounts, published in June 1971, to which the Chairman attached "a simple analysis of our accounts which I believe will facilitate their understanding". Included here was a consolidated cash flow statement, profit and loss account, and balance sheet. The consolidated balance sheet displayed both the book value and market value for each type of item as at December 1969 and 1970. This practice was repeated in 1971; amd in 1972 and 1973 the statement was incorporated into the report and accounts themselves, appearing at the back.[3]

In these published statements Costain's have attempted to approximate the market values of land and buildings, plant and equipment, investments - quoted and unquoted, and stocks - including land for housing.

In table A the consolidated balance sheets for the five years 1969, 1970, 1971, 1972 and 1973 are set out on a comparative basis showing the book values and market values of all items, with ordinary shareholders funds stated on a market value basis as well as a book value basis for each year. On a market value basis shareholders funds are £13,735m in 1969 compared to a book value of £9.571m; in 1970, £18,693m compared to £11,190m; in 1971, £29,685m compared to £15,723m; in 1972, £36,432m compared to £20,478m; and in 1973, £42,392m compared to £24,965m.

These market value figures were specifically stated as being "estimated" with respect to 1969, 1970 and 1971; and as "assessed" in 1972, but in 1973 they were stated simply at "market value". However, the notes to all of the statements indicate that the market values given must vary as to objectivity, and hence verifiability, because of the degrees of reliability of the different sources used. From 1969 to 1972 the market values were based on estimates or assessments (a) by independent valuers, (b) partly by independent valuers and partly by directors, (c) by directors, and (d) by stock exchange sources. In 1973, however, all items were assessed by directors with the exception of quoted investments which were valued on the basis of stock market valuations.

TABLE A

RICHARD COSTAIN LIMITED AND SUBSIDIARIES — CONSOLIDATED BALANCE SHEET

	1969 Book Value £'000	1969 Market Value £'000	1970 Book Value £'000	1970 Market Value £'000	1971 Book Value £'000	1971 Market Value £'000	1972 Book Value £'000	1972 Market Value £'000	1973 Book Value £'000	1973 Market Value £'000
Land and buildings										
-United Kingdom-valued	(6,615	9,115	7,986	13,006	8,614	16,187	8,381	14,652	9,344	18,599
-miscellaneous	(				58	58	418	418		
-Overseas	2,371	2,371	2,305	2,500	1,723	2,704	2,397	3,473	3,135	3,754
Plant and Equipment	5,635	5,635	7,192	8,000	11,845	15,758	13,616	18,053	17,082	21,393
Investments-quoted	626	1,354	762	1,635	973	2,352	1,840	3,412	1,939	2,055
unquoted	1,442	1,500	1,730	1,730	1,699	1,699	2,090	2,685	2,500	3,624
Debtors and work in progress	19,374	19,374	18,149	18,149	16,989	16,989	20,767	20,767	28,949	28,949
Stocks-including land for housing	10,022	10,900	9,683	10,750	9,241	12,811	17,745	26,212	24,314	33,176
Cash in hand, at bank and on deposit	2,844	2,844	2,581	2,581	4,957	4,957	5,707	5,707	8,301	8,301
Total Assets	48,929	53,093	50,388	58,351	56,279	73,515	72,761	95,379	95,564	119,851
Borrowed money	18,840	18,840	17,725	17,725	15,051	15,051	15,086	15,086	24,341	24,341
Deferred taxation	411	411	838	838	1,322	2,679	2,808	7,142	3,386	7,994
Current liabilities & provisio provisions	18,940	18,940	19,400	19,400	22,807	22,807	31,046	31,046	38,841	38,841
Minority interests in subsidiaries	467	467	535	1,049	676	2,593	2,643	4,973	3,331	5,583
Preference share capital	700	700	700	700	700	700	700	700	700	700
Total Liabilities	39,358	39,358	39,198	39,712	40,556	43,820	52,283	58,947	70,599	77,459
Equity Share Capital	1,795	1,795	1,811	1,811	2,728	2,728	4,112	4,112	6,168	6,168
Reserves	7,776	11,940	9,379	16,828	12,995	26,957	16,366	32,320	18,797	36,224
	9,571	13,735	11,190	18,639	15,723	29,685	20,478	36,432	24,965	42,392

It can perhaps be agreed that the reliability of market value information provided by independent valuers and stock exchange sources is sufficiently objective, and hence verifiable, for the purposes of approximating market values. But what of those valuations made by directors? It is the subjective element in such valuations which must lay them open to question as to their reliability, though the directors' view may well be accurate and certainly they are well placed to make such an assessment. Whilst professional valuations are desirable there is of course the question of cost and Costain's directors accordingly chose to make some assessments themselves taking into account available professional valuations as well as sales data. An interesting point in this connection is that the auditors did not disapprove of Costain's market value figures. However, the potential limitations of the data as to accuracy must be noted, and the results of this application of "continuously contemporary accounting" treated with some caution. If however, the market value figures given can be accepted as approaching realism, as seems likely, then the results of the application must closely indicate the real dimensions of business fortune and changes in it.

General questions concerning the assessment of market values have now been considered but what of the valuation details in respect of particular items?

Land and Buildings: In 1969, the market values of all land and buildings were assessed by directors. In 1970 the market values of U.K. land and buildings were estimated by independent valuers whereas those overseas were estimated by directors. In 1971 and 1972, the "valued" U.K. land and buildings was estimated or assessed by independent valuers, the U.K. "miscellaneous" by directors, and the "overseas" partly by independent valuers and partly by directors. In 1973, the market values of all land and buildings were assessed by directors. The basis adopted in making all of these valuations was that of a willing buyer/willing seller in the open market. Only significant items were dealt with in the valuation process. Overall, it seems certain that the valuations made were conservative.

Plant and Equipment: In 1969, the valuation basis was that of depreciated original cost, but in 1970 the market values of plant and equipment were estimated by directors, in 1971 and 1972 partly by independent valuers and partly by directors, and in 1973 again by directors. The basis of the market valuations, as with land and buildings, was that of willing buyer/willing seller in the open market. Only major items were included in the valuation. In the case of dredgers, draglines, and mining equipment a world market exists and so world wide market values were adopted. A ready second-hand market exists for such items and they are often sold or traded-in before their effective useful lives are over. There is a point here concerning the market from which a multi-national company should obtain market value information. In the Chambers' system the company should obtain the information from the markets in which it conventionally deals, and this would seem consistent with Costain's experience. There is also the question of aggregation on a multi-national scale. However, this would not seem to be a problem so long as the market values adopted are an approximation of current cash equivalent and hence measure the adaptability of the enterprise in the various markets in which it operates.

Investments: In each of the years from 1969-73, quoted investments were consistently valued on the basis of stock market quotations at the middle market price. Unquoted investments, on the other hand, were valued on the basis of the share of equity held taken at book value.

Stocks: In 1969, stocks were valued by directors. In 1970, 1971, and 1972, stocks were valued partly by independent valuers and partly by directors. In 1973, the valuations were made entirely by the directors. In all cases the valuation basis was that of willing buyer/willing seller in the open market. The largest single item in this category consisted of land for housing.

Deferred Taxation: In the Chambers' system deferred taxation is not recorded because it is considered to be an intangible item which cannot affect the adaptability of the enterprise at the date of the report because it is not a legal obligation. In the application that follows the deferred taxation account has, therefore, been removed as a liability and included in shareholders equity. An elimination of the deferred taxation account does, of course, increase the measure of "continuously contemporary" profits, given that this account is a growing one as it is in this instance.

Foreign Currency Translation: In the 1973 accounts it is stated that "assets and liabilities in foreign currencies and the results of overseas subsidiaries and associated companies have been converted into sterling at the rates of exchange ruling at 31 December". This is also the approach used with the market value figures for each year which have been translated at current rates of exchange. This is consistent with the idea of providing relevant up-to-date information. Current market values must be translated at current rates if they are to say anything about existing existing capacity to adapt and survive, and grow.

There is a problem here though with regard to adjustments for changes in the general price level as required by the Chambers' system. Is it sufficient to adjust the shareholders equity in the home country by the home price level index, as is done in the following application, or is this too much of a simplification? If resources are deployed in various countries, as are perhaps shareholders too, then possibly local indexes should additionally be used, prior to the currency translation, to ascertain whether or not resources have been maintained in each area of activity, and not just in terms of the home country's inflationary experience. This is grounds for providing a more comprehensive disaggregation of performance data by multinational companies according to activity and geographical market, in addition to providing aggregate consolidated data.

If the users of financial reports are to be fully informed then they must surely require information of the success or otherwise of a business in maintaining the purchasing power of its resources in each geographical market. Any difference between the total of the general price level adjustments in each of the geographical markets and the amount of the home price level adjustment on the basis of the consolidated shareholders equity could be reconciled in the consolidated financial statements by making changes in the inflation adjustment as appropriate. Such changes would be necessary only if the total of the individual general price level adjustments was greater than the amount of the home-based consolidated price level adjustment, thus necessitating a further reduction of profit to maintain the general purchasing power of the business in multinational terms.

The Calculation of "Continuously Contemporary" Profits

The assessment of the market values of all assets readily provides a basis for the calculation of "continuously contemporary" profits. This calculation in respect of Richard Costain Ltd. for 1969-70, 1970-71, 1971-72, and 1972-73 is set out in Table B. The process was as follows: (1) the assessment of the shareholders equity at the beginning and end of each period, on the basis of current market values. These figures have been, of course, provided by the company but in addition the closing equity figure will have to be

TABLE B
COMPANY PROFITS: A 'CONTINUOUSLY CONTEMPORARY' CALCULATION

RICHARD COSTAIN LTD.		1969-70 £'000	1970-71 £'000	1971-72 £'000	1972-73 £'000
A. 1	Opening Equity: market value basis	13,735	18,639	29,685	36,432
2	Add: Deferred Taxation	+ 411	+ 838	+ 2,679	+ 7,142
A.	Opening Equity:adjusted (market value basis)	14,146	19,477	32,364	43,574
B. 1	Closing Equity: market value basis	18,639	29,685	36,432	42,392
2	Add: Deferred Taxation	+ 838	+ 2,679	+ 7,142	+ 7,994
3	Add: Dividends (ordinary)	+ 396	+ 816	+ 1,021	+ 885
4	Deduct: increases in share capital (incl. premiums)	- 70	- 2,769	- 225	-
B.	Closing Equity:adjusted (market value basis)	19,803	30,411	44,370	51,271
B-A	Equity Change:adjusted (market value basis)	+ 5,657	+10,934	+12,006	+ 7,697
C.	Deduct:Inflation Adjustment* (based on change in general price level as it affects Opening Equity:adjusted)	- 1,116	- 1,760	- 2,477	- 4,608
D.	Profit Result:Adjusted (after tax)	+ 4,541	+ 9,174	+ 9,529	+ 3,089
	Profit Result:Published	+ 1,902	+ 3,044	+ 4,940	+ 4,828

* Retail Price Index:ratio of change for the year: $\frac{145.0}{134.4}$ $\frac{158.1}{145.0}$ $\frac{170.2}{158.1}$ $\frac{188.2}{170.2}$

TABLE C : COMPANY PROFITS : A STATEMENT AND A RECONCILIATION

		a Published Profit £'000	b Asset Price Gains/Losses Not Recorded £'000	c Equity Change at Market Value (a + b) £'000	d Inflation Adjustment £'000	e Adjusted Profit (c + d) £'000	Published Dividends £'000	Published Retentions £'000
	1969-70	+1,902	+3,775	+ 5,657	-1,116	+4,541	396	1,506
RICHARD	1970-71	+7,890	+7,890	+10,934	-1,760	+9,174	816	2,228
COSTAIN	1971-72	+4,940	+7,066	+12,006	-2,477	+9,529	1,021	3,919
LTD.	1972-73	+4,828	+2,869	+ 7,697	-4,608	+3,089	885	3,943

TABLE D : PERFORMANCE COMPARISONS

		RATE OF RETURN ON OPENING EQUITY	
		PUBLISHED	ADJUSTED
	1969-70	19.87%	29.75%
RICHARD	1970-71	27.20%	43.20%
COSTAIN	1971-72	31.42%	27.35%
LTD.	1972-73	23.58%	6.41%

adjusted by any dividend payments (to be added back) and any increases in Share Capital (to be deducted). Further, an adjustment for deferred taxation will have to be made to the opening and closing equity figures. These adjustments are necessary to show the real growth in equity for the period. (2) The calculation of the net change in equity on a market value basis; an increase being a gain, a decrease being a loss. (3) The deduction from this figure of the amount necessary to be charged as an "inflation adjustment" to maintain the opening equity; this being based on the change in the retail price index for the year. Note that it has been assumed here as a simplification that dividend payments and shares issues coincide with the year end. A final adjusted profit result (after tax) for each year was thus arrived at and can be compared with the published profit results (after tax).

An Evaluation of Results

The effect of this application of the "continuously contemporary" accounting system to Richard Costain Ltd. can be seen in tables C and D which set out the results in summary form. In Table C the calculation of company profits on a "continuously contemporary" basis is summarised in a way which reconciles the published profit results with those on the adjusted basis. This reconciliation is achieved by adding or deducting the net amount of the asset price gains or losses not recorded in the "conventional" system, and by the deduction of the amount to be charged as an "inflation adjustment". Note that the asset price gains or losses, or net change in the market value of assets held, must be calculated by deduction since the outsider will not have access to the detailed records of specific assets held by the business. This figure is necessarily the change in equity at market values not already accounted for a published profit. In Table D the "rates of return on opening equity" are set out on the basis of published and adjusted profit results. The rate of return is calculated on the basis of profit as a percentage of the opening equity figure adjusted by the retail price index to end year prices.

Significant differences between the published and adjusted results are evident from a study of tables C and D. The range of adjusted profits from 1969-73 is +£9,529,000 to +3,089,000 compared to the published range of +£4,940,000 to +£1,902,000. Correspondingly, the range of adjusted rates of return are +43.20% to +6.41% compared to the published range of +31.42% to 19.87%.

An examination of the results for individual years reveals that "conventional" profit calculations both overestimate and underestimate the actual situation given that "continously contemporary" accounting is an accurate reflection of the impact of price changes on business fortunes. In 1969-70, 1970-71 and 1971-72 the published profit figures are an underestimate in contrast to the adjusted results (but note, in contradiction, that in 1971-72 the published rate of return figure is an overestimate). However, in 1972-73 the position is reversed; the published result is an overestimate.

The situation according to the published results is in fact one of growth with a peak in 1971-72 and a slight decline in 1972-73. The "continuously contemporary" situation, however, depicts more dramatic growth and subsequent decline; from a position of strength in 1970-71 to one of considerably reduced profitability in real terms in 1972-73. This is supported by the "rate of return" figures which show an adjusted return of 29.75% in 1969-70, peaking to 43.20% in 1970-71, but then declining to 27.35% in 1971-72 and 6.41% in 1972-73. This can be compared to the published returns of 19.87%, 27.20%, 31.42% and 23.58% for the four years in question.

It is interesting to note from table C that despite this decline in profitability the company has in fact maintained its equity capital in terms of general purchasing power. Moreover, the company's retentions policy has in fact had the effect of not paying dividends out of capital though the margin of safety in 1972-73 was reduced.

Conclusions

The feasibility and effect of a "continuously contemporary" accounting system has been successfully demonstrated in a comprehensive application to Richard Costain Ltd., a multinational company, for the period 1969-73.

If it is accepted that such a system is more realistic than the "conventional" approach, then the results of this application support the view that published profit results have the capacity to mislead in the dynamic situation of changing prices. The "continuosly contemporary accounting" proposal, in contrast, is successful, at least in this instance, in recording the impact of both changes in relative prices and changes in the general price level on the fortunes of business. This must surely be qualification enough to present it as a viable alternative to the "replacement cost" and "current purchasing power" proposals. The viability of a proposal does not, of course, make it necessarily valid or preferable in relation to others. This latter aspect has not been investigated here and in fact there is a dearth of evidence, as opposed to argument, bearing on the relative "usefulness" of the various alternatives which have been proposed. There would seem to be a clear need now for some effort in this area before any final conclusions can be drawn as to an appropriate system of accounting for price changes and inflation.

Notes

1 Note that this study is conducted in the context of reporting achievements and not expectations. See Barton (2) for a clarification of the functions of ex-post and ex-ante data in the decision-making process.

2 The following discussion also benefits from a meeting with Mr. B.C. Moss, Group Chief Accountant, Richard Costain Limited whose help on points of information is gratefully acknowledged.

3 Subsequent to the completion of this case study for the period 1969-73 it is noted from the 1974 report that this practice has now been discontinued. The Directors state that "having regard to the valatile market conditions prevailing in a number of areas, it is not considered appropriate to follow the practice of recent years and provide a detailed assessment of the aggregate excess of market values over book values. Nevertheless, your board is satisfied that the overall worth to the Group of the underlying net tangible assets is not less than that applicable at 31 December 1973". But volatile market conditions must surely be just the situation where knowledge is crucial; and if precision is not possible then estimates would be useful with some indication as to probable accuracy.

A further point is that however valatile the state of a market it must always be possible to make some assessment of the position at a particular point in time. That is, of course, the function of a balance sheet; but that is not omitted even though it is known that the position will be different the very next day.

References

(1) Chambers, Raymond J., ACCOUNTING EVALUATION AND ECONOMIC BEHAVIOUR, (Prentice-Hall, Englewood Cliffs) 1966;

and "Second Thoughts on Continuously Contemporary Accounting", ABACUS, September 1970, pp. 39-55.

(2) Barton, A.D., "Expectations and Achievements in Income Theory", THE ACCOUNTING REVIEW, October 1974, pp 664-681

(3) Chambers, R.J., "Continuously Contemporary Accounting", THE ACCOUNTANT, April 30th, 1970. pp. 644-645.

VIII British Developments in Current Cost Accounting

26 The Sandilands Report

W. T. Baxter

It is one of the features of British public life that, when we want an opinion on pressing problems, we entrust its formulation to a group of laymen who have no personal acquaintance with the matter. The system may work remarkably well when the opinion reflects the general feeling and sense of justice, but less well when it deals with the abstract or intricate. Thus a jury may reach a wise verdict on whether a book offends today's views on obscenity, but an unwise one when faced with complexities. Accounting principles involve both general feeling and complex analysis, so we ought not to be surprised if a government committee, doing its best to re-think principles, should produce a report that is excellent in some parts, less so in others. In my view, the Sandilands report has this curate's egg quality.

VALUABLE CONTRIBUTIONS BY THE REPORT

First the good news. In its analysis of the nature of income, and its effort to build upon the Hicksian definition, the report reaches a level far above that usually found in public pronouncements on accounting. Its support for the unravelling of operating profit from holding gain is at once valuable and daring. Its stress on the irrelevance of historical cost for decisions, and the importance of current cost, is admirable. Above all, it deserves immense credit for its choice of the Bonbrightian concept of a selective "value to the owner" (deprival value) for valuing assets.

The report explains these matters with clarity, and backs up its explanation with samples and statistics. As a text-book on accounting principles, it bids fair to be a best seller for many a day. We academics must ruefully concede that it succeeds in publicising matters that we have tried for years to put across with much less success.

But academics can take pleasure at least in noting how much our colleagues have contributed to the report. Its discussion frequently acknowledges the weight of the views in their evidence, even where it rejects these. And, after all, most of the report's innovations are based on three books by American academics: Sweeney (1) introduced inflation accounting to English-speaking readers (and receives brief mention); Bonbright (2) fathered "value to the owner" (handsomely acknowledged); and, if I am not mistaken, Edwards and Bell (3) did the first important writing on holding gain and operating profit (ignored).

CCA VERSUS CPP

Many of the discussions (including that in the report) on inflation accounting treat the "current cost" and "current purchasing power" approaches as if they were mutually exclusive. This is a pity: both should play a part in improved accounts.

Reform should cure defects in four areas:

1. Asset Values

   During inflation, the historical figures in a balance sheet must tend to understate the firm's resources. As the report argues forcefully, managers and investors are thereby handicapped. Conversion of the historical figures with a general index may be better than nothing, but there is no guarantee that a given asset's value moves in harmony with general prices; for instance, the price of stocks in the linen-hire industry went up some five times as fast as general prices in 1973-4. So the CCP proposal of SSAP7 is a rather feeble cure for the balance sheet. Here, current value is far better.

2. Costs for Management decision

   A manager must from time to time make decisions on some proposed activity by comparing its revenues with its costs, including the sacrifice of assets (already owned) that will be used up. If his values for the assets are wrong, his decision is less likely to be right. Here again, CCP correction of historical cost may yield an answer remote from the assets' current worth to the firm.

In both (1) and (2) above, the aim is to show net assets at a given moment, and here we have just found CCA (interpreted as deprival value) to be vastly more helpful than CCP. But in (3) and (4) the aim is instead to compare the total net assets (whether valued at CCA or anything else) at different dates, i.e. to see if the owner has maintained his capital. So now we face an additional problem - that of selecting the unit of comparison over time. We may choose the £, or a CCP unit, or a physical unit, i.e. we may define maintenance in terms of money capital, real capital, or physical capital. It is on this choice that most of the argument centres:

3. Income and the time-lag error

If, during inflation, there is a time-lag between the cost date of an input and the sale date of the corresponding output, then the use of historical cost exaggerates the surplus of revenue over cost, i.e. throws up a bigger profit. Here the accountant is flouting logic by subtracting units of different kinds (bad cost £s from worse revenue £s). Typically the error occurs in three types of calculation: for capital gains; where stocks are held; and where depreciating assets are held.

To cure the error, one must translate the cost of £s into their counterparts at revenue date. The translator appears best to satisfy logic (i.e. subtracts £s of most nearly the same ilk) if he can say for instance:

"The £1 spent in March seems just as good, in the eyes of the owner, as £1.1 earned in July; so let us raise the March cost by 10%." This view means that one plumps for the concept of real capital maintenance, and uses the index that most nearly reflects the owner's purchases of things-in-general. SSAP7 backs this general index (GI) concept. The alternative is to translate the cost by revaluation or use of the special index (SI) of the particular input's prices, i.e. to say that capital has been made good if the firm can restore the physical units - regardless of whether they are worth more in real terms, or indeed are now worthless. The report backs this physical concept when it highlights operating profit alone, and relegates holding gain into a dim background. The GI view stresses the man and economic reality; the SI view, the firm and physical attributes. To those who accept that the chief reason for measuring income is to aid man's decisions on consumption and investment, there cannot be much doubt which concept is the winner.

4. Real appreciation (or loss) on assets

When prices are fluctuating dramatically, the values of some assets (or liabilities) may rise or fall far more than GI movement suggests. News of such real change (i.e. the difference between general and special movements) may be important to investors and managers, sometimes alerting them to incompetence and to such dangers as the likelihood of a takeover. If the reformed statements use both the SI and the GI, the hidden real appreciation comes into view automatically; because the assets are revalued with the SI, but the owners' claims (capital, retained profits, etc.) with the GI) the real gains emerge as a difference.

Similarly, where the GI is applied to the owners' claims but the figures for net money assets are not adjusted, the accounts throw up the gain or loss on money. This is a particularly important figure. If the accounts of trustees and charities let alone the commercial firms, had shown inflation's ravages over the post-war period, the public outcry might well have stung the government out of its inertia.

Lenders would have seen how philanthropic they were, and borrowers how much they gained from gearing. Instead of shrill outcry when interest rates rise, there would be recognition that the rates should be far higher (even after tax) if they are to offset the real but hidden transfers of wealth from lender to borrower.

Accounts that ignore such movement are indefensible.

In recognising holding gain, the report does us a great service. In refusing to distinguish real from nominal holding gains, or to recognise gain and loss on money, it does us a great disservice.

COMBINING CCA VALUES WITH CPP PROFIT

It may be objected that there is a clash between my use of current cost under (1) and (2) above, and of CPP under (3) and (4). If current cost is the right figure for decision costs, is it not also the most informative charge in income calculations? And is not CPP income thereby pushed out? The answers to these two questions are yes and no. Current cost is indeed the most telling figure for the debit to the profit and loss account (and dovetails best with current balance sheet values). But, by the simple device of crediting real holding gain to the account (instead of relegating all holding gain to reserves and a note, as the report does on page 190), the profit balance can be restored to CPP level.

THE REPORT'S REJECTION OF THE GENERAL INDEX

Right at its start, the report denounces the GI. Its main reason (pages 12 and 13) is that "the concept of 'general price changes' in the abstract, unrelated to the purchasing pattern of any class of individuals or entities, is unquantifiable"; movement in the retail price index "measures the rate of inflation experienced on average by a broad range of middle income families" but not by the highest income group of companies.

I find this view astounding. Knowledgeable people readily admit the limitations of a composite index, yet find it informative for all manner of purposes. The publications of the Central Statistical Office - whose staff can hardly be accused of naivete in these matters - bristle with tables of CPP figures. Innumerable writers illuminate economic affairs with calculations based on composite indices. Various South American lands, plagued by inflation, have for years been using composite indices to adjust contracts, accounts and tax - and seem well pleased with the arrangement. I am ready to bet that, when the members of the Sandilands committee open their morning paper, most of them turn to the Financial Times index, and feel that it tells them something worth knowing.

Final accounts normally contain some figures that cannot be guaranteed as incontrovertibly accurate. They should aim to give a picture that is as comprehensive as possible, and approximate data can often be far better than none. Sophisticated readers are not unaware of the figures' limitations, and accept Keynes' saying that it is better to be vaguely right than precisely wrong. If the introduction of CPP figures gives helpful insight into matters of major importance, some slight fuzziness is not too high a price.

ILL-RESULTS OF IGNORING CPP

Its doctrinaire rejection of the GI robs the report of much of its potential value. The first and most obvious aim of inflation accounts is to tell readers about money loss or gain; without the GI, this is impossible. Many of the other aims are also frsutrated. The committee's attitude has not only weakened its analysis, but has led it to shift its ground and evade the chief issue. The Inflation Accounting report is not on inflation accounting.

The report's attitude may do more harm in a much broader context. Increasingly we are coming round to the view that, where we cannot halt inflation, we had better learn to live comfortably with it. The most successful steps to this end (as tested for instance in Brazil for the last dozen years) are based on indexation of bonds, other long term contracts, wages, tax, etc. These steps seem fairly effective in abating the most harmful results of inflation, i.e. personal suffering and resource misallocation. The whole programme of "monetary correction" rests on the acceptability of a composite index. Thus the report's disparagement of the GI may have ill-consequencies far removed from accounting.

RELEVANT ISSUES IN THE ABSENCE OF INFLATION

However, the report's by-passing of the GI does yield an indirect gain in understanding. Some of the problems thrown up during discussions of inflation accounting are not really problems of inflation: they are more general, and might have been solved long before inflation became noticeable. In other words, the right way to start a study of inflation accounting is to ask how to draft the accounts of a firm whose assets change in value during a year when general prices are fairly stable.

Here, the two main problems concern the concept of physical capital maintenance, and the treatment of money gain or loss.

1. Physical Capital and the Finance of Expansion.

LIFO is the best-known application of the concept of physical capital maintenance: if the number of tons, etc., of stock stays constant, change in stock value is ignored (even when there is a disastrous loss); only change in the number of units is recognised. The report's adjustment of the cost-of-sales and depreciation with the SI comes to much the same thing (though it is more defensible in that the suggested "summary statement" gives some clue to the size of the holding gains, under the unlikely heading "movements on reserves net of tax").

The main argument in favour of the physical capital concept is of course that it obviates the payment of tax and dividend on holding gain, and thus helps the firm to pay for replacement without cash strain. The report founds its case largely on this notion of gains "that may prudently be regarded as distributable" (p.28). The doctrine is at first sight appealing; but it soon lands us in a mess. It subordinates income measurement to cash budgeting. Cash distributions may be imprudent for all manner of reasons; where do we draw the line in deciding whether imprudence changes income? If I commit myself to buying a car, the budgetary strain may be agonizing; but does it cut down my salary?

It is tempting to answer these questions by distinguishing physical replacement from physical expansion. This brings us to the most difficult point of the argument - the contrast between physical and economic attributes. We feel superior when told that a primitive tribe ranks a man's wealth by the number of his cattle, with no regard to whether the beasts are too decrepit to yield meat and milk. But are we not falling into just the same trap if, when recording outlay on stock, we treat it in one way if it is for extra physical units, and in another if it is for replacement of the same number of units whose price has gone up? (Remember that we are still assuming money's value to be stable). Surely the right criterion of asset expansion is that the outlay is expected to improve the cash flow. Dearer units are just as likely as more units to do this (unless the firm is very queerly placed). Both types of outlay are investment in extra resources, and so bring expansion in the economic sense.

If this view is sound, the events germane to our discussion flow as follows. The owner of stocks (or for that matter other kinds of assets, such as securities) first sells the appreciating asset, and thus augments his income. He next decides to plough these earnings back, i.e. henceforth to keep the firm at its expanded size. He may do so by physical replacement or by investment in different assets; both courses leave his wealth at its new level, and so do not reduce his income. Where a company report hides the expansion by failing to stress holding gain, it denies shareholders their right to say whether the investment serves their best interest.

It is doubtless exceedingly unfortunate when tax payments jeopardise economic-expansion-cum-physical stability; physical shrinkage may bring disproportionate inefficiency. loss, and unemployment. But the fault lies with tax rates and rules, not income measurement. It is against tax that reformers should aim their fire.

Moreover if tax is grounded on dubious theory, as it will be if the report is put into effect, there will be anomalies and injustice. The man-in-the-street will feel bitter at his own stern assessment when firms with big holding profits are let off; he may well find it odd that a socialist government should treat business so handsomely. Persons liable to capital gains tax will ask why, when so many other holding gains are exempt, their gain should attract tax. Much ingenuity will be expended on dressing up speculative ventures as trade in stocks. When special prices turn downwards (and here comes the most serious flaw in the system), business-men will be outraged on finding that they may not deduct holding loss from taxable profit; the harm done at this stage will probably be so great that the government will be forced to junk the whole system.

2. Change in the Value of Money Assets and Liabilities.

Even when the general value of money is stable, the value of a given set of money-rights can change. Thus we may reduce a debt to us as a concession to a semi-bankrupt debtor; likewise our creditors may in hard times allow a reduction in the sum due by us on redemption of a loan.

The report's rules for such loss and gain are not clear. Is the reduction of the asset a realised or an unrealised loss? Probably most of us would treat it - if for no reason other than prudence - as realised. Does it come from holding or operations (ordinary or extraordinary)? Presumably the answers depend largely on whether the debt originated in ordinary trade or financial dealings; compare normal bad debts with default on bonds. The rules for gain on liabilities are even vaguer. There would be simple logic in saying that what is sauce for the goose is sauce for the gander - that the timing and classification of gain should be the counterparts of those for loss. But the reduction of a remote liability does seem more nebulous than other gains, and in the meantime provides no liquid resources. A cut today in my budgeted loan repayment in 1996 is certainly a form of gain to me, but yields no cash with which to pay a current tax. Probably such gain should be kept quite separate from other forms of profit.

RELEVANT ISSUES DURING INFLATION

Once the ground-rules have been laid down for measuring income in times of price stability, we can readily adapt them to inflation. The holding gains of stability are real gains. Inflation accounting should identify such gains - the gap between general (nominal) and special appreciation - and treat them according to the ground-rules; and it should drain away the nominal gains from income. To unravel real from nominal, it needs the GI.

The two main problems can be re-stated briefly.

1. Physical capital, real capital, and expansion.

Because the real capital concept concentrates on the owners' balances rather than the net assets, it greatly simplifies many of the issues. It avoids difficulties when a replacement is physically dissimilar to the old asset. It interprets expansion and replacement in terms of effects on the owners' purchasing power. It clarifies discussions of backlog depreciation. It dispenses with the awkward, perhaps meaningless, notion of "the entity's well-offness".

When a firm makes a real holding gain during inflation, GI correction of income will lessen the cash strains of replacement, though it will not relieve them completely; thus some case for tax concession will persist. On the other hand, the firm suffering real holding loss will be far better placed with GI correction.

It will be a thousand pities if a new way of measuring profit, deemed vastly more informative to all parties save the tax inspector, has to be thrown away for the sake of tax concessions. If the national interest demands aid for expanding firms, the aid should be direct and explicit, and not a hidden by-product of distorted accounts. There would not be much harm in continuing to have a double set of profits - one for the taxman, one for the rest. The tax profit could be reduced by allowances for new plant, etc., as at present - and (to be consistent, and give even more aid for expansion) by comparable allowances for all investment in stock.

2. Inflationary gain and loss on money

Inflation changes the worth of money rights just as inexorably as the debt reductions mentioned before, but without the clear evidence of formal agreements½ Good accounts should show the change, and can do so with GI help.

More than any other kind of holding gain and loss, however, the value change seems remote from operating profit in both its nature and "realisation". Accounts should therefore keep it far removed from other profit. While SSAP7 was sound on this point in its argument, its numerical illustration unfortunately lumped money gain with other profit: this treatment can give a distorted impression of the firm's progress (as subsequent published statistics show) and raises the spectre of a new tax on money gain. I think that money gain or loss should not affect taxable income; there would be gross inequity in letting business charge the loss on the money in its till (as Brazil does), and not letting the private person charge the loss on the £ in his pocket. The Sandilands committee's distaste for GI adjustment was no doubt strengthened by its recognition of the tax hazard.

RECOMMENDATIONS

The government has now ordered the accounting profession to work out a detailed programme, presumably in line with the Sandilands views. A steering committee is charged with this task. We must hope that it will draft counter-proposals. They should include these major points:

1. Final accounts should be adjusted by both the SI and GI - the former for assets, the latter for income. There is no great difficulty in using both within a set of (one-column) accounts.

2. Gain or loss on money should be included in accounts but not lumped with any other profits.

3. Taxable profit should be based on GI profit. If further encouragement is needed for real investment, it should take the form of allowances that are unrelated to the accounts.

PRINCIPLES AND INDEPENDENCE.

"Recommendations" and "standards" have their disadvantages - sapping of independent judgement, constraint on enquiry and education, the risk of ossification. Another item must, it now seems, be added to the list. Thanks to the existence of standards, government can tell the profession to change "generally accepted principles". But a profession that prizes its independence and integrity should not (indeed cannot) change principles at an outsider's behest. We must trust that the steering committee will be firm on this issue, and will have the wit and determination to proffer a better programme.

FOOTNOTES

(1) Sweeney, H.W., STABILIZED ACCOUNTING, (New York: Harper & Bros.), 1936; (republished by Hold, Rinehart and Winston), 1964.

(2) Bonbright, J.C., VALUATION OF PROPERTY, (New York: McGraw-Hill), 1937; (reprinted Charlotteville, Virginia: Michie Company), 1965.

(3) Edwards, E.O. and Bell, P.W., THE THEORY AND MEASUREMENT OF BUSINESS INCOME, (Berkeley: University of California Press), 1960.

27 Recommendations for Practice: Extracts from U.K. Exposure Draft 18

(The extracts printed here are taken from the British Exposure Draft 18 on Current Cost Accounting. To reduce this excerpt to manageable proportions, we have omitted the now redundant implementation proposals (paras. 1-6 of the original draft), the extensive definitions and explanatory notes (paras. 101-232), the treatment of taxation and government grants (paras. 18-21, 47-48, 71-75) and material on group accounts (paras. 80-84). The remaining text encapsulates the basic essentials of the proposal, and has been illustrated with pro forma statements taken from the original Appendices. Eds.)

CONTENT OF ACCOUNTS

6. Annual Accounts prepared and presented on the bases set out in this Standard should contain a profit and loss account, an appropriation account and a balance sheet. Except for wholly-owned subsidiaries, there should be included in the notes to the accounts a statement of the change in shareholders' net equity interest after allowing for the change in the value of money. Accounts of enterprises within the scope of SSAP 10 will also include a statement of source and application of funds.

PROFIT AND LOSS ACCOUNT

7. The profit and loss account should show (inter alia)

(a) the operating profit or loss for the year;
(b) interest payable less receivable;
(c) the current cost profit or loss before taxation;
(d) taxation;
(e) the current cost profit or loss before

Table 1.

X. Ltd. and its Subsidiaries

Year ended 31st December, 197 .

Consolidated Profit and Loss Account

	See Note	£000s	Paragraph in Standard	
Turnover		X		
Operating profit/(loss) for the year	1.	X	129	
Interest payable less receivable		X	17	
		X		
Share of profits/(losses) of associated companies		X	86	
CURRENT COST PROFIT/(LOSS) BEFORE TAXATION AND BEFORE EXTRAORDINARY ITEMS		X		7
Taxation	2.	(X)	20	
		X		
Minority interest		(X)		
Current cost profit/(loss) before extraordinary items		X		
Extraordinary items (net of tax and minority interest)	3.	X		
CURRENT COST PROFIT/(LOSS) FOR THE YEAR		X	130	

Consolidated Appropriation Account

	See Note		£000s	Paragraph in Standard
Current cost profit/(loss) for the year			X	
Net surplus for year on revaluation of assets	4.	X		
Appropriated to revaluation reserve		(X)	X	22
Available for distribution and general reserve			X	
Dividends			(X)	
Added to/(deducted from) general reserve			X	

extraordinary items;

(f) extraordinary items; and

(g) the current cost profit or loss for the year.

The operating profit or loss is arrived at after charging depreciation and the cost of sales on the basis of the current value to the business of the physical assets consumed during the year.

Depreciation: plant and machinery

8. The charge to the profit and loss account for depreciation should equal the value to the business of the assets consumed during the period. When assets are valued on the basis of their net current replacement cost, the value consumed increases as the replacement cost of the asset increases, but since it will not normally be possible to identify individual price movements within an accounting period, the charge may be based on average values for the period, calculated before charging depreciation for the current period. It may be based on end-of-period values if this basis does not produce a materially different charge from one calculated on average values.

9. Where average values are used, the charge for depreciation is obtained by apportioning the asset's average value over a period equal to the expected remaining useful life of the asset at the beginning of the period.

10. A review of asset lives should be regularly undertaken on a consistent basis so that the depreciation charge is realistic in relation to the expected life of the asset.

11. Backlog depreciation should be charged against the related revaluation surpluses, rather than to the profit and loss account.

12. In a period when the basis of valuing an asset is changed from its net current replacement cost to its economic value or net realisable value, depreciation should first be calculated by the normal method adopted by the company on the assumption of the continuing application of a net current replacement cost basis of valuation. The further write down required should be treated in accordance with the provisions of paragraph 28.

Depreciation: land and buildings

13. Depreciation is not normally required for freehold land,

but is required for freehold buildings. Depreciation should be based on:

(a) the depreciable amount;
(b) the estimated remaining economic useful life of the buildings at the year end,

both of which will be advised by the valuer, after consultation with the directors.

14. Depreciation of leasehold land and buildings will be required on both the depreciable amount and the residual amount. If the valuer, after consultation with the directors, estimates that the remaining economic useful life of the buildings exceeds the remaining term of the lease, the entire value of the land and buildings should be depreciated over the remaining term of the lease. Where the remaining economic useful life of the buildings is estimated to be less than the remaining term of the lease, the depreciable amount should be depreciated over the estimated remaining economic useful life of the buildings, and the residual amount should be depreciated over the remaining term of the lease.

Cost of stock and work in progress consumed

15. The amount charged to the profit and loss account for the period for stock and work in progress consumed should be the value to the business, at the date of consumption, of the stock and work in progress consumed during the period.

16. Where a cost of sales adjustment is calculated (see appendix 3) to revise to current cost a cost of sales determined on another basis, the adjustment should be added to or, where appropriate, deducted from the cost of sales charged to the profit and loss account for the period and included as part of the surplus or deficit arising on revaluation of stock.

Interest

17. The net amount of interest paid and interest received should be shown separately in the profit and loss account as a deduction from, or addition to, the operating profit for the period. The separate amounts of interest paid and received should be disclosed in a note to the accounts.

APPROPRIATION ACCOUNT

22. The appropriation account should show:

(a) the current cost profit or loss for the year;
(b) the amount of:
  (i) the surpluses or deficits for the year (net of minority interests) arising from the revaluation of assets; plus or minus
  (ii) the amount appropriated by the directors to or from revaluation reserve;
(c) the dividends for the year; and
(d) the balance, being a transfer to or from general reserve.

23. The net surplus or deficit for the year arising from the revaluation of assets should be analysed according to whether the revaluation arose from:

(a) fixed assets;
(b) investments;
(c) stock and work in progress; and
(d) exchange translation differences.

The total surpluses and the total deficits should be shown in arriving at the net surplus or deficit under each of the above headings. Exceptional surpluses or deficits should be disclosed separately.

24. The directors should explain the basis and the reasons for the amounts appropriated to or from revaluation reserve.

Classification of changes in the value to the business of an asset.

25. The change in the value to the business of an asset should be dealt with either in the profit and loss account or as a revaluation surplus or deficit in accordance with the following paragraphs.

Land and buildings.

26. A change in the value of land and buildings held as fixed assets should normally be treated as a revaluation surplus or deficit except that:

(a) depreciation should be charged to the profit and loss account; and
(b) where the basis of valuing land and buildings is changed from:
  (i) the open market value for their existing use, or

(ii) the depreciated replacement cost for the building and the open market value for existing use for the bare land, to the open market value for any alternative use, then the surplus or deficit should be shown in the profit and loss account as an extraordinary item;

(c) where land and buildings are written down to be included in a group of assets for which an economic value is calculated, this write-down should be charged to the profit and loss account.

Plant and machinery and other fixed assets.

27. A change in the value of an item of plant and machinery or other fixed asset such that the old and new values are both based on its gross current replacement cost should normally be credited or charged, net of backlog depreciation, as a revaluation surplus or deficit.

28. A change in the value of an item of plant and machinery or other fixed asset, other than one arising directly from a movement in the gross replacement cost of the asset, should be credited or charged to the profit and loss account, disclosed if appropriate as an exceptional or an extraordinary item.

Government Grants.

29. Any change in the value of a fixed asset resulting from a change in the rate of Government grant receivable should be treated as a revaluation surplus or deficit.

Stock and work in progress.

30. A change in the value of an item of stock and work in progress such that the old and new values are both on a replacement cost basis should normally be treated as a revaluation surplus or deficit.

31. A change in the value of an item of stock and work in progress, other than a change resulting from a movement in replacement cost, should be credited or charged to the profit and loss account, disclosed if appropriate as an exceptional or extraordinary item.

Investments.

32. A change in the value of an investment should be treated as a revaluation surplus or deficit except either:

(a) where the investment represents liquid funds temporarily invested in which case it should be credited or charged to the profit and loss account; or

(b) where the treatment of the investment is covered by the section on stock.

The exception in (a) relating to liquid funds temporarily invested does not apply to organisations a principal part of whose business is the holding of investments.

Inclusion of certain revaluation surpluses and deficits in the profit and loss account.

33. The profit and loss account should be credited or charged with revaluation surpluses or deficits which can be clearly shown to have arisen as a result of:

(a) the purchase or holding of an asset solely with a view to gaining the benefit of an increase in its market value
(b) a decision to make a significant departure from a normal buying pattern by purchasing stock in advance of normal requirements in order to avoid an expected increase in price
(c) the purchase of stock at a price substantially different from the relevant market buying price at the date of purchase.

The composition of amounts so treated, and the reason for including the amounts as part of the operating result, should be disclosed in a note to the accounts.

BALANCE SHEET

Land and buildings.

34. The following paragraphs relate to land and buildings held by both property and non-property companies except where property companies are specifically excluded. The procedures peculiar to property companies are outlined in Part 4 of this Standard (omitted Eds.)

35. The value to the business of land and buildings in owner occupation will normally be the open market value for their existing use, plus estimated attributable acquisition costs.

36. If in the valuer's opinion an open market valuation cannot be made, the value to the business should be the total of the depreciated replacement cost of the buildings and the open market value plus estimated attributable acquisition costs of the bare land for its existing use. This value must be reviewed in the context of the overall profitability of the business

Table 2.

X Ltd. and its subsidiaries

Balance Sheet at 31st December, 197 .

	See Note	Group £000s	Company £000s	Paragraph In Standard
ASSETS EMPLOYED:				
Fixed assets	5.			44/46
Interest in subsidiaries	6.			82
Interest in associated companies	7.			84
Other investments	8.			63/64
Intangible assets (including goodwill)	9.			50-53/58
Net current assets				
Stock and work in progress				69
Debtors				68
Cash				
Creditors				70
Current taxation				71
Short-term borrowings				70
Dividends				
FINANCED BY:				
Issued share capital				
Share premium account				
Revaluation reserve	10.			
General reserve				
Minority interests				
Deferred taxation	11.			72-75
Long-term loans	12.			70

activity for which the buildings are used, and if appropriate the land and buildings should be included in the group of assets for which an economic value is calculated.

37. Land and buildings owned by non-property companies should be valued by a professionally qualified valuer at intervals of not more than five years, and more frequently if:

(a) the assets represent a major proportion of the company's gross assets; or
(b) there have been considerable market variations or major changes in the property assets since the previous professional valuation.

38. In the years between full-scale professional valuations, the directors should estimate the value of land and buildings after consultation with their professional valuers, taking into account, inter alia, market variations and changes in construction costs.

39. Where leasehold land and buildings have a negative value (eg because of the onerous provisions of the lease), this should be reflected in the balance sheet either as a provision or as a deduction from the positive value of other leasehold interests.

40. Any land and buildings owned by companies but not for their own occupation (eg rental producing properties) should be valued at their open market value plus estimated attributable acquisition costs. Land and buildings which have become surplus to the company's requirements and for which there is an intention to sell, should be valued at their open market value less estimated disposal expenses.

Plant and machinery.

41. Plant and machinery should be shown in the accounts at its value to the business at the balance sheet date. This will be its net current replacement cost except where this is greater than both the economic value and the net realisable value, in which case the value to the business will be the higher of the economic value and the net realisable value.

42. Where the gross current replacement cost of plant and machinery is estimated by reference to the cost of a substantially identical asset, that cost should be calculated by reference to one or more of the following sources of data. Those listed higher in the order are likely to give a closer

approximation to the required figure:

(a) suppliers' official price lists, catalogues etc., with appropriate deductions for trade discounts;
(b) the company's own replacement cost estimates, based on expert opinion;
(c) an index compiled by the company from its own purchasing experience;
(d) authorised external price indices analysed by asset type
(e) authorised external price indices analysed by using industry.

Disclosure requirements relating to plant and machinery and land and buildings.

43. The statement of accounting policies should disclose the bases on which the company has valued its fixed assets, and the basis on which depreciation has been provided.

44. There should be separate disclosure of plant and machinery valued at net current replacement cost, economic value, and net realisable value respectively. The gross current replacement cost and the accumulated depreciation to date should be shown for those assets that are valued on the basis of their net current replacement cost. For assets valued at their economic value or their net realisable value, only this net figure should be shown; no attempt should be made to construct and disclose any related gross value.

45. The value of land and buildings valued at open market value should be disclosed separately from the value of land and buildings which includes buildings valued on a depreciated replacement cost basis.

46. The tabulated statement of fixed assets should show the assets at their value to the business (disclosing gross values where appropriate) at the beginning and end of the year, additions at cost, the disposal of assets at their value to the business, the depreciation charge for the year and the transfers to and from the revaluation reserve.

Intangible assets (including research and development expenditure but excluding goodwill)

50. Intangible assets should be shown in the balance sheet at their value to the business only where this value can be established. Where such a value cannot be established, the intangible assets should be written off in the profit and loss account.

51. Where intangible assets are shown in the accounts, they should be revalued each year and depreciated through the profit and loss account in the same manner as other fixed assets.

52. The existence of assets for which a quantifiable value cannot be established should be noted in the accounts although no value should be placed on them.

53. Research and development expenditure carried forward should be valued on a current cost basis. This will normally involve revaluing at current costs the constituent elements of the expenditure in accordance with the appropriate provisions of this Standard. Any excess of this value over the amount which it is expected can be recovered out of future earnings should be written off in the profit and loss account.

Goodwill.

54. In determining the amount of goodwill arising on a purchase:

(a) the net assets acquired are to be valued at their value to the acquiring entity according to the principles of CCA; and

(b) any shares or loan stock issued as whole or part consideration are to be valued at their market value.

55. In any year in which an acquisition gives rise to a material amount of goodwill, such goodwill should be disclosed in the accounts, separate amounts being shown for each such acquisition.

56. No account should be taken of any increase after acquisition in the value of purchased goodwill. No value should be placed in accounts on internally generated goodwill.

57. The policy adopted by companies for accounting for purchased goodwill should be disclosed and consistently applied.

58. Goodwill should be shown separately in the balance sheet at cost less amounts written off. Any amount written off should be shown on the face of the profit and loss or appropriation account. The amount written off goodwill in each of the last five years should be shown in a note to the accounts.

59. It has been a common practice under historical cost accounting to calculate goodwill by reference to the book value of the assets acquired. If, at the time of purchase, the assets had a higher value to the business than their book value the revaluation of these assets and the inclusion of goodwill at

the amount recorded in the historical accounts would result in double counting. On changing to CCA any goodwill which is brough forward from the historical cost accounts and which arose initially from a difference between the value to the business of the acquired assets at the date of acquisition and the value used in the computation of such goodwill should be written off against surpluses arising on revaluation. Where this is not practicable and where it is still possible to identify the business originally acquired the goodwill element may be calculated by reference to:

(a) the net assets of the subsidiary, as shown in the current cost accounts at the time of changeover;
(b) the carrying value of the investment in the subsidiary at the time of changeover.

Where (a) exceeds (b) the balance should be treated as a surplus arising on revaluation. Where (b) exceeds (a) the balance should be deemed to be purchased goodwill and treated accordingly. Any other goodwill brough forward from the historical cost accounts should be treated in accordance with paragraph 58. Any write off of goodwill required by this section should be made in both the consolidated and the holding company's accounts.

60 On first changing from historical cost accounts to current cost accounts the goodwill element in the purchase price of an investment in an associated company should be calculated by reference to the value to the business of the attributable portion of the net assets of an associated company at the time of the acquisition and the value to the business of the consideration. Where this is not practicable the goodwill element should be calculated by reference to:

(a) the net assets of an associated company, as shown in the current cost accounts at the time of changeover;
(b) the carrying value of the investment at the time of changeover.

Where (a) exceeds (b) the balance should be treated as a surplus arising on revaluation. Where (b) exceeds (a) the balance should be deemed to be purchased goodwill and treated accordingly.

Investments.

61. For the purpose of the following paragraphs investments include trade investments but exclude subsidiary and associated companies.

62. The following paragraphs do not deal with businesses which trade in investments with the purpose of making a trading profit on increases in market value. The treatment of investments in this case should be in accordance with the provisions of this Standard on stock and work in progress.

63. Quoted investments should be valued at their mid-market price. In exceptional circumstances when the directors consider mid-market price to be unrepresentative of the value to the business the directors may use another method of valuation, in which case there must be shown in a note to the accounts:

(a) the value at mid-market price and the reasons the directors consider it to be unrepresentative of the value to the business;
(b) the basis that they have used to value the investment.

64. Unquoted investments should be stated at their value to the business as determined by the directors. This would normally be related to:

(a) the net asset value of the company on a CCA basis; and/or
(b) the value of the stream of income from the investment.

Where in the opinion of the directors, the above is unrealistic they should explain the bases they have used.

Where a material amount of unquoted investments is held the basis of valuation should be stated in a note to the accounts.

65. A gain or loss in value of an investment which is classified as liquid funds temporarily invested should be credited or charged in arriving at the operating profit.

66. A gain or loss in value of an investment which is not classified as liquid funds temporarily invested should be included in surpluses and deficits arising from revaluation of assets.

67. Income from investments should be included in operating profit. The Companies Act 1967 requires that there shall be shown the amounts respectively of income from quoted investments and income from unquoted investments.

Non-current debtors.

68. Non-current debtors should be valued as hitherto, that is, normally at face value less a provision for any expected losses. Where discounting is the present practice, this should be continued.

Stock and work in progress.

69. The amount at which stock and work in progress is stated in the balance sheet should be the total of the value to the business, at the accounting date, of the separate items of stock and work in progress or of groups of similar items.

Liabilities (excluding deferred tax)

70. (a) Liabilities should continue to be shown on the same basis as hitherto, that is, normally at face value.
(b) Where a liability is also a listed security the value of the outstanding amount, based on the mid-market price at the balance sheet date, should be shown by way of note.

STATEMENT SHOWING EFFECT OF CHANGE IN THE VALUE OF MONEY

76. The accounts should include a statement, by way of note, setting out prominently the gain or loss for the period of account in the shareholders' net equity interest after allowance has been made for the change in the value of money during the period. In the case of a holding company the note should relate to the group accounts only.

77. The statement should show:

(a) the net equity interest as shown in the balance sheet at the beginning of the period, plus any amount brought into the accounts in respect of new equity capital introduced during the period, plus or minus, the amount of the allowance needed to compensate these amounts for the change in the value of money during the period;
(b) the net equity interest at the end of the period before provision for dividends on the equity capital;
(c) the net gain or loss in the net equity interest during the period, being the difference between the amounts referred to in (a) and (b);
(d) the dividends on the equity capital for the year.

Table 3.

STATEMENT OF CHANGE IN SHAREHOLDERS' NET EQUITY INTEREST AFTER ALLOWING FOR THE CHANGE IN THE VALUE OF MONEY	£000s	Paragraph in Standard
		76
Net equity interest at beginning of year	X	77(a)
New equity capital introduced during year	X	77(a)
	X	
Amount required to compensate for the change in the value of money during year	X	
	X	
Net equity interest at end of year before dividends on equity capital	X	77(b)
Gain/(loss) for year after allowing for the change in the value of money	X	77(c)
Dividends on equity capital for year	X	77(d)
Gain/(loss) for year after allowing for the change in the value of money and after dividends	X	

ANALYSIS OF THE GAIN/(LOSS) ON MONETARY ASSETS AND LIABILITIES AFTER ALLOWING FOR THE CHANGE IN THE VALUE OF MONEY:		78
Long-term liabilities	X	
Bank overdrafts	X	
Non-equity share capital	X	
Other	X	
Total gain or loss	X	

The allowance for the change in the value of money was made by applying the general index of retail prices, based on January 1974 = 100. At 1.1.197 the index stood at X, and at Y at 31.12.197 . 79

78. An analysis of the gain or loss on holding monetary assets and liabilities during the period should also be provided, showing separately the figures for:

(a) long-term liabilities;
(b) bank overdrafts;
(c) non-equity share capital.

79. The allowance for the change in the value of money should be made by applying a general price index as follows:

(a) for companies registered in the United Kingdom; the general index of retail prices;
(b) for companies registered in the Republic of Ireland; the official consumer price index.

The name of the relevant index, the figures of the index at the beginning and end of the period, and the base date of the index, should be stated.

28 Current Cost Accounting: U.K. Controversies and Overseas Solutions

D. P. Tweedie

INTRODUCTION

"To be effective, accounting standards must be generally acceptable to all preparers and users of accounts...It is clear...that substantial simplification and modification of ED 18 will be necessary before ASC can propose to the accountancy bodies a generally acceptable system of CCA for introduction as standard practice."

With these words, taken from its statement of June 29, 1977 the ASC effectively stopped the development of the ED 18 version of current cost accounting. The ASC, however, confirmed that it had not altered its view "that a generally acceptable system of current cost accounting is urgently necessary". What now appears likely to happen is that the ASC will move more slowly towards a complete changeover to CCA and future CCA exposure drafts or standards will incorporate only those aspects of the system for which a broad measure of consensus has been achieved. The more contentious proposals of ED 18 are almost certain to be subjects for further intensive professional debate before inclusion in any future ASC pronouncement.

The arguments over accounting for inflation are not of course unique to the United Kingdom. The debate is now raging worldwide. Within the last few years, however, there has been a general movement towards a limited agreement in the developed world as a trend has developed towards CCA as an acceptable system for accounting for inflation. It is the purpose of this article briefly to trace this movement and then to consider what lessons can be learned from the three overseas countries which have moved furthest towards current cost accounts by assessing how they have dealt with the two major criticisms levelled against the ED 18 proposals, namely,

(a) the problem of asset valuation caused by the concept of the value to the business (deprival value); and (b) the difficulties of determining distributable profit resulting from the failure of the ED 18 system to define a capital maintenance concept.

THE TREND TOWARDS CCA

Of the seven countries examined in this brief survey, five - Australia (1974), Canada (1974), New Zealand (1975), South Africa (1975), and the United States of America (1974) - have, like the UK, produced either an exposure draft or a discussion paper advocating the use of current purchasing power accounting (CPPA). In South Africa no further publications have been issued but current cost accounting has since been proposed in various forms in the other four countries. Australia (1975) and New Zealand (1976) have both issued exposure drafts on current cost accounting. Australia has also produced a provisional standard on the subject (1976) but in New Zealand, the question of a standard is still under consideration following the report of the Government's Committee of Inquiry into Inflation Accounting (the Richardson Report - 1976), which recommended a different form of CCA from that proposed in the earlier exposure draft.

Canada and the United States have moved towards CCA in rather different ways. The United States Financial Accounting Standards Board (FASB), having decided to defer consideration of a standard based on its CPPA exposure draft, published a discussion paper (1976) which outlined the advantages and disadvantages of different systems of price-level accounting. The Securities and Exchange Commission, however, had already begun a move away from CPPA by issuing, in March 1976, Accounting Series Release No. 190. The Release required large companies to disclose, as additional information, the estimated current replacement cost of stock and productive capacity at the end of each financial year and the approximate amount of cost of sales and depreciation based on replacement cost for the two most recent financial years.

In Canada the Accounting Research Committee of the Canadian Institute "realised that general price-level accounting(was) not a remedy for all the limitations of historical cost based financial reporting", and while still reviewing the comments received on its CPPA exposure draft, it issued a discussion paper on current value accounting in 1976. Like the FSAB's 1976 discussion paper, the paper's aim was to provide a better understanding of the various approaches to current value accounting. Unlike its American equivalent, however, the paper revealed a preliminary position stating its authors' opinion that current value accounts should be shown as supplementary information and giving their views on asset and liability valuation and income determination.

In Europe, too, supplementary current value statements have been proposed. In the Netherlands, where accounting practice allows companies to produce either historic cost or current value financial statements, the Council of the Nederlands Instituut van Registeraccountants, in a note appended to the IASC's Exposure Draft on Accounting Treatment of Changing Prices, expressed strong approval for the proposal that information in the annual accounts may be based on current values and also raised serious objections to CPPA. The Council, however, recognised that inflation exposed the equity of enterprises to the risk of erosion of capital through inflation, and proposed that a supplementary statement should be appended to accounts which would not only show net income on current value and historical cost bases but would also indicate whether the purchasing power of shareholders' equity had been maintained.

The proposed West German supplementary statement was somewhat different in nature. This statement would indicate to shareholders "how much of the annual profit in the interest of preserving the operating capacity capital should not be distributed". The information to be disclosed reveals the "fictional profit", and consists of the additional depreciation expense and cost of goods sold if a replacement cost (derived from specific indices) rather than an historic cost basis had been used, reduced by the proportion of fixed assets and inventories that are financed by sources other than equity capital. The statement, therefore, does not show the entire "fictional profit", but only that proportion of it which is assumed to be generated by equity capital.

It can be seen, therefore, that only three of the countries surveyed have explored CCA to the extent that accounts based on such a system were proposed.[1] The remainder of this article, therefore, concentrates on the publications advocating CCA in Australia, Canada and New Zealand and compares their proposals on the question of asset valuation and income measurement to those propounded in ED 18.

ASSET VALUATION

The Problems

Two major criticisms have been levelled at ED 18's proposals on asset valuation: first, the problems caused by the concept of value to the business, and secondly, and of lesser importance, the subjectivity involved in estimating the degree of technological change when seeking the cost of modern equivalent assets.

The concept of value to the business proposed in ED 18 involves the calculation of three different values for each asset. Apart from the time taken and the expense of such a valuation procedure, the measure of economic value involves subjective assessments of both the size and the timing of future cash flows emanating from an asset (or a group of assets) and the selection of a suitable discount rate. The subjective and anticipatory nature of the calculation of economic value has seriously alarmed many of those concerned with financial reporting in the United Kingdom.[2] The problems caused by the use of the value to the business concept have also been considered overseas, and in all three countries considered here the concept has been abandoned as a valuation basis for non-monetary assets.

The Overseas View

In Australia, economic value was discussed in the exposure draft on current value accounting and then dismissed as a general valuation basis for use in financial statements on the grounds that it was a subjective notion based on management's expectations of future events and would, in any case, be impossible to calculate in practice.

Instead of the concept of the value to the business as proposed by ED 18, the Australian exposure draft recommended a less complex formula for the valuation of non-monetary assets. If an asset was essential to the continuance of operations it would be worth to the entity no more than it would cost to replace the operating capability which it provided. If the asset was not essential to operations then it would be worth no more than its net realisable value. The resulting provisional standard noted that this method contravened the long-established principle that no asset should be carried in the balance sheet at an amount greater than that expected to be recovered as the asset is consumed in operations and/or when it is sold. Consequently, the standard produced an amended valuation procedure for assets continuing in use. This involved asking two questions about each asset:

(1) Is the asset to continue in use?
If yes - answer question 2.
If no - value at net realisable value.

(2) Can the current cost (or in the case of a depreciable asset - written down current cost) be expected to be recovered (a) through charges as the asset is consumed and (b) by its sale? If yes - value at replacement cost (or written down replacement cost). If no - value at the amount of replacement cost that can be recovered (the recoverable amount).

The recoverable amount concept is not new - the UK's ED 17, for example, recommends similar treatment for development expenditure (para 21 (d)). For current cost accounting in Australia, however, it fulfils a new role by giving a valuation in those cases where an asset is to be retained for use but where it is unlikely to be replaced - a role which would frequently have been filled by an economic value under the value to the business concept. (It should be noted that the recoverable amount still demands, like economic value, the estimation of future cash flows relating to the asset).

On the practicalities of deriving replacement cost the Australian publications were similar to ED 18, though greater stress was placed on the use of indices. The exposure draft proposed that land and buildings were to be professionally valued periodically (with suitable indices used for intermediate years). Stock and work in progress were to be valued at current buying prices and reproduction cost respectively. The current cost of other fixed assets was to be determined (in order of preference) by - (a) specific prices of comparable new or second hand assets; (b) estimates of current reproduction costs; (c) expert valuation; (d) cost or a value calculated in accordance with (a), (b) or (c) above adjusted by use of a specific price index to reflect subsequent price changes; and (e) as (d) but adjusting by means of a general price index instead of a specific index.

The provisional standard was not so explicit but merely mentioned that, ideally, current cost would be determined by reference to the market buying prices or, if that were not possible, an approximation of current cost such as that achieved by specific indices. In both the exposure draft and the provisional standard allowance was to be made for technological changes; a simple formula was given for this purpose in the provisional standard.

The New Zealand proposals on asset valuation were similar in nature to those of their Australian neighbours. Both the exposure draft and the Richardson Report rejected the economic value concept. The former publication simply declared that economic value estimates were insufficiently objective to be applied in external financial statements while the latter agreed with this criticism and, in addition, condemned the amount of time and expense involved in making three valuations (including economic value) in order to decide which of the three should be employed to value an individual asset (or group of assets).

Having rejected economic value, both the exposure draft and the Richardson Report opted (like the Australians) for current replacement cost and net realisable values for asset valuation purposes. The Richardson Report adopted the Australian exposure draft's "essential to the business" criterion to decide whether an asset should be valued at replacement cost or net realisable value. The exposure draft opted for a similar basis of "impairment of operating capability". This implied that, if the loss of the asset (again a form of deprival value) would materially impair the operating capability of the business, its value to the business was replacement cost, since continuing replacement of its operating capability was implied. Where the loss of the asset would not impair the operating capability of the business, its replacement cost would not normally be the relevant value to the business since the business could continue its normal operations without the particular asset. In this situation net realisable value was considered to be the most appropriate and objective valuation.

The exposure draft advocated the same five bases of arriving at replacement cost of fixed assets as the Australian exposure draft, and, in addition, as a practical measure, stated that the value of land and buildings could be based on the Government Valuation adjusted where necessary for the time lag or locality, by reference to the relevant Valuation Department index (thereby saving the expense of valuation to be incurred under the ED 18 proposals). The Richardson Report, too, favoured the use of indices and, while recognising that specific valuations could give a more accurate measure of current costs than indices, indicated that such valuations would be difficult to verify and expensive for the enterprise. For these reasons the report advocated as a long-term goal, the development of a full range of official indices which should be used where a measure of replacement cost was required and which should only be departed from in exceptional circumstances. Technological changes, the Report recommended, should be incorporated in the production of the official indices.[3] (The West German specific indices attempt to account for technological change.)

The Canadian Accounting Research Committee's "preliminary Position", outlined in its discussion paper did not, like the British Australian and New Zealand proposals advocate an overall approach to asset valuation. Instead, it considered each type of asset separately and suggested the use of a combination of values including discounted cash flows. In general, fixed assets, stock (unless obsolete) and long-term inter-company investments were to be valued at replacement cost, which could be market cost or derived by means of specific indices. (The problem of technological change was recognised and it was suggested that, in some cases, this would be reflected in the second-hand market price.) Marketable securities were to be valued at net realisable values, while monetary assets and liabilities in the balance sheet should be shown at discounted cash flow values except for short-term items where the time value of money effect was small. (For liabilities, a quoted market price would in many cases provide an acceptable equivalent value.) The discounting approach suggested for monetary assets and liabilities (other than marketable securities,) in the balance sheet was quite unique: none of the Australian or New Zealand pronouncements mentioned earlier advocated any change from existing practices.

The overseas proposals for asset valuation were (apart from the Canadian proposals on monetary assets and liabilities) concerned with only two measures of value - replacement cost (including Australia's "recoverable amount") and net realisable value, the former being used when the assets were vital to the business and the latter when the assets were not essential to business requirements. Many of the complexities found in ED 18 would undoubtedly be removed if a similar system were to be introduced un the UK. A further point for the ASC to note when assessing the future of CCA is the readiness of the overseas publications to accept specific indices as surrogates of a "true" replacement cost thereby simplifying markedly the valuation process from that proposed in ED 18 and consequently easing the difficulties faced by auditors in verifying replacement cost valuations.

DISTRIBUTABLE PROFIT

The Main Problem

One of the greatest weaknesses of ED 18 was its failure to define distributable profit. In what appeared to be an attempt to satisfy all shades of opinion the appropriation account proposed in ED 18 allowed directors to choose their own capital maintenance concept, thereby enabling each company to come to its individual definition of distributable income.

Corporate income can be defined as the amount the company can distribute to the owners of its equity at the end of the year and be as well off at the end of the year as at the beginning. The major problem facing accountants, of course, is the definition of "welloffness".

If prices do not move, under the historical cost convention the accountant calculating the year's distributable profit does not have to concern himself with the decision of whether to measure "welloffness" in terms of either the shareholders' equity capital or the physical assets of the enterprise. Provided that the costs of the assets were charged against profit, the company would then retain sufficient funds to replace its assets when their useful life expired. Shareholders' real capital, too would be maintained, as it would retain its purchasing power from one year to the next.

Remove the constraint of zero price movement, however, and a quite different picture emerges. Now the accountant has to chose between two quite distinct capital maintenance concepts - the proprietary and the entity view points.

(1) Invested Financial Capital (The Proprietary View)

In this case it is argued that the capital to be maintained is measured by the amount of cash (including undistributed earnings) invested by the shareholders in the past. In inflationary situations this concept has been developed by restating capital in terms of changes in the purchasing power of money, ie. the maintenance of real financial capital. Profit can only be derived after the equity has been maintained.

This concept is not confined to historical cost accounts or to those based on a CPP index restatement. Wealth acquired from capital gains can be spent just as readily as wealth acquired by trading activities, and consequently the concept can be employed when current costs are used by including the holding gains and losses on assets in earnings rather than in a revaluation reserve and then deducting the appropriate amount from income to maintain equity capital in real (current purchasing power) terms.

(2) Invested Physical Capital (The Entity View)

This view considers capital not from the viewpoint of

the shareholder interested in his cash investment but in terms of the operating capability of the enterprise. In this case the costs to be recovered before profit is calculated are the current replacement costs of assets with the same productive capabilities as those used in the business. The changes in replacement prices of the company's assets are not considered to be earnings but an adjustment to owners' equity in order to maintain the physical capital of the enterprise. It should be noted that the notion of maintaining capital in terms of operating capability is simply used for the purpose of profit measurement and does not imply commitment to any specific action regarding eventual replacement or future use of resources.

The argument over whether the proprietary or entity view should be preferred is unlikely to be settled in the near future. Ultimately one's viewpoint depends upon which frame of reference is used to consider the shareholders' role in relation to the firm, and one's opinion of the fundamental objectives of the firm.[4] (It is because of the conflicting views on these basic questions that the proposal of presenting accounting information in more than one form is receiving increasing support - note, for example, the suggestion in ED 18 of a Statement of Change in Shareholders' Net Equity Interest in addition to the current cost statement.[5])

Both the proprietary and entity viewpoints have their advantages. Owners of businesses, for example, would find the proprietary concept extremely useful. The owner would almost certainly consider his stake in the firm as an integral part of his own wealth and would be extremely interested in measuring the total increment to his wealth generated by the firm during the course of the year. Accordingly, he would not only be interested in his company's trading profits but also in capital gains made by holding assets. Such a person would almost certainly wish to compare his capital gains with the rise in prices of other commodities purchased by him (ie. the real capital gains would be important to him) since if the rise in value of his assets coupled with his trading profits failed to keep pace with the rate of inflation of the prices of goods and services purchased by him, then his real wealth would be decreasing. In a case such as this Professor Baxter's[6] elegant concept of "ideal" income would be invaluable to the owner.

Many investors in public companies, however, do not remain with a particular enterprise over a long period[7] and probably do not equate their wealth directly to the company's performance but rather study the company at a distance by examining the stock market prices and, for the future, its ability to generate future dividends. They, and management, it has been argued,[8] are possibly more concerned with the firm's competitive survival and consequently with the preservation of the entity's stock of resources, ie. the maintenance of its overall ability to provide goods and services (the entity approach).

The Overseas View

The two Australian and two New Zealand publications favoured the use of the entity concept. They suggested that revaluation gains should be taken to a capital reserve in the balance sheet to adjust owner's equity and should not, therefore, be included in profit, thereby preventing the distribution of funds needed to preserve operating capacity. The Canadian discussion paper, however, rejected this view, arguing that it did not seem appropriate for the purposes of external financial reporting since it has not been proven that in the long run an enterprise necessarily should survive. Instead, the discussion paper proposed that holding gains on assets should be included in the income statement and profit struck after a deduction had been made to ensure that the general purchasing power of shareholders' equity had been maintained, ie. a proprietary approach was adopted.

The Canadian discussion paper, therefore, presented an entirely different measure of income from the other four publications (see Table). The others did not, however, hold unanimous views on income measurement and capital maintenance. All four attempted to maintain physical capital by charging revenue with the current cost of sales and with depreciation derived from the current costs of the assets utilised in the business. The bases for depreciation were not, however, identical. While the Australian publications based depreciation (like ED 18) on the average replacement cost of the assets during the year, the New Zealand exposure draft and the Richardson Report proposed depreciation based on year end replacement values, the former on the grounds of practicality and prudence, the latter because its tests had established "that for most activities the end-of-period basic calculation would not produce a materially different result from the average-for-the-period base". This, however, was only a minor difference in the type of entity approach preferred in the Australian and New Zealand publications; two major disagreements (both of which have been the subject of fierce debate in the United Kingdom) revealed fundamental differences in the measurement of distributable profits, namely - (1) the problems of accounting for backlog depreciation and (2) the gain or loss on holding monetary assets and liabilities.

SUMMARY OF DEFINITION OF PROFIT

AUSTRALIA

Provisional Standard

Historic Cost Profit adjusted for the current cost of sales and depreciation (based on average replacement cost values)

Net gain on the revaluation of assets taken to a revaluation reserve

Exposure Draft

Historic Cost Profit adjusted for the current cost of sales and depreciation (based on average replacement cost values)

Gross gain on the revaluation of assets taken to a revaluation reserve

NEW ZEALAND

Exposure Draft

Historic Cost Profit adjusted for the current cost of sales and depreciation (based on year and values)

Gross gain on the revaluation of assets taken to a revaluation reserve

Richardson Report

(a) Current Cost Operating Profit -
Historic cost of sales
Historic cost of sales
Less: cost of sales adjustment (current costs)
Less:historic cost expenses
Less: current cost depreciation based on year end values
Less: loss in purchasing power of monetary assets

(b) Profit attributable to owners
Current Cost Operating Profit
Less: interest on borrowed Profit
Plus: movements in revaluation reserves financed from borrowed fund

CANADA

Discussion Paper

Historic Cost Profit adjusted for the current cost of sales and current depreciation Plus: gains (losses) on revaluation of assets and liabilities Less: amount required to maintain the purchasing power of equity capital.

(1) Backlog Depreciation

The Problem

The problem of backlog depreciation can be illustrated

very simply. Suppose a company purchases for £100 an asset which has a two-year service life at the beginning of year 1. The replacement cost of the asset rises to £150 at the beginning of year 2 and remains at that price. In years 1 and 2 the annual depreciation charges on a replacement cost basis would have been £50 and £75 respecitvely.

A new machine, however, would have cost £25 more than the total depreciation provided (£125) and consequently if all profits had been distributed, the operating capacity of the business would not have been maintained without recourse to further financing. Consequently an accounting system based on the entity concept of maintaining operating capability has to decide whether or not distribution of the backlog depreciation will result in a reduction in operating capacity.

There are three main ways of dealing with the problem of backlog depreciation in current cost accounts.

(a) Charge it to revaluation reserve - (the Sandilands approach), ie. the revaluation reserve is credited with the rise in gross replacement cost of the asset and debited with the backlog depreciation. In this situation no attempt is made to reduce distributable earnings to ensure that the total of the asset's replacement cost is retained in the business. Instead it is argued that it is the net book value of the asset which is being restated as this represents the value assigned to the remaining service potential. It can also be argued (a) that the investment of the previous depreciation expense can offset this backlog; and (b) that in the event of regular replacement, backlog depreciation is irrelevant, eg. in the example given above, if the company owned two machines and replaced one each year the depreciation charge in year 2 would have enabled the company to replace the asset without recourse to further financing.

(b) Charge it against the profit for the period in which the replacement cost arises. The replacement cost of the asset is retained in the business by reducing the current year's profit by the amount of the backlog depreciation. (Presumably the charge would be shown separately from the normal depreciation charge to avoid conflicting with the matching principle.)

(c) Charge it against retained earnings. In this case distributable reserves are reduced to ensure the retention of the asset's replacement cost.
ED 18, which allowed companies to choose either the

proprietary or any form of entity concept to maintain capital did draw attention to the problem of backlog depreciation (ED 18 Appendix 2) but unlike the Australian and New Zealand publications no recommended treatment was suggested.

The Overseas View

Both the Australian and New Zealand exposure drafts proposed that backlog depreciation should be charged against retained earnings. (The New Zealand exposure draft did state, however, that in the first year of current cost accounts backlog depreciation could be charged against the revaluation reserve and the amount so treated disclosed in a note each year.) The Australian provisional standard and the Richardson Report in New Zealand, however, rejected this approach and both stated that backlog depreciation should be debited to the revaluation reserve. The former argued that the charge against retained earnings could represent an unreasonable restriction on the availability of retained earnings for distribution while the latter stated that the treatment proposed in the exposure drafts invalidly implied that the depreciation charges in previous years had been incorrect.

(2) Gains and Losses on Holding Monetary Assets and Liabilities.

The Problem

To devotees of the proprietary concept the gain or loss arising through the holding of monetary items is invariably considered to be an essential feature of the loss to the owners in times of inflation. Supporters of the entity notion, however, are frequently only concerned with non-monetary assets, ie. they regard capital maintenance in terms of physical units such as a machine. Cash is also considered in physical £1 units, and since a £1 note at the beginning of a year is a £1 note at its end, losses caused by holding cash are not recorded in the accounts. The entity concept is, however, now usually considered to be concerned with the maintenance of operating capability not replacement with identical machines. It could be argued, therefore, that monetary assets should also be considered in terms of service capacity and, consequently, as rising prices result in a company requiring an increase in the £ investment in fixed assets and stock, so too will it require a greater £ investment in monetary assets to service the level of its existing operations. Consequently, it could be argued that an adjustment should be made to operating profit in the profit and loss account to record the increased amount required to be retained to maintain the company's existing operations[9] (the revaluation reserve/capital maintenance reserve would show the corresponding entry).

The Overseas View

The Australian exposure draft and provisional standard adopted the same position as ED 18 on the question of monetary items; all three recommended further study on this complex question but no adjustments were to be made to accounts in the meantime. The New Zealand exposure draft, however, did not appear to accept that further research was necessary. It stated that, while it was obvious that there was a loss in general purchasing power of net monetary items held in a period of inflation, it was equally obvious that monetary items were already expressed in the monetary unit and therefore no adjustment for any gain or loss in purchasing power was required. The Richardson Committee fundamentally disagreed with this position. It argued that "if the ability of the monetary assets to carry out their function is affected by changes in prices....this should be measured and taken into account in arriving at the current cost operating profit of the enterprise". Consequently, the Richardson Report recommended that an adjustment should be made to operating profit in respect of the purchasing power change in circulating monetary assets.

It should be noted that the Report rejected the notion that any gain on liabilities should be set off against the loss on monetary assets in the adjustment to operating profit. It argued that the operating profit should measure the return on assets employed; monetary liabilities were merely a means of financing these assets in general and could not, therefore, be attributed to the financing of particular assets (such as monetary assets).[10]

The Committee did believe, however, that the increases in the capital maintenance reserve (similar to ED 18's revaluation reserve) attributable to the revaluation of assets, represented real gains to the owners to the extent that they were financed from borrowed funds. If, to maintain operating capability, distributions to the shareholders were limited to operating profit and if inflation continued, the debt/equity ratio would be gradually reduced to zero as the capital maintenance reserve increased the equity base. Such a policy, the Report stated, would be taking financial conservatism to extreme levels. To combat this it was suggested that the profit and loss account should be divided into two sections - current operating profit and distributable profit. In the latter section of the account the gain attributable to borrowing based on the movements in the capital maintenance reserve (rather than on purchasing power change) should be rought back into the income statement[11] - the assumption being that operating capacity would be maintained by additional borrowing in the future to maintain the debt/equity ratio.

This approach could well be considered to be counter to the aim of the entity concept in that if the assumption proves to be incorrect the company could have distributed funds needed to maintain its operating capability. It could be argued, therefore, that a more conservative approach is necessary and that the gains on holding assets should only be distributable when additional finance had been raised on the basis of the increased value of the assets of the enterprise. Logically, distributions could also be made to the extent to which the maintenance of the operating potential of monetary assets had been financed by borrowing. If, for example, the increased sums required to maintain the same level of monetary working capital could be financed by increases in trade credit obtained, then the company would not have to retain such amounts as its operations were being financed by outside sources.

CONCLUSIONS

It is clear that no simple solution to the United Kingdom's CCA problems are to be found overseas. The worldwide debate appears to be as heated and possibly as acrimonious as in these islands. Several points from the overseas attempts to outline a desirable current cost accounting system could, however, be useful to the ASC when they consider how to modify ED 18.

(1) Economic value as a basis for valuing non-monetary assets has been rejected as impractical in Canada, Australia and New Zealand, and in the case of the two latter countries a far simpler approach has been adopted.

(2) Specific indices appear to be acceptable to these three countries as a means of determining replacement cost.[12] (Indices adapted to account for technological change, as proposed in the Richardson Report, would appear to be especially valuable.)

(3) In relation to overseas proposals ED 18 compared unfavourably in failing to define a capital maintenance concept and consequently in allowing various concepts of

profit. In Australia and New Zealand the entity concept appears to have been accepted, the later publications in both countries charging backlog depreciation to the revaluation reserve.

(4) Little agreement has yet been reached on the treatment of gains or losses caused by holding monetary assets and liabilities.

ED 18 was perhaps a victim of its attempt to pacify the conflicting opinions in the United Kingdom about price-level accounting. While the Exposure Draft proposed that the presentation of a defined current operating profit should be compulsory, its Appropriation Account allowed companies to produce their own definition of income. (All the Australian, Canadian and New Zealand forms of profit discussed in this paper, and summarised in the Table at page could have been produced under ED 18's guidelines.) This was an impossible situation for financial reporting. What now appears to be necessary is a vastly simplified and less flexible version of CCA than that proposed in ED 18.

The overseas proposals outlined in items 1-3 above would seem to be a suitable basis for simplification. The question of the loss on monetary items is still a matter of contention abroad, although it has been argued in the Richardson Report that if the entity approach is accepted the maintenance of operating capacity (and operations) necessitates the maintenance of the purchasing power of monetary assets essential to the business. "Gains" on borrowed funds, which simply finance the asset base, should not, according to the overseas publications favouring the entity concept, be included in operating profit. In this regard, a lesson could perhaps be drawn from the Richardson Committee's proposals in the division of the profit and loss account into two sections - the first section showing current operating profit (including a deduction for the maintenance of monetary assets) and the second showing the amount potentially distributable to shareholders.[13] This should include operating profit and the extent to which the maintenance of operating capacity required (including the maintenance of monetary service potential) has, while maintaining the debt/equity ratio, actually been financed by long-term and/or short-term borrowing.

As one of the pacemakers in the field of price-level accounting, the United Kingdom gave an impetus to accounting for inflation throughout the world. Instead of now trying to produce a unique form of current cost accounting the United Kingdom could benefit by listening to the international debate. Attention should now be paid to the progress made in countries which had the advantage of following the British pronouncements in the early years and which now seem to be on the way to genuine participation in the world-wide experiment with price-level accounting.

FOOTNOTES

(1) It should be remembered that in one of these three countries - Canada - only supplementary statements were proposed.

(2) See, for example, Auditing Practices Committee, The Audit Implications of ED 18: Current Cost Accounting, 1977, pages 10-11; J.C. Shaw: "ED 18: The Implications for Auditors", The Accountant's Magazine, January 1977, pages 11-12; and E. Stamp: "ED 18 and Current Cost Accounting: A Review Article", Accounting and Business Research, Spring 1977, page 85.

(3) The Exposure Draft mentioned the technological problems and then proceeded to ignore them.

(4) See R.S. Gynther: "Accounting Concepts and Behavioural Hypotheses", Accounting Review April 1967, pages 274-290.

(5) The New Zealand Exposure Draft proposed a similar form of statement.

(6) See W.T. Baxter: "Brave New Standard: Inflation Accounting, Mark 3", The Accountant's Magazine, April 1977, pages 137-140.

(7) See R.J. Briston and C.S. Greensted: "Shareholder Behaviour in the New Issue Market: A Final Progress Report", Accounting and Business Research, Spring 1976, pages 125-134.

(8) Gynther, op. cit.

(9) For the sake of simplicity the retail price index could be used to measure the amount required to maintain monetary assets. Ideally, the maintenance of debtors should be based on the increase in the company's selling prices and the maintenance of actual cash on the loss in the company's specific purchasing power.

(10) See also R.S. Gynther: "Why Use General Purchasing Power?", Accounting and Business Research, Spring 1974, practicularly pages 154-5, J. Perrin: "Why CCP is not the Answer", Accountancy, May 1976, page 60 and G. Briscoe and G. Hawke: "Long term

Debt and Realisable Gains in Shareholder Wealth: an Empirical Study", Journal of Business Finance and Accounting, Spring 1976, pages 125-135.

(11) Note the similarity to the West German supplementary statement which only shows the "fictional profit" in terms of that financed by shareholders.

(12) For an example of the difficulties experienced when indices are not used see S. Hamilton: "Field Testing ED 18: the Practical Reality", The Accountant's Magazine, May 1977, pages 192-195.

(13) This would be similar to - though less flexible than - ED 18's appropriation account.

Official Publications of Overseas Inflation Accounting Proposals

A. The Institute of Chartered Accountants of Australia and Australian Society of Accountants, Statement of Provisional Accounting Standards "Current Cost Accounting", 1976.

B. The Institute of Chartered Accountants of Australia and Australian Society of Accountants, Preliminary Exposure Draft, "A Method of Current Value Accounting", 1975.

C. New Zealand Society of Accountants, ED 14, "Accounting in terms of Current Costs and VAlues", 1976.

D. Report of the Committee of Inquiry into Inflation Accounting, New Zealand, 1976.

E. Accounting Research Committee of the Canadian Institute of Chartered Accountants, Discussion Paper, "Current Value Accounting" 1976.

29 Alternative Recommendations for Practice: the Hyde Guidelines

The Accounting Standards Committee recommends that the published financial statements of companies listed on The Stock Exchange should include a prominent separate statement showing the financial results as amended by the adjustments described below. Wherever practicable, it is recommended that the statement should be prepared for accounting periods ending on or after December 31st, 1977.

While this recommendation is directed primarily to listed companies, its wider adoption is urged in the interests of more informative reporting.

It is recommended that three adjustments should be made to the financial results as computed on the historical cost convention. Each adjustment should be shown separately.

Depreciation

An adjustment should be made for the difference between depreciation based upon the current cost of fixed assets and the depreciation charged in computing the historical cost result.

Cost of Sales

An adjustment should be made for the difference between the current cost of stock at the date of sale and the amount charged in computing the historical cost result.

'Gearing'

It is recognised that there are differing views on the question of how monetary items should be dealt with in inflation adjusted statements and that such differences are unlikely to be resolved quickly or without experiment. Nevertheless, it is considered that it would not be acceptable for the statement recommended to be limited to adjustments for depreiation and cost of sales. Such limitation would result in an incomplete and potentially misleading picture being given to shareholders and other users of accounts. Accordingly, the description of the gearing adjustment given below and the proposals which follow in paragraphs 16 to 20 are intended as an interim guide as to how this adjustment might be approached.

There are two different situations to be met, each of which calls for a different treatment:

(a) If the total liabilities of the business, including for this purpose preference share capital, exceed its total monetary assets so that part of its operating capability is effectively financed by the net monetary liabilities, an adjustment should be made to reflect the extent to which the depreciation and cost of sales adjustments do not need to be provided in full from the current revenues of the business in showing the profit attributable to the shareholders.

(b) If the total monetary assets of the business exceed its total liabilities, an adjustment should be made to reflect the increase in the net monetary assets needed to maintain its scale of operation.

The form of each of these three adjustments is described below.

Depreciation

Where the business has already developed appropriate methods of computing current cost depreciation it is recommended that such methods should be used for the purpose of computing the adjustment.

Where other appropriate methods have not been developed, the charge for current cost depreciation may be computed by use of an appropriate index of price movements. For this purpose, the historical cost gross and net book values and current year depreciation charge should be analysed by reference to the year of purchase of each asset concerned. These amounts should be revised in accordance with the change in appropriate indices between the revised current year depreciation charge and the historical cost depreciation charge.

For assets in the United Kingdom the index, or indices, used may be selected from the industry specific or asset specific indices published in the Central Statistical Office booklet Price index numbers for Current Cost Accounting. For assets in the Republic of Ireland the index, or indices, used may be selected from those published by the Central Statistics Office of the Republic of Ireland. For buildings the index of the cost of new construction may be used.

For assets located in other countries, corresponding indices should be used where available. The Central Statistical Office booklet Current Cost Accounting - Guide to price indices for Overseas Countries may be helpful in indicating the indices available in certain overseas countries. If suitable specific indices for overseas assets cannot be obtained, a general price index for the country concerned may be used.

The method used to compute the depreciation adjustment, and the indices employed, should be disclosed in a brief note to the statement.

Cost of Sales

Where the business has already developed appropriate methods of computing the current cost of sales, it is recommended that such methods should be used for the purpose of computing the adjustment. For example, where accounting information is available from standard costing systems, or from base stock or last-in-first-out methods, it may be possible easily to compute the current cost of sales without resort to other methods. Where a more appropriate method cannot be devised and implemented in the time available it is recommended that, wherever possible, the cost of sales adjustment should be computed using the averaging method.

Using the averaging method, the current cost of sales may be computed by revising the historical cost of opening and closing stock to the average current cost for the year by use of an appropriate index. The index, or indices, used for this calculation may be selected from the same sources as indicated for depreciation.

Where progress payments are received from customers, the cost of sales adjustment should be computed on the amount of stock and work in progress after deduction of such payments. To avoid duplication, the progress payments deducted from stock and work in progress should be excluded from the calculation of the gearing adjustment.

The method used to compute the cost of sales adjustment, and the indices employed, should be disclosed in a brief note.

Gearing

It is acknowledged that some companies have already drawn up current cost statements including a gearing adjustment calculated by a method different from that described below, and that others may be planning to do so. Recognizing that circumstances will differ, such companies are not discouraged from following their own methods providing these are disclosed in a note to the statement. The simple approach to the calculation of a gearing adjustment outlined below is recommended unless another method is preferred.

Where the total liabilities of the business, including preference share capital, exceed its total monetary assets, a calculation should be made of the proportion of:

(a) the net balance of monetary liabilities to
(b) the net balance of monetary liabilities plus the equity share capital and reserves.

In computing the amount of reserves to be used in this calculation, the difference between the current values and historical cost amounts for fixed assets and, if material, for stocks, should be added to the reserves shown by the historical cost accounts.

An amount equal to this proportion of the depreciation and cost of sales adjustments should be credited as a separate adjustment in the statement.

Where the total monetary assets of the business exceed its total liabilities, and adjustment should be calculated by applying to the net balance of monetary assets the percentage change in an appropriate index during the accounting year. This adjustment should be charged as a separate item in the statement.

In order to relate these adjustments as closely as possible to the current year's results, averages from the opening and closing balance sheets of the accounting year should be used, unless an alternative averaging method is considered necessary to give a fairer view. For the first year for which this calculation is made, it should be based upon the closing balance sheet if an appropriate average position cannot be obtained without an undue amount of work.

The method used to compute the adjustment, and the index employed, should be disclosed in a brief note to the statement.

Comments

The Accounting Standards Committee will be grateful to receive comments as soon as practicable, particularly from preparers and users of accounts in which the proposals contained in this interim recommendation are implemented, to assist them in considering how the evolution of inflation accounting should progress.

(Appendices 1 to 3, illustrating the cost of sales and gearing adjustments and a suggested format for the statement of adjustments, are not reproduced.)

IX On Some Radical Proposals

30 Cash Flow Accounting

G.H. Lawson

It is indeed perhaps a little unfortunate that the expression cash-flow accounting should have passed into common usage, though I must admit that a name more accurately describing the nature of the beast does not readily suggest itself - at least not to me.

What is Cash-Flow Accounting?

As I understand things, or perhaps more precisely as I have hitherto attempted to argue the case for cash-flow accounting, it constitutes the analytical framework for linking past, present, and prospective financial performance. It is, therefore, a vehicle which may be used to disclose the past development of the finances of business and therefore the determinants of the true return actually received by proprietors or shareholders in the past. (Hereafter I shall refer to company and shareholders rather than to a business and its proprietors.) Alternatively it may be used as a system for disclosing the determinants of the true return shareholders are likely to receive in the future. Cash-flow accounting may therefore also be regarded as an aid to investor decision-making.

Thus, because the logic of the method, which derives from financial and economic theory, dictates that all financial transactions be specified as cash-flows to facilitate an allowance for the time-value of money as one of the costs of resource utilization (or, alternatively, as a prerequisite to the incorporation of an allowance for shareholder time-preference), there is quite clearly no valid reason for the inference that cash-flow accounting is synonymous with receipts and payments accounting in the traditional sense of that expression.

In the light of these introductory remarks it should now be apparent that most of my subsequent comments will be concerned little with the specification of a company as a total cash-flow model, but mainly with the nature, use, derivation, and disclosure of the data which should be enshrined within a cash-flow system. It may nevertheless be useful to have a company depicted as a cash-flow model in front of us (illustration I).

I take it I am on pretty firm ground in suggesting that one of the desiderata of a satisfactory method of disclosure is that the method should be capable of revealing the components of the true past and prospective return to shareholders and that, nowithstanding statement V 8 (formerly S8) (The Accountant, August 7th, 1965) the purpose for which annual accounts are normally prepared ought to be to enable individuals to take investment decisions. Thus the true return obtainable by shareholders is directly and obviously related to the financial relationship subsisting between a company and its shareholders which is par excellence an example of the investment decision. A shareholder who commits capital now, thereby foregoing current consumption, obtains the opportunity to consume and/or reinvest an uncertain stream of benefits or net disposable receipts in the future.

In the case of a limited company, which enjoys a potentially indefinite life, the stream of net disposable receipts obtainable by the chain of successive generations of shareholders is an infinite stream of dividends (net of new injections of external equity finance). It is in this infinite stream of dividends that the return to shareholders truly resides and this applies equally to shareholders who do not propose to retain their shares indefinitely or, indeed, who propose to sell now. Individuals who invest for a finite time-period obtain an exit share price, the magnitude of which (assuming rational and informed investor behaviour), will depend upon the incoming shareholders' estimates of the dividend stream to be received thereafter.

Now it is easy to argue that, if companies were obliged to disclose their prospective dividend streams and the expected inflows and outflows of cash whence that dividend stream will ultimately emerge, investors would be able to deduce more accurate and objective share values, and simultaneously would be more capable of assessing relative financial efficiency. In addition to more rationally-based share prices, we might also expect the

Illustration 1

FRAMEWORK FOR A TOTAL CASH-FLOW FINANCIAL SYSTEM

End Year	1	2	3	etc.	etc.
(1) Increase or decrease in	+	+	+	+	+
bank balance or overdraft	−	−	−	−	−
(2) Net operating cash-flows	+	+	+	+	+
(3) Corporation taxes paid (based on assessable profits)	−	−	−	−	−
(4) Capital expenditure (including portfolio investment)	−	−	−	−	−
(5) (i) cash grants; and	+	+	+	+	+
(ii) tax rebates resulting from tax depreciation allowances on (4)	+	+	+	+	+
(6) Long term debt flows (in and out)	+	+	+	+	+
including interest payments on debt	−	−	−	−	−
(7) Tax rebates on debt interest payments	+	+	+	+	+
(8) External equity finance	+	+	+	+	+
(9) Sales of surplus assets	+	+	+	+	+
(10) Tax rebates on existing assets and losses brought forward	+	+	+	+	+
(11) Dividends less dividend tax	$D_1(1-d)$	$D_2(1-d)$	$D_3(1-d)$	etc.	etc.
(12) Less External equity finance	E_1	E_2	E_3	etc.	etc.
(13) Shareholders. cash-flow stream	$D_1(1-d)$ $-E_1$	$D_2(1-d)$ $-E_2$	$D_3(1-d)$ $-E_3$	etc. etc.	etc. etc.

Operating cash-flow statement

(subheading (2))

End Year	1	2	3	etc.	etc.
(i) Sales receipts	+	+	+	+	+
(ii) Materials	−	−	−	−	−
(iii) Labour	−	−	−	−	−
(iv) Works overhead	−	−	−	−	−
(v) Administrative overhead	−	−	−	−	−
(vi) Selling overhead	−	−	−	−	−
Transfer to (2) above	+	+	+	+	+

latter to become inherently more stable and, as a further consequence, a more accurate relationship between equity returns and the structure of fixed interest rates. Thus, with a much more efficient capital market it is not unreasonable to conclude that there would be an improvement in the whole process of economic organization in our market economy.

In a much more realistic mood, one is perhaps compelled to concede that an obligation to disclose all the information to which I have just referred - that is, future plans and estimates in full financial detail - would create an impossible situation for the majority of companies. But, accepting that it may not be possible to have fully detailed and quantified estimates of the components of an infinite dividend stream, one should not then leap to the inference that in the absence of complete information about the future, there is little point in having any more than we currently receive. Nor should we give up the attempt to develop new methods of presenting current information and managerial intentions, thus enabling investors to infer much more than is currently possible about the magnitudes and time-profile of a company's future dividend stream.

Determinants of the Future Dividend Stream.

Whilst it may be difficult, not to say impossible, to quantify all the determinants of a company's future dividend stream, they can, however, be specified. Such a specification, which is exemplified by the cash-flow model in front of you, is illuminating because it clearly suggests the manner in which all available information ought to be presented if the shareholder is to be helped to infer the maximum about the level and growth of future dividends.

The dimensions of a future dividend stream clearly depend upon a number of factors of which, leaving aside taxes, investment incentives, and additional injections of equity finance, the following are perhaps the most important:

(a) the level of earnings generated by existing assets net of any capital expenditure (hereafter referred to as replacement expenditure) necessary to maintain the trading and productive capacity of those assets intact;

(b) the allocation of that earnings level between dividends and retentions, i.e. the pay-out ratio or plough-back ratio;

(c) the average rate of return which can be obtained by reinvesting retentions in new capital projects i.e., capital expenditure over and above replacement expenditure, within the firm or, for that matter, in investments outside it;

(d) the time-profile of cash-flows expected from new capital projects;

(e) the level of debt-financing and debt-raising capacity.

Assuming for the moment that the foregoing information was available for the latest and previous accounting years, it would be possible to draw a set of logically-based numerical inferences about a company's future dividend stream.

Now it may be tempting to argue that, apart from two or three magnitudes which can be sensibly estimated, namely (i) capital expenditure necessary to maintain trading and productive capacity intact and (ii) the expected rate of return on new capital projects including their expected cash-flow time profiles, most of the foregoing information can already be derived from the conventional profit and loss account (or a series thereof) and balance sheets, and that it is entirely open to whomsoever wishes to have this information to undertake the necessary analysis for himself.

Such a contention ought to be challenged for at least two reasons. First, if it is the case that published accounting data needs first to be further analysed before thay can be used by investors to facilitate further inferences for decision-making purposes, the accountant has not completed his task.

A second and much more pertinent consideration is that even among accountants themselves, to say nothing of the armies of other professionals who lack the accountant's technical skill but nevertheless analyse accounts as a matter of daily routine, there is nothing like unanimity as to what further analysis ought to be undertaken. The simple, but nevertheless vital, point I am leading up to is this: if, as seems to be widely accepted, earnings are taken to be the funds which can be allocated between dividends and the finance to be utilized for new investment from which future earnings and dividend growth can be expected, earnings must necessarily be measured on a cash-flow basis.

Illustration 2

TEN-YEAR PERIOD ENDED SEPTEMBER 30th, 1969

Conventional accounts (i.e., accounting flows)	£	£	Cash-flows
Profit before depreciation (i.e., conventional cash-flow)	+69,266	+45,333	Pre-tax operating cash-flow
Historical cost depreciation	-20,020	-25,000	Estimated replacement capital expenditure (see note)
Taxation charged in profit and loss account	-19,171	-13,551	Taxes paid
Cumulative post-tax retained profit	+£30,075	+£6,782	Distributable cash-flow

As the following illustration suggests, £25,000 is probably a very conservative estimate of depreciation calculated on a current cost basis.

Assumptions

(i) Average asset life: seven years

(ii) Weighted average cost of finance in money terms (i.e. company employs a mixture of debt and equity)): 10 per cent per annum.

To recover current capital expenditure of £1,000 over a period of seven years it would be necessary to make a (constant) annual depreciation charge, a, of £205.4 given by:

$$£1{,}000 = a\left\{\frac{1-(1+0.1)^{-7}}{0.1}\right\}$$

whence, a = £205.4

On a fixed instalment basis, annual depreciation of £1,000÷7 = £143 would be charged. The latter constitutes approximately 70 per cent of the £205.4 annual depreciation calculated on a current cost basis whereas the historical cost depreciation embodied in the 10 year illustration represents 80 per cent of the (£25,000) current cost depreciation estimate. To this extent the £25,000 estimate is conservative.

In an inflationary world, that is in the real world, for any given rate of growth of output the deviation between true and 'conventional' cash-flows is magnified to the extent that a company is able to pass on price increases into selling prices. Hence the higher the rate of 'shifted' cost escalation, the higher is the inflationary contribution to the deviation. At this juncture it is perhaps important to give a real world example of the deviation to which I have just referred (Illustration 2).

In Illustration 2, retained earnings conventionally measured overstate retentions truly available for redeployment in new investments by a factor of approximately 4½. Had the company made a dividend payment of (say) £3,000 - superficially a very modest or conservative proportion of post-tax profits over the 10-year period in question-true retentions would have been overstated by a factor of about 8. It is also of significance, for a reason to which I shall refer in a moment, that in this particular case the year-by-year percentage deviation between 'conventional' cash-flow and true cash-flow was by no means consistent.

The relevance of the fact that the application of the conventional rules of accounting will generally result in a very serious overstatement of earnings truly retained for re-investment should now be apparent. It is this: if an accounting system does not provide an accurate measure of the earnings truly retained by a company on behalf of its shareholders it follows that the appraisal or estimation by shareholders of the effect of the plough-back decision on future earnings and dividend levels is systematically undermined from the start.

I strongly suspect that this state of affairs, conjoined with the fact that the deviation between 'conventional' and 'true' cash-flows is not a consistent percentage, explains why more than one member of the academy has found little or no positive correlation between plough-back and future earnings growth. Thus, using conventionally measured retentions as an implicit or explicit proxy for new capital investment, these researchers have correlated the former with future earnings levels, in an attempt to determine inter alia how profitably funds had been reinvested within the firm. But, as the accountant may prefer to put it, in so far as in circumstances of turnover growth (measured in money terms), some proportion of these (conventional) retentions has already been absorbed in the form of extra working capital in supporting a past turnover increase, this proportion is clearly not available for investment once again. It is in my view a major weakness of the accruals system of accounting that it facilitates this kind of confusion between capital and revenue; or, in other words that it falsely gives the impression that certain funds which effectively have already become fixed capital investment are still available for distribution or reinvestment. As already stated, this possibility clearly has important implications for individuals who attempt to draw inferences about the growth of future earnings and dividends.

Sources and applications of funds

Now it will doubtless be objected that I am making too much of a song and dance about the extent to which the conventional system of accounting overstates the funds truly available for reinvestment in projects that will contribute to future earnings growth, and that the position can, in any event, be clearly elucidated by the 'appropriate' use of source and application of funds statements. Whilst this latter assertion is absolutely correct, it is obviously important that the nature of the 'appropriate' use of source and application of funds statements should be clearly understood. There is also the pertinent but unresolved question as to how the investing public might be given sufficient guidance about the 'appropriate' usage of source and application of funds statements - and it is hardly necessary to add that at present companies are not legally obliged to disclose source and application of funds statements.

It is now perhaps important to state quite explicitly that the substance of the foregoing remarks amounts to a contradiction of the commonly held view that the difference between the cash-flow and accruals bases of measuring profits is merely a question of a difference in timing, and that both systems will disclose the same total profits in the long run. Apart from the fact that the question of timing is by no means a trivial consideration, the sum of cash-flow profits can only equal the sum of accrued profits in virtually only one very special case - namely, when on the winding-up of a business all assets and liabilities are realized at balance sheet values. For all practical purposes this, and one or two other highly restricted situations, can be ignored.

In summing up my comments under the first two subheadings of this lecture, I would merely like to suggest that cash-flow accounting, as I understand it, constitutes the analytical framework in which should be embodied all financial information about the past, present, and future whence a company's proprietors can attempt to infer the magnitudes and time-profile of a potentially infinite dividend stream.

As I have attempted to show, in order to estimate the shareholders' expected cash-flows and expected cash-flows and especially the growth therein, it is necessary to infer another set of cash-flows, namely, a company specified as a cash-flow model. Whether one cares to admit it or not, the analysis of conventional accounting data as a pre-requisite to the inferring of a future dividend stream amounts to the conversion of accounting flows into cash-flows. It is a curious paradox that whereas when engaging in forward planning the accountant will readily allow for extra working capital but then, in disclosing data to investors who fundamentally are engaging in the same forward planning exercise, acts as though he no longer believes that the working capital corrective is necessary. Thus, in the latter case the accountant effectively shifts the line of demarcation between revenue and capital thereby overstating the former and understating the latter.

The main purpose of the first part of this paper was to suggest that cash-flow accounting, as I have attempted to describe it, is justifiable in its own right in the logic of economics and finance.

As should now be apparent, and unlike the conventional accruals system of accounting, cash-flow accounting explicitly recognizes that a company's cash-generating and profit-making abilities are integrally related. Indeed, if we first allow for the time-value of money using a discounting or compounding procedure, the ability to generate cash and the capacity to earn profit are not merely integrally-related considerations but are in fact synonymous. If this is so, and in so far as inflation contributes to the deviation between 'conventionally-measured' (i.e., accrued) profits and profits measured on a cash-flow basis, the conventional method of accounting becomes increasingly less useful for managerial purposes in an inflationary world. The higher the rate of inflation the more acute the managerial problem, and the greater the motivation to switch to cash-flow accounting. This is my diagnosis of the causes of the recent renaissance of cash-flow accounting in its new forward-looking guise.

In cash-flow accounting an alternative to accounting for inflation, or merely a reaction to it? In offering a brief answer to this question, I would say that cash-flow accounting is logically defensible in any circumstances but that as a managerial tool it is inherently more capable of demonstrating or accounting for the impact of inflation on company profits and finances than any other system. Hence, whilst the recent revival of interest in cash-flow accounting may have been stimulated by the present alarming rate of inflation which I suppose really began in 1969, cash-flow accounting per se is, in my view at least, much more than a mere pragmatic reaction to what I sincerely hope will soon be seen as a transient phenomenon.

Perhaps I may now refer to some of the wider aspects of inflation which have implications for the accounting process, that is to say, the accounting process as I understand it.

Future Dividends

The actual return provided for a shareholder is delivered in actual money terms. The successive dividends in which this return truly resides are therefore not directly comparable in an inflationary world. Should a shareholder wish to ascertain whether a dividend is being maintained in terms of purchasing power, he must in some way correct for the rise in the general level of prices, or perhaps more accurately, for the rises in the prices which are relevant to his own pattern of expenditure.

It is in my view a mistake to conclude that because we live in a world characterized by endemic inflation, we must abandon accounting in money terms. (It is, of course, important that we should be in accord on matters of definition, though by now my own interpretation of accounting in money terms ought to be pretty clear). It is not obvious to me that, in order to provide a shareholder with the information from which he can attempt to infer the magnitude and growth rate of future dividends, it is necessary to correct an array of magnitudes in the latest set of accounts with index numbers. Provided replacement expenditure is reasonably accurately measured in terms of current prices and, additionally, provided operating earnings have been calculated on a cash-flow basis (i.e., in the jargon of the accountant, working capital adjustments have been effected), the fund which is truly divisible between (a) dividends and (b) finance for redeployment in new investments, can always be measured in terms of current prices, that is, in actual money prices.

Something which, in my view, ought readily to suggest itself is that explicit attempts should be made to inform shareholders about the nature of the impact of inflation on a company's finances and how, in consequence, future dividends are likely to be affected.

In speaking of (say) 5 per cent annual inflation or a 5 per cent rise in the general level of prices between one year and the next, we are in fact making use of a weighted arithmetic average. Thus, if the average annual increase is 5 per cent, there must be many prices, of which wages and salaries are a notable example, that are rising at a faster annual rate than 5 per cent. Concurrently, other prices in the economy must, by definition, be increasing at less than 5 per cent annually. As an example of the latter, one can perhaps point to the unit capital costs of successive generations of fixed assets. In general it is to be expected that technological advance will cause a continuous decline in asset prices in real terms. Indeed one can go further and legitimately suggest that, generally speaking, for any given shareholder expectations about future inflation, escalating wage rates constitute a long run bias in favour of capital intensive manufacturing processes.

The extent to which the individual company is affected by inflation and price changes vis-a-vis other companies will obviously depend upon at least three things. First, the relative proportions of wage, salary, materials, overhead, and capital costs in the structure of its total annual cash outflows; secondly, the ability and inclination of the company to vary the ratio of the aforementioned factor costs; and thirdly, the ability and inclination of the company to pass on inflationary and other cost increases into selling prices. All three of these factors represent important considerations for any management which attempts to forecast the future development of its company's finances, or, in other words, the determinants of the cash-flow stream ultimately available for shareholders.

Equally they are considerations which ought to be held clearly in view by shareholders who attempt to deduce their future dividend streams. In the absence of an obligation to publish detailed and fully quantified financial plans, explicitly allowing for anticipated price changes, the impact of the latter on company finances should at least be the subject of a commentary in a company's annual report and accounts. Such a commentary would attempt an economic analysis along the lines I have just proposed and, contributing information about expected relative price changes would be of importance not only to shareholders but also from the standpoint of resource allocation at the macroeconomic level. Until the problems of inflation and rising prices are first explicitly and universally recognized for what they are, namely phenomena which ought to be taken into account in all current decisions and estimates by both management and shareholders, the whole process of resource allocation is less than efficient because all are attempting to optimize in relation to the wrong set of prices.

Supplemented by further actual data, an enlarged version (Illustration 3) of the previous illustration clearly suggests that the appropriate use of a source and application of funds statement requires, in effect, that it be converted into a cash-flow statement.

Thus, referring to the source and application of funds statement on the left-hand side of Illustration 3 and again assuming replacement expenditure to be £25,000 (this, as explained earlier, is probably a conservative estimate of the capital expenditure which was necessary to maintain trading and productive capacity intact) the amount of retentions truly available for reinvestment in new capital projects is evidently equal to 'conventional' cash-flow <u>minus</u> replacement expenditure minus taxes provided <u>minus</u> increase in working capital, i.e., £69,266- £25,000 - £19,171 - £18,313 = £6,782. This latter number is clearly given by operating cash-flows <u>minus</u> replacement expenditure <u>minus</u> taxes paid, i.e., £45,333 - £25,000 - £13,551 = £6,782.

Given the importance which is almost universally attached to the conventional profit figure, the lay reader of the accounts of the company in question could, even if fortunate enough to be provided with a source and application of funds statement, be forgiven for assuming that the company had earned (net of tax) £49,246 - £19,171 = £30,075 for its shareholders, but proposed to retain this profit for reinvestmenton their behalf in order to raise the future level of earnings. In general the lay reader would not be told that two correctives, one in respect of depreciation and the other in respect of working capital, usually need to be applied to (conventionally-measured) retentions before the finance truly available for raising the earnings level can be ascertained.

Had the company in question paid a dividend in excess of £6,782, as would have been legally possible more would have been distributed to shareholders than had actually been generated from trading and production.

In these circumstances the dividend would obviously have been subvented from non-equity cash which was probably intended as finance for fixed-capital formation - though again shareholders would not normally be informed of such a state of affairs. Furthermore, this situation could continue for as long as a company had access to external debt or equity cash sources. Thus the fact that it would not continue indefinitely would be due not to the operation of any inbuilt safeguard within the accruals system of

Illustration 3

TEN-YEAR PERIOD ENDED SEPTEMBER 30th 1969

Source and application of funds statement				Source and application of cash statement	
Source of funds	£	£	£		Source of cash
Share capital		500	500		Share capital
Bank overdraft..		24,822	24,822		Bank overdraft
Short-term loan		6,263	6,263		Short-term loan
Hire-purchase credit ..		4,013	-		
"Conventional" cash-flow:					
Pre-tax profit..	49,246				
Depreciation	20,020				
		69,266	45,333		Operating cash-flow
Total		£104,864	£76.918		Total
Application of funds	£	£	£	£	Application of cash
Capital expenditure:					Capital expenditure
Replacement	25,000			25,000	Replacement
New projects	40,272			36,259	New projects
		65,272	61,259		
Investment in associated company		1,894	1,894		Investment in associated company
Taxes on profit..		19,171	13,551		Taxes paid
Increase in working capital		18.313	-		
Increase in cash balance		213	213		Closing cash balance
Total		£104.864	£76.918		Total

accounting but because, in the long run, creditors and shareholders would, in the absence of a commensurate return on capital invested, refuse to provide further finance.

The fact that in a situation of indefinite turnover growth it is possible for 'conventional cash-flow' consistently to exceed 'true cash-flow' (and therefore to mask an uncovered dividend situation) also raises the presumption that for a particular rate of growth of turnover and selling price level, 'true cash-flow' may be persistently negative. In that case, trading and production are permanently subsidized by some other source of cash, whilst 'conventional profits' (net of depreciation) are persistently positive.

Again, it can be said that such a situation would not continue indefinitely becuase external sources of finance would sooner or later dry up. But once more the crux of the matter is the absence of a safeguard within the accruals system of accounting. In this case there is nothing, apart from the ultimate sanction just mentioned, to prevent the system disclosing a situation which on common-sense grounds alone ought to be rejected, namely, one in which a persistent negative operating cash-flow is apparently consistent with truly profitable business activity.

It is clearly necessary to emphasize that the duration and extent to which the accruals system of accounting may mask an adverse situation may be such that a substantial amount of capital may be eroded before the reality of the situation becomes patently obvious.

Contrary to widespread belief, the measurement of earnings on a cash-flow basis is not merely a matter of adding back depreciation to conventional profit before deducting replacement capital expenditure. Converting conventional profit back to cash-flow earnings is in fact quite a detailed operation involving adjustments in respect of so-called working capital changes, between one accounting period and the next, i.e., changes in trade debtors, trade creditors, inventory, debtors and creditors in respect of overheads and so on. In a situation in which there is turnover growth in money terms, a failure to make working capital adjustments to conventional profit can result in very significant and seriously misleading deviations between true cash flow and what is popularly believed to be cash-flow.

It would also follow from what I have been saying about the relative impact of inflation as between one company and the next, that the problem cannot be handled merely by the application of a corrective in the form of a single index number.

Extra Cash for Replacement

My previous suggestion that escalating wage rates constitute an effective long-run bias in favour of capital-intensive manufacturing processes is entirely consistent with the fact that the replacement cost of an asset may substantially exceed its historical cost. If the rise in the general level of prices is accompanied by changes in the relative prices of labour and capital goods, the technological possibilities of (capital-labour) substitution will always offer advantageous opportunities. The fact that asset replacement costs may, in absolute terms, exceed their historical costs is a financial problem which, to a greater or lesser extent, characterizes all economically-valid investment decisions.

The important distinction which therefore needs to be held clearly in view is the difference between relative and absolute price changes. All this is perhaps best described with the use of an example which, as will be shown, can also be used to draw out important implications from an accounting standpoint.

Illustration 4

Assumptions

(i) In a non-inflationary world investors require a discounted cash-flow rate of return of 5 per cent per annum from the ordinary shares of company X. (For illustrative convenience personal taxes are ignored).

(ii) The shareholders of company X anticipate annual inflation at the rate of 5 per cent per annum, i.e., they expect their initial (money) capital invested to be eroded at the annual rate of 5 per cent.

(iii) Given the shareholders' required rate of return and their expectations about future inflation, the directorate of company X aims to provide its shareholders with a rate of return of at least 10 per cent per annum in money terms.

(iv) Company X has the opportunity to invest shareholders' capital in Project Y which has the following (expected) characteristics:

Capital cost in terms of 1971 prices
- £3.352 (outflow)
Expected life - five years

Annual wage savings resulting from this investment in terms of 1971 prices - £1,000 (annual end-year inflow).

(v) Wage rates are expected to rise at an annual rate of 8 per cent.

Analysis

(a) In terms of 1971 prices, the discounted cash-flow rate of return provided by project Y is given by the value of r which satisfies the equation:

$$£3,352 = \frac{1,000}{1+r} + \frac{1,000}{(1+r)^2} + \frac{1,000}{(1+r)^3} + \frac{1.000}{(1+r)^4} + \frac{1.000}{(1+r)^5}$$

$$= 1.000 \quad \frac{1 - (1+r)^5}{r}$$

whence, using tables to solve for r,

r = 15 per cent per annum.

(b) In the absence of inflation and rising wage rates, and given the requirement of a shareholders' (minimum) rate of return of 5 per cent per annum, shareholders' capital would be maintained intact if project Y were capable of generating an annual cash-flow, a, given by:

$$£3,352 = \frac{a}{1+0.05} + \frac{a}{(1+0.05)^2} + \frac{a}{(1+0.05)^3} + \frac{a}{(1+0.05)^4} + \frac{a}{(1+0.05)^5}$$

$$= a \left(\frac{1-(1+0.05)^{-5}}{0.05}\right)$$

whence, again using tables,

$$a = £3,352 \div 4.3295$$

$$= £774$$

(i.e. a five-year annuity of £774 (paid in arrears) purchased at a price of £3,352 provides a rate of interest of 5 per cent in addition to the full recovery of capital).

If, in this case, depreciation disclosed in the accounts were based on the assets' historical cost and calculated on a fixed instalment basis, the annual charge would be £3,352 ÷ 5 = £670.

Annual depreciation actually charged would therefore represent only 670 ÷ 774 = 87 per cent of the provision which would be necessary to maintain the shareholders' initial capital of £3,352 intact.

(c) Taking into account the expected annual increases in wages, the discounted cash-flow rate of return provided by project Y is given by the value of r* which satisfies the equation:

$$\pounds 3{,}352 \quad \frac{1{,}000}{1+r^*} + \frac{1{,}000(1+0.08)}{(1+r^*)^2} + \frac{1{,}000(1+0.08)^2}{(1+r^*)^3}$$

$$+ \frac{1{,}000\ (1+0.08)^3}{(1+r^*)^4} + \frac{1.000(1+0.08)^4}{(1+r^*)^5}$$

$$= \frac{1{,}000}{r^*-0.08} \left(1 \; \frac{(1+0.08)^5}{(1+0.r^{*3}} \right)$$

whence, r^*= 22 per cent per annum.

(d) Taking into account shareholder expectations about future inflation in addition to their required rate of return shareholders' capital would be maintained intact if project Y was capable of generating an annual cash-flow, a*, given by:

$$\pounds 3{,}352 = a^* \quad \frac{1-(1+0.1)^5}{0.1}$$

whence,

$$a^* = \pounds 3.352 \div 3.7908$$

$$= \pounds 884$$

Assuming the same conventional depreciation charge as in (b) namely, £670, the latter would, in this case, represent only 670 ÷ 884 = 76 per cent of the provision which would be necessary to maintain the shareholders' initial capital of £3,352 intact.

(e) The nature of the bias in favour of capital intensive assets can now be drawn into sharper perspective. With reference to (a) to (d) above, and assuming again (i) that wage rates will continue to rise at an annual rate of 8 per cent, (ii) that shareholders continue to entertain the expectation of 5 per cent annual inflation (i.e. a required money return of 10 per cent), the proposition is that so long as the annual rate of increase in capital costs is less than 8 per cent, the generations of assets which succeed project Y will, ceteris paribus, become more profitable. This may be demonstrated in the following manner.

Given 8 per cent (expected) annual wage rate escalation and a shareholder (minimum) required rate of return of 10 per cent per annum, in money terms, the net present value of project Y is given by:

$$\frac{£1.000}{0.1-0.08}\left(1-\frac{(1+0.08)^5}{(1+0.1)^5}\right)-£3.352 \qquad (1)$$

Assuming the capital cost, of such a project as this, increases at the annual rate of 6 per cent, its net present value if adopted one year later would, other things being the same, be equal to:

$$\frac{£1,000(1+0.08}{0.1-0.08}\left(1-\frac{(1+0.08)^5}{(1+0.1)^5}\right)-£3.352(1+0.06) \qquad (2)$$

Given that the value of (1) is positive, which necessarily follows from part (c), mere inspection shows that the value of (2) exceeds the value of (1).

Assuming, as seems to be suggested by what evidence there is, that the previous assumptions are realistic, it would follow as already stated, that the level of economically viable capitalintensive projects in the economy as a whole will tend to rise in relation to the level of viable labour -intensive projects.

Conclusion

Perhaps I may now conclude this section, and indeed the paper itself, by drawing your attention to the fact that I have not attempted a direct answer to the question of how to provide the extra cash for the replacement of fixed assets at prices exceeding acquisition cost. It seems to me that the crux of the matter must, given that the relationship between a company and shareholders is par excellence an example of the investment decision, be concerned with the prevention of the erosion of shareholders' capital. As I understand things, it is this particular concept of the inviolability of proprietors capital which ought to suggest the basis for measuring the cost of maintaining earning-power intact. In other words, in attempting to lay down a theoretical basis for company accounting, attention should be focused preeminently on the economic relationship between a company and its shareholders. There is no reason whatsoever for assuming that because a joint stock enterprise is endowed with a separate legal personality that a company directorate is accountable to that person as such or, perhaps more to the point, that in attempting to measure profits we may adopt an entity concept which allows us to pretend that shareholders no longer exist.

As I have attempted to show, if we start from the assumption that before earnings can be reckoned shareholdrs' capital must first be maintained intact, it is then clearly necessary for company decision makers to ensure that rising prices are correctly allowed for in investment decisions, that shareholders expectation about future inflation are also sensibly embodied in the analysis, and, last but not least, that due recognition is given to the time-value of money - which is another way of saying that we should explicitly recognize from the outset that shareholders have time-preferences.

31 The Case for Current Cost of Capital Accounting

D.A.R. Forrester

Assets or Affairs

Advocates of inflation accounting have exaggerated the pretensions of historical accounts to give meaningful asset values. The theory underlying most financial accounting is not one of 'constant money values' but one of costs charged to management and charged off when expired, of cash cycles, complete or incomplete (as the Trueblood Report views it), of a series of complete or incomplete 'transactions' or affairs.

Interpreted thus, the balance sheet is seen as simply collecting the varied 'accruals' and 'prepayments' necessary to adjust cash inflows and outflows for period calculation. This model is useful in so far as it relates owners' dated investments and returns to management decisions in like terms. Specifically, it must avoid using future cash-cycle possibilities in valuing those completed, or imputing replacement costs either to base stock or base plant units used up. It is coherently based on an alternative valuation and matching principle, yielding a logical and widely understood view of profits.

Two modifications of this 'affairs' model are possible. One, commended to Germans[1], suggests that the profits so derived may not be distributable to shareholders without reduction in net worth in inflationary times. The additional retention may be separately calculated by notionally attributing the more 'fixed' assets to this net worth, and revaluing these only at specific replacement prices. Other assets are considered to be financed indefinitely and at changing price-levels by renewable borrowing. By such a calculation, the Germans propose neat and logical modification of traditional profits which are there subject to minimum as well as maximum legal regulation: in other words, profit and distribution theory and law are not separable.

But an alternative modification of the cash-cycles model has a very long history and wide application. Robert Hamilton of Aberdeen wrote in 1788 that the merchant's gain or loss should be established by the excess of gross profit above the interest of his stock, such interest being calculated on the money laid out until it is recovered[2]. Only fairly recently has imputed interest been excluded from costs and from accounts, not only because auditors preferred to trace only cash transactions, but also because the theory of profit maximisation prescribes the use in decision-making of marginal costs rather than average or very full absorption costs, including cost of capital. Marginal costs, of course, can be distinguished as a constituent element even in stock valuations in accordance with SSAP 9, and cost of capital elements need not blur certain decisions while beneficially informing others.

Arguments for cost-of-capital accounting may include:

(a) the logical preferability of net residual income to returns on capital employed;

(b) the incongruence of incorporating a time value for money in investment, batch size and other decisions without reflecting it in accounts;

(c) the superiority of a model prompting a single profit statement, which may disclose the contributions rather than the appropriations of all factors of production, and the super-profits or losses resulting from management's use of these factors;

(d) the preferability, at the present time, of suggesting fair levels of reward for all elements in all firms whether geared or ungeared, regulated, nationalised or whatever. (Interestingly, co-operatives' accounts have continued to charge interest to departments, although at rates so insensitive to those of the market as to deprive employees' pension funds[3].)

Problems

In pursuit if an acceptable cost-of-capital accounting system, problems emerge both in principle and detailed applications. Notable among such problems are the establishment of an appropriate cost-of-capital rate, the capital or assets base to which such a rate is applicable, and whether this imputed interest is to be regarded as a cost, expense or appropriation of profit.

We shall argue here for use of the open market rate appropriate to one-year, risk-free loans and for its reflection in addition to depreciation as a cost of facilities used, and as a 'holding cost' for stocks and work-in-progress. We shall also argue in favour of its application to unexpired or unliquidated values reflecting the original expense and decisions, rather than to assessed values. Nevertheless, revaluations may with advantage be reflected thoroughly and systematically in the books at time of company takeover, major managerial change, or nationally when a new firm currency is being established.

The arguments against annual revaluations arise from resistance to the inventory approach, whereby physical assets are listed and considered to be evaluatable at any time in objective and unambiguous manner[4]. Not only very different values but very different groupings will be appropriate on liquidation and on thorough-going replacement. For the going concern, the incomplete cycles model is more relevant, although management should never be ignorant of past, present and future prices, particularly for its standard stock items; but it cannot be held rigidly accountable in one-year time spans of discretion. Its decisions with horizons of several months or several years are in terms of cash out anticipating future cash receipts appropriately discounted. Interim notional holding gains and losses confuse the situation except perhaps in certain speculative situations[5].

We thus argue for an imputation of interest, such as that recommended by the British Master Printers as recently as 1959, but against the perpetual updating of plant costs, defensible perhaps for a uniform costing system but not for accountability purposes. We may also learn something from Limperg's emphasis on the current cost of all elements, including capital, which were totalled to establish a current deprival value. At this cost, goods would be sold in a 'steady state' economy, requiring to be immunised from price-changes which, apparently, Limperg felt had little adaptive function[6]. (Where Sandilands ignored the cost of capital but accepted other aspects of the Limperg cost theory, we will adopt the inverse!).

In France, after the War, there was experience of nationwide revaluations, as in Germany in 1948. Thereafter there has been resistance to inflation accounting, partly through experience of years of totalitarian manipulation of prices, so that indices did not reflect a balancing of supply and demand. Today in this country many prices reflect monopoly market power, the least effective answer to which is to maintain one's demand schedule through implied replacement. Instead of reflecting in the accounts replacement prices or current labour rates (achieved despite high unemployment), it may be wise to focus on key prices or rates which have long been held to have a stabilising and contra-cyclical tendency. In place of indices of general or specific price-levels available at three provisional stages prior to finalisation twelve weeks after the balance sheet date, as recommended by ED 18, we may find an earlier and preferable modifier in the interest rate struck by the market for a risk-free loan covering the period.

Advocates of cost-of-capital accounting have argued for average, marginal, historical or other interest rates, specific to the firm or industry. We suggest that it is more important to establish a single, firm rate of general application than to search for a rate or rates theoretically appropriate to each circumstance and decision. A rate based on current one-year local authority loans should thus be standardised by an appropriate regulating body. This will be called accounting interest applicable in a system we may christen current cost of capital accounting, or CCCA. Specific risks and opportunities will thus be reflected both in net present valuations in advance, and in residual income profits.

Method

Let us illustrate its application to a company floated on 1 January with a simple balance sheet as in Figure 1. Two identidal contracts are commenced, one on 1 October and the other on 1 January, the latter being delivered, and paid for on 31 December. Materials, labour and expense are paid for evenly each month, so that the cash account appears as in Figure 2.

The traditional profit and loss account would be as in Figure 3. One notes that labour and materials are recorded at current market rates but that the interest paid to the lenders is in accordance with possibly an earlier contractual commitment. The majority of overheads and depreciation has been charged in cost of sales but, in accord with SSAP 9, a proportion based

1. Opening balance sheet, 1 January

Ordinary shares	400	Fixed assets	100
10% Loan stock	100	Cash	400
	500		500

2. Cash account for year

Opening balance		400
Less Direct labour	250	
Direct materials	625	
Expense	100	975
		(575)
Add Sales receipts		1000
		425
Less Loan interest		10
Closing balance		415

3. Traditional profit and loss account for year

Sales		1000
Less Cost of sales		
Direct labour	200	
Direct material	500	
Expense	80	
	780	
Depreciation	16	796
Operating profit		204
Less Interest paid		10
Profit before tax and extra-ordinary items		194

4. Traditional stock valuation

Direct labour	50
Direct materials	125
Expense	20
Depreciation	4
	199

5. CCCA stock valuation

Direct labour	50
Direct materials	125
Expense	20
	195
Accounting interest (on average stock at 4% per quarter)	4
Cost of facilities (depreciation and interest)	7.2
	206.2

on normal activities and including expenditure accruing wholly or partly on a time basis is included in stocks (Figure 4.) Interest charges have not been similarly handled, although the standard requires that expenditure incurred in the normal course of business in bringing the product to its present location and condition be not reduced by the exclusion of selected overheads. But if these contracts had been considered long-term, a treatment closely in line with that about to be illustrated would have had to be adopted.

Let us now hypothesise that inflation during the year has run at 20 per cent for these fixed assets (equalling depreciation in our example), at 10 per cent for stocks and at 15 per cent for retail prices, with 16 per cent accounting interest. A medley of adjustments could be presented to 'maintain capital' as variously interpreted. What we argue, however, is that management should be fully charged with all resources committed to their care, and that this will reveal the rewards of risk-taking and enterprise.

Interest should be charged to work-in-progress on all resources from the time of acquistion, and credited to the accounting interest account, either on monthly balances or, in our example of smooth flows, on average levels. In the CCCA year end stock account (Figure 5), we show direct costs and expense incurred over three months and totalling £195, being increased by accounting interest on the average or half that sum for this quarter year. Conservatives may object that the realisation principle has been abandoned, but there is little logic in their arguments for the inclusion or exclusion of any cost element from stock values.

In all circumstances, provisions may be needed against future losses: here we aim to maximise the benefits of full cost valuation, reduced as neccessary by full provisions. As in stocks, so in cost of sales, interest on average product costs is included, plus a cost-of-facilities charge bringing together interest and depreciation of fixed assets (see flow chart, Figure 6).

While decisions to duplicate or sell facilities must be based on appropriate prices, depreciation and interest on fixed assets could be based on acquisition cost, on depreciated value, on some realisable value or on replacement cost. The treatment adopted here finds precedent and support in American Cost Accounting Standards.[7] These, of course, are applicable to government contractors,

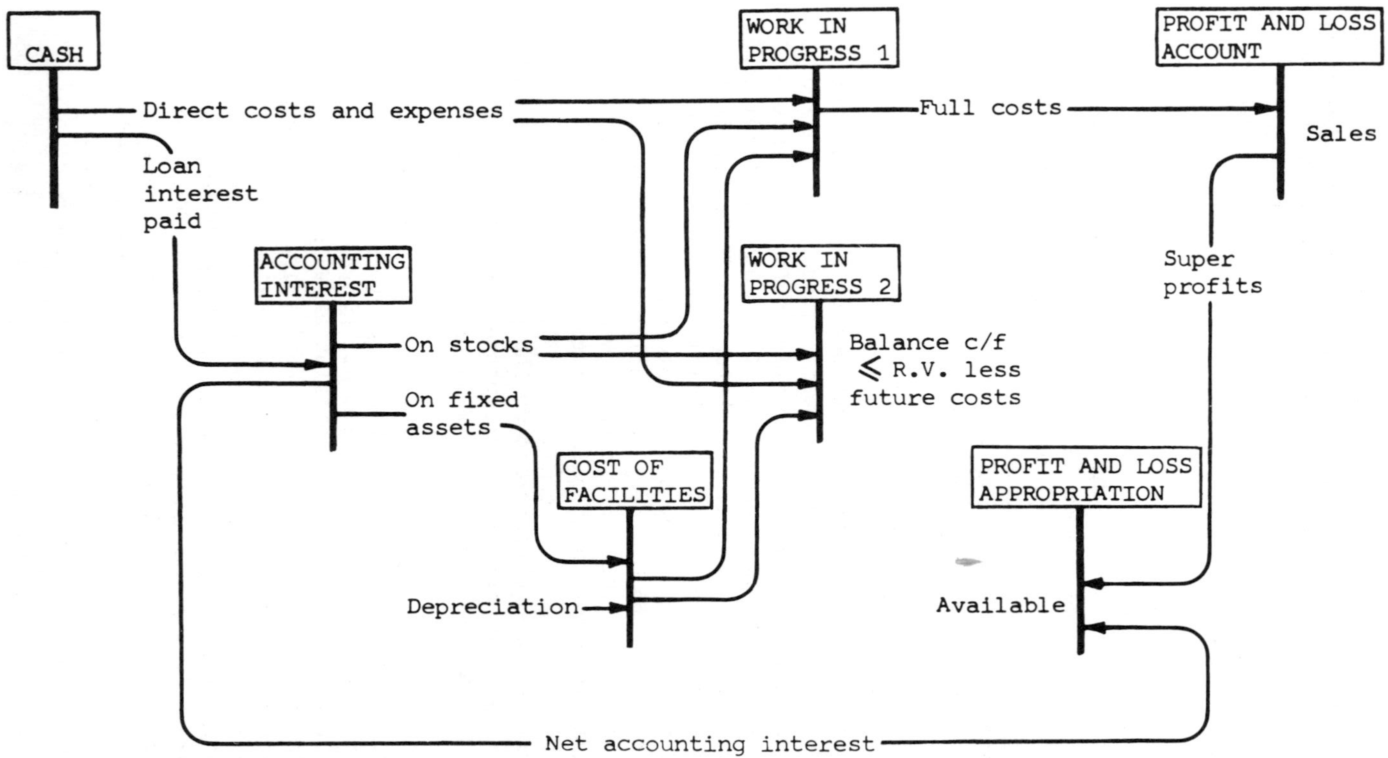

6 Flow chart of CCCA entries

on whose behalf argument was made that depreciation charges allowed should be based on asset replacement costs and this was incorporated in an October 1975 Exposure Draft[3] . In March 1976, the proposal was reversed, however, as a result of suggestions that an interest rate used in recognising the contract cost of capital employed could be designed to cover the impact of inflation as well as the time value of maney. For facilities utilised and valued at historical cost, charges are made to contracts for depreciation and for 'cost of money' at semi-annual rates set by the Secretary of the Treasury in relation to current commercial five-year borrowing rates. Accordingly, our cost-of-facilities account is debited with depreciation and with accounting interest for the year, and this is charged to the two work-in-progress contracts on the basis of machine or plant usage.

A CCCA profit and loss account is given in Figure 7. Attention will be directed to the surplus from operations, particularly where profits are subject to regulation but in general as a measure of managerial success in dealing with paricular risks and opportunities. In this sense the surplus represents 'super profits'. But the traditional picture is largely restored in the appropriation section, where the contra-entries to the holding costs are shown as credits and reduced by actual interest payments to reveal the gains to ordinary shareholders, including that arising from the difference between current and historical interest rates paid to outside capital.

Critics could concentrate on the possibility not only of holdings gains but of a real interest element being included in stocks and yet shown as profits available for appropriation. Safeguards have been described, however, against overanticipation of profits. Indeed, the future cost deductible from realisable values for contract 2 should not only include direct costs and overhead, but the cost of capital attributable in the future. There is provision, therefore, for safeguarding future profitability (and not merely loss avoidance) on contracts in progress. Critics may also see from the closing balance (Figure 8) that management has been charged with no interest on working capital apart from stocks. Our illustration could have been extended to show perhaps imputed cost under this heading, matched with interest earned or paid, together perhaps with cash discounts to reveal gains or losses incurred in relation to monetary items.

7. CCCA profit and loss account for year

Sales		1000
Less Cost of sales (memo detail)		
Direct labour	200	
Direct material	500	
Expense	80	
	780	
Accounting interest (Average 16% p.a.)	62.4	
Cost of facilities	28.8	871.2
Surplus from operations (=£0.322 per £1 share)		128.8
Accounting interest		
Charged to work-in-progress (£62.4 + £4)	66.4	
Charged on facilities (£12.8 + £3.2)	16.0	
	82.4	
Less Interest paid	10	
Net to shareholders (+£0.181 per share)		72.4
Available for appropriation before tax and extra-ordinary items		201.2

8. Closing balance sheet - CCCA basis

Ordinary Shares	400	Fixed assets, at cost		100
Appropriation account		Less Depreciation		20
Surplus from operations	128.8			80
Accounting interest - net	72.4	Stocks	206.2	
	601.2	Cash	415	
10% loan stock	100			621.2
	701.2			701.2

9. Balance Sheet of a fully geared company

Share capital	5	Fixed assets	500
15% loan stock	995	Stocks	500
	1000		1000

10. CCA profit statement

Operations profits (say)		300
Less Interest		150
		150
Revaluation surplus	200	
Less charged to reserves ?		

Memorandum note

Gain on loan $\frac{995 \times 100}{120} - 995 = 170$

Views in conflict

Sandilands and ED18, we have suggested, adopted Limperg's theory and model with the significant exception of current costs of capital. This omission produces fundamental flaws and weaknesses which they have attempted to play down and hope may be resolved during the exposure period. We must examine the choices open to them and the reasons given for a treatment which ignores the right and ability of lenders to secure their interest with its essential role in counter-inflationary policies.

Once again, an illustration may help, based this time on a very highly geared firm experiencing, let us say, specific and general price inflation of 20 per cent, while historic interest is payable at 15 per cent. The balance sheet is given in Figure 9 and a CCA profit and loss account in Figure 10, along with memorandum note of holding gains on the loan stock.

Three choices were open. If the lenders were thought to have anticipated specific price inflation of assets which they may be later called on to refinance, then the revaluation surplus of £200 should have been reduced by actual interest paid. If, on the other hand, we ignore any real interest receivable by the lender (after taxation and after providing for the maintenance of his capital), then actual interest paid could have been offset against the so-called gain through holding a monetary liability repayable in reduced CPP terms. Only if all monetary liabilities are considered to be indexed and interest rates contractually payable are seen as appropriations of CCA profits before tax is the recommended treatment a logical one.

Sandilands's argument is dogmatic in the extreme: 'charges in labour, interest and expenses other than depreciation and cost of sales will reflect cost incurred during the year' and will be at the value to the business of such items whether the rate paid is above or below current market rates (para. 536). Interest payments is money terms should be charged against current-cost profit to which it would be 'incorrect' to add back any inflation element in the actual interest paid. It is then argued that, even though interest rates are lower than inflation (and therefore must all be charged against holding gains), the feasibility of identifying real and fictitious interest is doubtful (para. 539). These are presumably the 'matters of principle' basic to their argument in addition to the 'severe difficulties for tax' referred to later (par. 689-

691). Observing the final stages of a British economy unable to regulate itself, the Committee found no strong relations between rates of inflation and interest, for the latter had just fallen and still appeared to be influenced by international rates[8].

Sandilands pursued immediate solutions, in particular tax relief on stock appreciation: if interest payments fully chargeable against tax included an inflationary expectation then, when stock is financed by borrowing, the same cost would be allowed twice. They held these to be two separate matters and were unable to find rational means to allocate sources of finance to assets[9]. (We may note the preconcern of the Committee with the effect of taxation on the nominal profits of the firm, and its silence concerning the taxation as income of interest receipts the rate of which, to maintain capital after tax, would be very high, given recent inflationary trends.)

ED18 is clear that interest received less interest paid should be added to operating profits (para. 17). Explanatory Note 172 refers to the argument that rates assume an element to compensate for inflation and that this element should be matched against capital gearing gains and charged against revaluation reserves. The logic behind this and a similar treatment of part of interest received is recognised but felt to raise the problem of analysing interest to real and fictitious elements, and of inconsistency with proposed treatments of gains and losses on monetary items. The Guidance Manual attempts elucidation by describing interest as the 'cost to the company of operating at a level above that which has not been financed by means other than specific borrowing' and as 'a charge for the use of the money to finance assets which earn the company's trading revenue'. Interest is to be regarded as a trading expense unless capitalised in property development where it may be added to costs before a revaluation surplus is earned. Capitalised interest then becomes part of the depreciation charge against revenue when earned. (par. 313-316).

We referred earlier to the choice for current cost of capital accounting as to whether the costs should be capitalised, treated as an addition to conversion costs or shown as a period charge against profits. This last treatment is the simplest method of indicating residual income. The very full absorption cost technique, which we illustrated, is feasible and approximately congruent with decision models for larger contracts or stocks with slow turnovers. It certainly has advantages over the ED18 proposal that such contracts be treated as monetary assets, with only memorandum CPP calculations thereon, unless they be property developments financed by specific borrowings. Under CCCA, the full cost of building or creating facilities would be capitalised until commissioning and thereafter would become subject to depreciation and to interest charges to users. (When the fixed asset becomes redundant, such charges would, of course, be expensed until the asset is sold).

Our proposals may be compared to those advanced by Defliesse of New York and described by Anthony in his "Accounting for the Cost of Interest" (Lexington, 1975). He writes with experience of American regulated industries and government contracts but seeks recognition by the Financial Accounting Standards Board of interest in maturing stocks, developed oil reserves and self-made plant, as an initial step. The interest rate he prefers is the firm's weighted average cost of capital.

We have obviously gone further. We have set against a proposal to base accounting on physical assets perpetually revalued at replacement cost an alternative which sees the firm's business as cash cycles, complete, incomplete and potential. All should be subject to a cost-of-capital charge and to a rate which will vary primarily with inflation expectations. Actual borrowing and lending or return rates may be expected to vary round this base rate, as for banks. These institutions have sought a system of inflation accounting which would facilitate the maintenance of their capital and financial stability.

The solutions to the problem of capital maintenance are not to be found in CCCA or in CCA, where the most approximate and subjective guides are given for adding to or subtracting from revaluation surplus. The Germans, we suggested, have rightly clarified that the problem can only be logically resolved if expressed in terms of present assets and capital structure.

After decades of 'the growth of the firm', our present situation explains renewed efforts to elaborate a steady state theory and to clarify measures for taxation and distribution which will prevent erosion of the 'substance' of the firm. Interpretations of this have been varied, of course, although mostly related to assets or net worth rather than to earning or employment capacity. This last can best be guaranteed, it would appear, by ensuring the continued willing co-operation of labour and capital. In place of capital maintenance we would be wise to develop a theory and procedures prompting management reliance not on a permanent but on a precarious capital, which demands real earnings and distribution rates, disseminated as costs throughout each organisation and certainly not postponable to other inflationary claims. Such capital would be flexible and renewable, of course, and would attract the savings of oil exporters, pension funds and wage earners alike.

When profits can exceed holding costs and these costs exceed holding gains, then we are on the way to maintain and perhaps to restore previous purchasing powers and parities to the pound. Pessimists may suggest that Brazil's example and thorough-going indexation provide the only solutions for the UK. But it is wrong to pretend that this country, with widespread economic problems focused in worse inflation than almost anywhere else in Europe, can give a lead by inflation accounting proposals now exposed and justified by expectations of continuing inflation[10]. Accounting systems should reflect not the 'noise' of manipulated specific prices but the full effects of key variables, such as the time value of money.

Notes

1. By a Technical Committee of the Institute of Auditors; cf. COENENBERG AND MACHARZINA: Journal of Business Finance and Accounting, Spring 1976.

2. Quoted in YAMEY, EDEY and THOMSON (Eds.): Accounting in England and Scotland to 1800, p.87.

3. See decision in Evans v London Cooperative Society (1976).

4. Such valuation and indexation may be necessary for national accounts and statistics. Fisher's innovative work in imputing market values is criticised by Bonbright: The Valuation of Property: I, p.47.

5. Speculation against the pound can justify even 'Headquarters of which to be proud', Management Accounting, June 76, p.220, and D.A.R. FORRESTER: 'Stop-Inflation Accounting', The Accountant, 10 June 1976.

6. The background to his views is clarified in A. MEY:

'Le theorie de la valeur et du calcual rationnel de l'economie industriel' 'La Revue Economie Politiquie 1960'.

7. Similarly, in 1974, the British Review Board on the pricing of non-competitive contracts chaired by Sir William Slimmings recommended historically high target rates of return on capital employed only until the Sandilands Committee recommendations could promote common procedures for all sectors. Profits, they said, should be sufficient to meet taxation, interest payments, and to provide shareholders with returns comparable to those elsewhere, taking risk into account, and also to maintain capital in real terms (indeed such must be the cost of all capital).

8. While 'cost push' theorists analyse the anticipations of inflation incorporated in organised wage demands, a study of the relationship netween anticipated inflation and nominal interest rates has become a 'growth industry' in America. Fisher divided nominal interest into real and inflation-anticipatory elements, but Keynsians have observed slow adjustments to experienced price changes, Recent studies include those by Sargent in Quarterly Journal of Economic Review, June 1975. The longer-term health of the capital market requires after-tax inflation proofing which cannot be achieved by rates on a market so manipulated and confined as that in Britain. Overpriced labour is currently replaced by underpriced capital; cf. S. BRITTAN: 'What to do with a stronger pound', Financial Times, 30 December 1976.

9. Para. 690 reads 'to particular expenditure'. The Germans have clarified several alternative modes of allocation.

10. Cf. M.J. Lafferty's remarks to the Financial Times conference reported 17 December 1976.

X Review of Worldwide Developments

32 Worldwide Developments in Inflation Accounting

In the following paragraphs, we look first at the latest proposals for CCA in the United Kingdom, and then review the recent progress made in various other countries of the world towards a system of inflation accounting, pointing out any significant differences from the British proposals.

THE UNITED KINGDOM

Recent years have seen a dramatic increase in the rates of inflation suffered by Britain. One result of this has been that accounts prepared on the basis of historical cost are less able to convey a true and fair view of a company's financial position. Thus, inflation accounting, having been a subject for theoretical discussion among British accountants for many years, has now become a matter of some urgency. As far back as 1949, proposals were made to modify historical cost accounting in an attempt to deal with the problems created by changing prices. Fixed assets, notably property, have increasingly been shown at revaluation, for instance, rather than at cost.

In the early 1970's it became clear that more comprehensive proposals for dealing with the problem needed to be considered and, in January 1973, Exposure Draft 8, "Accounting for Changes in the Purchasing Power of Money" ("ED.8"), was issued. The proposals in that exposure draft were for the adoption of a Current Purchasing Power ("CPP") method, which was intended to be supplementary to figures based on historical cost. Under this system, a general price level index is used to convert the historical cost of non-monetary assets to pounds of current purchasing power, and to calculate the holding gain or loss on monetary items.

The Sandilands Committee, while acknowledging the valuable contribution of ED.8 to the subject, concluded in 1975 that the most fruitful line of development for a United Kingdom system of inflation accounting would be one based on replacement costs and recommended that a system to be known as CCA should be developed. The proposals outlined by Sandilands were essentially very simple, and were evolutionary rather than revolutionary in their effect on existing standards and practices. Two adjustments were initially proposed for the historical cost profit and loss account to reflect the "value to the business" of assets consumed in the production of income; these were a "cost of sales adjustment" and an adjustment so as to base depreciation charges on the year-end valuation of fixed assets. Both adjustments were to be made by reference to a series of published price indices. There were also to be consequential changes in the balance sheet valuations of assets.

Following acceptance of the Sandilands Report by the accounting profession and by Government, a steering group was set up to prepare an initial standard on CCA which would apply first to listed companies and later to all other companies. The steering group, under Mr. Douglas Morpeth, embodied their proposals in Exposure Draft 18 (ED.18) which was issued in November 1976 by the Accounting Standards Committee.

Readers of this booklet will already be familiar with the contents of ED.18 and it is therefore unnecessary to describe its proposals in any detail here. The following indicates the general scope of ED.18:-

(a) Fixed assets are to be shown in the balance sheet at their value to the business (normally written down replacement cost) and not at their depreciated original cost; stocks are to be shown in the balance sheet at their value to the business (normally replacement cost) and not at the lower of their original cost and net realisable value.

(b) Depreciation for the year is to be calculated on the value to the business of the fixed assets concerned.

(c) The cost of stock consumed during the year is to be calculated on the value to the business of the stock at the date of consumption and not at the date of purchase.

(d) The effects of the loss or gain from holding monetary assets, or from financing the business with borrowed money, are to be shown in the "statement of the gain or loss in the value of the shareholders' net equity interest after allowing for the change in the value of money".

(e) The distinction between real and apparent growth in so far as the equity interest is concerned is to be made clear in the "statement of the gain or loss in the value of the shareholders' net equity interest after allowing for the change in the value of money".

(f) Directors may appropriate to a revaluation reserve amounts required to maintain the scale of the business. The main components of this appropriation are likely to be:-

  (i) increased replacement cost of fixed assets and stock;
  (ii) increased requirements for monetary working capital; and
  (iii) depreciation underprovided in the past on fixed assets because prices have risen since the depreciation was provided.

ED.18 proposes a phased programme for introducing CCA. According to the timetable, all listed companies and other companies and nationalised industries with assets or sales exceeding £10 million (except those with more than 50% of their assets outside the United Kingdom) will adopt CCA for accounting periods starting after 1st July, 1978. Six months later, all limited companies and nationalised industries with assets or sales in excess of £1 million will adopt CCA for their accounts. Finally, from 1980 onwards, all businesses whose turnover or assets exceed £100,000 are expected to produce accounts on a CCA basis. Ultimately, every business is expected to be using CCA.

The exposure draft is open for comment until 31st May, 1977. Discussion is likely to be extensive. The complexity of the exposure draft and the extent of familiarisation necessary should not be under-rated. If past precedents are followed, a major revision of the exposure draft could result in a further period of exposure and discussion.

BELGIUM

For over thirty years, Belgium has had a system of indexing wages and rents to the cost of living - changes generally being made in any month following a 2% rise or fall in the index. It might therefore be expected that index-linked financial statements are only a short step away. Until recently, however, there has been little emphasis in Belgium on sophisticated financial reporting and there were no standard accounting principles. A company's financial statements are the sole responsibility of the directors, who can be held liable for over-valuation, so there is a natural tendency towards a conservative accounting treatment.

The Belgians are now making a determined effort to reform their company law on the basis of the draft Fourth Directive of the European Commission and thus their progress towards a system of inflation accounting will probably be closely in step with EEC legislation.

FRANCE

In France, Government institutions dominate the capital market, with approximately 80% of medium and long term finance passing through the hands of the State. The country has traditionally had a codified concept of managing business affairs and, in the absence of pressure from the investing public, the form and content of financial statements have been influenced primarily by the requirements of Government and fiscal authorities. Tax declarations have to agree with published financial statements, and so, for all practical purposes, French accounting principles reflect the tax laws. The national accounting plan, "Plan Compatable", drawn up in 1957, codified the principles to be followed.

Since 1958, when a once and for all revaluation of fixed assets was permitted on the introduction of the New Franc, there have in general been no tax-free revaluations. Except for some recognition through temporary tax deferral on the increased cost of stocks (which did not result in a change in balance sheet values), French accounting practice has been based on the exclusive use of historical costs.

The 1977 Finance Law makes provision for a one-time revaluation of non-depreciable assets included in balance sheets at 31st December 1976 or the first subsequent balance sheet. Revaluation is compulsory for quoted companies and their subsidiaries but optional for other companies. For tax purposes, this adjustment will have no effect and historical cost will continue to be used. As regards depreciable assets, the Government has not so far permitted revaluation. This dichotomy in approach to balance sheet items poses problems to the auditor in forming an opinion on the true and fair view.

The wider question of inflation accounting is still being considered by the Government. The report of a committee under M. Delmas Marsalet, published in November 1976, proposed that companies should be required to publish supplementary statements based on the CPP system as a first step to a complete changeover to CPP accounts. Selection of the CPP concept would be against the trend in most other major industrial countries. The report also concluded that, because of conflict with the existing tax system, the use of CCA, if adopted at all, should be restricted to supplementary information. These recommendations have not yet been accepted or rejected.

GERMANY

Germany has made determined and successful efforts to maintain a strong currency and to avoid inflation. As a result, the level of inflation has recently declined to an annual rate of 4%, and comparatively little attention has been given to any type of inflation accounting. The financial statements of German companies tend to follow the fiscal and legal requirements, as is the case in France and Belgium. The depreciation shown in the accounts, for example, is normally that allowable for tax purposes. Since 1965 there has been a mandatory format for the financial statements of companies incorporated as an AG (Aktien Gesellschaft). Other companies frequently follow this format.

Although no mandatory accounting standard has been published, a statement issued by the Accounting Principles Committee in October 1975 proposed that the effect of changing prices should be reported by a supplementary note in the directors' annual report. The statement recommends the voluntary disclosure of the amount of annual income which should be set aside to maintain the productive capacity of the business, consisting of additional depreciation based on the replacement cost of plant and equipment, determined by applying the official indices to the historical cost of each category of fixed assets, and as adjustment to cost of sales using the replacement cost of materials consumed. The statement also recommends that the supplementary note should disclose the basis of calculating the amount which should be set aside, and that it should be subject to audit.

Two aspects of the German system are of particular importance. Firstly, neither the current values of fixed assets nor of inventories need to be disclosed; and secondly, a distinction is made between equity-financed and debt-financed assets. Only equity-financed assets are brought into the calculation of the sum to be set aside. For simplicity the statement assumes that equity capital is first used to finance non-mpnetary fixed assets, and subsequently monetary fixed assets (such as loans and investments), inventories and other assets, in that order.

Although these proposals have been issued as a formal statement by the German Institute, the extent to which the recommendations will be followed cannot be predicted. It seems unlikely that a system of accounting for changing prices will be adopted in the mainstream accounts - at least in the foreseeable future - bearing in mind the emphasis on the retention of historical cost accounts.

HOLLAND

In Holland the existence of a strong auditing profession and active stock exchange have proved important influences on the layout of financial statements, the general form of which was prescribed in 1971 by the Annual Accounts of Enterprises Act. The Dutch approach to inflation accounting relies heavily on the observation of general principles and on notions such as "sound business practice". For this reason, the concept of replacement cost accounting has up to now, at least, remained comparatively unfettered by standard rules.

The outstanding example of replacement cost accounting in Holland, and indeed in Europe, has been that of the Philips group, which has used replacement costs not only for internal purposes but also for external reporting. The system operated by Philips is restricted to adjusting financial statements for changes in replacement costs, no account being taken of the gain arising from a fall in purchasing power of net monetary liabilities. The group does not have a published accounting policy for dealing with losses on net monetary assets, but for local management purposes, any losses from holding net monetary assets are charged to the profit and loss account. Philips started using replacement cost theory in the late 1930's. However the most recent count shows that only about one Dutch company in six has adopted some type of replacement cost accounting, and that some of these companies limit their replacement concepts to the depreciation charge. There is no statutory requirement to adopt replacement cost theory, and replacement cost accounts are not accepted as a basis for computing taxable profits.

Recent levels of inflation have increased the pressure in Holland for more general acceptance of replacement cost accounting. The Tripartite Study Group - a committee representing employers, trade unions and the Dutch Institute of Accountants - has published a series of "draft considerations". A recent draft, published in December 1976, recommended that the result of operations on the basis of current values should be shown in financial statements, and that the result on the basis of historical costs should be indicated in a note to the accounts.

AUSTRALIA

There is, in general, a close affinity between Australian and British accounting practice. As in Britain, Australian companies have been able to incorporate asset revaluations in their financial statements; as in Britain also, the 1976 Federal Budget introduced tax relief for the element of profits attributable to stock appreciation. The legislation necessary to give effect to this tax relief has not yet been enacted.

As regards the basis of preparing financial statements, the accounting profession has long recognised the need for a fundamental change in accounting practice in the face of continuing inflation. Two "preliminary exposure drafts" were issued on the subject. The first of these, published in 1974 and incorporating CPP theory, failed to gain much support. At about this time, a Government committee on the taxation implications of inflation, under Professor Russell Mathews, whose report was published in May 1975, specifically recommended that the current value concept should be adopted for tax purposes. In June 1975, the second preliminary exposure draft was issued, based on current value accounting. It soon became apparent that the second draft represented the preferred approach - both of industry and of the accounting profession - and in October 1976 the Australian Accounting Standards Committee issued a provisional accounting standard based on the current value concept.

The provisional accounting standard is in many respects similar to ED.18 although the drafting approach has been different. The Australian proposals only set out a broad framework, whereas ED.18 attempts to deal with as many of the known problems of implementing CCA as possible. A significant difference of principle relates to the revaluation of non-monetary assets. The Australian procedure is that when a non-monetary asset is revalued in terms of current cost, the profit arising is taken through a statement of change in shareholders' equity to a revaluation reserve (termed current cost adjustment account) which is shown as a separate item in shareholders' equity. In Britain, revaluation surpluses are routed via an appropriation account, where it is for the directors to use their discretion in deciding what proportion is taken to revaluation reserves.

The provisional standard recommends that companies should use CCA for accounting periods beginning on or after 1st July 1977, and it is planned to make it mandatory for periods starting on or after 1st July 1978. In the first year in which the provisional standard is adopted, companies are recommended to present CCA accounts as a supplement to the financial statements. This recommendation has been supported in a letter from the Stock Exchange to all listed companies, but it has not yet been followed in many published accounts.

NEW ZEALAND

Since 1973, New Zealand has experienced annual inflation rates consistently above 10%. Progress towards inflation accounting has closely followed U.K. developments, but has included a Government commission on the subject and university-based research to find the procedure most suitable to New Zealand. An exposure draft on CPP published in March 1975 by the New Zealand Society of Accountants has been dropped in favour of CCA. In August 1976, the Society published its CCA proposals in an Exposure Draft ("ED.14"); this is much along the lines of the U.K. proposals in ED.18, one exception being the requirement for a separate revaluation reserve to be maintained for inventories as distinct from other assets.

The Richardson Committee, appointed by the New Zealand Government to assess alternative methods of inflation accounting and broader issues, reported in December 1976. Its main recommendations are that a CCA system should be adopted for financial reporting, pricing and taxation purposes and that operating profit should include an adjustment to reflect changes in the value of monetary items. This adjustment would be restricted, however, to changes in the purchasing power of short term monetary assets and of borrowings used to finance assets which have been revalued during the accounting period. The Committee recommended a phased introduction of CCA, starting with accounting periods beginning after 31st March 1978 for some companies and extending to all companies three years later. Meanwhile, a research programme on inflation accounting is in progress at the University of Waikato, including the field testing of CPP, CCA and Continuous Contemporary Accounting ("COCOA").

SOUTH AFRICA

Despite an annual rate of inflation which has recently exceeded 10%, South African accounts continue to be presented as if this major distortion did not exist. Only a few South African public companies have published supplementary financial statements adjusted for inflation - on the basis of changes in current purchasing power. Other companies have embarked on programmes of revaluing fixed assets in their financial statements and basing depreciation on the revalued amounts; but no companies have published financial statements on a current value or replacement cost basis.

In January 1975, the National Council of Chartered Accountants (South Africa) issued an exposure draft prepared by Professor W.A. Joubert of Orange Free State University. This paper, which failed to receive widespread support, advocated a technique of accounting for inflation which was based partly, but not entirely, on CPP concepts; the exposure draft did however recognise that, for non-monetary assets, the carrying values arrived at should be compared with their current values and adjusted if significantly different. The income statement was to include, as a transfer to non-distributable reserves, the amount required to maintain the general purchasing power of shareholders' equity.

Later in 1975, the National Council of Chartered Accountants issued a statement recommending that, until such time as a particular method of accounting for inflation gains general acceptance either in South

Africa or abroad, companies should adopt any method of reflecting the impact of inflation on financial statements. There have also been suggestions that the National Council may also set up a working party to consider the requirements of the investing public. Until an accounting standard is published, taxation computations must continue to be based on historical cost figures. The Department of Internal Revenue has said, however, that if and when the accounting profession in South Africa decides on a method of inflation accounting, it will give serious consideration to using the method adopted as the basis for tax assessments.

THE UNITED STATES OF AMERICA

In the United States, a great deal of thought has been given to the problem of adjusting financial statements for the effects of inflation. In 1969 the Accounting Principles Board published its statement No. 3 ("APB Statement No. 3"). This statement recommended publication of supplementary statements showing the effect of general price level changes; it was not mandatory, however, and few companies followed its recommendations. In December, 1974, broadly similar proposals were put forward in an exposure draft published by the Financial Accounting Standards Board ("FASB"). The preface to this exposure draft stated that the FASB was taking action on general price level accounting because the necessary techniques had been well developed; but that current value accounting was also being considered within the scope of another project - "Conceptual Framework for Accounting and Reporting" - as a result of which a further exposure draft might be issued.

In considering the development of inflation accounting in the United States, it is as well to recognise the effect of the income tax laws as regards depreciation of fixed assets and the valuation of inventories. Since 1954, for instance, the Internal Revenue Service has permitted the use of various accelerated depreciation methods, enabling companies to obtain tax and cash flow benefits. Secondly, for the valuation of inventory, the last-in, first-out ("LIFO") method is acceptable for tax purposes; the effect of this is that the amount charged to cost of sales is approximately the replacement cost of the goods sold. In the last few years there has been a trend towards wider adoption of LIFO. A distinction between these concessions is that, unlike accelerated depreciation, LIFO must be used for financial statement purposes if it is to be used for tax purposes.

The views of the Securities and Exchange Commission ("SEC") have also been significant in the development of inflation accounting. The SEC has traditionally been opposed to companies recording assets at more than historical cost or disclosing (except in limited situations) the fair value of assets if that amount is in excess of book value, on the grounds that such methods were contrary to generally accepted accounting principles. However, in August 1975, the SEC proposed that financial statements should include footnote disclosure of the current cost of replacing inventories and productive capacity, as well as cost of sales and depreciation based on current replacement cost.

The SEC rules were issued formally in March 1976, and relate to financial statements for years ended on or after 25th December 1976. The rules apply initially to most of the 1,000 or so largest non-financial companies in the United States; it is intended that at a later stage the requirements will be extended more widely. For companies in the extractive industries, certain mineral resource assets are exempt for one year. Companies are also required to disclose how they compute the replacement cost data. At present there is no requirement for replacement cost figures to be audited, although the SEC has said that it will regard the auditor as being "associated" with the disclosures made. However, recognising that the required data will be imprecise and that subjective estimates will be involved, the SEC has introduced a "safe harbour" rule to protect companies from legal action resulting from justifiable imprecision.

The rules issued by the SEC are thus in sharp contrast to the CPP methods proposed in the still outstanding FASB exposure draft, further consideration of which has been deferred indefinitely on the grounds that the method is not well understood and the need for it not sufficiently demonstrated to justify the costs of preparing the information.

CANADA

Canada has recently succeeded in reducing its inflation rate to single digit levels. This may be partly attributable to a complex Government anti-inflation programme, scheduled to run until October 1978, under which certain large companies are required to report quarterly deviations from permitted profit levels to the Anti-Inflation Board.

In the past Canadian financial statements have been based on historical costs and on accounting principles similar to those followed in the United States and in the United Kingdom. In 1972 the Canadian Institute of Chartered Accountants commissioned a research study of current value accounting and price level restatements. This led to the publication in November 1974 of a guideline of the use of general price level adjusted supplementary statements, a method which closely reflected U.K. thinking at that time. In July 1975, by which time the annual inflation rate was about 10%, an exposure draft based on the general purchasing power concept was issued. No pressure was placed on companies to follow the method described in the exposure draft, however, since it was recognised that many aspects were still subject to debate; meanwhile, Canada continued to watch the progress of the discussion in other countries - particularly the United States and the United Kingdom - and to gather data on the purpose of financial statements.

In August 1976, following further research, a discussion paper on current value accounting was issued and the guideline on general price level adjusted statements fell into abeyance. The discussion paper is intended to encourage companies to experiment with the current value approach put forward and indeed with other methods as well. The discussion paper favours the general purchasing power capital maintenance approach even though the productive capacity approach has been adopted by several other countries such as Australia and the U.K.

Perhaps the most significant view expressed in the discussion paper is that all holding gains or losses, including the charge necessary to maintain the general purchasing power of shareholders' equity, should be shown in the income statement; this is a view which has not found favour elsewhere in the world, unless of course it has been done in the rather abstract CPP supplements where it has been coupled with warnings that readers are not to assume distributabily of such income. It is also interesting to note that, for the valuation of mining assets, the paper has suggested that an estimate of future cash flow should be discounted at a rate appropriate to the business. It remains to be seen whether further study of the problem will confirm the practicality of this solution.

It is evident that Canada is unlikely to adopt a final position on inflation accounting until the Canadian Institute study of the objectives of financial statements is completed. A parallel study into the practical problems of current value accounting is also being undertaken by the Accounting Research Committee, with the co-operation of some sixty Canadian companies who are experimenting with various current value accounting methods. It is expected that both of these studies will have been completed by the end of 1977.

THE PROSPECTS FOR INTERNATIONAL CO-ORDINATION

International co-ordination on any subject is seldom easy and sometimes impossible. This is particularly true of so vexed a question as inflation accounting, although the need for co-ordination is clearly important. If a multi-national company is raising money on world markets, for instance, there should be some international yardstick by which its operations can be judged. It would be absurd if the financial statements of companies in one country were expressed on the basis of historical cost; those in another by reference to changes in general purchasing power; and others on the basis of current value accounting - with or without an adjustment for changes in the worth of monetary items.

What are the prospects of avoiding this confusion? Consider first the "catalysts" available - those forces which may act as a helpful influence. The most significant development in the consideration of accounting problems on an international scale has been the formation in 1973 of the International Accounting Standards Committee ("IASC"). This committee originally comprised sixteen leading accountancy bodies in nine nations (Australia, Canada, France, Germany, Japan, Mexico, Holland, the U.K. and the U.S.A.), but has since been enlarged to include forty-nine accountancy bodies drawn from thirty seven countries. The IASC has already published a number of international standards on basic accounting topics, and its members are committed to a policy of compliance in their own countries. As regards inflation accounting, the IASC issued early in 1976 an exposure draft recommending that financial statements should reflect changing prices in one way or another. As yet, however, it has not progressed to the stage of expressing a view that one particular method should be adopted internationally to the exclusion of other methods.

There are several other spurs to standardisation. The stock exchanges of the world, for instance, have a common interest in ensuring that fair comparisons can be made and thus preventing a false market in stocks and shares.

There is also a general feeling of impatience for a simple and universal solution to the problem of inflation accounting. Public opinion moves slowly but it is a powerful force once it gets under way.

There are two main obstacles to the adoption of a uniform policy. Firstly, once the standard-setting body of a country has adopted a particular point of view, it is normally reluctant to change. The second obstacle is that accounting for inflation is something which vitally affects governments; each country's efforts are therefore affected to a greater or lesser degree by the search for a politically acceptable solution.

SUMMARY OF WORLD-WIDE TRENDS

Let us now try to sum up the world-wide trends in inflation accounting. There are three approaches to the problem. First, in those countries where financial statements are linked to the legal and taxation framework and historical cost principles are firmly entrenched, little is being done to introduce inflation accounting on a widespread basis. This approach is found mainly in Europe - particularly in France, Germany and Belgium. Secondly, there is the approach which has originated from countries such as Britain, Holland and the United States, involving the recognition either of specific price changes or of general price level changes. This approach has been followed, or is under discussion, in many of the countries covered in this booklet. The third approach consists of indexing a wide range of items, both in financial statements and in most monetary transactions. This approach has been adopted in high inflation countries such as Brazil, where the need for a ready solution to the problem has been more pressing than the demand for sophistication.

There is no denying the world-wide trend. Strict historical cost accounting is widely accepted as being inadequate and outdated, and a change to some form of current value accounting is favoured in most industrialised countries of the world. In Britain and Australia, the accounting professions have gone a long way towards adopting CCA and, unless there is some reversal in the next year, fundamental changes in accounting practices will soon be made. Even so, until 1980 or even later, British companies will still be required to record historical costs both for tax purposes and to satisfy EEC requirements - although such information may be supplementary to mainstream accounts prepared on a CCA basis.

CONCLUSIONS

It can be seen that there is a clear trend towards some form of current value accounting, which may also reflect changes in general purchasing power. Different countries will decide on the form of inflation accounting which they think is appropriate. No country in the world seems likely to have its selected method fully established and operating much before 1980 and, in many countries, the process will take substantially longer. Nevertheless, some form of current value accounting seems inevitable. An international accounting standard, setting out a detailed method of inflation accounting for universal acceptance, might possibly emerge ten years from now.

Bibliography

So much has been written on inflation accounting that any bibliography is inevitably highly selective. This bibliography concentrates most heavily on articles and books published within the last ten years, and a great deal of space is devoted to material describing developments in the United Kingdom and U.S. but case studies in other parts of the World are well represented, and several elderly but classic studies are included. The compiler apologises in advance to anyone who feels that any item has been undeservedly omitted.

The bibliography is divided into 12 sections, as follows:

SECTION A: INFLATION ACCOUNTING - GENERAL.

Australian Accounting Research Foundation 'An Evaluative Paper: A Comparison of Accounting Measurement Systems.' Insert to 'The Chartered Accountant in Australia' September 1975.

S.S. Alexander 'Income Measurement in a Dynamic Economy' (revised by D. Solomons) in 'Studies in Accounting Theory' ed. W.T. Baxter and S. Davidson, London, Sweet and Maxwell, 1962. A classic study, investigating different concepts and methods involved in income measurement, drawing heavily on economic theory.

S. Basu and J.R. Hanna 'Inflation Accounting: alternatives, implementation issues and some empirical evidence.' Research Monograph published by the Society of Industrial Accountants of Canada, Hamilton, Canada, 1975.

W.T. Baxter 'Inflation and Accounts' Investment Analyst, Dec. 1962, pp 3-13; reprinted in 'Studies in Accounting for Management Decision' ed. A.M. Bourn, McGraw-Hill, London, 1969; also in 'Modern Financial Management' ed. B.V. Carsberg and H.C. Edey, Penguin, 1969. Valuable summary of the defects of historical-cost accounts in times of inflation, and of the merits of 'stabilised accounting.'

W.T. Baxter 'Accounting Values and Inflation' McGraw-Hill, London, 1975. Extensive and exhaustive on all aspects of inflation accounting; written from a British perspective.

A.M. Bourn 'Valuation and Profit' in 'Studies in Accounting for Management Decision' ed A.M. Bourn, McGraw-Hill, London, 1969. Good discussion of various concepts of profit and value - historic cost, price-level adjusted, net realisable value, replacement cost, etc.

William D. Bradford 'Inflation and the Value of the Firm-Monetary and Depreciation Effects' Southern Economic Journal, Vol. 40, 1974, pp 414-428. Meticulous breakdown of the defects of historical-cost accounting.

John A. Bullard 'Price-level restatement and valuation reporting' Management Accounting (U.S.) Vol. 57, Feb. 1976, pp 15-18, 26. Short review and evaluation.

R.J. Chambers 'Elements of Price Variation Accounting' The Accountant Vol. 162, 1970, pp 299-304. Examines how the effects of price variations might be brought into accounts.

R. J. Chambers 'Historical Cost Accounting and its Variants' The Accountant Vol. 162, 1970, pp 341-346. Critical of both historical-cost accounting and partial asset revaluations.

F.L. Clarke 'Accounting for Inflation-a Bibliography' The Chartered Accountant in Australia, Vol 46, March 1976, pp 22-26. Covers articles in the Chartered Accountant in Australia 1962-1975.

T.K. Cowan 'Progress through Dilemma-A Compromise Solution to the Problem of Accounting for Changing Prices and Values' Accounting and Business Research No. 5, Winter 1971, pp 38-46. Suggests that inflation accounting has not received popular support because it would reduce reported profits. If reserves were revalued annually, this revaluation could be used to absorb asset revaluations, thus only affecting the balance-sheet, not the income statement.

John R. Croll 'General Price-level Indexing-a delusion, a snare, a mockery?' C.A. Magazine, Vol. 106, March 1975, pp 29-34. Argues that G.P.A. does not improve accounting disclosure.

M.F. Desmarchelier, L. Hall, and R. Willing 'A User's View of C.P.P., C.V.A., and C.C.A.' Chartered Accountant in Australia, Vol. 46, pp 14-17, 19. A brief survey.

R.C. Dochweiler 'The Practicability of Developing Multiple Financial Statements - A Case-Study.' Accounting Review, Vol. 44, 1969, pp 729-742. Attempt to produce financial statements incorporating historical cost, price-level adjusted and replacement cost information, G.P.A. data was relatively easy and cheap to produce, but it was prohibitively difficult to obtain market prices on which to base replacement costs; only 3% of H.C. values could be adjusted in this way.

David F. Drake and Nicholas Dopuch 'On the Case for Dichotomising Income.' Journal of Accounting Research, Vol. 2, 1964, pp 192-205. Critique of Edwards and Bell's proposal to partition income into holding gains and operating profit.

Edgar O. Edwards 'The State of Current Value Accounting.' Accounting Review Vol. 50, 1975, pp 235-245. Retrospective and simplified summary of the Edwards and Bell approach.

E.O. Edwards and P.W. Bell 'The Theory and Measurement of Business Income.' Univ. of California Press, 1961. A careful analysis of different concepts of business income, how they should be measured and what they would mean. A very influential book, which has influenced all aspects of inflation accounting; especially the 'general price-level adjustment' -v- 'replacement cost' debate. E. & B. argue that a rise in replacement cost is a cost saving or holding gain which should be reported separately from operating profit. If the general price-level is rising, the holding gains should be partitioned into 'real' and 'ficitious' components.

R.S. Gynther 'Accounting for Price-level Changes-Theory and Procedures' Pergamon Press, Oxford, 1966. A readable survey of the field, also incorporates Gynther's views on the subject.

R.S. Gynther 'Accounting Concepts and Behavioural Hypotheses.' Accounting Review, Vol. 42, 1967, pp 274-290. Argues that different asset valuation conventions involve different concepts of capital; these concepts depend on various assumptions about the behaviour of the accounting entity.

R.S. Gynther 'Capital Maintenance, Price Changes and Profit Determinations.' Accounting Review, Vol. 45, 1970, pp 712-730. Further develops the ideas of Gynther 1967.

R.S. Gynther 'Accounting for Changing Prices; Some Recent Thinking, Recommendations and Practice.' Chartered Accountant in Australia, Vol. 42, Dec. 1971, pp 12-24. Discusses several proposals for accounting for inflation, paying special attention to the concept of capital on which they are based. Includes a short section on methods actually used by companies. See Chambers' response, same periodical, March 1972.

Palle Hansen 'The Accounting Concept of Profit.' North-Holland Publishing Co., Amsterdam, 1962. A careful exploration of the concept of profit, drawing on economic as well as accounting theory.

E.S. Hendriksen 'Purchasing-power and Replacement Cost Concepts - Are They Related?' Accounting Review, Vol. 39, 1963, pp 483-491. Argues that G.P.A. is not the only method concerned with the maintenance of a quantum of purchasing-power; replacement cost is also concerned, since it reflects the purchasing-power of the firm which is the accounting entity.

G.S. Kirk 'A Practical Examination of the Alternative Approaches to Accounting for Price Changes. 'Chartered Accountant in Australia, Vol. 46, Sept. 1975, pp34-37; Oct. 1975, pp47-52; Nov. 1975, pp 47-51.

Patrick R.A. Kirkman 'Accounting under Inflationary Conditions.' Allen & Unwin, London, 1974. A lengthy and detailed work, which delves firmly and without hesitation into both theoretical debate and discussion of practical problems.

P.R.A. Kirkman 'Inflation Accounting: a Guide for Non-accountants' John Wiley & Sons, New York, 1975.

James A. Largay III and John Leslie Livingstone 'Accounting for Changing Prices.' John Wiley & Sons, New York, 1976. Wide and thorough coverage of C.C.A. and C.P.P., illustrated with examples drawn from actual company accounts. Mechanics of adjustments dealt with in detail and depth, with meticulously worked examples.

Kenneth W. Lemke 'Capital Maintenance and Confusion.' Abacus Vol. 10, 1974, pp 26-38. Argues that current price reflects how much purchasing-power is currently embodied in an asset, so C.V.A. reveals whether the purchasing-power of capital has been maintained better than C.P.P. does.

Ronald Ma and M.C.Miller 'Inflation and the Current Value Illusion' Accounting and Business Research, No. 24, Autumn 1976, pp 250-263. C.P.P. is preferred to C.V.A., since C.P.P. retains historic cost valuation, and better serves the objectives of accountability and verifiability.

R.L. Mathews 'Income, Price Changes, and the Valuation Controversy in Accounting.' Accounting Review, Vol. 43, 1968, pp 509-516. Good short discussion.

R. Mattesich 'The Market-value Method According to Sterling: a Review Article' Abacus, Vol. 7 1971, pp 176-193. Review of R.R. Sterling's 'Theory of the Measurement of Enterprise Income.'

M.F. Morley 'The Fiscal Implications of Inflation Accounting.' Institute for Fiscal Studies and Institute of Chartered Accountants in England and Wales, London, 1974. Very thorough study of the economic consequences of taxing inflation-adjusted profit, of how such a reform would affect the fairness of the tax system, and implications for capital gains taxation.

National Association of Accountants 'Inflation Accounting - a Bibliography.' New York, 1976; covers 1968 to mid-1976.

National Association of Accountants 'The Inflation Dilemma.' 2 vols. 1. Managing Price-level Accounting. 2. Management Reporting under Inflation. New York, 1975.

R.H. Parker and G.C. Harcourt 'Readings in the Concept and Measurement of Income.' Cambridge University Press, 1969. An indispensable and excellent collection of classic articles. The introduction gives a valuable summary of issues, especially with regard to the choice of asset values.

W.A. Paton 'Observations on Inflation from an Accounting Stance.' Journal of Accounting Research, Vol. 6, 1968, pp 72-86. Survey of several aspects of the measurement problem which inflation causes for accountants.

S.H. Penman 'What Net Asset Value?' Accounting Review, Vol. 45, 1970, pp 333-346. Discussion of different concepts of asset value.

A.J. Platt 'The Replacement of Fixed Assets.' Accountancy, Vol. 85, March 1974, pp 40-50. A careful consideration of how depreciation should be calculated during inflation. Illustrated with worked samples.

J.A. Priddice 'Current-value Accounting and Price-level Restatements - Where Do We Stand?' Chartered Accountant in Australia, Vol. 44 Sept. 1973, pp 4-16. Summarises some important issues in the inflation accounting debate, and suggests reasons why countries like the U.K. and Australia have been so slow to adopt any method of inflation accounting.

L.S. Rosen 'Current-value Accounting and Price-level Restatements.' Canadian Institute of Chartered Accountants, Toronto, 1972. A research monograph which simplifies and summarises many of the issues. Includes a chapter on Canadian price indices, and one on case-studies of Canadian companies.

K. Schwayder 'The Capital Maintenance Rule and Net Asset Valuation Rule.' Accounting Review, Vol. 44, 1969, pp 304-316. Discussion of how the definition of capital effects the choice of asset valuation rule.

George J. Staubus 'Price-level Accounting - Some Unfinished Business.' Accounting and Business Research, No. 21, Winter 1975, pp 42-47. Excellent short discussion of various capital maintenance concepts.

R.R. Sterling 'Theory of the Measurement of Enterprise Income.' University Press of Kansas, 1969. A carefully argued book, which examines the reasons for income measurement by studying the experiences of an enterprise and its hypothetical transactions; Sterling comes out in favour of realisable values as measures of costs and values in accounting.

R.R. Sterling 'Asset Valuation and Income Determination.' Scholars' Book Co., Lawrence, Kansas, 1971. A valuable collection of essays.

Robert R. Sterling 'Relevant Financial Reporting in an Age of Price Changes.' Journal of Accountancy, Vol. 139, Feb. 1975, pp 42-51. Supports price-level adjusted financial statements because they allegedly, meet the primary needs of accounting-relevance and accountability. Response by R.J. Chambers, 'N.O.D., C.O.G. and Pu.P.U.: See How Inflation Teases.' Same journal, Sept. 1975, pp 56-62; comment by Paul Rosenfield, Dec. 1975, pp 90-93; reply by Chambers, same issue, pp 93-94.

Richard F. Vancil 'Inflation Accounting: the Great Controversy.' Harvard Business Review, Vol. 54, March/April 1976, pp 58-67. A survey article. Letters in reply in May/June issue, pp 174, 176, 178.

SECTION B.: INFLATION ACCOUNTING-EXPERIENCE OF VARIOUS COUNTRIES

Michael O. Alexander and Douglas Barrington 'A Feasible Method of Current-Value Accounting.' C.A. Magazine, Vol. 107, Sept. 1975, pp 33-39. Draws on the experience of several Canadian firms which have adopted current-value accounting.

F.L. Clarke (ed.) 'Accounting for Inflation.' Chartered Accountant in Australia, Vol. 46, Oct. 1975, pp 41-52. A collection of three articles, surveying inflation accounting developments in U.S, U.K., South Africa, New Zealand and Canada.

F.L. Clarke 'Australia's Current Cost Accounting: A Touch of This and a Dash of That.' The Accountant, Vol. 176, Feb. 17th 1977, pp 190-192. Report of Australia's current cost proposals, which apparently embody some elements of Sandilands but also incorporate additional features.

A Coenenburg and K. Macharzina 'Accounting for Price Changes: an Analysis of Current Developments in Germany.' Journal of Business Finance and Accounting Vol. 3, No. 1, 1976, pp 53-68

Robert W. Comer 'Brazilian Price-level Accounting. 'Management Accounting (U.S.) Vol. 57, Oct. 1975, pp 41-42,46.

Max I Epps 'Realistic Accounting under South American Inflation.' Journal of Accountancy, Vol. 111, Jan. 1961, pp 67-73.

Robert Fleming 'Accounting for Inflation in Brazil. 'The Accountant's Magazine, Vol. 73, Feb. 1974, pp 58-60.

John C. Getzelman 'Financial Analysis in an Inflationary Environment.' Management Accounting (U.S.), Vol. 56, March 1975, pp 31-35. A Brazilian perspective on inflation accounting.

J. Hammond 'Notes on the Calculation of Business Profit during the Present Inflationary Period in France. 'Accounting Research, Vol. 3, 1952, pp 346-352.

Per V.A. Hanner 'Accounting and Taxation in Sweden in Relation to the Problem of Inflationary Profits.' "Accounting Research Vol. 1, Jan. 1950.

Geoffrey Holmes 'C.C.A.: Irish Company Shows the Way.' Accountancy, Vol. 88, March 1977, pp 74, 76-77. C.C.A. in the accounts of P.J. Carroll & Co. Ltd.

P. Holzer and H. Schonfeld 'The German Solution to the Postwar Price-level Problem. 'Accounting Review, Vol. 39, 1963, pp 377-381.

P. Holzer and H. Schonfeld 'The French Approach to the Postwar Price-level Problem. 'Accounting Review, Vol. 39, 1963, pp 382-388.

Pearson Hunt 'A System Developed in Countries with Persistent Inflation.' Journal of Business Finance and Accounting, Vol. 3, No. 1, 1976, pp 161-165. A brief description of an inflation accounting method developed by Professor Emmerico Paternost, which grew out of his business experience in Chile and Brazil.

International Accounting Standards Committee "Exposure Draft 6: International Accounting Standard: Proposed Statement: Accounting Treatment of Changing Prices." 'London, 1976: available from the Institute of Chartered Accountants in England and Wales.

International Accounting Standards Committee 'The Treatment of Changing Prices in Financial Statements: a Summary of Proposals'. London, 1977. Available from the Institute of Chartered Accountants in England and Wales. Covers recent proposals in I.A.S.C. member countries.

W.J. Kenley 'Accounting under Conditions of Inflation: Important Developments in New Zealand.' Australian Accountant,

Vol. 46, June 1976, pp 280-285.

Felix P. Kollaritsch ' Austria's Answer to Inflationary Profits and Taxation.' Accounting Review, Vol. 36, 1961, pp 439-445

Michael Lafferty 'International Moves in Inflation Accounting.' The Accountant Vol. 176, Jan. 27th 1977, pp 104-106. Covers recent developments in Australia, U.S., Canada, South Africa, the E.E.C., South America and New Zealand.

James H. MacNeill 'Accounting for Inflation Abroad; a Study of Government-approved Applications of Price-level Accounting in Twelve Different Countries. 'Journal of Accountancy Vol. 112, Aug. 1961, pp 67-73.

E.J. Mann 'Inflation and Accounting in Brazil. 'Journal of Accountancy, Vol. 124, Nov. 1967, pp 49-54.

New Zealand Correspondent 'Current Costs in New Zealand.' The Accountant, Vol. 176, Jan. 13th 1977, pp 46-47.

R.W. Scapens 'The Treatment of Inflation in the Published Accounts of Companies in Countries Overseas.' Institute of Chartered Accountants in England and Wales, London, 1973.

Peter Standish 'Inflation Accounting Down Under.' Accountancy, Vol. 87, March 1976, pp 48,50,52. Developments in Australia.

D.G. Trow 'The New Zealand Approach to Inflation Accounting.' The Accountant's Magazine, Vol. 81, Feb. 1977, p 65.

C.A. Westwick and N.J. Ballanger 'How Companies Account for Inflation.' The Accountant, Vol. 172, 1975, pp 455-461, 496-500. Survey of 60 British companies which have adopted some method of accounting for inflation.

SECTION C:
GENERAL PRICE-LEVEL ADJUSTED ACCOUNTING - THEORY

Simon Archer 'Inflation Accounting: Right and Wrong Use of a G.P.I.' Accountancy, Vol. 87, Nov. 1976, pp 51-53.

Australian Society of Accountants 'Accounting for Price-level Changes: a symposium.' Melbourne, 1974.

John M. Boersema 'Can General Price-level Adjusted Statements Be Approximated By the Outsider?' Accountancy, Vol.

85, May, 1974, pp 72-74. Compares figures for two U.S. companies obtained by a short-cut method with those obtained by a more detailed method, based on movements of stocks, asset records, etc. For one company, there was close agreement between the two sets of figures, but there were considerable discrepancies in the other case.

John M.Boersema 'Reporting Price-level Gains on Long-term Debt.' C.A. Magazine, Vol. 106, May, 1975, pp 24-27. Explores various issues, especially the problem of when such gains are realised.

Michael Bourn 'The Gain on Borrowing'. Journal of Business Finance and Accounting, Vol. 3, 1976, pp 167-182. Argues that the gain on borrowing is largely illusory, but the loss from holding money during inflation is real. Therefore, these items deserve different treatment in inflation accounting.

William D. Bradford 'Price-level Accounting and the Measurement of Inflation Gains and Losses.' Accounting Review, Vol. 49, 1974, pp 296-306. Careful analysis of the sources of gains and losses on monetary items during inflation. See Beshara's Comment, same journal, Vol. 50, 1975, p 582-585, and Reply by Bradford, same issue, pp 586-587.

G. Briscoe and G. Hawke 'Long-term Debt and Realisable Gains in Shareholder Wealth: an Empirical Study.' Journal of Business Finance and Accounting, Vol. 3, No. 1, 1976, pp 125-135. The authors find no correlation between 'gains on debt' and increases in shareholder wealth in a sample of 120 large British companies. They conclude that such gains are not commonly realised and should not be included in inflation-adjusted profit.

M. Bromwich 'Individual Purchasing-power Indices and Accounting Reports: a Comment on a Suggestion by Professor Gynther.' Accounting and Business Research, No. 18, Spring 1975, pp 118-122. Critique of proposals to use specific, rather than general, price indices in price-level accounting.

R.J. Chambers 'Price-level Adjusted Accounting.' The Accountant, Vol. 162, 1970, pp 408-413. Simple discussion of the cases for and against.

F.L. Clarke 'A Closer Look at Sweeney's Stabilised Accounting Proposals.' Accounting and Business Research, No. 24 Autumn 1976, pp 264-275. An examination and reinterpretation of H.W. Sweeney's 'Stabilized Accounting.'

Murray L. Davies 'The Case Against G.P.L. Statements.' C.A. Magazine, Vol. 107, Sept. 1975, pp 40-44. Alleges that asset values reported under G.P.A. are misleading.

James C. Dyer 'An Alternative Method for Determining General-Price-level Gains and Losses.' Chartered Accountant in Australia, Vol. 43, Feb. 1973, pp 4-8. Compares two methods of Computing gains or losses on monetary items.

D.A. Egginton and R.C. Morris 'Borrowing Costs, Price-level Change and E.D.8.' The Accountant, Vol. 169, 1973 pp 463-466. Argues that, in inflation, geared companies gain not only from the decline in the real value of loan principle, but also gain when nominal interest rates do not fully anticipate inflation; this gain is already included in conventional profit, but should be reported separately.

John R. Grinyer 'Holding Gains on Long-term Liabilities: a Rigorous Analysis.' Accounting and Business Research, No. 20, Autumn 1975, pp 292-297. Argues that the gain on debt should be incorporated into the calculation of real interest cost, and that the usual method of dealing with such gains in C.P.P. accounting is likely to give rise to serious errors. See Comment by D.A. Egginton and R.C. Morris, same journal, No. 23, Summer 1976, pp 177-181, who argue that Grinyer's approach is based on certain misconceptions.

R.S. Gynther 'Accounting for Inflation: The Treatment of Borrowing.' The Accountant, Vol. 169, 1973, pp 48-50. Opposes the inclusion of gains on long-term debt in profit, because they are a transfer from holders of debt to shareholders, and should be dealt with in shareholders' personal accounts, not in the accounts of a firm.

R.S. Gynther 'Why Use General Purchasing-power?' Accounting and Business Research, No. 14, Spring 1974, pp 142-156, Attacks the relevance and usefulness of price-level accounting.

Nils H. Hakansson 'On the Relevance of Price-level Accounting.' Journal of Accounting Research, Vol. 7, 1969, pp 22-32. Concludes that price-level accounting has little relevance. Discussion is partly framed in mathematical terms.

Loyd C. Heath 'Distinguishing Between Monetary and Non-monetary Assets and Liabilities in General Price-level Accounting.' Accounting Review, Vol. 47, 1972, pp 4568-469. Draws attention to the lack of a clear-cut distinction between monetary and non-monetary items.

A.J.A. Hinds 'Inflation Accounting for Companies: a Practical

Solution.' The Accountant's Magazine, Vol. 78, 1974, pp257-63. A simplified approach to G.P.A. See also Reply by J.A.W. Moir, same Vol., pp 433-436; response by Hinds pp 475-79.

A. Hope 'More Problems in Inflation Accounting.' Accountancy, Vol. 84, Oct, 1973, pp 10-13. Describes some practical problems which arose in producting price-level adjusted financial statements as part of an experiment carried out at Manchester University.

Yuji Ijiri 'The Price-level Restatement and its Dual Interpretation.' Accounting Review, Vol. 51, 1976, pp 227-243. The conventional view of G.P.A. is that the unit of account is charged, so measurements are made in real, not nominal, terms. Ijiri argues that the unit of account remains the same, but the accounting principles guiding the preparation of the financial statements are changed.

H. Levy 'Inflation and Price-level Accounting - the Challenge of the 70s.' Chartered Accountant in Australia, Vol. 41, May, 1971, pp 9-12. Brief but readable survey of the case for G.P.A.

R. Ma 'A Comparative Review of some Price-level Accounting Systems.' Abacus Vol. 1, 1965, pp 107-131.

Perry Mason 'Price-level Changes and Financial Statements - Basic Concepts and Methods.' American Accounting Association. Evanstown, Illinois, 1956. A classic study, influencing later thinking and work in the U.S.

A.M.C. Morison A Model for Accounting for Inflation.' Accounting and Business Research, No. 17, Winter, 1974, pp 41-52. Attacks C.P.P. for not dealing adequately with relative price changes. Special attention is paid to stock profits which should only be included in profit if the company has earned them through good pricing policies.

D.R. Myddleton 'Short-cuts in Adjusting Accounts for Currency Debasement.' Investment Analyst, No. 29, May 1971, p 8-16. A simplified method which can be used by 'outsiders'.

Enrico Petri and Roland Minch 'Contemporary Inflation Accounting Proposals and an Alternative.' Abacus, Vol. 11, 1975, pp 182-192. Argues for specific, rather than general, price indices; but advocates inclusion of holding gains on assets in profits.

A.J. Platt 'The Gain on Long Money - a Different View.' Accountancy, Vol. 84, Oct. 1973, pp 15-17. Opposes the inclusion of such gains in profit, on realisation grounds.

Paul Rosenfield 'General Price-level Accounting and Foreign Operations.' Journal of Accountancy, Vol. 131, Feb. 1971, pp 58-65. Deals with consolidation of domestic G.P.A. statements with foreign currency statements.

J.B. Ryan 'Myth of Purchasing-power as a Constant Unit of Measurement.' The Australian Accountant, Nov. 1972, pp 383-9. On the imperfections of indices.

Keith Schwayder 'Expected and Unexpected Price-level Changes.' Accounting Review, Vol. 46, 1971, pp 307-320. Argues that, under certain circumstances, G.P.A. may be more misleading than historical cost accounting, especially where the firm anticipates inflation and the accounts reflect this.

Alan D. Stickler and Christina S.R. Hutchins 'General Price-level Accounting Described and Illustrated.' 'Canadian Institute of Chartered Accountants, Toronto, 1975.

H.W. Sweeney 'Stabilized Accounting.' Holt, Rinehart and Wilson, New York, 1964. Reprint of Sweeney's 1936 text, one of the earliest English-language works on the subject. Very influential. Also includes a case-study.

Jerold Zimmerman 'Price-level Restatements: A Technical Note.' Journal of Accounting Research, Vol. 12, 1974, pp 372-382. Deals with how price-level restatements can allow for seasonal fluctuations in sales, purchases, etc.

SECTION D: G.P.A.: U.S. THEORY AND RECOMMENDATIONS FOR PRACTICE

Accounting Principles Board Statement No. 3 'Financial Statements Restated for General Price-level Changes.' New York, American Institute of Certified Public Accountants. 1969.

American Institute of Certified Public Accountants 'Reporting the Financial Effects of Price-level Changes.' Research Study No. 6. New York, 1962. Prepared by the Institute's Research Staff. Surveys the issues involved in G.P.A., giving examples drawn from company accounts. Background to later A.P.B. and F.A.S.B. proposals.

Sydney Davidson, Clyde P. Stickney and Roman L. Weil 'Inflation Accounting: A Guide for the Accountant and the Financial Analyst.' McGraw-Hill, New York, 1976. Deals with the F.A.S.B.'s proposals for general price-level accounting, explains the prodcedures and gives guidelines for auditors and statement users.

James B. Edwards 'Inflation Accounting for Utilities.' Management Accounting (U.S.) Vol. 58, August, 1976, pp 92-23. G.P.A. for public utilities.

Solomon Fabricant 'Inflation and Current Accounting Practice: an Economist's View.' Journal of Accountancy, Vol. 132, Dec. 1971, pp 39-44. Critical appraisal of A.P.B. Statements No. 3 (Financial Statements Restated for General Pricelevel Changes) and No. 4 (Basic Concepts and Accounting Principles Underlying Financial Statements).

Financial Accounting Standards Board 'Discussion Memorandum Reporting the Effects of General Price-level Changes in Financial Statements.' Feb. 1974.

William H. Hannum and W. Wasserman 'General Adjustments and Price-level Measurement.' Accounting Review, Vol. 43, 1968, pp 295-302. Discusses which particular U.S. price index should be used in G.P.A.

R.C. Jones 'The Effects of Price-level Changes on Business Income, Capital and Taxes.' American Accounting Association, Evanstown, Illinois, 1956. A classic and influential study.

Perry Mason 'Price-level Changes and Financial Statements: Basic Concepts and Methods.' See Section C.

R.L. Mathews 'Price-level Changes and Useless Information.' Journal of Accounting Research, Vol. 3, 1965, pp 133-148. A spirited critique of A.I.C.P.A. Research Study No. 6.

Joseph P. Matoney Jr. 'Mandatory Price-level Adjusted Financial Statements: the F.A.S.B. Proposals.' National Public Accountant, Vol. 20, Dec. 1975, pp 16-20.

National Association of Accountants 'Price-level Adjustments: a M.A.P. Committee Interim Report.' Management Accounting (U.S.) Vol. 56, June 1975, pp 45-50.

Lawrence Revsine and Jerry L. Weygandt 'Accounting for Inflation - the Controversy' Journal of Accountancy, Vol. 138, Oct. 1974, pp 72-78. Concentrates especially on G.P.A. vs. the use of specific indices.

P. Rosenfield 'Accounting for Inflation - a Field-test.' Journal of Accountancy Vol. 127, June 1969, pp 46-50. Reports on the results of 'field-testing' of general price-level accounting by 18 U.S. companies. The method is that discussed in A.I.C.P.A. Research Study No. 6.

Leonard M. Savoie 'Price-level Accounting. Practical Politics, and Tax Relief.' Management Accounting (U.S.) Vol. 58, Jan. 1977, pp15-18. Discusses the political opinions towards inflation accounting in the U.S.

H.W. Sweeney 'Stabilized Accounting.' See Section C.

SECTION E:
G.P.A.: U.K. THEORY AND RECOMMENDATIONS FOR PRACTICE

R.S. Allen 'Purchasing-power or Replacement Cost? E.D.8. Has Feet of Clay.' The Accountant, Vol. 168, 1973 pp 459-461. Critique of U.K. proposals on G.P.A.

R.J. Chambers 'General Purchasing-power Accounting: E.D.8. Is Not the Answer.' The Accountant, Vol. 169, 1973, pp 15-18.

F.L. Clarke 'Some Observations on the Indexation of Accounts.' Abacus, Vol. 11, 1975, pp 107-121. A survey of approaches to C.P.P. accounting in U.K. published accounts.

David Damont 'Inflation Accounting - More Problems.' Accountancy, Vol. 86, 1975, pp 42-43. On the relevance of C.P.P. accounts to the investment analyst.

D.A. Egginton and R.C. Morris 'Borrowing Costs, Price-level Changes and E.D.8.' See section C.

Institute of Chartered Accountants in England and Wales 'Accounting for Stewardship in a Period of Inflation.' London 1968. The first contribution by this Institute.

Institute of Chartered Accountants in England and Wales 'Inflation and Accounts.' London, 1971. Brief discussion of G.P.A., illustrated by worked examples.

Institute of Chartered Accountants in England and Wales (on behalf of the Accounting Standards Steering Committee) 'Proposed Statement of Standard Accounting Practice E.D.8: Accounting for Changes in the Purchasing-power of Money.' London, 1973.

Institute of Chartered Accountants in England and Wales 'Accounting for inflation: a Working Guide to the Accounting Procedures.' London, 1973. An guide to the details of implementing E.D.8.

Institute of Chartered Accountants in England and Wales (on behalf of the Accounting Standards Steering Committee) 'Provisional Statement of Standard Accounting Practice P.S.S.A.P.7: Accounting for Changes in the Purchasing-power of Money.' London, 1974. E.D.8 never achieved the status of an accounting standard; it was made provisional until the Sandilands Committee reported, and then dropped. (For Sandilands, see section J.)

P.R.A. Kirkman 'A Weakness of E.D.8' The Accountant, Vol. 168, 1973, pp 535-538. Discusses the appropriate treatment of gains on long-term debt.

Bryan Lund 'The Manager and Inflation Accounting.' Accountancy Vol. 85, Oct. 1974, pp 36-40. Discusses what the introduction of general price-level adjusted accounting would mean for managers. Lund criticises G.P.A. for retaining the defects of historical cost accounting and not being forward-looking.

P.W. Parker and P.M.D. Gibbs 'Accounting for Inflation - Recent Proposals and their Effects.' Journal of the Institute of Actuaries, Vol. 101, 1974, pp 353-403. Long discussion of the need for inflation accounting, principles applying C.P.P. accounting to major U.K. companies. Audience discussion included.

John Perrin 'Why C.P.P. is not the Answer.' Accountancy, Vol. 87, May 1976, pp 56,58,60.

Scottish Chartered Accountant 'Inflation Accounting' The Accountant's Magazine, Vol. 77, 1973, pp 472-480. A suggestion for simplifying the method for preparing general price-level adjusted accounts, with special reference to the A.S.S.C. proposals.

R.G. Wilson 'Practical Aspects of Inflation Accounting. 'The Accountant, Vol. 181 1974, pp 170-172. Comparison of P.S.S.A.P.7 with replacement cost accounting.

SECTION F: CASE - STUDIES OF G.P.A.

John M. Boersema 'Can General Price-level adjusted Statements Be Approximated by the Outsider?' See Section C.

G. Briscoe and G. Hawke 'Long-term Debt and Realisable Gains in Shareholder Wealth: an Empirical Study.' See Section C.

Vincent C. Bremner and James J. Benjamin 'Financial Reporting in Units of General Purchasing-power. 'Management Accounting (U.S.) Vol. 57, June, 1976, pp 15-18. Report on a questionnaire survey which suggests there is a need for education in price-level accounting among both issuers and users of financial statements.

F.L. Clarke 'Some Observations on the Indexation of Accounts.' See section E.

R.S. Cutler and C.A. Westwick 'The Impact of Inflation Accounting on the Stock Market.' Accountancy, Vol. 83, March 1973, pp15-24. Application of C.P.P. Accounting to 104 quoted U.K. companies. Analyses the relative importance of the components of the differences between H.C. and C.P.P. results.

T.R. Dyckman 'Investment Analysis and Price-level Restatements: a Behavioural Study.' American Accounting Association, Evanston, Illinois, 1969. An investigation of whether the availability of price-level adjusted information affected per share valuations made by a group of investment analysts. The availability of adjusted information made a significant difference to valuations and Dyckman concludes that the availability of such information could alter the allocation of resources.

T.R. Dyckman 'The Effects of Restating Financial Statements for Price-level Changes: a Comment.' Accounting Review, Vol. 50, 1975, pp 796-808. Critical analysis and comparison of 3 studies designed to discover whether price-level restatements affect economic decisions. Replies by Heintz and McIntyre, same issue, pp 809-817.

R.W. Estes 'An Assessment of the Usefulness of Current Cost and Price-level Information by Financial Statement Users.' Journal of Accounting Research Vol. 6, 1968, pp 200-207. This study suggests quite a lot of interest in such information, especially in a supplementary form.

James A. Heintz 'Price-level Restated Financial Information and Investment Decision-making.' Accounting Review, Vol. 48, 1973, pp 679-690. Availability of price-level restated information made no difference to financial forecasts in this study. See Comment by Dyckman, same journal, Vol. 50 1975, pp 796-808: Reply by Heintz, same issue, pp 809-814.

Eldon S. Hendrikson 'Price-level Adjustments of Financial Statements.' Washington State University Press, 1961. Evaluation of price-level adjustments and a cast-study of two U.S. public utilities 1937-56. Includes a section on the selection of a price-index and the appropriateness of specific or general price indices.

A. Hope 'more Problems in Inflation Accounting.' See section C.

R.C. Jones 'Price-level Changes and Financial Statements - Case-studies of Four Companies.' American Accounting Association Evanston, Illinois, 1955. The companies are Armstrong Cork Co., New York Telephone Co., Reece Corporation, and Sargent And Co.

R.C. Jones 'The Effects of Price-level Changes on Business Income, Capital and Taxes.' See section D.

Thomas W. McRae and Richard Dobbins 'Behavioural Aspects of the Inflation Accounting Controversy.' Accounting and Business Research, No. 14, Spring, 1974, pp 135-140. Survey of attitudes towards inflation accounting among auditors, management accountants, civil servants, academics and shareholders.

D.R. Myddleton 'The Effects of Currency Debasement as Illustrated by Gas Industry Accounts.' The Accountant, Vol. 162, 1970, pp 689-694.

D.R. Myddleton 'Consolidated Nationalised Industries Accounts, 1948-1970: Published Figures Adjusted for Currency Debasement.' Accounting and Business Research, No. 6, Spring 1972, pp 83-101.

James E. Parker 'Impact of Price-level Accounting.' Accounting Review, Vol. 52,1977, pp 69-96. An extensive study of the impact of price-level accounting (as per the F.A.S.B. recommendations) on the summary balance-sheets and income statements of 1,050 U.S. companies for each of 3 subsequent years. The impact varied substantially among firms and among industries.

P.W. Parker and P.M.D. Gibbs 'Accounting for Inflation - Recent Proposals and their Effects.' See section E.

P.W. Parker and P.M.D. Gibbs 'Inflation Accounting and its Effects.' Accountancy Vol. 85, September 1974, pp 58-63. Summary of work reported at length in previous reference.

Russell J. Petersen 'Interindustry Estimation of General Price-level Impact on Financial Information.' Accounting Review, Vol. 48, 1973, pp 34-44. Study of the magnitude of the impact of price-level adjustments.

Russell J. Peterson ' A Portfolio Analysis of General price-level Restatements.' Accounting Review, Vol. 50, 1975, pp 525-533. Further work on the magnitude of the impact of restatements.

Boris Popoff 'The Price-level Restatement and Accounting Realism - a Case-study of a New Zealand Company.' International Journal of Accounting Education and Research, Vol. 6, No. 2, 1971, pp15-37.

Robert F. Randall 'Finally - Inflation Accounting' Management Accounting (U.S.) Vol. 56, Nov. 1974, pp 57-59. Report of the inflation accounting used by the Indiana Telephone Corporation since 1954.

P. Rosenfield 'Accounting for Inflation: a Field-test.' See section D.

Richard A. Samuelson 'Prediction and Price-level Adjustment.' Journal of Accounting Research, Vol. 10, 1972, pp 322-345. Compares the ability of historical cost and price-level adjusted data to predict future dividends and capital gains. No clear advantage in prediction emerged.

George J. Staubus 'The Effects of Price-level Restatements on Earnings.' Accounting Review, Vol. 51, 1976, pp 574-589. Explores the question of whether there is any simple relationship between historical cost and price-level adjusted profits, and whether thedifferences between them are significant.

P.T. Wanless 'Current Purchasing-power Accounting: a Study of a Co-operative Venture.' Abucus, Vol. 12, 1976, pp 61-72. Application of C.P.P. accounting to a large Scottish wholesale co-operative 1959-1973.

P.T. Wanless 'Inflation and the Comparability of Accounts.' Journal of Business Finance and Accounting, Vol. 3, No 1, 1976, pp 69-84. Compares impact of C.C.P. accounting on the profits of 20 Scottish companies with the results reported by Cutler and Westwick (see this section).

C. A. Westwick and N.J. Ballanger 'Inflation Accounting: the Institute's field-test Results.' Accountancy, Vol. 86, August, 1975, pp 32-33,36. C.P.P. accounting was field-tested by 80 U.K. companies; particular attention is paid to the time involved in preparation and to the magnitude of differences between H.C. and C.P.P. figures.

James S. Winarchick and Robert E. Malcolm 'General Purchasing-power Accounting.' Management Accounting (U.S.) Vol, 58, July, 1976, pp 38-40. Application of G.P.A. to ten U.S. steel companies.

SECTION G: CURRENT COST ACCOUNTING - THEORY

Morton Backer (with Richard Simpson) 'Current Value Accountant.' Financial Executives Research Foundation, New York, 1973.

W.T. Baxter 'Depreciating Assets: the Forward-looking Approach.' The Accountant's Magazine, Vol. 75, 1971, pp 159-165. Argues that fixed assets should be valued at their replacement cost because this measures their 'deprival value' - i.e. the advantage of already owning the asset and not having to buy it.

W.T. Baxter and N.H. Carrier 'Depreciation, Replacement Price and the Cost of Capital.' Journal of Accounting Research, Vol. 9, 1971, pp 189-214. Further discussion of deprival value.

N.M. Bedford and J.C. McKeown 'Comparative Analysis of Net Realisable Value and Replacement Costing.' Accounting Review, Vol. 47, 1972, pp 333-338.

J. Bonbright 'The Valuation of Property.' New York, 1937. Widely and probably erroneously believed to be one of the first English language works to support the use of replacement cost in accounts. The book was concerned with valueations for insurance rather than for use in balance-sheets or for measuring costs.

Michael Bromwich 'Asset Valuations with Imperfect Markets.' Accounting and Business Research, No. 20, Autumn 1975, pp 242-253. Discusses how well net realisable value and replacement cost indicate economic value (net present value) when markets are imperfect.

John W. Buckley and James R. Goode 'Inventory Valuation and Income Measurement An Improved System of Analysis.' Abacus Vol. 12, 1976, pp 34-48. A proposal for isolating holding gains on inventory in order to measure profit better.

R.J. Chambers 'Accounting, Evaluation and Economic Behaviour.' Prentice-Hall, Englewood Cliffs, New Jersey, 1966. An attempt to develop a dynamic accounting and to replace the static 'going concern' approach to income measurement and asset valuation with one which sees the firm as continually adapting to a changing environment. Chambers recommends the use of net realisable values (current cash equivalents) as these best reflect the firm's changing external opportunities.

R.J. Chambers 'Continuously Contemporary Accounting.' The Accountant, Vol. 162, 1970, pp 643-647. A very brief outline of the proposals in Chambers, 1966.

R.J. Chambers 'Second Thoughts on Continuously Contemporary

Accounting.' Abacus Vol. 6, 1970, pp 39-56. Clarifies some of the issues raised by Chambers, 1966.

R.J. Chambers 'Continuously Contemporary Accounting: Misunderstandings and Misrepresentations.' Abacus, Vol. 12, 1976, pp 137-151. Chambers replies to many critics; he claims his ideas have been widely misunderstood and attempts further clarification.

John S. Cook and Oscar J. Holzmann 'Current Cost and Present Value in Income Theory.' Accounting Review, Vol. 51, 1976, pp 778-787. Argues that market price measures economic value only in perfectly competitive markets.

George J. Foster 'Mining Inventories in a Current Price Accounting System.' Abacus, Vol. 5, 1969, pp 79-119. Discusses the problems of applying continuously contemporary accounting in extractive industries.

K.P. Gee 'A Pragmatic Defence of Replacement Cost.' Accounting and Business Research, No. 24, Autumn 1976, pp242-249. Upholds replacement cost as the only measure of deprival value and discusses aggregation problems.

Myron J. Gordon 'The Valuation of Accounts at Current Cost.' Accounting Review Vol. 28, 1953, pp 373-384. An early statment of the ideas later developed systematically by Edwards and Bell (see section A).

S.J. Gray and M.C. Wells 'Asset Values and Ex Post Income.' Accounting and Business Research, No. 11, Summer 1973, pp 163-168. Attacks the view (popularised by Solomons and Stamp) that assets which the firm intends to keep should be valued at replacment cost. Stimulated many articles in subsequent issues.

S.J. Gray and M.C. Wells 'A Further Comment on Asset Valuation and Income Measurement.' Accounting and Business Research, No. 18, Spring 1975, pp 91-95. Reply to the controversy stirred up by their 1973 article.

John R. Grinyer and Richard W. Lewis 'Valuation and Meaningful Accounts.' Accounting and Business Research, No. 8, Autumn 1972, pp 275-284. Discusses how well different kinds of asset valuations aid investment decisions.

M.H. Hunter 'Gains on Monetary Liabilities under Current Value Accounting.' Australian Accountant, Vol. 46, May, 1976, pp 204-206, 209-213.

E.R. Iselin 'Chambers on Accounting Theory.' Accounting Review, Vol. 43, 1968, pp 231-235. A short critique of Chambers, 1966.

Kermit Larson and R.W. Schattke 'Current Cash Equivalent, Additivity and Financial Action.' Accounting Review, Vol. 41, 1966, pp 634-641. Alleges that the current cash equivalents recommended by Chambers are not additive, because Chambers presumes separate realisation. Reply by Chambers, same journal, Vol. 43, 1967, pp 751-757.

Kenneth W. Lemke 'Capital Maintenance and Confusion.' See section A.

Ronald Ma 'On Chambers' Second Thoughts! Abacus, Vol. 10, 1974, pp 124-128. Reflections on establishing current cash equivalents. Reply by Chambers pp 129-137.

Ronald Ma 'Value to the Owner Revisited.' Abacus, Vol. 12, 1976, pp 159-165. Disputes that 'value to the owner' should always be identified with replacement cost.

Graeme Macdonald 'Deprival Value; its Use and Abuse.' Accounting and Business Research, No. 16, Autumn 1974, pp 263-269. Critique of Gray and Wells, 1973.

B. Popoff 'Current Value Accounting.' Chartered Accountant in Australia, Vol. 44 Dec. 1973, pp 4-14. Argue for splitting income into holding gains and operating profit. Includes Popoff's own empirical works.

Boris Popoff 'The Information Value of Replacement Cost Accounting for External Company Reports.' Accounting and Business Research, No. 17, Winter 1974, pp 61-71. Favours replacement cost accounting as indicating economic viability and surplus over opportunity costs (sic).

L. Revsine 'On the Correspondence Between Replacement Cost Income and Economic Income.' Accounting Review, Vol. 45, 1970, pp 513-523.

L. Revsine 'Replacement Cost Accounting.' Prentice-Hall Englewood Cliffs, New Jersey, 1973. Evaluates replacement cost accounting, especially in terms of the system's ability to predict future distributable cash flows, the availability and verifiability of replacement costs, and the interpretation of replacement cost accounting ratios.

A.R. Robinson 'Current-value Accounting by Value-in-use.'

Chartered Accountant in Australia, Vol. 44, August 1973, pp 4-13. An argument for market prices in asset valuations, based on J.B. Canning's idea of 'value-in-use.'

Paul Rosenfield 'Current Replacement Value Accounting: a Dead End.' Journal of Accountancy, Vol. 140, Sept. 1975, pp 63-73. Attack on replacement cost accounting. Reply and challenge by Tom. K. Cown, same journal, June 1976, pp 83-86; response by Rosenfield, same issue, pp 86-87.

Howard Ross 'Financial Statements - a Crusade for Current Values.' Sir Issac Pitman (Canada) Ltd., 1969. A provocative and emotive call for current value accounting as an aid to better decision making.

H.J. Snavely 'Current Cost for Long-lived Assets.' Accounting Review, Vol. 44, 1969, pp 344-353. Attacks the inclusion of holding gains on fixed assets in profit, because an increase in replacement cost does not necessarily mean an increase in the firm's future cash flows.

D. Solomons 'Economic and accounting Concepts of Cost and Value.' in 'Modern Accounting Theory.' ed. M. Backer, Prentice-Hall, Englewood Cliffs, New Jersey, 1966; and in 'Readings in the Concept and Measurement of Income.' Cambridge University Press, 1969. An influential paper in the N.R.V.vs. R.C. debate. Sets out the conditions under which N.R.V. and R.C. are appropriate asset valuations.

E. Stamp 'Income and Value Determination: an Essay towards a Theory.' The Accountant's Magazine, Vol. 75, 1971, pp 277-293. Similar but simpler arguments to Solomons.

George J. Staubus 'Current Cash Equivalents for Assets; a Dissent.' Accounting Review, Vol. 42, 1967, pp 650-661. Argues that current cash equivalents are better measured by the asset's likely contribution to the firm's cash flow than by net realisable value; N.R.V. is only useful in sell-or-hold decisions.

Touche Ross and Co. 'Current Value Accounting; Economic Reality in Financial Reporting.' New York, 1975.

Brian F. Trump and Robert J. Flew 'Establishment of Replacement Values with Particular Emphasis on Technological Change.' Australian Accountant, Vol.45, Dec. 1975, pp 652-656.

P.T. Wanless 'Reflections on Asset Valuation and Value to

the Firm' Abacus, Vol. 10, 1974, pp 160-164. Explores the relationship between economic value, replacement cost and net realisable value in conditions of market disequilibrium.

G. Whittington 'Asset Valuation, Income Measurement and Accounting Income.' Accounting and Business Research, No. 14, Spring 1974, pp 96-101. A contribution to the debate over replacement cost stimulated by Gray and Wells, 1973.

F.K. Wright 'Depreciation and Obsolescence in Current Value Accounting.' Journal of Accounting Research, Vol. 3, 1965, pp 167-182. Wright is another well-known advocate of replacement costs, which he regards as measures of 'value to the owner'.

F.K. Wright 'A Theory of Financial Accounting.' Journal of Business Finance Vol. 2, 1970, pp 57-69. Fuller explanation of 'value to the owner'.

F.K. Wright 'The Relationship Between Present Value and Value to the Owner.' Journal of Business Finance, Vol. 5, 1973, pp 19-26. Further explanation and analysis of value to the owner.

Hiroshi Yoshida 'Value to the Firm and the Asset Measurement Problem.' Abacus Vol. 9, 1973, pp 16-21. Critique of Stamp's 1971 paper.

SECTION H: DUTCH CURRENT VALUE ACCOUNTING

Morton Backer 'Valuation Reporting in the Netherlands: a Real Life Example.' Financial Executive, Vol. 4. Jan. 1973, pp 40-50. Report on the current value accounts produced by the international Philips group of companies.

R. Burgert 'Reservations about Replacement Value Accounting in the Netherlands.' Abacus, Vol. 8, 1972, pp 111-127. A critique of Limperg's theory of replacement cost accounting, which was very influential in Dutch accounting theory. An appendix gives details of how few Dutch firms actually use replacement cost accounting.

A. Goudeket 'An Application of Replacement Value Theory.' Journal of Accountancy Vol. 110, July 1960, pp 37-47: also in 'Reading in International Accounting.' ed. K.B. Berg et al., Houghton Mifflin, Boston, 1969. The classic article on Philips current value accounting.

Geoffrey Holmes 'Replacement Value Accounting.' Accountancy,

Vol. 83, March 1972, pp 4-9. A short article on the Philips system of accounting.

Alfred W. Knol 'Accounting in Holland.' Accountancy, Vol. 84, Jan. 1973, pp 32-38. Fits current values into the general picture of accounting in Holland.

A. Mey 'Theordore Limperg and his Theory of Values and Costs.' Abacus, Vol. 2, 1966 pp 3-24. An explanation of Limperg's influential theories.

A. Mey 'On the Application of Business Economics and Replacement Value Accounting in the Netherlands.' Graduate School of Business Administration, University of Washington, Seattle, Washington, 1970.

W. Poldervaart 'Replacement Value Accounting.' in 'Studies in Accounting for Management Decision.' ed. A.M. Bourn, McGraw-Hill, London, 1969. A senior employee describes the Philips system of accounting.

L.S. Rosen 'Replacement Value Accounting.' Accounting Review, Vol. 42, 1967, pp 106-113.

George M. Scott 'A Business Economics Foundation for Accounting: the Dutch Experience.' International Journal of Accounting Education and Research, Vol. 5, No. 2, 1970, pp 177-131. (Also in Accounting and Business Research, No. 4, 1971 pp309-318.)

A. van Sventer 'The Continuity Postulate in Dutch Current Value Accounting.' International Journal of Accounting Education and Research, Vol. 4, No. 1, 1969.

J. Vos 'Replacement Value Accounting.' Abacus, Vol. 6, 1970, pp 132-144, Explains the theoretical basis and practical implementation of Philips current value accounting.

SECTION J: CURRENT COST ACCOUNTING IN THE UNITED KINGDOM

W.T. Baxter 'The Sandilands Report.' Journal of Business Finance and Accounting, Vol. 3, No. 1, 1976, pp 115-124. A scholarly survey of the merits and short-comings of the Sandilands Report.

Adrian Buckley 'Back to Sandilands: Spurious Precision of E.D.18.' The Accountant, Vol. 176, April 21st 1977. pp444-447. Claims that the A.S.S.C. current cost proposals are impractical, too complex and produce unverifiable figures.

R.J. Chambers 'Accounting for Inflation - part or whole?' The

Accountant's Magazine, Vol. 80, March 1976, pp 86-89 Critical of the Sandilands Report.

F.L. Clarke 'C.C.A./C.P.P.: a Technical Impossibility.' The Accountant's Magazine, Vol. 80, 1976, pp 394-397. Opposes the feasibility of combining C.C.A. and C.P.P. in one set of accounts.

Martin Gibbs, Keith Percy and Richard Saville 'Inflation Accounting:Sandilands - the Effect on Dividends.' Accountancy, Vol. 87, August, 1976, pp 62-64,66.

John Grinyer 'Sandilands; From the Frying - pan into the Fire?' Accountancy Vol. 87, Jan. 1976, pp 34-40.

Geoffrey Holmes 'Sandilands Summarised,' Accountancy, Vol. 86, Oct. 1975, pp 22-31.

Inflation Accounting Steering Group 'Proposed Statement of Standard Accounting Practice E.D.18: Current Cost Accounting.' Institute of Chartered Accountants in England and Wales, London, 1976. The British accountancy profession's proposals for currend cost accounting, under the influence of the Sandilands Report. These proposals are currently under revision.

Inflation Accounting Steering Group 'Guidance Manual on Current Cost Accounting.' Tolley Publishing Co. and Institute of Chartered Accountants in England and Wales, London, 1976. The authorised and authoritative guide to implementing E.D.18; massive and detailed, but now out-of-date.

Inflation Accounting Steering Group 'The Legal Implications of C.C.A.' Accountancy, Vol. 88, Feb. 1977, pp 98, 100, 102, 104, 106: and The Accountant's Magazine, Vol. 81, Feb. 1977 pp 50-54.

Pat Kirkman and Chris Nobes 'Inflation Accounting: Dividend Policy and Inflation.' Accountancy, Vol. 87, Oct. 1976, pp 71-72, 75-76. Discusses the likely impact of C.C.A. on dividend policies, especially in sectors where historical cost accounting substantially overstates profit.

P.R.A. Kirkman and C.W. Nobes 'Inflation Accounting: Problems of Depreciation under a C.C.A. System.' Accountancy, Vol. 88, Feb. 1977, pp 40-41, 44-45.

G.H. Lawson 'Sandilands: Holding Gains, Debt Financing, Working Capital and Current Cost Accounting.' Journal of Business Finance and Accounting, Vol. 3. No. 1 1976, pp 105-114. Argues that the Sandilands proposals for the treatment of holding gains and debt financing seriously overstate profits because unrealised gains are included in profit.

T.A. Lee 'Sandilands and User Comprehension.' Journal of Business Finance and Accountancy, Vol. 3. No. 1, 1976, pp 85-95. Alleges Sandilands pays too much attention to problems of measurement and not enough to communication problems.

Thomas D. Lynch 'Accounting for Inflation: Fiscal and Other Implications.' The Accountant's Magazine, Vol. 81, March 1977, pp 95-99. Implication of C.C.A.

Andrew McCosh 'Implications of Sandilands for non- U.K. Accountants.' Journal of Accountancy, Vol. 141, March 1976, pp42-51.

Andrew McCosh and Richard F. Vancil 'Reconciling Sandilands with Current Purchasing-power Adjustments.' Accounting and Business Research, No. 23, Summer 1976, pp162-170. Argues that accounts should include both Sandilands C.C.A. adjustments and a conversion from C.C.A. to C.P.P.

D.R. Myddleton 'Why Sandilands is Unacceptable.' Journal of Business Finance and Accounting, Vol. 3, No. 1, 1976, pp97-104. Argues firmly and convicingly that 'Sandilands mixes up the question of whether to allow for inflation in accounts with the question of what basis to use in measuring costs... Sandilands agrees that the accounting unit of measurement should have a constant value through time, but nevertheless proposes to continue to use the monetary unit.....we have to assume that the members of the Sandilands committee have completely misunderstood the essential nature of a market economy.'

David Rudd 'The Best is the Enemy of the Good.' Accountancy, Vol. 87, Sept. 1976, pp 42-44, 46. Condemns Sandilands for inconsistencies and proposes a simpler alternative.

J. Timothy Sale and Robert W. Scapens 'Sample of Sandilands' C.A. Magazine, Vol. 110, Jan. 1977, pp 45-48. How the U.K. C.C.A. proposals might look in practice.

'Sandilands Report' Inflation Accounting. Report of the Inflation Accounting Committee. Cmd. 6625, London, H.M.S.O., 1975.

J.C. Shaw 'Sandilands: a Practising Accountant's View.' The Accountant's Magazine, Vol. 80, Jan. 1976, pp 9-13.

Angus Sibley 'The Investment Scene - Sandilands and the Investor.' The Accountant's Magazine, Vol. 80, Feb. 1976, pp 53-55.

Philip Sober 'E.D.18 and Property Investment Companies.' The Accountant, Vol. 176, April 14th 1977, pp 417-419. Alleges that E.D.18 is not suitable for property companies, especially with respect to its depreciation proposals.

Edward Stamp 'Sandilands - Some Fundamental Flaws.' The Accountant's Magazine Vol. 79, 1975, pp 408-411.

Peter Standish 'Inflation Accounting: Can Auditing Survive Sandilands?' Accountancy, Vol. 87, Nov. 1976, pp 44,46-49.

Chris Westwick 'Sandilands, P.S.S.A.P.7, but what Now.' Accountancy, Vol. 86, Dec. 1975, pp 38-39. Arguments in favour of combining C.C.A. and C.P.P. in accounts. Illustrated by a worked example.

Chris Westwick 'How did the Steering Group Tackle the Problem of C.C.A.,' Accountancy, Vol. 88, Jan. 1977, pp 42-44. Explains the background to E.D.18 and compares E.D.18 with proposals made earlier for price-level accounting.

SECTION K: REPLACEMENT COST IN THE UNITED STATES.

Ettore Barbatelli and Carl W. Hagelin 'Replacement Cost Estimating for Financial Reporting.' Management Accounting (U.S.) Vol. 57, June, 1976, pp 21-25. Suggestions on estimating replacement costs to conform with new S.E.C. disclosure requirements.

Stephen F. Black and Albert A. Koch 'Replacement Cost - Charting the Uncharted Seas' Journal of Accountancy, Vol. 142, Nov. 1976, pp 72-76. How to assess replacement costs to comply with S.E.C. rules about replacement cost disclosure.

Donald R. Brinkman and Paul H. Prentiss 'Replacement Cost and Current Value Measurement: How To Do It.' Financial Executive, Vol. 43, Oct. 1975, pp 20-26.

Paul E. Cheney 'A Review of Some Objections to Fair Value Accounting.' Management Accounting (U.S.) Vol. 57, June 1976, pp 29-31,37.

Sydney Davidson and Roman L. Weil 'Inflation Accounting: the S.E.C. proposal for Replacement Cost Disclosure.' Financial Analysts' Journal, Vol. 32, March/April 1976, pp 57-66.

L. Todd Johnson and Philip W. Bell 'Current Replacement Costs: a Qualified Opinion.' Journal of Accountancy, Vol. 142, Nov. 1976. Critique of the S.E.C. disclosure rule on replacement costs and some suggested improvements.

Richard Krol and Roy D. Thylin 'S.E.C. Requires Large Corporations to Disclose Replacement Cost.' Financial Executive, Vol. 44, June 1976, pp 28-32, 37.

National Association of Accountants 'S.E.C. Adopts Replacement Cost' Management Accounting (U.S.) Vol. 57, June 1976, p19-20.

Richard A. Samulson 'Estimating the Replacement Cost of Inventories and Cost of Sales.' Management Accounting (U.S.) Vol. 58, March 1977, pp 29-32. Advice on how to conform with S.E.C. disclosure requirements.

H.J. Trienans 'Legal Aspects of Fair Value Accounting' Financial Executive, Vol. 41, Jan. 1973, pp 30-36.

SECTION L: CASE STUDIES OF CURRENT COST ACCOUNTING

James Benjamin 'The Accuracy of the Period-end Method of Computing the Current Cost of Materials Used.' Abacus, Vol. 9, 1973, pp 73-81. Uses computer simulations to show the errors which can arise if the method of measuring the current cost of materials assumes an even flow of purchases and the actual patterns of purchasing are seasonal or irregular.

James Benjamin'The Effects of Using Current Cost in the Measurement of Business.' Accounting and Business Research, No. 11, Summer 1973, pp 213-218. Investigates the effects of differences in asset lives, growth rates, stock turnover, etc. on the gap between historical and current costs.

Vincent C. Brenner 'Financial Statement Users' Views of the Desirability of Reporting Current Cost Information.' Journal of Accounting Research, Vol. 8, 1970, pp 159-167. Reveals a lack of interest in current cost among this sample.

Adrian Buckley 'C.C.A. and Management Accounting.' The Accountant, Vol. 176, March 24th 1977, pp 338-340. Sandilands proposals are alledged to provide information useful for internal as well as external financial reporting. This study of 130 U.K. companies suggests that only a few companies actually use a current cost approach to internal reporting.

JOhn Fisher 'Current Cost Accounting.' The Accountant, Vol. 174, 1976, pp 528-530, 556-558. Surveys some problems of current cost accounting and reports on a field test in which the Sandilands recommendations were applied to five U.K. Companies.

Werner Frank 'A Study of the Predictive Significance of Two

Income Measures.' Journal of Accounting Research, Vol. 7, 1969, pp 123-136. An experiment to see whether predictions of current cost income or conventional income are more accurate; no difference between them emerges. Study covers six industries and a large number of firms.

S.J. Gray 'Price Changes and Company Profits in the Securities Market.' Abacus Vol. 11, 1975, pp 71-85. An application of Chamber's system of continuously contemporary accounting to major Australian investment companies 1970-73.

S.J. Gray 'Accounting for Price Changes: a Case-study of a Multinational Company.' Journal of Business Finance and Accounting, Vol. 3, No. 1, 1976, pp 1-14. Application of continuously contemporary accounting.

E.J. Gress 'Application of Replacement Cost Accounting: a Case-Study.' Abacus Vol. 8, 1972, pp 3-13. R.C. accounts for 1968 and 1969 for an Australian company. Discusses the method used in some detail.

Geoffrey Holmes 'Published Accounts: Experimenting with C.C.A.' Accountancy Vol. 87, 1976, pp 76-79. C.C.A. in the accounts of Record Ridgeway Ltd.

D.L. McDonald 'A Test Application of the Feasability of Market-based Measures in Accounting.' Journal of Accounting Research, Vol. 6, 1968, pp 38-49. One group of accountants was asked to value an automobile on the basis of market prices and one group on the basis of the conventional historic cost approach to depreciation. There was more agreement on the market-based measures than the historic cost. McDonald concludes that the use of market-based measures in accounting is feasible.

Edward V. McIntyre 'Current Cost Financial Statements and Common Stock Investment Decisions.' Accounting Review, Vol. 48, 1973, pp 575-585. Investigation of whether the type of accounting information available influences investment decisions. See also Dyckman, 1975, (section F)

James C. McKeown 'An Empirical Test of a Model Proposed by Chambers.' Accounting Review, Vol. 46, 1971, pp 12-36. Is it feasible to use current cash equivalents as accounting valuations? McKeown makes the attempt for a medium-sized firm and finds that information on which to base current cash equivalents is readily available and verifiable.

James C. McKeown 'Comparative Application of Market and Cost-based Accounting Models.' Journal of Accounting Research, Vol.

11, 1973, pp 72-79. To evaluate cost-based and market-based models, published prices were compared with prices observed in auctions; it seems published prices could be very misleading.

J.R. Perrin 'Inflation Accounting: Survey of Academic Opinion.' Journal of Business Finance and Accounting, Vol. 3, No. 1. 1976, pp 183-199. A limited survey covering the views of 30 professors of accounting: but what it lacks in scientific method is made up for by the detailed nature of the questions asked and the interesting responses. The survey is particularly concerned with reactions to Sandilands.

Robert R. Sterling and Raymond Radosvitch 'A Valuation Experiment.' Journal of Accounting Research, Vol. 7, 1969, pp90-95. What are the practicalities of using market values in accounting? This study asked practising accountants to produce a historical cost book value and a fair market value for a single piece of equipment. Authors conclude that 'historical costs are more objective but are not univocal or verifiable.'

Robert R. Sterling, John O. Tolefson and Richard E. Flaherty 'Exchange Valuation: an Empirical Test' Accounting Review, Vol. 47, 1972, pp 709-721. An interesting paper, peripherally related to current cost, which attempts to discover the 'de facto, as opposed to de jure generally accepted accounting principles' by asking subjects to account for particular events.

Chris Westwick and Rex Bush 'Getting Down to the Job of Inflation Accounting.' Accountancy, Vol. 87, June 1976, pp 42-49. Describes how C.C.A. adjustments were made to the accounts of the Institute of Chartered Accountants in England and Wales (as well as C.P.P. adjustments).

SECTION M: CASH FLOW ACCOUNTING

Raymond Ashton 'Cash Flow Accounting; a Review and Critique.' Journal of Business Finance and Accounting, Vol. 3, No. 4, 1976, pp 63-82.

Diran Bodenhorn 'A Cash Flow Concept of Profit.' Journal of Finance, Vol. 19, 1964, pp 16-31.

Diran Bodenhorn 'An Entity Approach to the Measurement of Wealth, Income and Product.' Abacus, Vol. 8, 1972, pp127-145. Detailed justification of cash flow accounting based on a model of the behaviour of the firm.

G.H. Lawson 'Cash Flow Accounting' The Accountant Vol. 165, 1971, pp 586-620-622. Lawson defends cash flow accounting for its simplicity, its verifiability, and its close connection with D.C.F. decision models.

G.H. Lawson 'Some Arguments for Cash Flow Accounting.' Certified Accountant Vol. 65, 1973, pp 217-221, 269-273.

G.H. Lawson 'The Rationale of Cash Flow Accounting.' Investment Analyst, No. 46, Dec. 1976, pp 5-12. Explains the case for cash flow accounting with the aid of simple models and some mathematical notation.

T.A.Lee 'The Nature and Purpose of Cash Flow Accounting.' South African Chartered Accountant, Vol. 8, 1972, pp 429-431. Clear well-written and simple.

T.A. Lee 'The Relevance of Accounting Information Including Cash Flows.' The Accountant's Magazine, Vol. 74, 1972, pp30-34.

T.A. Lee'A Case for Cash Flow Accounting.' Journal of Business Finance, Vol. 4, 1972, pp 27-37.

George J. Staubus 'The Relevance of Evidence of Cash Flows.' in 'Asset Baluation and Income Determination' ed. R.R. Sterling. Scholars Book Co., Lawrence, Kansas, 1971.

Acknowledgements

Reading 1 is a paper given at a Conference on Inflation Accounting at the University of Strathclyde in 1974; reprinted by permission of the author.

Reading 2 appeared in "Issues in Accountability" No.1, Oct. 1977; reprinted by permission of Strathclyde Convergencies.

Reading 3 is reprinted by permission of the Harvard Business Review: "The Case for Historical Costs" by Robert N. Anthony, Nov/Dec 1976. Copyright C 1976 by the President and Fellows of Harvard College; all rights reserved.

Reading 4 from "Asset Valuation and Income Determination" ed. R.R. Sterling, Scholars' Book., Kansas, 1971; reprinted by permission of the author and the publisher.

Reading 5 from the G.A.O. Review, Winter 1977; reprinted by permission of the authors and the G.A.O. Review.

Reading 6 is reproduced by permission of the Institute of Chartered Accountants in England and Wales.

Reading 7 from the Journal of Accounting Research, Vol. 3, 1965; reprinted by permission of the Editor of the Journal of Accounting Research.

Reading 8 from Accounting and Business Research, No.21, 1975; reprinted by permission of the Institute of Chartered Accountants in England and Wales.

Reading 9 from "Inflation and Company Accounts in Mechanical Engineering" NEDO, London, 1973; reprinted by permission of the Controller of H.M.S.O.

Reading 10 from the Accounting Review, Vol.47, 1972; reprinted by permission of the American Accounting Association and the author.

Reading 11 is an extract from "Current Purchasing-Power Accounting; a Case-Study of a Co-operative Venture" Abacus Vol.12, 1976; reprinted by permission of Sidney University Press and the author.

Reading 12 from the Accounting Review, Vol. 50, 1975; reprinted by permission of the American Accounting Association and the author.

Reading 13 from the Journal of Accounting Research, Vol.2, 1964; reprinted by permission of the Editor of the Journal of Accounting Research.

Reading 14 is an extract from "Income and Value Determination; an Essay Towards a Theory" The Accountant's Magazine, Vol. 85, 1971; reproduced by permission of the author and the Editor of the Accountant's Magazine.

Reading 15 from Abacus Vol.9, 1973; reprinted by permission of the author and Sidney University Press.

Reading 16 from the Accounting Review, Vol.47, 1972; reprinted by permission of the American Accounting Association and the author.

Reading 17 from the Accountant, 1970; reprinted by permission of the Accountant and the author.

Reading 18 from Abacus, Vol.2, 1966; reprinted by permission of Sidney University Press.

Reading 19 reprinted by permission of the author.

Reading 20 is a shortened version of an article of the same name in Abacus, Vol. 8, 1972; reprinted by permission of Sidney University Press and the author.

Reading 21 from Accountancy, Vol.83, 1972; reprinted by permission of the Institute of Chartered Accountants in England and Wales.

Reading 22 is a shortened version of an article of the same name in the Journal of Accounting Education and Research, Vol. 5, 1970; reprinted by permission of the University of Illinois.

Reading 23 from the Journal of Accounting Research, Vol. 6, 1968; reprinted by permission of the Editor of the Journal of Accounting Research.

Reading 24 from Abacus, Vol.8, 1972; reprinted by permission of Sidney University Press and the author.

Reading 25 from the Journal of Business Finance and Accounting, Vol.3, 1976; reprinted by permission of Basil Blackwell Ltd.

Reading 26 from the Journal of Business Finance and Accounting, Vol.3, 1976; reprinted by permission of Basil Blackwell Ltd.

Reading 27 reprinted by permission of the Institute of Chartered Accountants in England and Wales.

Reading 28 from the Accountant's Magazine, Vol.91,1977; reprinted by permission of the author and the Editor of the Accountant's Magazine.

Reading 29 reprinted by permission of the Institute of Chartered Accountants in England and Wales.

Reading 30 from the Accountant, 1971; reprinted by permission of the author and the Editor of the Accountant.

Reading 31 from Management Accounting, March 1977; reprinted by permission of the author and the Editor of Management Accounting.

Reading 32 from "Worldwide Developments in Inflation Accounting", Coopers and Lybrand, 1977; reprinted by permission of Coopers and Lybrand.

INDEX

Proposed statement of standard accounting practice 30 April 1979 ED24

Current Cost Accounting

Issued for comment by persons interested in financial reporting by the

Accounting Standards Committee

Comments should quote reference ED 24 and be addressed to:

The Accounting Standards Committee,
PO Box 433,
Chartered Accountants' Hall,
Moorgate Place,
London, EC2P 2BJ

and should be despatched so as to be received not later than **31 October 1979.** All replies will be regarded as on public record unless confidentiality is requested by the commentator.

The draft is issued for comment only by the

Accounting Standards Committee of

The Institute of Chartered Accountants in England and Wales
The Institute of Chartered Accountants of Scotland
The Institute of Chartered Accountants in Ireland
The Association of Certified Accountants
The Institute of Cost and Management Accountants and
The Chartered Institute of Public Finance and Accountancy

and does not necessarily represent the views of the Councils of these bodies. It should be noted that the draft may be modified in the light of comment received before being issued in the form of an accounting standard.

Proposed statement of standard accounting practice 30 April 1979 ED24

Current Cost Accounting

Summary

1 Prolonged and acute inflation has shown that the traditional historical cost (HC) accounting system has serious defects for many purposes. There has been a great deal of debate on what kind of system should replace or supplement it. No agreed solution has been reached in any part of the world. The Accounting Standards Committee (ASC) nevertheless recognises the important need in present conditions to disclose information about the effects of changing prices. The accompanying exposure draft follows the ASC's statement of intent issued in July 1978 and evolves from the interim recommendation published in 1977 (the 'Hyde' guidelines). The aim of the exposure draft is to propose a practical and workable standard which will be a move forward in the evolution of the subject.

2 The exposure draft proposes that the standard would apply, with certain exceptions, only to listed companies and to other entities with an annual turnover of £5,000,000 or more.

3 Annual financial statements would include, in addition to historical cost accounts, a current cost profit and loss account, a current cost balance sheet (which may be in summarised form) and explanatory notes.

4 The current cost profit and loss account would show:

(a) the current cost operating profit derived after making depreciation, cost of sales and monetary working capital adjustments; and

(b) the current cost profit attributable to shareholders derived after making a gearing adjustment.

5 In the current cost balance sheet, fixed assets and stock would generally be included at their value to the business. Value to the business would normally be net current replacement cost.

6 The proposed standard is brief and confined to principles. Separate Guidance Notes are published which contain practical methods intended to help companies to implement CCA. The Guidance Notes are not mandatory and do not form part of the proposed standard.

7 The exposure draft is open for comment until 31 October 1979. It is proposed that the standard should be effective for accounting periods beginning on or after 1 January 1980 but this date will be kept under review in the light of comments received.

Current cost accounting

Contents

Proposed statement of standard accounting practice 30 April 1979 ED24

Current cost accounting

Preface

General

1 In July 1978 the Accounting Standards Committee ('ASC') issued a 'statement of intent' setting out its plans for the further development of price level accounting. The statement indicated that:

— an exposure draft would be prepared with the assistance of the Inflation Accounting Steering Group ('IASG') and published not earlier than the spring of 1979;

— it would propose that published financial statements drawn up under the historical cost ('HC') convention should be supplemented by statements providing profit and loss account and balance sheet information on a current cost ('CCA') basis;

— these statements would evolve from the interim recommendation issued in November 1977 (subsequently known as the 'Hyde' guidelines) and take into account comments on it and on ED18 'Current cost accounting';

— it would be proposed that the standard should apply only to listed companies and other large undertakings (the relevant size criterion being a matter for public discussion and comment);

— the exposure draft would be confined to principles and objectives: separate guidance notes, not forming part of the standard, would be published setting out suitable methods for implementing the principles and objectives.

2 The accompanying exposure draft (ED24) conforms to the statement of intent. ED24 replaces ED18 which is now withdrawn. Persons interested in financial reporting are urged to study ED24 and send comments (favourable as well as critical) to the Secretary of ASC by 31 October 1979. If the nature of the discussion which develops indicates the need, public hearings will be held so that people who wish to do so may present their views orally.

Background

3 The traditional historical cost accounting system has proved acceptable for most purposes in times of relative price stability. Prolonged and acute inflation however has shown it to have serious defects for many purposes. Indeed its limitations have already led to departures from the strict historical cost convention. For example, in the UK and Ireland many businesses have revalued their fixed assets and provided additional depreciation thereon, and in some countries a LIFO basis has been adopted for stock valuation so as to produce a measurement of cost of goods sold—though not of stock values—which is similar to those under a current cost system.

4 There has been a great deal of debate of what kind of accounting system or systems should replace or supplement the traditional HC system in a period of significant price changes. In the UK and Ireland the first definitive proposals were issued as ED8 in January 1973, followed by PSSAP7 in May 1974, entitled 'Accounting for changes in the purchasing power of money'. They were based on the method known as 'current purchasing power' or 'CPP' which involves the translation of all the basic HC figures for a given year into currency units of a common purchasing power at a specific date. It was intended that the proposals should apply mainly to listed companies and called for supplementary statements on a CPP basis.

5 In July 1973 the UK Government announced that an independent committee of enquiry was to be set up to consider the various methods of adjusting company accounts and whether, and if so how, company accounts should allow for changes in costs and prices. This committee, which became known as the Sandilands Committee, reported in September 1975. It recommended that a system of current cost accounting should be developed which dealt with the effect of specific price changes on individual businesses as opposed to the effect of changes in the general purchasing power of money. This aim was to be achieved by charging against revenue the 'value to the business' of assets consumed, which in normal circumstances would be based upon replacement cost. The committee recommended that current cost accounts should replace historical cost accounts and that the proposals should be incorporated into an accounting standard to apply from 1978.

6 Following the publication of the Sandilands Report, the Inflation Accounting Steering Group was constituted to draft for the ASC a proposed standard based on the Sandilands recommendations. This proposed standard was published as ED18. It became clear that the Sandilands recommendations, and ED18 which stemmed from them, were not acceptable. Among other things there was considerable objection to the replacement of HC by a new untested system; the proposals were considered too complicated; and the profit figure was considered misleading without adjustment for monetary items.

The Interim Recommendation (the 'Hyde' Guidelines)

7 The ASC however recognised the urgent need in present conditions to show how HC accounts are affected by changing prices. To this end it published the interim recommendation in November 1977. The document outlined a simplified form of CCA and recommended that companies listed on The Stock Exchange should include in their financial statements a prominent statement showing the profit or loss calculated on a current cost basis. It took into account the widely held view that an adjustment—called a 'gearing adjustment'—was necessary to show, in addition to adjustments for depreciation and cost of sales, how the method of financing the business could affect the impact of price level changes.

8 The response to the interim recommendation by the larger companies has been encouraging. However, it is evident from comments made in annual reports, and from comments to the ASC, that many companies are reluctant to include price level information in their annual financial statements until an acceptable accounting method is proposed as a standard, and until more detailed guidance is available on problem areas. The accompanying exposure draft is developed from the interim recommendation and takes into account comments received on it and on ED18.

Evolution from the 'Hyde' Guidelines

9 In common with the Hyde guidelines, the exposure draft proposes that a separate statement be given showing the current cost adjustments made to the HC profit in respect of depreciation, cost of sales and 'gearing'. The exposure draft however goes further in:

(a) introducing, separate from the 'gearing adjustment', an adjustment (here called the monetary working capital adjustment—'MWCA') which in effect extends the cost of sales adjustment to the other working capital items:

(b) calling for a current cost balance sheet (which may be in summarised form); and

(c) calling for current cost earnings per share to be shown by listed companies.

The Monetary Working Capital Adjustment

10 The ASC believes that a separate monetary working capital adjustment is an important development from the interim recommendation in determining the current cost operating profit; that is the surplus after allowing for the effect of price changes on all the net operating assets of the business of which monetary working capital is a component. The nature of the MWCA is illustrated in a footnote to this preface. The ASC considers that the MWCA is necessary in arriving at a useful indicator of the business results, but appreciates that there may be practical difficulties in defining the items which should be included. The proposed definition attempts to strike a practical balance and provides that the adjustment will normally be confined to trade debtors and trade creditors but permits the inclusion of an element of cash and overdraft where this is necessary to avoid giving a misleading result.

Current Cost Balance Sheet

11 The ASC believes that a current cost balance sheet (which may be in summary form) is necessary to form a basis for estimating return on capital employed on a current cost basis. Most of the information required for its preparation would already be required to prepare the current cost profit and loss adjustments.

Scope

12 The exposure draft proposes that the standard should apply to all listed companies and other entities with a turnover of £5 millions or more (subject to a number of specific exceptions). The threshold of £5 millions turnover coincides with the threshold defining larger companies in the EEC Fourth Directive on company law.

13 There are about 2,500 listed companies in the United Kingdom and Ireland which will be affected by the standard. It is estimated that a threshold of £5 millions turnover would bring roughly 3,000 more unlisted companies within the scope of the proposed standard, making 5,500 in all. If higher thresholds were set it is estimated that the following numbers of companies would fall within the scope of the standard:

£10m turnover: 3,800
£15m turnover: 3,450
£20m turnover: 3,100

14 It is proposed that insurance, property investment and dealing companies and investment and unit trusts should be excluded from compliance with the standard on the grounds that the CCA method does not appear to be wholly appropriate to them. Further research and discussion is necessary to determine whether a suitable system can be established for such businesses.

Guidance Notes

15 The exposure draft itself is brief and confined to a statement of the principles of the CCA system and the disclosure requirements. Separate Guidance Notes are also published which suggest practical methods intended to help companies implement CCA. The ASC holds the view that flexibility is necessary at this stage to assist further development; the Guidance Notes are therefore not mandatory and do not form part of the proposed standard. The ASC will nevertheless be pleased to receive comments on the content of these Guidance Notes.

16 The methods suggested in the Guidance Notes do not cover all the practical difficulties relating to particular industries. Where such problems arise generally in a particular industry companies may well find it useful to consult together and through their trade association with a view to establishing suitable guidelines for use in that industry.

Conclusion

17 Whilst the proposed standard applies only to annual financial statements it is hoped that current cost information will eventually be included in other statements such as interim accounts, preliminary results and prospectuses. The ASC also considers it desirable that the preparation of CCA information for annual financial statements should provide a basis upon which managements may develop CCA information for their internal use where they have not already done so.

18 Despite years of study and debate the problem of price level accounting has not reached an agreed solution in any part of the world (except perhaps in one or two areas of hyperinflation where the differences between various systems of accounting pale into insignificance). There is no perfect solution to the problem and many alternatives have attractive features. The aim has been to provide a practical and workable standard which will represent a real move forward in the evolution of the subject.

19 The ASC believes that there is now an urgent need to produce an accounting standard. It is proposed that the standard should be effective for accounting periods beginning on or after 1 January 1980 but this date will be kept under review in the light of comments received. Persons interested in financial reporting are urged to submit their comments (critical and favourable) on the exposure draft as soon as possible and at the latest by 31 October 1979. In particular, views will be welcomed on:

(a) the monetary working capital adjustment;

(b) the turnover limit of £5 millions; and

(c) the problems of particular industries.

ED24 30 April 1979

Footnote on the Monetary Working Capital Adjustment

(a) In the course of informal discussions, the ASC has found that the reasons for the monetary working capital adjustment are not well understood. Broadly speaking, if the MWCA is added to (or deducted from) the cost of sales adjustment (COSA), the resulting adjustment deals with the whole of the net working capital and not stocks alone. The general intention is that current cost operating profit should be struck after allowing for the 'maintenance' of net working capital rather than just stocks.

(b) It may be helpful to give examples which illustrate the need for the adjustment in arriving at current cost operating profit. These relate to a 'supermarket', a 'bank' and a 'manufacturing company'.

(c) *'Supermarket':*

			£M
Balance Sheet includes—Stock			48.0
—Creditors			(47.0)
			1.0
Profit and Loss Account—			
	HC Profit		23.0
	CC adjustments for:		
	Cost of sales	10.0	
	Monetary working capital	(9.8)	
		0.2	
	Depreciation	3.0	3.2
	CC operating profit		19.8

The COSA provides for the extra funds needed to replace, at current prices, stock which has been consumed during the year. However, when suppliers allow credit, the amount of credit allowed increases as the prices increase. This reduces the need for the business to provide additional working capital from its own resources. In this 'supermarket' example, the stocks are almost entirely financed by creditors, a COSA is largely unnecessary and is almost wholly cancelled out by the MWCA.

(d) *'Bank'*

			£M
Balance Sheet includes—	Advances and other liquid assets less deposits		490
			490
Profit and Loss Account—			
	HC Profit		158
	CC adjustments for:		
	Monetary working capital	93	
	Depreciation	9	102
	CC operating profit		56

There is no COSA since there is no trading stock in the ordinary sense. A bank provides financial services which depend upon its having available an adequate amount of liquid funds; monetary working capital in this example therefore includes cash on the grounds that a bank has to keep a certain proportion of its assets in that form. In a period of rising prices, the scale of a bank's activities in real terms would be reduced, unless it increases its working capital. The MWCA makes provision for this extra working capital which is required to maintain the substance of the business.

(e) *'Manufacturing company'*

			£M
Balance Sheet includes—	Stock		180
	—Debtors less creditors		21
			201
Profit and Loss Account—			
	HC profit		101
	CC adjustments for:		
	Cost of sales	57	
	Monetary working capital	7	
		64	
	Depreciation	10	74
	CC operating profit		27

In this example the net amount of trade debtors and creditors is relatively small; this may often be so in a manufacturing business. In these circumstances the amount of the MWCA will be quite small in comparison with the 'supermarket' and 'bank' examples given earlier.

ED24 30 April 1979

Current Cost Accounting

Part 1 Explanatory note

Introduction

1 In most systems of accounting profit is determined after making charges against revenue to provide for the maintenance of capital. Since the definition of capital varies according to the accounting system adopted, the method of determining profit also varies.

2 The proposed standard provides for current cost information to be included in annual financial statements in addition to historical cost (HC) accounts. It sets out a current cost accounting (CCA) system based upon a concept of capital which is represented by the net operating assets of a business. These net operating assets (fixed assets, stock and monetary working capital) are the same as those included in the historical cost accounts, although in the current cost accounts the fixed assets and stock are normally expressed at current cost. The net operating assets, in accounting terms, can be said to represent the operating capability of the business and usually will have been financed by both shareholders and borrowings.

3 A change in the prices of goods and services used by the business will affect the amount of funds required to maintain the operating capability derived from the net operating assets. In contrast to historical cost accounts, the current cost accounting system is designed to reflect this in the determination of profit.

The Objective of CCA

4 The objective of the current cost system is to reflect the impact of specific price changes on the business when:

(a) determining profits for an accounting period; and

(b) preparing the balance sheet.

5 In determining profits the objective is achieved in two stages:

The *current cost operating profit* is determined as the surplus after allowing for the impact of price changes on the funds needed to continue the existing business and maintain its operating capability, whether financed by share capital or borrowings; and

The *current cost profit attributable to shareholders* is then determined after allowing for the effect of financial gearing.

6 In the balance sheet the objective is met by including, where appropriate, the assets at their value to the business (normally net current replacement cost). This provides a realistic statement of the assets employed in the business and enables a relationship to be established between the current cost profit and the net assets employed.

Current Cost Operating Profit

7 Three adjustments to the historical cost trading profit before interest are normally required to arrive at current cost operating profit. These are called the depreciation, cost of sales and monetary working capital adjustments.

Depreciation Adjustment

8 The depreciation adjustment allows for the impact of price changes when determining the charge against revenue for that part of fixed assets consumed in the period. It is the difference between the value to the business of fixed assets consumed and the amount of the depreciation charge in the historical cost accounts. The resulting total depreciation charge thus represents the value to the business of that part of fixed assets consumed in earning the revenue of the period.

Cost of Sales Adjustment

9 The cost of sales adjustment (COSA) allows for the impact of price changes when determining the charge against revenue for stock consumed in the period. It is the difference between the value to the business of stock consumed and the cost of stock charged in the historical cost accounts. The resulting total charge thus represents the value to the business of stock consumed in earning the revenue of the period.

Monetary Working Capital Adjustment

10 Most businesses have other working capital besides stock involved in their day-to-day operating activities. For example, when sales are made on credit the business has funds tied up in debtors. Conversely, if the suppliers of goods and services to the business allow a period of credit, the amount of funds needed to support working capital is reduced. This monetary working capital is an integral part of the net operating assets of the business which form the basis of the capital maintenance concept in current cost accounts. Thus, in order to allow for the impact of price changes on the total net operating assets, the proposed standard provides for an adjustment in respect of monetary working capital when determining current cost operating profit.

11 In a business which holds stocks, the monetary working capital adjustment (MWCA) supplements the COSA and together they allow for the impact of price changes on the total amount of working capital used by the business. For example, the relationship between the MWCA made in respect of trade debtors and trade creditors and the COSA is as follows:

(a) when sales are made on credit the business has to finance the price changes in its inputs until the sales result in a receipt of cash. The part of the MWCA related to trade debtors, in effect, extends the COSA to allow for this; and

(b) conversely, when materials and services are purchased from suppliers who offer trade credit, price changes are financed by the supplier during the credit period. To this extent extra funds do not have to be found by the business and this reduces the need for a COSA and in some cases for a MWCA on debtors. The part of the MWCA related to trade creditors reflects this reduction.

A MWCA may be equally necessary in a business which does not hold stocks.

12 In principle, monetary working capital might include cash and overdraft to the extent that these are directly related to the day-to-day operating activities of the business. However, in order to limit the subjectivity involved in defining items to be included in monetary working capital, the proposed standard requires that it should normally be based on trade debtors and trade creditors. Monetary working capital will include cash or overdraft only in those circumstances where their exclusion can be shown to give a misleading calculation of current cost profit.

13 The proposed standard allows for the COSA and MWCA to be combined in the current cost profit and loss account when the method of calculation does not enable them to be separately identified.

Current Cost Profit Attributable to Shareholders

14 The net operating assets shown in the balance sheet usually will have been partly financed by borrowings. Where such borrowings are fixed in monetary terms, any liability to repay is not affected by changes in the prices of assets which they have partly financed. This provides a benefit to shareholders during a period of increasing prices, or a loss should they decline, which is not brought into current cost operating profit.

15 In determining the current cost profit attributable to shareholders, this benefit is recognised by a 'gearing adjustment'. This reduces the total of the adjustments for depreciation, cost of sales, and monetary working capital in the proportion which net operating assets financed by borrowing bear to the total net operating assets. The calculation is based upon the adjustments made when assets are consumed and this complies with the prudence concept and the EEC Fourth Directive requirement that the credit should not be taken to profit until it is realised.

16 The gearing adjustment, together with the other adjustments to historical cost profit, result in a current cost profit attributable to shareholders after making provision for the effect of price changes on that proportion of the net operating assets which has been financed by the shareholders. The current cost profit attributable to shareholders should be shown after interest, tax and extraordinary items.

17 The provisions of SSAP15 'Accounting for deferred taxation' apply equally to the current cost accounts as well as to the historical cost accounts.

The Capital Maintenance Reserve

18 The current cost balance sheet includes a capital maintenance reserve. This reflects revaluation surpluses and deficits arising from changes in the prices of fixed assets and stock (to the extent that they are not already included in the HC accounts), and the monetary working capital adjustment. If such amounts were distributed this would imply that the operating capability of the business had been eroded. The capital maintenance reserve also includes the gearing adjustment which will reduce the total balance on the reserve. The net balance relates to the extent to which price changes have affected the proportion of net operating assets which have been financed by shareholders.

Distributable Profit

19 The amounts that can prudently be distributed depend not only on profitability, but also on the availability of cash. This is so with all systems of accounting. When determining distribution policy, consideration must be given to factors not reflected in profit, such as capital expenditure plans, changes in the volume of working capital, the effect on funding requirements of changes in production methods and efficiency, liquidity, and new financing arrangements, as well as the effect of price changes on the finance required. The current cost profit attributable to shareholders does not necessarily measure the amount that can prudently be distributed since, although it will reflect the impact of price changes on the profits reported under the historical cost system, other factors still need to be considered. Even if the effect of such factors is neutral, a full distribution of the current cost profit attributable to shareholders may make it necessary to arrange additional finance (equal to the gearing adjustment) to avoid an erosion of the operating capability of the business. However, an increase in the value to the business of the assets may provide increased cover for such financing.

Annual Financial Statements

20 The proposed standard sets out the current cost information which should be disclosed to provide the user with a clearer picture of the results for the period and the financial state of the business at the balance sheet date. This consists of a current cost profit and loss account and a current cost balance sheet together with appropriate notes.

21 Statements of Standard Accounting Practice issued for use with historical cost accounts also apply to current cost accounts except where a conflict exists due to the conceptual difference between the systems. In particular, the fundamental accounting concepts set out in SSAP2 apply, i.e. the 'going concern', 'accruals', 'consistency' and 'prudence' concepts. The 'going concern' concept is particularly appropriate to CCA which relates profit to the maintenance of operating capability. As regards the 'accruals' concept, CCA is based upon the matching of current cost with current revenue.

Methods Appropriate to the Preparation of Current Cost Accounts

22 At this stage the ASC does not believe that it would be right to be prescriptive about the methods which should be adopted by all businesses when preparing current cost accounts. Guidance Notes have been published which the ASC hopes will be helpful, since they offer practical solutions to the more common situations. However, they do not form part of the proposed standard and accordingly are not mandatory.

Uses and Limitations

23 Since the CCA system set out in the proposed standard is predominantly cost based, it is expected that the accounting policies adopted will be generally the same as those used in the HC accounts. In particular, the current cost accounts do not encompass assets which are not covered by the HC accounts.

24 The CCA system allows for the impact of specific price changes on the net operating assets, and thus the operating capability, of the business. It does not seek to allow for the impact of other factors, such as a change in the nature of the business. The system does not measure the effect of changes in the general value of money or translate the figures into currency of purchasing power at a specific date. Because of this it is not a system of accounting for general inflation. Further, it does not show changes in the value *of* the business as a whole or the market value of the equity.

25 Whilst the current cost system allows for the effect of price changes in the accounts of a particular period and thus gives a more realistic measure of results, it does not directly provide for meaningful comparisons between the figures of different periods. As with historical cost accounts, the figures for profit and capital employed in different years are not comparable unless they are adjusted to a common basis. This problem can be mitigated by using ratios or indexing the profits and dividends of earlier years.

Part 2 Definition of terms

26 *Net operating assets*
The net operating assets comprise the fixed assets, stock and monetary working capital which are included in the historical cost balance sheet. They represent, in accounting terms, the operating capability of the business which is broadly the quantum of goods and services that the business is currently able to supply with its existing resources.

27 *Value to the business*
This is:

(a) the net current replacement cost;

or, if a permanent diminution in the value of the asset to below net replacement cost has been recognised:

(b) its recoverable amount.

28 *Recoverable amount*
This is the greater of the net realisable value of the asset and, where applicable, the amount recoverable from its further use.

29 *Monetary working capital*
This is the aggregate of:

(a) trade debtors, prepayments and trade bills receivable, plus

(b) stocks not subject to a cost of sales adjustment, less

(c) trade creditors, accruals and trade bills payable,

insofar as they arise from the day-to-day operating activities of the business as distinct from transactions of a capital nature.

In those situations where their exclusion can be shown to be misleading when calculating current cost profit, it can also include:

(a) cash floats, and

(b) that part of bank balances or overdrafts arising from fluctuations in the volume of stock, trade debtors and trade creditors.

In the case of banks and other financial businesses this definition is extended to cover other current assets and other current liabilities insofar as they also arise from the day-to-day operating activities of the business as distinct from transactions of a capital nature.

30 *Net borrowing*
This is the excess of:

(a) the aggregate of all liabilities and provisions (including convertible debentures and deferred tax but excluding proposed dividends) other than those included within monetary working capital

over

(b) the aggregate of all current assets other than those subject to a cost of sales adjustment and those included within monetary working capital.

Part 3 Proposed Standard Accounting Practice

Scope

31 This accounting standard applies to the annual financial statements of the following entities:

A. All companies (other than those in paragraph B(iii) below) having a listing on The Stock Exchange for any class of share or loan capital.

B. All other entities where the annual financial statements are intended to give a true and fair view of the financial position and profit or loss except for the following:

(i) Entities (or a group of entities) with a turnover of less than £5,000,000 per annum.

(ii) Wholly owned subsidiaries of companies registered in the UK or Republic of Ireland.
This exemption does not apply where the parent company is exempted under (iii) below. Where this is the case the group accounts of the holding company should include current cost information in respect of such subsidiaries (not themselves exempted under (iii)) if their combined turnover exceeds £5,000,000 per annum.

(iii) The following types of entity:

(a) insurers;

(b) property investment and dealing with the exception of such companies which hold the properties of another entity within the group to which this Standard does apply; and

(c) investment and unit trusts.

(iv) Entities whose long term financial objective is other than to achieve an operating profit; examples of such entities are charities, building societies, friendly societies, trade unions and pension funds.

32 Annual financial statements of companies coming within the scope of the standard should include, in addition to historical cost accounts, current cost accounts prepared in accordance with the procedure set out in paragraphs 33-40. The current cost accounts should contain a profit and loss account and balance sheet, together with explanatory notes, disclosing the information set out in paragraphs 41-45.

The Current Cost Profit and Loss Account

33 When calculating the current cost operating profit and the current cost profit attributable to shareholders, the following procedures should be adopted.

34 The current cost operating profit should be derived by making the following main adjustments to historical cost trading profit (before interest) to provide for the impact of price changes on the net operating assets* of the business:

(a) A depreciation adjustment, to allow for the difference between the value to the business* of the fixed assets consumed in the period and the depreciation charged in the historical cost accounts.

(b) A cost of sales adjustment, to allow for the difference between the value to the business* of the stock consumed in the period and the cost of stock charged in the historical cost accounts.

(c) A monetary working capital adjustment, to allow for the effect of price changes on the monetary working capital* needed to support the operating capability.

Each of these adjustments may be positive or negative.

35 Where a proportion of the assets of the business is financed by net borrowing*, a gearing adjustment is required in arriving at the current cost profit attributable to shareholders. This should be calculated by:

(a) determining the proportion of the net operating assets which has been financed by net borrowing; and

(b) multiplying the total of the charges or credits made to allow for the impact of price changes on the net operating assets of the business by the proportion determined at (a).

Other Matters Relating to Current Cost Profit

36 The treatment within the current cost profit and loss account of gains and losses on asset disposals, extraordinary and exceptional items, prior year items, income from associates, group consolidation adjustments and the translation of foreign currencies, should where practicable, be consistent with the principles of CCA as explained in Part 1—Explanatory Note. Where this is impracticable the treatment adopted should be disclosed in a note to the current cost accounts.

---

*As defined in the Definitions Section of the Standard.

37 The taxation charge in the current cost accounts should be based on the principles set out in SSAP15 'Accounting for deferred taxation'.

The Current Cost Balance Sheet

38 Assets and liabilities should be included in the balance sheet, as far as practicable, on the following bases:

(a) *Land and buildings, plant and machinery and stocks subject to a cost of sales adjustment*—at their value to the business.

(b) *Investments in associated companies*—either at the applicable proportion of the associated company's net assets stated under this standard and allowing for goodwill paid on acquisition computed in accordance with CCA principles or, where such information is not readily available, at directors' best estimate thereof.

(c) *Other investments (excluding those treated as current assets)*—at directors' valuation. Where the investment is listed and the directors' valuation is materially different from mid-market value, the basis of valuation and the reasons for the difference should be stated.

(d) *Intangible assets (excluding goodwill arising on consolidation)*—either at their current replacement cost or, if this is impracticable, on the basis adopted in the historical cost accounts.

(e) *Goodwill arising on consolidation*—this should be reduced from the amount shown in the historical cost accounts to the extent that it represents revaluation surpluses existing at the date of acquisition.

(f) *Current assets, other than those subject to a cost of sales adjustment*—at the amounts shown in the historical cost accounts.

(g) *All liabilities*—at the amounts shown in the historical cost accounts.

The Capital Maintenance Reserve

39 A reserve, called the capital maintenance reserve, should be included in the current cost balance sheet to reflect:

(a) revaluation surpluses (or deficits) arising from:

(i) price changes in respect of fixed assets; and

(ii) price changes in respect of stock, and investments other than those included as current assets;

to the extent that they are not already included in the historical cost accounts

(b) the monetary working capital adjustment; and

(c) the gearing adjustment.

Amounts to reduce assets from current replacement cost to recoverable amount* should be charged to the profit and loss account.

40 A debit balance on the capital maintenance reserve should be shown as a deduction from the total of capital and reserves and not charged to the profit and loss account.

Contents of Accounts

Profit and Loss Account

41 The current cost profit and loss account should show:

(a) the current cost operating profit or loss;

(b) the gearing adjustment and interest/income relating to the net borrowing on which the adjustment has been based;

(c) share of current cost profits or losses of associated companies;

(d) current cost profit or loss before taxation and extraordinary items;

(e) taxation;

(f) current cost profit or loss before extraordinary items;

(g) extraordinary items; and

(h) current cost profit or loss (after tax) attributable to shareholders.

---

*As defined in the Definitions Section of the Standard.

42 A reconciliation should be provided between the current cost operating profit and the profit or loss before charging interest and taxation as shown in the historical cost accounts giving the respective amounts of the following:

(a) additional depreciation adjustment;

(b) cost of sales adjustment;

(c) monetary working capital adjustment and interest relating to monetary working capital, where appropriate; and

(d) other material adjustments made to the historical cost accounts when determining current cost operating profit.

The adjustments for cost of sales and monetary working capital may be combined if, owing to the method of calculation, they cannot be separately identified.

Balance Sheet

43 The current cost balance sheet (which may be in summarised form) should show the group's assets and liabilities on the bases required by this standard. It should be supported by summaries of the fixed asset accounts and the capital maintenance reserve.

Explanatory Note

44 The notes attached to the current cost accounts should indicate the bases and methods adopted in arriving at:

(a) the valuation of fixed assets and the depreciation thereon;

(b) the valuation of stock and work in progress and the cost of sales adjustment;

(c) the monetary working capital adjustment;

(d) the gearing adjustment;

(e) the basis of translating foreign currencies and dealing with gains or losses arising; and

(f) other material adjustments to the historical cost accounts.

Earnings per Share

45 Listed companies should show the current cost earnings per share for the current and corresponding period. It should be based on the current cost profit attributable to equity shareholders before extraordinary items. In other respects the calculation should be consistent with that used in the historical cost accounts.

Group Accounts

46 A company which is a holding company of a group and which is required to produce group accounts, should produce current cost group accounts in accordance with the principles set out in this standard but need not produce current cost accounts for itself as a single company.

Corresponding Amounts

47 In all accounts prepared in accordance with this standard, corresponding amounts for the preceding period should be stated. They should normally be included at the same figure as shown in the previous period's accounts.

48 For the first year for which current cost accounts are prepared, corresponding amounts need only be included if they are readily available.

Relationship with Other Standards

49 Existing standards issued for use with historical cost accounts apply to current cost accounts except where a conflict exists caused by the conceptual difference between the systems.

Date from which Effective

50 The accounting practices set out in this standard should be adopted as soon as possible and regarded as standard for annual financial statements relating to accounting periods starting on or after 1 January 1980.

Appendix 1 Example of presentation of current cost accounts

This appendix does not form part of the Statement of Standard Accounting Practice. The methods of presentation used are illustrative of the accounts of a manufacturing company. They are in no way prescriptive and other methods of presentation may equally comply with the standard.

Y Limited and Subsidiaries
Group Current Cost Profit and Loss Account
for the year ended 31st December, 1980

1979 *£'000*		*£'000*
18,000	Turnover	20,000
2,420	Profit before interest and taxation as in the historical cost accounts	2,900
1,320	*Less:* Current cost adjustments (Note 2)	1,510
1,100	CURRENT COST OPERATING PROFIT	1,390
340	Gearing adjustment	370
180	Interest	200
160		170
1,260	Current cost profit before taxation	1,560
610	Taxation	730
650	CURRENT COST PROFIT ATTRIBUTABLE TO SHAREHOLDERS	830
400	Dividends	430
250	Retained current cost profit for the year	400
21.7p	Current cost earnings per share	27.7p

Where applicable the share of current cost profits of associated companies, minority interests and extraordinary items should be presented in a manner consistent with the historical cost accounts.

Y Limited and Subsidiaries
Summarised Group Current Cost Balance Sheet
as at 31st December 1980

1979 £'000	1979 £'000		£'000	£'000
		Assets Employed:		
	7,130	Fixed assets (Note 3)		8,530
		Net current assets:		
3,200		Stock and work in progress	4,000	
700		Trade debtors less trade creditors	800	
(1,000)		Other current liabilities (including taxation)	(1,000)	
	2,900			3,800
	10,030			12,330
		Financed by:		
		Capital and reserves		
3,000		Issued share capital	3,000	
1,180		Capital maintenance reserve (Note 4)	3,030	
3,900		Retained profit	4,300	
	8,080			10,330
	1,950	Loan capital		2,000
	10,030			12,330

Where applicable other relevant items not shown in the above balance sheet should be presented in a manner consistent with the historical cost accounts.

Y Limited and Subsidiaries
Matters arising from application of the Standard
which should be included in the Notes to the
Current Cost Accounts
for the year ended 31st December 1980

1 *Explanatory notes*
(See paragraph 44 of Standard)

2 *Current cost adjustments*

1979 £'000		£'000
400	Cost of sales	460
70	Monetary working capital	100
470		560
850	Additional depreciation	950
1,320		1,510

3 *Fixed assets*

	Gross	*Depreciation*	*Net*	*Previous Year*
	£'000	*£'000*	*£'000*	*£'000*
Land and buildings	1,780	680	1,100	1,070
Plant and machinery	16,780	9,350	7,430	6,060
	18,560	10,030	8,530	7,130

4 *Capital maintenance reserve*

	£'000
Balance at 1st January	1,180
Surplus on revaluations	
Land and buildings	200
Plant and machinery	1,430
Stock and work in progress	490
Monetary working capital adjustment	100
	2,220
Gearing adjustment	370
	1,850
Balance at 31st December	3,030

Where applicable surpluses or deficits arising on the following should also be shown as a movement in the capital maintenance reserve.

(1) the revaluation of investments (other than those included in current assets).

(2) The revaluation of investments in associated companies.

(3) Consolidation differences arising on foreign currency translations.

Movements on the capital maintenance reserve should, where relevant, be shown net of minority interest.

Current position of ASC subjects

April 1979

Publication		Price	Date
Statements of Standard Accounting Practice issued			
SSAP	Explanatory foreword (Revised May 1975)	30p	Jan 71
SSAP 1	Accounting for the results of associated companies (Amended Aug. 1974)	45p	Jan 71
SSAP 2	Disclosure of accounting policies	45p	Nov 71
SSAP 3	Earnings per share (Revised Aug. 1974)	45p	Feb 72
SSAP 4	The accounting treatment of government grants	30p	Apr 74
SSAP 5	Accounting for value added tax	30p	Apr 74
SSAP 6	Extraordinary items and prior year adjustments (Revised April) 1975)	45p	May 74
SSAP 8	The treatment of taxation under the imputation system in the accounts of companies (Revised December 1977)	45p	Aug 74
SSAP 9	Stocks and work in progress	45p	May 75
SSAP 10	Statements of source and application of funds	45p	July 75
SSAP 12	Accounting for depreciation	45p	Dec 77
SSAP 13	Accounting for research and development	45p	Dec 77
SSAP 14	Group Accounts	50p	Sept 78
SSAP 15	Accounting for deferred taxation	50p	Oct 78
Exposure Drafts issued			
ED 3	Accounting for acquisitions and mergers	45p	Jan 71
ED 16	Supplement to 'Extraordinary items and prior year adjustments'	45p	Sept 75
ED 21	Accounting for foreign currency transactions	45p	Sept 77
ED 22	Accounting for post balance sheet events	45p	Feb 78
ED 23	Accounting for contingencies	50p	Nov 78
Also available			
The Corporate Report		£2.00	Aug 75
Inflation Accounting an interim recommendation		50p	Nov 77
Setting Accounting Standards – a consultative document		£1.75	Sept 78
Guidance Notes on ED 24		£1.75	Apr 79

(Copies of the above may be obtained from the Publications Dept., The Institute of Chartered Accountants in England and Wales, P.O. Box 433, Chartered Accountants' Hall, Moorgate Place, London EC2P 2BJ. Cash with order. Cheques payable to Chartac).

Future programme

Accounting for leases – lessor and lessee
Accounting for pension costs in company accounts
Accounting for diversified operations
Statement of value added
Employment report
Simplified financial statements

Listing of a subject in the programme (which is periodically reviewed) is not necessarily a commitment to publish a standard, nor is any order of priority implied.